OpenGL
Programming Guide

*The Official Guide to Learning
OpenGL, Release 1*

OpenGL Architecture Review Board
Jackie Neider Tom Davis Mason Woo

Addison-Wesley Publishing Company
Reading, Massachusetts Menlo Park, California
New York Don Mills, Ontario Wokingham, England
Amsterdam Bonn Sydney Singapore Tokyo Madrid
San Juan Paris Seoul Milan Mexico City Taipei

Silicon Graphics, the Silicon Graphics logo, and IRIS are registered trademarks and OpenGL and IRIS Graphics Library are trademarks of Silicon Graphics, Inc. X Window System is a trademark of Massachusetts Institute of Technology. Display PostScript is a registered trademark of Adobe Systems Incorporated.

The authors and publishers have taken care in preparation of this book, but make no expressed or implied warranty of any kind and assume no responsibility for errors or omissions. No liability is assumed for incidental or consequential damages in connection with or arising out of the use of the information or programs contained herein.

Library of Congress Cataloging-in-Publication Data

Neider, Jackie.
    OpenGL programming guide : the official guide to learning OpenGL, release 1 / OpenGL Architecture Review Board ; Jackie Neider, Tom Davis, Mason Woo.
        p.   cm.
    Includes index.
    ISBN 0-201-63274-8
    1. Computer graphics.   2. OpenGL.   I. Davis, Tom.   II. Woo, Mason.   III. OpenGL Architecture Review Board.   IV. Title.
    T385.N435   1993
    006.6'765—dc20   93-3162
                                                                                            CIP

Authors: Jackie Neider, Tom Davis, and Mason Woo
Sponsoring Editor: David Rogelberg
Project Editor: Joanne Clapp Fullagar
Cover Image: Thad Beier
Cover Design: Jean Seal
Text Design: Electric Ink, Ltd., and Kay Maitz

Set in 10-point Stone Serif

5 6 7 8-MA-9998979695
Fifth printing, June 1995

For my family—Felicity, Max, Sarah, and Scout.

—JLN

For my family—Ellyn, Ricky, and Lucy.

—TRD

To Tom Doeppner and Andy van Dam, who started me along this path.

—MW

About This Guide

The OpenGL graphics system is a software interface to graphics hardware. (The GL stands for Graphics Library.) It allows you to create interactive programs that produce color images of moving three-dimensional objects. With OpenGL, you can control computer-graphics technology to produce realistic pictures or ones that depart from reality in imaginative ways. This guide explains how to program with the OpenGL graphics system to deliver the visual effect you want.

What This Guide Contains

This guide has the ideal number of chapters: 13. The first six chapters present basic information that you need to understand to be able to draw a properly colored and lit three-dimensional object on the screen:

- Chapter 1, **"Introduction to OpenGL,"** provides a glimpse into the kinds of things OpenGL can do. It also presents a simple OpenGL program and explains essential programming details you need to know for subsequent chapters.

- Chapter 2, **"Drawing Geometric Objects,"** explains how to create a three-dimensional geometric description of an object that is eventually drawn on the screen.

- Chapter 3, **"Viewing,"** describes how such three-dimensional models are transformed before being drawn onto a two-dimensional screen. You can control these transformations to show a particular view of a model.

- Chapter 4, **"Display Lists,"** discusses how to store a series of OpenGL commands for execution at a later time. You'll want to use this feature to increase the performance of your OpenGL program.

- Chapter 5, **"Color,"** describes how to specify the color and shading method used to draw an object.

- Chapter 6, **"Lighting,"** explains how to control the lighting conditions surrounding an object and how that object responds to light (that is, how it reflects or absorbs light). Lighting is an important topic, since objects usually don't look three-dimensional until they're lit.

The remaining chapters explain how to add sophisticated features to your three-dimensional scene. You might choose not to take advantage of many of these features until you're more comfortable with OpenGL. Particularly advanced topics are noted in the text where they occur.

- Chapter 7, **"Blending, Antialiasing, and Fog,"** describes techniques essential to creating a realistic scene—alpha blending (which allows you to create transparent objects), antialiasing, and atmospheric effects (such as fog or smog).

- Chapter 8, **"Drawing Pixels, Bitmaps, Fonts, and Images,"** discusses how to work with sets of two-dimensional data as bitmaps or images. One typical use for bitmaps is to describe characters in fonts.

- Chapter 9, **"Texture Mapping,"** explains how to map one- and two-dimensional images called *textures* onto three-dimensional objects. Many marvelous effects can be achieved through texture mapping.

- Chapter 10, **"The Framebuffer,"** describes all the possible buffers that can exist in an OpenGL implementation and how you can control them. You can use the buffers for such effects as hidden-surface elimination, stenciling, masking, motion blur, and depth-of-field focusing.

- Chapter 11, **"Evaluators and NURBS,"** gives an introduction to advanced techniques for efficiently generating curves or surfaces.

- Chapter 12, **"Selection and Feedback,"** explains how you can use OpenGL's selection mechanism to select an object on the screen. It also explains the feedback mechanism, which allows you to collect the drawing information OpenGL produces rather than having it be used to draw on the screen.

- Chapter 13, **"Now That You Know,"** describes how to use OpenGL in several clever and unexpected ways to produce interesting results. These techniques are drawn from years of experience with the technological precursor to OpenGL, the Silicon Graphics IRIS Graphics Library.

In addition, there are several appendices that you will likely find useful:

- Appendix A, **"Order of Operations,"** gives a technical overview of the operations OpenGL performs, briefly describing them in the order in which they occur as an application executes.

- Appendix B, **"OpenGL State Variables,"** lists the state variables that OpenGL maintains and describes how to obtain their values.

- Appendix C, **"The OpenGL Utility Library,"** briefly describes the routines available in the OpenGL Utility Library.

- Appendix D, **"The OpenGL Extension to the X Window System,"** briefly describes the routines available in the OpenGL extension to the X Window System.

- Appendix E, **"The OpenGL Programming Guide Auxiliary Library,"** discusses a small C code library that was written for this book to make code examples shorter and more comprehensible.

- Appendix F, **"Calculating Normal Vectors,"** tells you how to calculate normal vectors for different types of geometric objects.

- Appendix G, **"Homogeneous Coordinates and Transformation Matrices,"** explains some of the mathematics behind matrix transformations.

- Appendix H, **"Programming Tips,"** lists some programming tips based on the intentions of the designers of OpenGL that you might find useful.

- Appendix I, **"OpenGL Invariance,"** describes the pixel-exact invariance rules that OpenGL implementations follow.

Finally, an extensive **Glossary** defines the key terms used in this guide.

How to Obtain the Sample Code

This guide contains many sample programs to illustrate the use of particular OpenGL programming techniques. These programs make use of a small auxiliary library that was written for this guide. The section "OpenGL-related Libraries" on page 10 gives more information about this auxiliary library. You can obtain the source code for both the sample programs and the auxiliary library for free via ftp (file-transfer protocol) if you have access to the Internet.

First, use ftp to go to the host sgigate.sgi.com, and use *anonymous* as your user name and *your_name@machine* as the password. Then type the following:

```
cd pub/opengl
binary
get opengl.tar.Z
bye
```

The file you receive is a compressed *tar* archive. To restore the files, type:

```
uncompress opengl.tar
tar xf opengl.tar
```

The sample programs and auxiliary library are created as subdirectories from wherever you are in the file directory structure.

Many implementations of OpenGL might also include the code samples and auxiliary library as part of the system. This source code is probably the best source for your implementation, because it might have been optimized for your system. Read your machine-specific OpenGL documentation to see where the code samples can be found.

What You Should Know Before Reading This Guide

This guide assumes only that you know how to program in the C language and that you have some background in mathematics (geometry, trigonometry, linear algebra, calculus, and differential geometry). Even if you have little or no experience with computer-graphics technology, you should be able to follow most of the discussions in this book. Of course, computer graphics is a huge subject, so you may want to enrich your learning experience with supplemental reading:

- *Computer Graphics: Principles and Practice* by James D. Foley, Andries van Dam, Steven K. Feiner, and John F. Hughes (Reading, Mass.: Addison-Wesley Publishing Co.)—This book is an encyclopedic treatment of the subject of computer graphics. It includes a wealth of information but is probably best read after you have some experience with the subject.

- *3D Computer Graphics: A User's Guide for Artists and Designers* by Andrew S. Glassner (New York: Design Press)—This book is a nontechnical, gentle introduction to computer graphics. It focuses on the visual effects that can be achieved rather than on the techniques needed to achieve them.

Once you begin programming with OpenGL, you might want to obtain the *OpenGL Reference Manual* by the OpenGL Architecture Review Board (Reading, Mass.: Addison-Wesley Publishing Co., 1993), which is designed as a companion volume to this guide. The *Reference Manual* provides a technical view of how OpenGL operates on data that describes a geometric object or an image to produce an image on the screen. It also contains full descriptions of each set of related OpenGL commands—the parameters used by the commands, the default values for those parameters, and what the commands accomplish.

"OpenGL" is really a hardware-independent specification of a programming interface. You use a particular implementation of it on a particular kind of hardware. This guide explains how to program with *any* OpenGL implementation. However, since implementations may vary slightly—in performance and in providing additional, optional features, for example—you might want to investigate whether supplementary documentation is available for the particular implementation you're using. In addition, you might have OpenGL-related utilities, toolkits, programming and debugging support, widgets, sample programs, and demos available to you with your system.

Style Conventions

These style conventions are used in this guide:

- **Bold**—Command and routine names, and matrices

- *Italics*—Variables, arguments, parameter names, spatial dimensions, and matrix components

- Regular—Enumerated types and defined constants

Code examples are set off from the text in a monospace font, and command summaries are shaded with gray boxes.

Topics that are particularly complicated—and that you can skip if you're new to OpenGL or computer graphics—are marked with the Advanced icon. This icon can apply to a single paragraph or to an entire section or chapter.

☐ Advanced

Exercises that are left for the reader are marked with the Try This icon.

☐ Try This

Acknowledgments

No book comes into being without the help of many people. Probably the largest debt the authors owe is to the creators of OpenGL itself. The OpenGL team at Silicon Graphics has been led by Kurt Akeley, Bill Glazier, Kipp Hickman, Phil Karlton, Mark Segal, Kevin P. Smith, and Wei Yen. The members of the OpenGL Architecture Review Board naturally need to be counted among the designers of OpenGL: Dick Coulter and John Dennis of Digital Equipment Corporation; Jim Bushnell and Linas Vepstas of International Business Machines, Corp.; Murali Sundaresan and Rick Hodgson of Intel; and On Lee and Chuck Whitmore of Microsoft. Other early contributors to the design of OpenGL include Raymond Drewry of Gain Technology, Inc., Fred Fisher of Digital Equipment Corporation, and Randi Rost of Kubota Pacific Computer, Inc. Many other Silicon Graphics employees helped refine the definition and functionality of OpenGL, including Momi Akeley, Allen Akin, Chris Frazier, Paul Ho, Simon Hui, Lesley Kalmin, Pierre Tardiff, and Jim Winget.

Many brave souls volunteered to review this book: Kurt Akeley, Gavin Bell, Sam Chen, Andrew Cherenson, Dan Fink, Beth Fryer, Gretchen Helms, David Marsland, Jeanne Rich, Mark Segal, Kevin P. Smith, and Josie Wernecke from Silicon Graphics; David Niguidula, Coalition of Essential Schools, Brown University; John Dennis and Andy Vesper, Digital Equipment Corporation; Chandrasekhar Narayanaswami and Linas Vepstas, International Business Machines, Corp.; Randi Rost, Kubota Pacific; On Lee, Microsoft Corp.; Dan Sears; Henry McGilton, Trilithon Software; and Paula Womak.

Assembling the set of colorplates was no mean feat. The sequence of plates based on the cover image (Plates 1-9) was created by Thad Beier of Pacific Data Images, Seth Katz of Xaos Tools, Inc., and Mason Woo of Silicon Graphics. Plates 10-23 are snapshots of programs created by Mason. Gavin Bell, Kevin Goldsmith, Linda Roy, and Mark Daly (all of Silicon Graphics) created the fly-through program used for Plate 24. The model for Plate 25 was created by Barry Brouillette of Silicon Graphics; Doug Voorhies, also of Silicon Graphics, performed some image processing for the final image. Plate 26 was created by John Rohlf and Michael Jones, both of Silicon Graphics. Plate 27 was created by Carl Korobkin of Silicon Graphics. Plate 28 is a snapshot from a program written by Gavin Bell with contributions from the Inventor team at Silicon Graphics—Alain Dumesny, Dave Immel, David Mott, Howard Look, Paul Isaacs, Paul Strauss, and Rikk Carey. Plates 29 and 30 are snapshots from a visual simulation program created by the Silicon Graphics IRIS Performer team—Craig Phillips, John Rohlf, Sharon Fischler, Jim Helman, and Michael Jones—from a database produced for Silicon Graphics by Paradigm Simulation, Inc. Plate 31 is a snapshot from skyfly, the precursor to Performer, which was created by John Rohlf, Sharon Fischler, and Ben Garlick, all of Silicon Graphics.

Several other people played special roles in creating this book. If we were to list other names as authors on the front of this book, Kurt Akeley and Mark Segal would be there, as honorary yeoman. They helped define the structure and goals of the book, provided key sections of material for it, reviewed it when everybody else was too tired of it to do so, and supplied that all-important humor and support throughout the process. Kay Maitz provided invaluable production and design assistance. Kathy Gochenour very generously created many of the illustrations for this book. Tanya Kucak copyedited the manuscript, in her usual thorough and professional style.

And now, each of the authors would like to take the 15 minutes that have been allotted to them by Andy Warhol to say thank you.

I'd like to thank my managers at Silicon Graphics—Dave Larson and Way Ting—and the members of my group—Patricia Creek, Arthur Evans, Beth Fryer, Jed Hartman, Ken Jones, Robert Reimann, Eve Stratton (aka Margaret-Anne Halse), John Stearns, and Josie Wernecke—for their support during this lengthy process. Last but surely not least, I want to thank those whose contributions toward this project are too deep and mysterious to elucidate: Yvonne Leach, Kathleen Lancaster, Caroline Rose, Cindy Kleinfeld, and my parents, Florence and Ferdinand Neider.

—JLN

In addition to my parents, Edward and Irene Davis, I'd like to thank the people who taught me most of what I know about computers and computer graphics—Doug Engelbart and Jim Clark.

—TRD

I'd like to thank the many past and current members of Silicon Graphics whose accommodation and enlightenment were essential to my contribution to this book: Gerald Anderson, Wendy Chin, Bert Fornaciari, Bill Glazier, Jill Huchital, Howard Look, Bill Mannel, David Marsland, Dave Orton, Linda Roy, Keith Seto, and Dave Shreiner. Very special thanks to Karrin Nicol and Leilani Gayles of SGI for their guidance throughout my career. I also bestow much gratitude to my teammates on the Stanford B ice hockey team for periods of glorious distraction throughout the writing of this book. Finally, I'd like to thank my family, especially my mother, Bo, and my late father, Henry.

—MW

Contents

Figures

Tables

Listings

Chapter 1

Introduction to OpenGL

Chapter Objectives

After reading this chapter, you'll be able to do the following:

- Appreciate in general terms what OpenGL offers

- Identify different levels of rendering complexity

- Understand the basic structure of an OpenGL program

- Recognize OpenGL command syntax

- Understand in general terms how to animate an OpenGL program

This chapter introduces OpenGL. It has the following major sections:

- **"What Is OpenGL?"** explains what OpenGL is, what it does and doesn't do, and how it works.

- **"A Very Simple OpenGL Program"** presents a small OpenGL program and briefly discusses it. This section also defines a few basic computer-graphics terms.

- **"OpenGL Command Syntax"** explains some of the conventions and notations used by OpenGL commands.

- **"OpenGL as a State Machine"** describes the use of state variables in OpenGL and the commands for querying, enabling, and disabling states.

- **"OpenGL-related Libraries"** describes sets of OpenGL-related routines, including an auxiliary library specifically written for this book to simplify programming examples.

- **"Animation"** explains in general terms how to create pictures on the screen that move, or *animate*.

What Is OpenGL?

OpenGL is a software interface to graphics hardware. This interface consists of about 120 distinct commands, which you use to specify the objects and operations needed to produce interactive three-dimensional applications.

OpenGL is designed to work efficiently even if the computer that displays the graphics you create isn't the computer that runs your graphics program. This might be the case if you work in a networked computer environment where many computers are connected to one another by wires capable of carrying digital data. In this situation, the computer on which your program runs and issues OpenGL drawing commands is called the *client*, and the computer that receives those commands and performs the drawing is called the *server*. The format for transmitting OpenGL commands (called the *protocol*) from the client to the server is always the same, so OpenGL programs can work across a network even if the client and server are different kinds of computers. If an OpenGL program isn't running across a network, then there's only one computer, and it is both the client and the server.

OpenGL is designed as a streamlined, hardware-independent interface to be implemented on many different hardware platforms. To achieve these qualities, no commands for performing windowing tasks or obtaining user input are included in OpenGL; instead, you must work through whatever windowing system controls the particular hardware you're using. Similarly, OpenGL doesn't provide high-level commands for describing models of three-dimensional objects. Such commands might allow you to specify relatively complicated shapes such as automobiles, parts of the body, airplanes, or molecules. With OpenGL, you must build up your desired model from a small set of *geometric primitives*—points, lines, and polygons. (A sophisticated library that provides these features could certainly be built on top of OpenGL—in fact, that's what Open Inventor is. See "OpenGL-related Libraries" on page 10 for more information about Open Inventor.)

Now that you know what OpenGL *doesn't* do, here's what it *does* do. Take a look at the color plates—they illustrate typical uses of OpenGL. They show the scene on the cover of this book, drawn by a computer (which is to say, *rendered*) in successively more complicated ways. The following paragraphs describe in general terms how these pictures were made.

- Plate 1 shows the entire scene displayed as a *wireframe* model—that is, as if all the objects in the scene were made of wire. Each line of wire corresponds to an edge of a primitive (typically a polygon). For example, the surface of the table is constructed from triangular polygons that are positioned like slices of pie.

  Note that you can see portions of objects that would be obscured if the objects were solid rather than wireframe. For example, you can see the entire model of the hills outside the window even though most of this model is normally hidden by the wall of the room. The globe appears to be nearly solid because it's composed of hundreds of colored blocks, and you see the wireframe lines for all the edges of all the blocks, even those forming the back side of the globe. The way the globe is constructed gives you an idea of how complex objects can be created by assembling lower-level objects.

- Plate 2 shows a *depth-cued* version of the same wireframe scene. Note that the lines farther from the eye are dimmer, just as they would be in real life, thereby giving a visual cue of depth.

- Plate 3 shows an *antialiased* version of the wireframe scene. Antialiasing is a technique for reducing the jagged effect created when only portions of neighboring pixels properly belong to the image being drawn. Such jaggies are usually the most visible with near-horizontal or near-vertical lines.

- Plate 4 shows a *flat-shaded* version of the scene. The objects in the scene are now shown as solid objects of a single color. They appear "flat" in the sense that they don't seem to respond to the lighting conditions in the room, so they don't appear smoothly rounded.

- Plate 5 shows a *lit, smooth-shaded* version of the scene. Note how the scene looks much more realistic and three-dimensional when the objects are shaded to respond to the light sources in the room; the surfaces of the objects now look smoothly rounded.

- Plate 6 adds *shadows* and *textures* to the previous version of the scene. Shadows aren't an explicitly defined feature of OpenGL (there is no "shadow command"), but you can create them yourself using the techniques described in Chapter 13. *Texture mapping* allows you to apply a two-dimensional texture to a three-dimensional object. In this scene, the top on the table surface is the most vibrant example of texture mapping. The walls, floor, table surface, and top (on top of the table) are all texture mapped.

- Plate 7 shows a *motion-blurred* object in the scene. The sphinx (or dog, depending on your Rorschach tendencies) appears to be captured as it's moving forward, leaving a blurred trace of its path of motion.

- Plate 8 shows the scene as it's drawn for the cover of the book from a different viewpoint. This plate illustrates that the image really is a snapshot of models of three-dimensional objects.

The next two color images illustrate yet more complicated visual effects that can be achieved with OpenGL:

- Plate 9 illustrates the use of atmospheric effects (collectively referred to as *fog*) to show the presence of particles in the air.

- Plate 10 shows the *depth-of-field effect*, which simulates the inability of a camera lens to maintain all objects in a photographed scene in focus. The camera focuses on a particular spot in the scene, and objects that are significantly closer or farther than that spot are somewhat blurred.

The color plates give you an idea of the kinds of things you can do with the OpenGL graphics system. The next several paragraphs briefly describe the order in which OpenGL performs the major graphics operations necessary to render an image on the screen. Appendix A describes this order of operations in more detail.

1. Construct shapes from geometric primitives, thereby creating mathematical descriptions of objects. (OpenGL considers points, lines, polygons, images, and bitmaps to be primitives.)

2. Arrange the objects in three-dimensional space and select the desired vantage point for viewing the composed scene.

3. Calculate the color of all the objects. The color might be explicitly assigned by the application, determined from specified lighting conditions, or obtained by pasting a texture onto the objects.

4. Convert the mathematical description of objects and their associated color information to pixels on the screen. This process is called *rasterization*.

During these stages, OpenGL might perform other operations, such as eliminating parts of objects that are hidden by other objects (the hidden parts won't be drawn, which might increase performance). In addition, after the scene is rasterized but just before it's drawn on the screen, you can manipulate the pixel data if you want.

A Very Simple OpenGL Program

Because you can do so many things with the OpenGL graphics system, an OpenGL program can be complicated. However, the basic structure of a useful program can be simple: Its tasks are to initialize certain states that control how OpenGL renders and to specify objects to be rendered.

Before you look at an OpenGL program, let's go over a few terms. *Rendering*, which you've already seen used, is the process by which a computer creates images from models. These *models*, or objects, are constructed from geometric primitives—points, lines, and polygons—that are specified by their *vertices*.

The final rendered image consists of pixels drawn on the screen; a *pixel*— short for picture element—is the smallest visible element the display hardware can put on the screen. Information about the pixels (for instance, what color they're supposed to be) is organized in system memory into bitplanes. A *bitplane* is an area of memory that holds one bit of information for every pixel on the screen; the bit might indicate how red a particular pixel is supposed to be, for example. The bitplanes are themselves organized into a *framebuffer*, which holds all the information that the graphics display needs to control the intensity of all the pixels on the screen.

Now look at an OpenGL program. Listing 1-1 renders a white rectangle on a black background, as shown in Figure 1-1.

Figure 1-1   A White Rectangle on a Black Background

Listing 1-1   A Simple OpenGL Program

```
#include <whateverYouNeed.h>

main() {

    OpenAWindowPlease();

    glClearColor(0.0, 0.0, 0.0, 0.0);
    glClear(GL_COLOR_BUFFER_BIT);
    glColor3f(1.0, 1.0, 1.0);
    glOrtho(-1.0, 1.0, -1.0, 1.0, -1.0, 1.0);
    glBegin(GL_POLYGON);
        glVertex2f(-0.5, -0.5);
        glVertex2f(-0.5, 0.5);
        glVertex2f(0.5, 0.5);
        glVertex2f(0.5, -0.5);
    glEnd();
    glFlush();

    KeepTheWindowOnTheScreenForAWhile();
}
```

The first line of the **main()** routine opens a window on the screen: The **OpenAWindowPlease()** routine is meant as a placeholder for a window system-specific routine. The next two lines are OpenGL commands that clear the window to black: **glClearColor()** establishes what color the window will be cleared to, and **glClear()** actually clears the window. Once the color to clear to is set, the window is cleared to that color whenever **glClear()** is called. The clearing color can be changed with another call to **glClearColor()**. Similarly, the **glColor3f()** command establishes what color to use for drawing objects—in this case, the color is white. All objects drawn after this point use this color, until it's changed with another call to set the color.

The next OpenGL command used in the program, **glOrtho()**, specifies the coordinate system OpenGL assumes as it draws the final image and how the image gets mapped to the screen. The next calls, which are bracketed by **glBegin()** and **glEnd()**, define the object to be drawn—in this example, a polygon with four vertices. The polygon's "corners" are defined by the **glVertex2f()** commands. As you might be able to guess from the arguments, which are (x, y) coordinate pairs, the polygon is a rectangle.

Finally, **glFlush()** ensures that the drawing commands are actually executed, rather than stored in a buffer awaiting additional OpenGL commands. The **KeepTheWindowOnTheScreenForAWhile()** placeholder routine forces the picture to remain on the screen instead of immediately disappearing.

OpenGL Command Syntax

As you might have observed from the simple program in the previous section, OpenGL commands use the prefix **gl** and initial capital letters for each word making up the command name (recall **glClearColor()**, for example). Similarly, OpenGL defined constants begin with GL_, use all capital letters, and use underscores to separate words (like GL_COLOR_BUFFER_BIT).

You might also have noticed some seemingly extraneous letters appended to some command names (the **3f** in **glColor3f()**, for example). It's true that the **Color** part of the command name is enough to define the command as one that sets the current color. However, more than one such command has been defined so that you can use different types of arguments. In particular, the **3** part of the suffix indicates that three arguments are given; another version of the **Color** command takes four arguments. The **f** part of the suffix indicates that the arguments are floating-point numbers. Some OpenGL commands accept as many as eight different data types for their arguments. The letters used as suffixes to specify these data types for ANSI C implementations of OpenGL are shown in Table 1-1, along with the corresponding OpenGL type definitions. The particular implementation of

OpenGL that you're using might not follow this scheme exactly; an implementation in C++ or Ada, for example, wouldn't need to.

Suffix	Data Type	Typical Corresponding C-Language Type	OpenGL Type Definition
b	8-bit integer	signed char	GLbyte
s	16-bit integer	short	GLshort
i	32-bit integer	long	GLint, GLsizei
f	32-bit floating-point	float	GLfloat, GLclampf
d	64-bit floating-point	double	GLdouble, GLclampd
ub	8-bit unsigned integer	unsigned char	GLubyte, GLboolean
us	16-bit unsigned integer	unsigned short	GLushort
ui	32-bit unsigned integer	unsigned long	GLuint, GLenum, GLbitfield

Table 1-1 Command Suffixes and Argument Data Types

Thus, the two commands

```
glVertex2i(1, 3);
glVertex2f(1.0, 3.0);
```

are equivalent, except that the first specifies the vertex's coordinates as 32-bit integers and the second specifies them as single-precision floating-point numbers.

Some OpenGL commands can take a final letter **v**, which indicates that the command takes a pointer to a vector (or array) of values rather than a series of individual arguments. Many commands have both vector and nonvector versions, but some commands accept only individual arguments and others require that at least some of the arguments be specified as a vector. The following lines show how you might use a vector and a nonvector version of the command that sets the current color:

```
glColor3f(1.0, 0.0, 0.0);

float color_array[] = {1.0, 0.0, 0.0};
glColor3fv(color_array);
```

In the rest of this guide (except in actual code examples), OpenGL commands are referred to by their base names only, and an asterisk is included to indicate that there may be more to the command name. For example, **glColor*()** stands for all variations of the command you use to set the current color. If we want to make a specific point about one version of a particular command, we include the suffix necessary to define that version. For example, **glVertex*v()** refers to all the vector versions of the command you use to specify vertices.

Finally, OpenGL defines the constant GLvoid; if you're programming in C, you can use this instead of void.

OpenGL as a State Machine

OpenGL is a state machine. You put it into various states (or modes) that then remain in effect until you change them. As you've already seen, the current color is a state variable. You can set the current color to white, red, or any other color, and thereafter every object is drawn with that color until you set the current color to something else. The current color is only one of many state variables that OpenGL preserves. Others control such things as the current viewing and projection transformations, line and polygon stipple patterns, polygon drawing modes, pixel-packing conventions, positions and characteristics of lights, and material properties of the objects being drawn. Many state variables refer to modes that are enabled or disabled with the command **glEnable()** or **glDisable()**.

Each state variable or mode has a default value, and at any point you can query the system for each variable's current value. Typically, you use one of the four following commands to do this: **glGetBooleanv()**, **glGetDoublev()**, **glGetFloatv()**, or **glGetIntegerv()**. Which of these commands you select depends on what data type you want the answer to be given in. Some state variables have a more specific query command (such as **glGetLight*()**, **glGetError()**, or **glGetPolygonStipple()**). In addition, you can save and later restore the values of a collection of state variables on an attribute stack with the **glPushAttrib()** and **glPopAttrib()** commands. Whenever possible, you should use these commands rather than any of the query commands, since they're likely to be more efficient.

The complete list of state variables you can query is found in Appendix B. For each variable, the appendix also lists the **glGet*()** command that returns the variable's value, the attribute class to which it belongs, and the variable's default value.

OpenGL-related Libraries

OpenGL provides a powerful but primitive set of rendering commands, and all higher-level drawing must be done in terms of these commands. Therefore, you might want to write your own library on top of OpenGL to simplify your programming tasks. Also, you might want to write some routines that allow an OpenGL program to work easily with your windowing system. In fact, several such libraries and routines have already been written to provide specialized features, as follows. Note that the first two libraries are provided with every OpenGL implementation, the third was written for this book and is available using ftp, and the fourth is a separate product that's based on OpenGL.

- The OpenGL Utility Library (GLU) contains several routines that use lower-level OpenGL commands to perform such tasks as setting up matrices for specific viewing orientations and projections, performing polygon tessellation, and rendering surfaces. This library is provided as part of your OpenGL implementation. It's described in more detail in Appendix C and in the *OpenGL Reference Manual*. The more useful GLU routines are described in the chapters in this guide, where they're relevant to the topic being discussed. GLU routines use the prefix **glu**.

- The OpenGL Extension to the X Window System (GLX) provides a means of creating an OpenGL context and associating it with a drawable window on a machine that uses the X Window System. GLX is provided as an adjunct to OpenGL. It's described in more detail in both Appendix D and the *OpenGL Reference Manual*. One of the GLX routines (for swapping framebuffers) is described in "Animation" on page 14. GLX routines use the prefix **glX**.

- The *OpenGL Programming Guide* Auxiliary Library was written specifically for this book to make programming examples simpler and yet more complete. It's the subject of the next section, and it's described in more detail in Appendix E. Auxiliary library routines use the prefix **aux**. "How to Obtain the Sample Code" on page vii describes how to obtain the source code for the auxiliary library.

- Open Inventor is an object-oriented toolkit based on OpenGL that provides objects and methods for creating interactive three-dimensional graphics applications. Available from Silicon Graphics and written in C++, Open Inventor provides pre-built objects and a built-in event model for user interaction, high-level application components for creating and editing three-dimensional scenes, and the ability to print objects and exchange data in other graphics formats.

The OpenGL Programming Guide Auxiliary Library

As you know, OpenGL contains rendering commands but is designed to be independent of any window system or operating system. Consequently, it contains no commands for opening windows or reading events from the keyboard or mouse. Unfortunately, it's impossible to write a complete graphics program without at least opening a window, and most interesting programs require a bit of user input or other services from the operating system or window system. In many cases, complete programs make the most interesting examples, so this book uses a small auxiliary library to simplify opening windows, detecting input, and so on.

In addition, since OpenGL's drawing commands are limited to those that generate simple geometric primitives (points, lines, and polygons), the auxiliary library includes several routines that create more complicated three-dimensional objects such as a sphere, a torus, and a teapot. This way, snapshots of program output can be interesting to look at. If you have an implementation of OpenGL and this auxiliary library on your system, the examples in this book should run without change when linked with them.

The auxiliary library is intentionally simple, and it would be difficult to build a large application on top of it. It's intended solely to support the examples in this book, but you may find it a useful starting point to begin building real applications. The rest of this section briefly describes the auxiliary library routines so that you can follow the programming examples in the rest of this book. Turn to Appendix E for more details about these routines.

Window Management

Three routines perform tasks necessary to initialize and open a window:

- **auxInitWindow()** opens a window on the screen. It enables the Escape key to be used to exit the program, and it sets the background color for the window to black.

- **auxInitPosition()** tells **auxInitWindow()** where to position a window on the screen.

- **auxInitDisplayMode()** tells **auxInitWindow()** whether to create an RGBA or color-index window. You can also specify a single- or double-buffered window. (If you're working in color-index mode, you'll want to load certain colors into the color map; use **auxSetOneColor()** to do this.) Finally, you can use this routine to indicate that you want the window to have an associated depth, stencil, and/or accumulation buffer.

Handling Input Events

You can use these routines to register callback commands that are invoked when specified events occur.

- **auxReshapeFunc()** indicates what action should be taken when the window is resized, moved, or exposed.

- **auxKeyFunc()** and **auxMouseFunc()** allow you to link a keyboard key or a mouse button with a routine that's invoked when the key or mouse button is pressed or released.

Drawing 3-D Objects

The auxiliary library includes several routines for drawing these three-dimensional objects:

sphere	octahedron
cube	dodecahedron
torus	icosahedron
cylinder	teapot
cone	

You can draw these objects as wireframes or as solid shaded objects with surface normals defined. For example, the routines for a sphere and a torus are as follows:

void **auxWireSphere**(GLdouble *radius*);

void **auxSolidSphere**(GLdouble *radius*);

void **auxWireTorus**(GLdouble *innerRadius*, GLdouble *outerRadius*);

void **auxSolidTorus**(GLdouble *innerRadius*, GLdouble *outerRadius*);

All these models are drawn centered at the origin. When drawn with unit scale factors, these models fit into a box with all coordinates from −1 to 1. Use the arguments for these routines to scale the objects.

Managing a Background Process

You can specify a function that's to be executed if no other events are pending—for example, when the event loop would otherwise be idle—with **auxIdleFunc()**. This routine takes a pointer to the function as its only argument. Pass in zero to disable the execution of the function.

Running the Program

Within your **main()** routine, call **auxMainLoop()** and pass it the name of the routine that redraws the objects in your scene. Listing 1-2 shows how you might use the auxiliary library to create the simple program shown in Listing 1-1.

Listing 1-2   A Simple OpenGL Program Using the Auxiliary Library: simple.c

```
#include <GL/gl.h>
#include "aux.h"

int main(int argc, char** argv)
{
    auxInitDisplayMode (AUX_SINGLE | AUX_RGBA);
    auxInitPosition (0, 0, 500, 500);
    auxInitWindow (argv[0]);

    glClearColor (0.0, 0.0, 0.0, 0.0);
    glClear(GL_COLOR_BUFFER_BIT);
    glColor3f(1.0, 1.0, 1.0);
    glMatrixMode(GL_PROJECTION);
    glLoadIdentity();
    glOrtho(-1.0, 1.0, -1.0, 1.0, -1.0, 1.0);
    glBegin(GL_POLYGON);
            glVertex2f(-0.5, -0.5);
            glVertex2f(-0.5, 0.5);
            glVertex2f(0.5, 0.5);
            glVertex2f(0.5, -0.5);
    glEnd();
    glFlush();

    sleep(10);
}
```

Animation

One of the most exciting things you can do on a graphics computer is draw pictures that move. Whether you're an engineer trying to see all sides of a mechanical part you're designing, a pilot learning to fly an airplane using a simulation, or merely a computer-game aficionado, it's clear that animation is an important part of computer graphics.

In a movie theater, motion is achieved by taking a sequence of pictures (24 per second), and then projecting them at 24 per second on the screen. Each frame is moved into position behind the lens, the shutter is opened, and the frame is displayed. The shutter is momentarily closed while the film is advanced to the next frame, then that frame is displayed, and so on. Although you're watching 24 different frames each second, your brain blends them all into a smooth animation. (The old Charlie Chaplin movies were shot at 16 frames per second and are noticeably jerky.) In fact, most modern projectors display each picture twice at a rate of 48 per second to reduce flickering. Computer-graphics screens typically refresh (redraw the picture) approximately 60 to 76 times per second, and some even run at about 120 refreshes per second. Clearly, 60 per second is smoother than 30, and 120 is marginally better than 60. Refresh rates faster than 120, however, are beyond the point of diminishing returns, since the human eye is only so good.

The key idea that makes motion picture projection work is that when it is displayed, each frame is complete. Suppose you try to do computer animation of your million-frame movie with a program like this:

```
open_window();
for (i = 0; i < 1000000; i++) {
    clear_the_window();
    draw_frame(i);
    wait_until_a_24th_of_a_second_is_over();
}
```

If you add the time it takes for your system to clear the screen and to draw a typical frame, this program gives more and more disturbing results depending on how close to 1/24 second it takes to clear and draw. Suppose the drawing takes nearly a full 1/24 second. Items drawn first are visible for the full 1/24 second and present a solid image on the screen; items drawn toward the end are instantly cleared as the program starts on the next frame, so they present at best a ghostlike image, since for most of the 1/24 second your eye is viewing the cleared background instead of the items that were unlucky enough to be drawn last. The problem is that this program doesn't display completely drawn frames; instead, you watch the drawing as it happens.

An easy solution is to provide *double-buffering*—hardware or software that supplies two complete color buffers. One is displayed while the other is being drawn. When the drawing of a frame is complete, the two buffers are swapped, so the one that was being viewed is now used for drawing, and vice versa. It's like a movie projector with only two frames in a loop; while one is being projected on the screen, an artist is desperately erasing and redrawing the frame that's not visible. As long as the artist is quick enough, the viewer notices no difference between this setup and one where all the frames are already drawn and the projector is simply displaying them one after the other. With double-buffering, every frame is shown only when the drawing is complete; the viewer never sees a partially drawn frame.

A modified version of the preceding program that does display smoothly animated graphics might look like this:

```
open_window_in_double_buffer_mode();
for (i = 0; i < 1000000; i++) {
    clear_the_window();
    draw_frame(i);
    swap_the_buffers();
}
```

In addition to simply swapping the viewable and drawable buffers, the **swap_the_buffers()** routine waits until the current screen refresh period is over so that the previous buffer is completely displayed. This routine also allows the new buffer to be completely displayed, starting from the beginning. Assuming that your system refreshes the display 60 times per second, this means that the fastest frame rate you can achieve is 60 frames per second, and if all your frames can be cleared and drawn in under 1/60 second, your animation will run smoothly at that rate.

What often happens on such a system is that the frame is too complicated to draw in 1/60 second, so each frame is displayed more than once. If, for example, it takes 1/45 second to draw a frame, you get 30 frames per second, and the graphics are idle for 1/30–1/45=1/90 second per frame. Although 1/90 second of wasted time might not sound bad, it's wasted each 1/30 second, so actually one-third of the time is wasted.

In addition, the video refresh rate is constant, which can have some unexpected performance consequences. For example, with the 1/60 second per refresh monitor and a constant frame rate, you can run at 60 frames per second, 30 frames per second, 20 per second, 15 per second, 12 per second, and so on (60/1, 60/2, 60/3, 60/4, 60/5, ...). That means that if you're writing an application and gradually adding features (say it's a flight simulator, and you're adding ground scenery), at first each feature you add has no effect on the overall performance—you still get 60 frames per second. Then, all of a sudden, you add one new feature, and your performance is cut in half because the system can't quite draw the whole thing in 1/60 of a second, so it misses the first possible buffer-swapping time. A similar thing happens when the drawing time per frame is more than 1/30 second—the performance drops from 30 to 20 frames per second, giving a 33 percent performance hit.

Another problem is that if the scene's complexity is close to any of the magic times (1/60 second, 2/60 second, 3/60 second, and so on in this example), then because of random variation, some frames go slightly over the time and some slightly under, and the frame rate is irregular, which can be visually disturbing. In this case, if you can't simplify the scene so that all the frames are fast enough, it might be better to add an intentional tiny delay to make sure they all miss, giving a constant, slower, frame rate. If your frames have drastically different complexities, a more sophisticated approach might be necessary.

Interestingly, the structure of real animation programs does not differ too much from this description. Usually, the entire buffer is redrawn from scratch for each frame, as it is easier to do this than to figure out what parts require redrawing. This is especially true with applications such as three-dimensional flight simulators where a tiny change in the plane's orientation changes the position of everything outside the window.

In most animations, the objects in a scene are simply redrawn with different transformations—the viewpoint of the viewer moves, or a car moves down the road a bit, or an object is rotated slightly. If significant modifications to a structure are being made for each frame where there's significant recomputation, the attainable frame rate often slows down. Keep in mind, however, that the idle time after the **swap_the_buffers**() routine can often be used for such calculations.

OpenGL doesn't have a **swap_the_buffers**() command because the feature might not be available on all hardware and, in any case, it's highly dependent on the window system. However, GLX provides such a command, for use on machines that use the X Window System:

```
void glXSwapBuffers(Display *dpy, Window window);
```

Listing 1-3 illustrates the use of **glXSwapBuffers**() in an example that draws a square that rotates constantly, as shown in Figure 1-2.

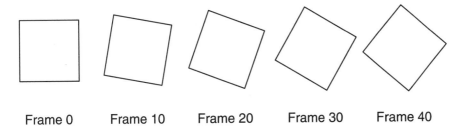

Frame 0   Frame 10   Frame 20   Frame 30   Frame 40

Figure 1-2   A Double-Buffered Rotating Square

Listing 1-3   A Double-Buffered Program: double.c

```
#include <GL/gl.h>
#include <GL/glu.h>
#include <GL/glx.h>
#include "aux.h"

static GLfloat spin = 0.0;

void display(void)
{
    glClear(GL_COLOR_BUFFER_BIT);

    glPushMatrix();
    glRotatef(spin, 0.0, 0.0, 1.0);
    glRectf(-25.0, -25.0, 25.0, 25.0);
    glPopMatrix();

    glFlush();
    glXSwapBuffers(auxXDisplay(), auxXWindow());
}

void spinDisplay(void)
{
    spin = spin + 2.0;
    if (spin > 360.0)
        spin = spin - 360.0;
    display();
}

void startIdleFunc(AUX_EVENTREC *event)
{
    auxIdleFunc(spinDisplay);
}
```

```
void stopIdleFunc(AUX_EVENTREC *event)
{
    auxIdleFunc(0);
}

void myinit(void)
{
    glClearColor(0.0, 0.0, 0.0, 1.0);
    glColor3f(1.0, 1.0, 1.0);
    glShadeModel(GL_FLAT);
}

void myReshape(GLsizei w, GLsizei h)
{
    glViewport(0, 0, w, h);
    glMatrixMode(GL_PROJECTION);
    glLoadIdentity();
    if (w <= h)
        glOrtho (-50.0, 50.0, -50.0*(GLfloat)h/(GLfloat)w,
            50.0*(GLfloat)h/(GLfloat)w, -1.0, 1.0);
    else
        glOrtho (-50.0*(GLfloat)w/(GLfloat)h,
            50.0*(GLfloat)w/(GLfloat)h, -50.0, 50.0, -1.0, 1.0);
    glMatrixMode(GL_MODELVIEW);
    glLoadIdentity ();
}


int main(int argc, char** argv)
{
    auxInitDisplayMode(AUX_DOUBLE | AUX_RGBA);
    auxInitPosition(0, 0, 500, 500);
    auxInitWindow(argv[0]);
    myinit();
    auxReshapeFunc(myReshape);
    auxIdleFunc(spinDisplay);
    auxMouseFunc(AUX_LEFTBUTTON, AUX_MOUSEDOWN, startIdleFunc);
    auxMouseFunc(AUX_MIDDLEBUTTON, AUX_MOUSEDOWN, stopIdleFunc);
    auxMainLoop(display);
}
```

Chapter 2

Drawing Geometric Objects

Chapter Objectives

After reading this chapter, you'll be able to do the following:

- Clear the window to an arbitrary color

- Draw with any geometric primitive—points, lines, and polygons—in two or three dimensions

- Control the display of those primitives—for example, draw dashed lines or outlined polygons

- Specify normal vectors at appropriate points on the surface of solid objects

- Force any pending drawing to complete

Although you can draw complex and interesting pictures using OpenGL, they're all constructed from a small number of primitive graphical items. This shouldn't be too surprising—look at what Leonardo da Vinci accomplished with just pencils and paintbrushes.

At the highest level of abstraction, there are three basic drawing operations: clearing the window, drawing a geometric object, and drawing a raster object. Raster objects, which include such things as two-dimensional images, bitmaps, and character fonts, are covered in Chapter 8. In this chapter, you learn how to clear the screen and to draw geometric objects, including points, straight lines, and flat polygons.

You might think to yourself, "Wait a minute. I've seen lots of computer graphics in movies and on television, and there are plenty of beautifully shaded curved lines and surfaces. How are those drawn, if all OpenGL can draw are straight lines and flat polygons?" Even the image on the cover of this book includes a round table and objects on the table that have curved surfaces. It turns out that all the curved lines and surfaces you've seen are approximated by large numbers of little flat polygons or straight lines, in much the same way that the globe on the cover is constructed from a large set of rectangular blocks. The globe doesn't appear to have a smooth surface because the blocks are relatively large compared to the globe. Later in this chapter, we show you how to construct curved lines and surfaces from lots of small geometric primitives.

This chapter has the following major sections:

- **"A Drawing Survival Kit"** explains how to clear the window and force drawing to be completed. It also gives you basic information about controlling the color of geometric objects and about hidden-surface removal.

- **"Describing Points, Lines, and Polygons"** shows you what the set of primitive geometric objects is and how to draw them.

- **"Displaying Points, Lines, and Polygons"** explains what control you have over the details of how primitives are drawn—for example, what diameter points have, whether lines are solid or dashed, and whether polygons are outlined or filled.

- **"Normal Vectors"** discusses how to specify normal vectors for geometric objects and (briefly) what these vectors are for.

- **"Some Hints for Building Polygonal Models of Surfaces"** explores the issues and techniques involved in constructing polygonal approximations to surfaces.

One thing to keep in mind as you read the rest of this chapter is that with OpenGL, unless you specify otherwise, every time you issue a drawing command, the specified object is drawn. This might seem obvious, but in some systems, you first make a list of things to draw, and when it's complete, you tell the graphics hardware to draw the items in the list. The first style is called *immediate-mode* graphics and is OpenGL's default style. In addition to using immediate mode, you can choose to save some commands in a list (called a *display list*) for later drawing. Immediate-mode graphics is typically easier to program, but display lists are often more efficient. Chapter 4 tells you how to use display lists and why you might want to use them.

A Drawing Survival Kit

This section explains how to clear the window in preparation for drawing, set the color of objects that are to be drawn, and force drawing to be completed. None of these subjects has anything to do with geometric objects in a direct way, but any program that draws geometric objects has to deal with these issues. This section also introduces the concept of hidden-surface removal, a technique that can be used to draw geometric objects easily.

Clearing the Window

Drawing on a computer screen is different from drawing on paper in that the paper starts out white, and all you have to do is draw the picture. On a computer, the memory holding the picture is usually filled with the last picture you drew, so you typically need to clear it to some background color before you start to draw the new scene. The color you use for the background depends on the application. For a word processor, you might clear to white (the color of the paper) before you begin to draw the text. If you're drawing a view from a spaceship, you clear to the black of space before beginning to draw the stars, planets, and alien spaceships. Sometimes you might not need to clear the screen at all; for example, if the image is the inside of a room, the entire graphics window gets covered as you draw all the walls.

At this point, you might be wondering why we keep talking about *clearing* the window—why not just draw a rectangle of the appropriate color that's large enough to cover the entire window? First, a special command to clear a window can be much more efficient than a general-purpose drawing command. In addition, as you'll see in Chapter 3, OpenGL allows you to set the coordinate system, viewing position, and viewing direction arbitrarily, so it might be difficult to figure out an appropriate size and location for a window-clearing rectangle. Also, you can have OpenGL use hidden-surface removal techniques that eliminate objects obscured by others nearer to the eye; thus, if the window-clearing rectangle is to be a background, you must make sure that it's behind all the other objects of interest. With an arbitrary coordinate system and point of view, this might be difficult. Finally, on many machines, the graphics hardware consists of multiple buffers in addition to the buffer containing colors of the pixels that are displayed. These other buffers must be cleared from time to time, and it's convenient to have a single command that can clear any combination of them. (All the possible buffers are discussed in Chapter 10.)

As an example, these lines of code clear the window to black:

```
glClearColor(0.0, 0.0, 0.0, 0.0);
glClear(GL_COLOR_BUFFER_BIT);
```

The first line sets the clearing color to black, and the next command clears the entire window to the current clearing color. The single parameter to **glClear()** indicates which buffers are to be cleared. In this case, the program clears only the color buffer, where the image displayed on the screen is kept. Typically, you set the clearing color once, early in your application, and then you clear the buffers as often as necessary. OpenGL keeps track of the current clearing color as a state variable rather than requiring you to specify it each time a buffer is cleared.

Chapter 5 and Chapter 10 talk about how other buffers are used. For now, all you need to know is that clearing them is simple. For example, to clear both the color buffer and the depth buffer, you would use the following sequence of commands:

```
glClearColor(0.0, 0.0, 0.0, 0.0);
glClearDepth(0.0);
glClear(GL_COLOR_BUFFER_BIT | GL_DEPTH_BUFFER_BIT);
```

In this case, the call to **glClearColor()** is the same as before, the **glClearDepth()** command specifies the value to which every pixel of the depth buffer is to be set, and the parameter to the **glClear()** command now consists of the logical OR of all the buffers to be cleared. The following summary of **glClear()** includes a table that lists the buffers that can be cleared, their names, and the chapter where each type of buffer is discussed.

void **glClearColor**(GLclampf *red*, GLclampf *green*, GLclampf *blue*, GLclampf *alpha*);

Sets the current clearing color for use in clearing color buffers in RGBA mode. For more information on RGBA mode, see Chapter 5. The *red, green, blue,* and *alpha* values are clamped if necessary to the range [0,1]. The default clearing color is (0, 0, 0, 0), which is black.

void **glClear**(GLbitfield *mask*);

Clears the specified buffers to their current clearing values. The *mask* argument is a bitwise-ORed combination of the values listed in Table 2-1.

Buffer	Name	Reference
Color buffer	GL_COLOR_BUFFER_BIT	Chapter 5
Depth buffer	GL_DEPTH_BUFFER_BIT	Chapter 10
Accumulation buffer	GL_ACCUM_BUFFER_BIT	Chapter 10
Stencil buffer	GL_STENCIL_BUFFER_BIT	Chapter 10

Table 2-1   Clearing Buffers

Before issuing a command to clear multiple buffers, you have to set the values to which each buffer is to be cleared if you want something other than the default color, depth value, accumulation color, and stencil index. In addition to the **glClearColor**() and **glClearDepth**() commands that set the current values for clearing the color and depth buffers, **glClearIndex**(), **glClearAccum**(), and **glClearStencil**() specify the color index, accumulation color, and stencil index used to clear the corresponding buffers. See Chapter 5 and Chapter 10 for descriptions of these buffers and their uses.

OpenGL allows you to specify multiple buffers because clearing is generally a slow operation, since every pixel in the window (possibly millions) is touched, and some graphics hardware allows sets of buffers to be cleared simultaneously. Hardware that doesn't support simultaneous clears performs them sequentially. The difference between

```
glClear(GL_COLOR_BUFFER_BIT | GL_DEPTH_BUFFER_BIT);
```

and

```
glClear(GL_COLOR_BUFFER_BIT);
glClear(GL_DEPTH_BUFFER_BIT);
```

is that although both have the same final effect, the first example might run faster on many machines. It certainly won't run more slowly.

Specifying a Color

With OpenGL, the description of the shape of an object being drawn is independent of the description of its color. Whenever a particular geometric object is drawn, it's drawn using the currently specified coloring scheme. The coloring scheme might be as simple as "draw everything in fire-engine red," or might be as complicated as "assume the object is made out of blue plastic, that there's a yellow spotlight pointed in such and such a direction, and that there's a general low-level reddish-brown light everywhere else." In general, an OpenGL programmer first sets the color or coloring scheme, and then draws the objects. Until the color or coloring scheme is changed, all objects are drawn in that color or using that coloring scheme. This method helps OpenGL achieve higher drawing performance than would result if it didn't keep track of the current color.

For example, the pseudocode

```
set_current_color(red);
draw_object(A);
draw_object(B);
set_current_color(green);
set_current_color(blue);
draw_object(C);
```

draws objects A and B in red, and object C in blue. The command on the fourth line that sets the current color to green is wasted.

Coloring, lighting, and shading are all large topics with entire chapters or large sections devoted to them. To draw geometric primitives that can be seen, however, you need some basic knowledge of how to set the current color; this information is provided in the next paragraphs. For details on these topics, see Chapter 5 and Chapter 6.

To set a color, use the command **glColor3f()**. It takes three parameters, all of which are floating-point numbers between 0.0 and 1.0. The parameters are, in order, the red, green, and blue components of the color. You can think of these three values as specifying a "mix" of colors: 0.0 means don't use any of that component, and 1.0 means use all you can of that component. Thus, the code

```
glColor3f(1.0, 0.0, 0.0);
```

makes the brightest red the system can draw, with no green or blue components. All zeros makes black; in contrast, all ones makes white. Setting all three components to 0.5 yields gray (halfway between black and white). Here are eight commands and the colors they would set:

```
glColor3f(0.0, 0.0, 0.0);       black
glColor3f(1.0, 0.0, 0.0);       red
glColor3f(0.0, 1.0, 0.0);       green
glColor3f(1.0, 1.0, 0.0);       yellow
glColor3f(0.0, 0.0, 1.0);       blue
glColor3f(1.0, 0.0, 1.0);       magenta
glColor3f(0.0, 1.0, 1.0);       cyan
glColor3f(1.0, 1.0, 1.0);       white
```

You might have noticed earlier that when you're setting the color to clear the color buffer, **glClearColor()** takes four parameters, the first three of which match the parameters for **glColor3f()**. The fourth parameter is the alpha value; it's covered in detail in "Blending" on page 196. For now, always set the fourth parameter to 0.0.

Forcing Completion of Drawing

Most modern graphics systems can be thought of as an assembly line, sometimes called a graphics *pipeline*. The main central processing unit (CPU) issues a drawing command, perhaps other hardware does geometric transformations, clipping occurs, then shading or texturing is performed, and finally, the values are written into the bitplanes for display (see Appendix A for details on the order of operations). In high-end architectures, each of these operations is performed by a different piece of hardware that's been designed to perform its particular task quickly. In such an architecture, there's no need for the CPU to wait for each drawing command to complete before issuing the next one. While the CPU is sending a vertex down the pipeline, the transformation hardware is working on transforming the last one sent, the one before that is being clipped, and so on. In such a system, if the CPU waited for each command to complete before issuing the next, there could be a huge performance penalty.

In addition, the application might be running on more than one machine. For example, suppose that the main program is running elsewhere (on a machine called the client), and that you're viewing the results of the drawing on your workstation or terminal (the server), which is connected by a network to the client. In that case, it might be horribly inefficient to send each command over the network one at a time, since considerable overhead is often associated with each network transmission. Usually, the client gathers a collection of commands into a single network packet before sending it. Unfortunately, the network code on the client typically has no way of knowing that the graphics program is finished drawing a frame or scene. In the worst case, it waits forever for enough additional drawing commands to fill a packet, and you never see the completed drawing.

For this reason, OpenGL provides the command **glFlush()**, which forces the client to send the network packet even though it might not be full. Where there is no network and all commands are truly executed immediately on the server, **glFlush()** might have no effect. However, if you're writing a program that you want to work properly both with and without a network, include a call to **glFlush()** at the end of each frame or scene. Note that **glFlush()** doesn't wait for the drawing to complete—it just forces the drawing to begin execution, thereby guaranteeing that all previous commands execute in finite time even if no further rendering commands are executed.

A few commands—for example, commands that swap buffers in double-buffer mode—automatically flush pending commands onto the network before they can occur.

---

void **glFlush**(void);

Forces previously issued OpenGL commands to begin execution, thus guaranteeing that they complete in finite time.

If **glFlush()** isn't sufficient for you, try **glFinish()**. This command flushes the network as **glFlush()** does and then waits for notification from the graphics hardware or network indicating that the drawing is complete in the framebuffer. You might need to use **glFinish()** if you want to synchronize tasks—for example, to make sure that your three-dimensional rendering is on the screen before you use Display PostScript to draw labels on top of the rendering. Another example would be to ensure that the drawing is complete before it begins to accept user input. After you issue a **glFinish()** command, your graphics process is blocked until it receives notification from the graphics hardware (or client, if you're running over a network) that the drawing is complete. Keep in mind that excessive use of **glFinish()** can reduce the performance of your application, especially if you're running over a network, because it requires round-trip communication. If **glFlush()** is sufficient for your needs, use it instead of **glFinish()**.

---
void **glFinish**(void);

Forces all previously issued OpenGL commands to complete. This command doesn't return until all effects from previous commands are fully realized.

Hidden-Surface Removal Survival Kit

When you draw a scene composed of three-dimensional objects, some of them might obscure all or parts of others. Changing your viewpoint can change the obscuring relationship. For example, if you view the scene from the opposite direction, any object that was previously in front of another is now behind it. To draw a realistic scene, these obscuring relationships must be maintained. If your code works something like this

```
while (1) {
    get_viewing_point_from_mouse_position();
    glClear(GL_COLOR_BUFFER_BIT);
    draw_3d_object_A();
    draw_3d_object_B();
}
```

it might be that for some mouse positions, object A obscures object B, and for others, the opposite relationship might hold. If nothing special is done, the preceding code always draws object B second, and thus on top of object A, no matter what viewing position is selected.

The elimination of parts of solid objects that are obscured by others is called *hidden-surface removal*. (Hidden-line removal, which does the same job for objects represented as wireframe skeletons, is a bit trickier, and it isn't discussed here. See "Hidden-Line Removal" on page 402 for details.) The easiest way to achieve hidden-surface removal is to use the depth buffer (sometimes called a z-buffer). (Also see Chapter 10.)

A depth buffer works by associating a depth, or distance from the viewpoint, with each pixel on the window. Initially, the depth values for all pixels are set to the largest possible distance using the **glClear()** command with GL_DEPTH_BUFFER_BIT, and then the objects in the scene are drawn in any order.

Graphical calculations in hardware or software convert each surface that's drawn to a set of pixels on the window where the surface will appear if it isn't obscured by something else. In addition, the distance from the eye is computed. With depth buffering enabled, before each pixel is drawn, a comparison is done with the depth value already stored at the pixel. If the new pixel is closer to the eye than what's there, the new pixel's color and depth values replace those that are currently written into the pixel. If the new pixel's depth is greater than what's currently'there, the new pixel would be obscured, and the color and depth information for the incoming pixel is discarded. Since information is discarded rather than used for drawing, hidden-surface removal can increase your performance.

To use depth buffering, you need to enable depth buffering. This has to be done only once. Each time you draw the scene, before drawing you need to clear the depth buffer and then draw the objects in the scene in any order.

To convert the preceding program fragment so that it performs hidden-surface removal, modify it to the following:

```
glEnable(GL_DEPTH_TEST);
...
while (1) {
   glClear(GL_COLOR_BUFFER_BIT | GL_DEPTH_BUFFER_BIT);
   get_viewing_point_from_mouse_position();
   draw_3d_object_A();
   draw_3d_object_B(); }
```

The argument to **glClear()** clears both the depth and color buffers.

Describing Points, Lines, and Polygons

This section explains how to describe OpenGL geometric primitives. All geometric primitives are eventually described in terms of their *vertices*—coordinates that define the points themselves, the endpoints of line segments, or the corners of polygons. The next section discusses how these primitives are displayed and what control you have over their display.

What Are Points, Lines, and Polygons?

You probably have a fairly good idea of what a mathematician means by the terms *point*, *line*, and *polygon*. The OpenGL meanings aren't quite the same, however, and it's important to understand the differences. The differences arise because mathematicians can think in a geometrically perfect world, whereas the rest of us have to deal with real-world limitations.

For example, one difference comes from the limitations of computer-based calculations. In any OpenGL implementation, floating-point calculations are of finite precision, and they have round-off errors. Consequently, the coordinates of OpenGL points, lines, and polygons suffer from the same problems.

Another difference arises from the limitations of a bitmapped graphics display. On such a display, the smallest displayable unit is a pixel, and although pixels might be less than 1/100th of an inch wide, they are still much larger than the mathematician's infinitely small (for points) or infinitely thin (for lines). When OpenGL performs calculations, it assumes points are represented as vectors of floating-point numbers. However, a point is typically (but not always) drawn as a single pixel, and many different points with slightly different coordinates could be drawn by OpenGL on the same pixel.

Points

A point is represented by a set of floating-point numbers called a *vertex*. All internal calculations are done as if vertices are three-dimensional. Vertices specified by the user as two-dimensional (that is, with only x and y coordinates) are assigned a z coordinate equal to zero by OpenGL.

OpenGL works in the homogeneous coordinates of three-dimensional projective geometry, so for internal calculations, all vertices are represented with four floating-point coordinates (x, y, z, w). If w is different from zero, these coordinates correspond to the euclidean three-dimensional point $(x/w, y/w, z/w)$. You can specify the w coordinate in OpenGL commands, but that's rarely done. If the w coordinate isn't specified, it's understood to be 1.0. For more information about homogeneous coordinate systems, see Appendix G.

Advanced

Lines

In OpenGL, *line* means *line segment*, not the mathematician's version that extends to infinity in both directions. There are easy ways to specify a connected series of line segments, or even a closed, connected series of segments (see Figure 2-1). In all cases, though, the lines comprising the connected series are specified in terms of the vertices at their endpoints.

 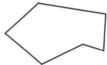

Figure 2-1   Two Connected Series of Line Segments

Polygons

Polygons are the areas enclosed by single closed loops of line segments, where the line segments are specified by the vertices at their endpoints. Polygons are typically drawn with the pixels in the interior filled in, but you can also draw them as outlines or a set of points, as described in "Polygon Details" on page 45.

In general, polygons can be complicated, so OpenGL makes some strong restrictions on what constitutes a primitive polygon. First, the edges of OpenGL polygons can't intersect (a mathematician would call this a *simple polygon*). Second, OpenGL polygons must be convex, meaning that they cannot have indentations. Stated precisely, a region is convex if, given any two points in the interior, the line segment joining them is also in the interior. See Figure 2-2 for some examples of valid and invalid polygons. OpenGL, however, doesn't restrict the number of line segments making up the boundary of a convex polygon. Note that polygons with holes can't be described. They are nonconvex, and they can't be drawn with a boundary made up of a single closed loop. Be aware that if you present OpenGL with a nonconvex filled polygon, it might not draw it as you expect. For instance, on most systems no more than the *convex hull* of the polygon would be filled, but on some systems, less than the convex hull might be filled.

Valid   Invalid

Figure 2-2   Valid and Invalid Polygons

For many applications, you need nonsimple polygons, nonconvex polygons, or polygons with holes. Since all such polygons can be formed from unions of simple convex polygons, some routines to describe more complex objects are provided in the GLU. These routines take complex descriptions and *tessellate* them, or break them down into groups of the simpler OpenGL polygons that can then be rendered. (See Appendix C for more information about the tessellation routines.) The reason for OpenGL's restrictions on valid polygon types is that it's simpler to provide fast polygon-rendering hardware for that restricted class of polygons.

Since OpenGL vertices are always three-dimensional, the points forming the boundary of a particular polygon don't necessarily lie on the same plane in space. (Of course, they do in many cases—if all the z coordinates are zero, for example, or if the polygon is a triangle.) If a polygon's vertices don't lie in the same plane, then after various rotations in space, changes in the viewpoint, and projection onto the display screen, the points might no longer form a simple convex polygon. For example, imagine a four-point quadrilateral where the points are slightly out of plane, and look at it almost edge-on. You can get a nonsimple polygon that resembles a bow tie, as shown in Figure 2-3, which isn't guaranteed to render correctly. This situation isn't all that unusual if you approximate surfaces by quadrilaterals made of points lying on the true surface. You can always avoid the problem by using triangles, since any three points always lie on a plane.

Figure 2-3   Nonplanar Polygon Transformed to Nonsimple Polygon

Describing Points, Lines, and Polygons   **31**

Rectangles

Since rectangles are so common in graphics applications, OpenGL provides a filled-rectangle drawing primitive, **glRect*()**. You can draw a rectangle as a polygon, as described in "OpenGL Geometric Drawing Primitives" on page 34, but your particular implementation of OpenGL might have optimized **glRect*()** for rectangles.

---

void **glRect**{sifd}(*TYPE x1, TYPE y1, TYPE x2, TYPE y2*);
void **glRect**{sifd}**v**(*TYPE *v1, TYPE *v2*);

Draws the rectangle defined by the corner points (*x1, y1*) and (*x2, y2*). The rectangle lies in the plane *z*=0 and has sides parallel to the *x*- and *y*-axes. If the vector form of the function is used, the corners are given by two pointers to arrays, each of which contains an (*x, y*) pair.

Note that although the rectangle begins with a particular orientation in three-dimensional space (in the *x-y* plane and parallel to the axes), you can change this by applying rotations or other transformations. See Chapter 3 for information about how to do this.

Curves

Any smoothly curved line or surface can be approximated—to any arbitrary degree of accuracy—by short line segments or small polygonal regions. Thus, subdividing curved lines and surfaces sufficiently and then approximating them with straight line segments or flat polygons makes them appear curved (see Figure 2-4). If you're skeptical that this really works, imagine subdividing until each line segment or polygon is so tiny that it's smaller than a pixel on the screen.

Figure 2-4   Approximating Curves

Even though curves aren't geometric primitives, OpenGL does provide some direct support for drawing them. See Chapter 11 for information about how to draw curves and curved surfaces.

Specifying Vertices

With OpenGL, all geometric objects are ultimately described as an ordered set of vertices. You use the **glVertex*()** command to specify a vertex.

---

void **glVertex**{234}{sifd}[v](*TYPE coords*);

Specifies a vertex for use in describing a geometric object. You can supply up to four coordinates (*x, y, z, w*) for a particular vertex or as few as two (*x, y*) by selecting the appropriate version of the command. If you use a version that doesn't explicitly specify *z* or *w*, *z* is understood to be 0 and *w* is understood to be 1. Calls to **glVertex*()** should be executed between a **glBegin()** and **glEnd()** pair.

Here are some examples of using **glVertex*()**:

```
glVertex2s(2, 3);
glVertex3d(0.0, 0.0, 3.1415926535898);
glVertex4f(2.3, 1.0, -2.2, 2.0);

GLdouble dvect[3] = {5.0, 9.0, 1992.0};
glVertex3dv(dvect);
```

The first example represents a vertex with three-dimensional coordinates (2, 3, 0). (Remember that if it isn't specified, the *z* coordinate is understood to be 0.) The coordinates in the second example are (0.0, 0.0, 3.1415926535898) (double-precision floating-point numbers). The third example represents the vertex with three-dimensional coordinates (1.15, 0.5, –1.1). (Remember that the *x, y,* and *z* coordinates are eventually divided by the *w* coordinate.) In the final example, *dvect* is a pointer to an array of three double-precision floating-point numbers.

On some machines, the vector form of **glVertex*()** is more efficient, since only a single parameter needs to be passed to the graphics subsystem, and special hardware might be able to send a whole series of coordinates in a single batch. If your machine is like this, it's to your advantage to arrange your data so that the vertex coordinates are packed sequentially in memory.

OpenGL Geometric Drawing Primitives

Now that you've seen how to specify vertices, you still need to know how to tell OpenGL to create a set of points, a line, or a polygon from those vertices. To do this, you bracket each set of vertices between a call to **glBegin()** and a call to **glEnd()**. The argument passed to **glBegin()** determines what sort of geometric primitive is constructed from the vertices. For example, the following code specifies the vertices for the polygon shown in Figure 2-5:

```
glBegin(GL_POLYGON);
    glVertex2f(0.0, 0.0);
    glVertex2f(0.0, 3.0);
    glVertex2f(3.0, 3.0);
    glVertex2f(4.0, 1.5);
    glVertex2f(3.0, 0.0);
glEnd();
```

GL_POLYGON   GL_POINTS

Figure 2-5   Drawing a Polygon or a Set of Points

If you had used GL_POINTS instead of GL_POLYGON, the primitive would have been simply the five points shown in Figure 2-5. Table 2-2 in the following function summary for **glBegin()** lists the ten possible arguments and the corresponding type of primitive.

void **glBegin**(GLenum *mode*);

Marks the beginning of a vertex list that describes a geometric primitive. The type of primitive is indicated by *mode*, which can be any of the values shown in Table 2-2.

Value	Meaning
GL_POINTS	individual points
GL_LINES	pairs of vertices interpreted as individual line segments
GL_POLYGON	boundary of a simple, convex polygon
GL_TRIANGLES	triples of vertices interpreted as triangles
GL_QUADS	quadruples of vertices interpreted as four-sided polygons
GL_LINE_STRIP	series of connected line segments
GL_LINE_LOOP	same as above, with a segment added between last and first vertices
GL_TRIANGLE_STRIP	linked strip of triangles
GL_TRIANGLE_FAN	linked fan of triangles
GL_QUAD_STRIP	linked strip of quadrilaterals

Table 2-2   Geometric Primitive Names and Meanings

void **glEnd**(void);

Marks the end of a vertex list.

Figure 2-6 shows examples of all the geometric primitives listed in Table 2-2. The paragraphs that follow the figure give precise descriptions of the pixels that are drawn for each of the objects. Note that in addition to points, several types of lines and polygons are defined. Obviously, you can find many ways to draw the same primitive. The method you choose depends on your vertex data.

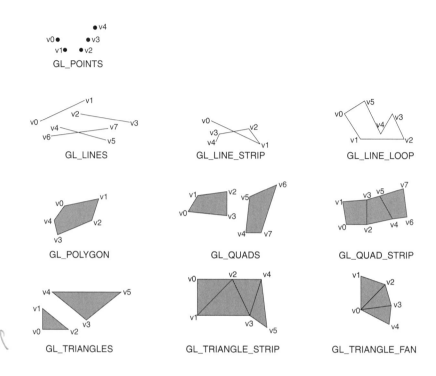

Figure 2-6   Geometric Primitive Types

As you read the following descriptions, assume that *n* vertices (v_0, v_1, v_2, ... , v_{n-1}) are described between a **glBegin()** and **glEnd()** pair.

GL_POINTS	Draws a point at each of the *n* vertices.
GL_LINES	Draws a series of unconnected line segments. Segments are drawn between v_0 and v_1, between v_2 and v_3, and so on. If *n* is odd, the last segment is drawn between v_{n-3} and v_{n-2}, and v_{n-1} is ignored.
GL_POLYGON	Draws a polygon using the points v_0, ... , v_{n-1} as vertices. *n* must be at least 3, or nothing is drawn. In addition, the polygon specified must not intersect itself and must be convex. If the vertices don't satisfy these conditions, the results are unpredictable.

GL_TRIANGLES	Draws a series of triangles (three-sided polygons) using vertices v_0, v_1, v_2, then v_3, v_4, v_5, and so on. If n isn't an exact multiple of 3, the final one or two vertices are ignored.
GL_LINE_STRIP	Draws a line segment from v_0 to v_1, then from v_1 to v_2, and so on, finally drawing the segment from v_{n-2} to v_{n-1}. Thus, a total of $n–1$ line segments are drawn. Nothing is drawn unless n is larger than 1. There are no restrictions on the vertices describing a line strip (or a line loop); the lines can intersect arbitrarily.
GL_LINE_LOOP	Same as GL_LINE_STRIP, except that a final line segment is drawn from v_{n-1} to v_0, completing a loop.
GL_QUADS	Draws a series of quadrilaterals (four-sided polygons) using vertices v_0, v_1, v_2, v_3, then v_4, v_5, v_6, v_7, and so on. If n isn't a multiple of 4, the final one, two, or three vertices are ignored.
GL_QUAD_STRIP	Draws a series of quadrilaterals (four-sided polygons) beginning with v_0, v_1, v_3, v_2, then v_2, v_3, v_5, v_4, then v_4, v_5, v_7, v_6, and so on. See Figure 2-6. n must be at least 4 before anything is drawn, and if n is odd, the final vertex is ignored.
GL_TRIANGLE_STRIP	Draws a series of triangles (three-sided polygons) using vertices v_0, v_1, v_2, then v_2, v_1, v_3 (note the order), then v_2, v_3, v_4, and so on. The ordering is to ensure that the triangles are all drawn with the same orientation so that the strip can correctly form part of a surface. Figure 2-6 should make the reason for the ordering obvious. n must be at least 3 for anything to be drawn.
GL_TRIANGLE_FAN	Same as GL_TRIANGLE_STRIP, except that the vertices are v_0, v_1, v_2, then v_0, v_2, v_3, then v_0, v_3, v_4, and so on. Look at Figure 2-6.

Restrictions on Using glBegin() and glEnd()

The most important information about vertices is their coordinates, which are specified by the **glVertex*()** command. You can also supply additional vertex-specific data for each vertex—a color, a normal vector, texture coordinates, or any combination of these—using special commands. In addition, a few other commands are valid between a **glBegin()** and **glEnd()** pair. Table 2-3 contains a complete list of such valid commands.

Command	Purpose of Command	Reference
glVertex*()	set vertex coordinates	Chapter 2
glColor*()	set current color	Chapter 5
glIndex*()	set current color index	Chapter 5
glNormal*()	set normal vector coordinates	Chapter 2
glEvalCoord*()	generate coordinates	Chapter 11
glCallList(), glCallLists()	execute display list(s)	Chapter 4
glTexCoord*()	set texture coordinates	Chapter 9
glEdgeFlag*()	control drawing of edges	Chapter 2
glMaterial*()	set material properties	Chapter 6

Table 2-3   Valid Commands between glBegin() and glEnd()

No other OpenGL commands are valid between a **glBegin()** and **glEnd()** pair, and making any other OpenGL call generates an error. Note, however, that only OpenGL commands are restricted; you can certainly include other programming-language constructs. For example, the following code draws an outlined circle:

```
#define PI 3.1415926535897;
GLint circle_points = 100;
glBegin(GL_LINE_LOOP);
for (i = 0; i < circle_points; i++) {
    angle = 2*PI*i/circle_points;
    glVertex2f(cos(angle), sin(angle));
}
glEnd();
```

Note: This example isn't the most efficient way to draw a circle, especially if you intend to do it repeatedly. The graphics commands used are typically very fast, but this code calculates an angle and calls the **sin()** and **cos()** routines for each vertex; in addition, there's the loop overhead. If you need to draw lots of circles, calculate the coordinates of the vertices once and save them in an array, create a display list (see Chapter 4), or use a GLU routine (see Appendix C).

Unless they are being compiled into a display list, all **glVertex*()** commands should appear between some **glBegin()** and **glEnd()** combination. (If they appear elsewhere, they don't accomplish anything.) If they appear in a display list, they are executed only if they appear between a **glBegin()** and a **glEnd()**.

Although many commands are allowed between **glBegin()** and **glEnd()**, vertices are generated only when a **glVertex*()** command is issued. At the moment **glVertex*()** is called, OpenGL assigns the resulting vertex the current color, texture coordinates, normal vector information, and so on. To see this, look at the following code sequence. The first point is drawn in red, and the second and third ones in blue, despite the extra color commands:

```
glBegin(GL_POINTS);
    glColor3f(0.0, 1.0, 0.0);     /* green */
    glColor3f(1.0, 0.0, 0.0);     /* red */
    glVertex(...);
    glColor3f(1.0, 1.0, 0.0);     /* yellow */
    glColor3f(0.0, 0.0, 1.0);     /* blue */
    glVertex(...);
    glVertex(...);
glEnd();
```

You can use any combination of the twenty-four versions of the **glVertex*()** command between **glBegin()** and **glEnd()**, although in real applications all the calls in any particular instance tend to be of the same form.

Displaying Points, Lines, and Polygons

By default, a point is drawn as a single pixel on the screen, a line is drawn solid and one pixel wide, and polygons are drawn solidly filled in. The following paragraphs discuss the details of how to change these default display modes.

Point Details

To control the size of a rendered point, use **glPointSize()** and supply the desired size in pixels as the argument.

> void **glPointSize**(GLfloat *size*);
>
> Sets the width in pixels for rendered points; *size* must be greater than 0.0 and by default is 1.0.

The actual collection of pixels on the screen that are drawn for various point widths depends on whether antialiasing is enabled. (Antialiasing is a technique for smoothing points and lines as they're rendered. This topic is covered in detail in "Antialiasing" on page 207.) If antialiasing is disabled (the default), fractional widths are rounded to integer widths, and a screen-aligned square region of pixels is drawn. Thus, if the width is 1.0, the square is one pixel by one pixel; if the width is 2.0, the square is two pixels by two pixels, and so on.

With antialiasing enabled, a circular group of pixels is drawn, and the pixels on the boundaries are typically drawn at less than full intensity to give the edge a smoother appearance. In this mode, nonintegral widths aren't rounded.

Most OpenGL implementations support very large point sizes. A particular implementation, however, might limit the size of nonantialiased points to its maximum antialiased point size, rounded to the nearest integer value. You can obtain this floating-point value by using GL_POINT_SIZE_RANGE with **glGetFloatv**().

Line Details

With OpenGL, you can specify lines with different widths and lines that are *stippled* in various ways—dotted, dashed, drawn with alternating dots and dashes, and so on.

Wide Lines

> void **glLineWidth**(GLfloat *width*);
>
> Sets the width in pixels for rendered lines; *width* must be greater than 0.0 and by default is 1.0.

The actual rendering of lines is affected by the antialiasing mode, in the same way as for points. (See "Antialiasing" on page 207.) Without antialiasing, widths of 1, 2, and 3 draw lines one, two, and three pixels wide. With antialiasing enabled, nonintegral line widths are possible, and pixels on the boundaries are typically partially filled. As with point sizes, a particular OpenGL implementation might limit the width of nonantialiased lines to its maximum antialiased line width, rounded to the nearest integer value. You can obtain this floating-point value by using GL_LINE_WIDTH_RANGE with **glGetFloatv()**.

Note: Keep in mind that by default lines are one pixel wide, so they appear wider on lower-resolution screens. For computer displays, this isn't typically an issue, but if you're using OpenGL to render to a high-resolution plotter, one-pixel lines might be nearly invisible. To obtain resolution-independent line widths, you need to take into account the physical dimensions of pixels.

With nonantialiased wide lines, the line width isn't measured perpendicular to the line. Instead, it's measured in the *y* direction if the absolute value of the slope is less than 1.0; otherwise, it's measured in the *x* direction. The rendering of an antialiased line is exactly equivalent to the rendering of a filled rectangle of the given width, centered on the exact line. See "Polygon Details" on page 45 for a discussion of the rendering of filled polygonal regions.

☐ Advanced

Stippled Lines

To make stippled (dotted or dashed) lines, you use the command **glLineStipple()** to define the stipple pattern, and then you enable line stippling with **glEnable()**:

```
glLineStipple(1, 0x3F07);
glEnable(GL_LINE_STIPPLE);
```

---

void **glLineStipple**(GLint *factor*, GLushort *pattern*);

Sets the current stippling pattern for lines. The *pattern* argument is a 16-bit series of 0s and 1s, and it's repeated as necessary to stipple a given line. A 1 indicates that drawing occurs, and 0 that it does not, on a pixel-by-pixel basis, beginning with the low-order bits of the pattern. The pattern can be stretched out by using *factor*, which multiplies each subseries of consecutive 1s and 0s. Thus, if three consecutive 1s appear in the pattern, they're stretched to six if *factor* is 2. *factor* is clamped to lie between 1 and 255. Line stippling must be enabled by passing GL_LINE_STIPPLE to **glEnable**(); it's disabled by passing the same argument to **glDisable**().

With the preceding example and the pattern 0x3F07 (which translates to 0011111100000111 in binary), a line would be drawn with 3 pixels on, then 5 off, 6 on, and 2 off. (If this seems backward, remember that the low-order bits are used first.) If *factor* had been 2, the pattern would have been elongated: 6 pixels on, 10 off, 12 on, and 4 off. Figure 2-7 shows lines drawn with different patterns and repeat factors. If you don't enable line stippling, drawing proceeds as if *pattern* were 0xFFFF and *factor* 1. (Use **glDisable**() with GL_LINE_STIPPLE to disable stippling.) Note that stippling can be used in combination with wide lines to produce wide stippled lines.

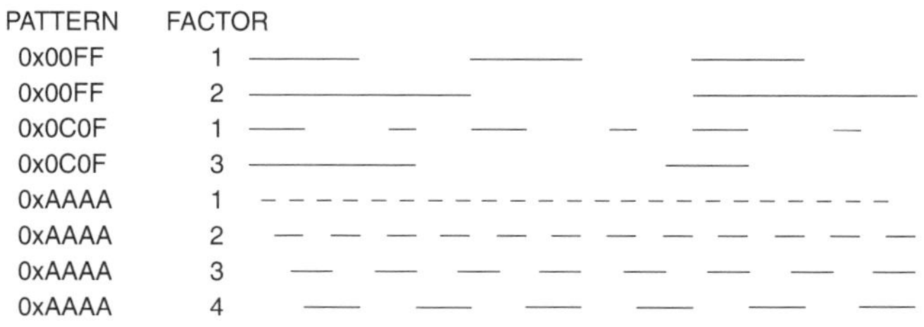

PATTERN	FACTOR	
0x00FF	1	
0x00FF	2	
0x0C0F	1	
0x0C0F	3	
0xAAAA	1	
0xAAAA	2	
0xAAAA	3	
0xAAAA	4	

Figure 2-7   Stippled Lines

One way to think of the stippling is that as the line is being drawn, the pattern is shifted by one bit each time a pixel is drawn (or *factor* pixels are drawn, if *factor* isn't 1). When a series of connected line segments is drawn between a single **glBegin**() and **glEnd**(), the pattern continues to shift as one segment turns into the next. This way, a stippling pattern continues across a series of connected line segments. When **glEnd**() is executed, the pattern is reset, and—if more lines are drawn before stippling is disabled—the stippling restarts at the beginning of the pattern. If you're drawing lines with GL_LINES, the pattern resets for each independent line.

Listing 2-1 illustrates the results of drawing with a couple of different stipple patterns and line widths. It also illustrates what happens if the lines are drawn as a series of individual segments instead of a single connected line strip. The results of running the program appear in Figure 2-8.

Figure 2-8   Wide Stippled Lines

Listing 2-1   Using Line Stipple Patterns: lines.c

```
#include <GL/gl.h>
#include <GL/glu.h>
#include "aux.h"

#definedrawOneLine(x1,y1,x2,y2) glBegin(GL_LINES); \
    glVertex2f ((x1),(y1)); glVertex2f ((x2),(y2)); glEnd();

void myinit (void) {
    /*  background to be cleared to black*/
    glClearColor (0.0, 0.0, 0.0, 0.0);
    glShadeModel (GL_FLAT);
}

void display(void)
{
    int i;

    glClear (GL_COLOR_BUFFER_BIT);
/*  draw all lines in white*/
    glColor3f (1.0, 1.0, 1.0);
```

```
/*  in 1st row, 3 lines, each with a different stipple*/
    glEnable (GL_LINE_STIPPLE);
    glLineStipple (1, 0x0101);/*  dotted*/
    drawOneLine (50.0, 125.0, 150.0, 125.0);
    glLineStipple (1, 0x00FF);/*  dashed*/
    drawOneLine (150.0, 125.0, 250.0, 125.0);
    glLineStipple (1, 0x1C47);/*  dash/dot/dash*/
    drawOneLine (250.0, 125.0, 350.0, 125.0);

/*  in 2nd row, 3 wide lines, each with different stipple */
    glLineWidth (5.0);
    glLineStipple (1, 0x0101);
    drawOneLine (50.0, 100.0, 150.0, 100.0);
    glLineStipple (1, 0x00FF);
    drawOneLine (150.0, 100.0, 250.0, 100.0);
    glLineStipple (1, 0x1C47);
    drawOneLine (250.0, 100.0, 350.0, 100.0);
    glLineWidth (1.0);

/*  in 3rd row, 6 lines, with dash/dot/dash stipple,*/
/*  as part of a single connected line strip*/
    glLineStipple (1, 0x1C47);
    glBegin (GL_LINE_STRIP);
    for (i = 0; i < 7; i++)
    glVertex2f (50.0 + ((GLfloat) i * 50.0), 75.0);
    glEnd ();

/*  in 4th row, 6 independent lines,*/
/*  with dash/dot/dash stipple*/
    for (i = 0; i < 6; i++) {
    drawOneLine (50.0 + ((GLfloat) i * 50.0),
        50.0, 50.0 + ((GLfloat)(i+1) * 50.0), 50.0);
    }

/*  in 5th row, 1 line, with dash/dot/dash stipple*/
/*  and repeat factor of 5*/
    glLineStipple (5, 0x1C47);
    drawOneLine (50.0, 25.0, 350.0, 25.0);
    glFlush ();
}
```

```
int main(int argc, char** argv)
{
    auxInitDisplayMode (AUX_SINGLE | AUX_RGBA);
    auxInitPosition (0, 0, 400, 150);
    auxInitWindow (argv[0]);
    myinit ();
    auxMainLoop(display);
}
```

Polygon Details

Polygons are typically drawn by filling in all the pixels enclosed within the boundary, but you can also draw them as outlined polygons, or simply as points at the vertices. A filled polygon might be solidly filled, or stippled with a certain pattern. Although the exact details are omitted here, polygons are drawn in such a way that if adjacent polygons share an edge or vertex, the pixels making up the edge or vertex are drawn exactly once—they're included in only one of the polygons. This is done so that partially transparent polygons don't have their edges drawn twice, which would make those edges appear darker (or brighter, depending on what color you're drawing with). Note that it might result in narrow polygons having no filled pixels in one or more rows or columns of pixels. Antialiasing polygons is more complicated than for points and lines; see "Antialiasing" on page 207 for details.

Polygons as Points, Outlines, or Solids

A polygon has two sides—front and back—and might be rendered differently depending on which side is facing the viewer. This allows you to have cutaway views of solid objects in which there is an obvious distinction between the parts that are inside and those that are outside. By default, both front and back faces are drawn in the same way. To change this, or to draw only outlines or vertices, use **glPolygonMode()**.

void **glPolygonMode**(GLenum *face*, GLenum *mode*);

Controls the drawing mode for a polygon's front and back faces. The parameter *face* can be GL_FRONT_AND_BACK, GL_FRONT, or GL_BACK; *mode* can be GL_POINT, GL_LINE, or GL_FILL to indicate whether the polygon should be drawn as points, outlined, or filled. By default, both the front and back faces are drawn filled.

For example, you can have the front faces filled and the back faces outlined with two calls to this routine:

```
glPolygonMode(GL_FRONT, GL_FILL);
glPolygonMode(GL_BACK, GL_LINE);
```

See the next section for more information about how to control which faces are considered front-facing and which back-facing.

Reversing and Culling Polygon Faces

By convention, polygons whose vertices appear in counterclockwise order on the screen are called *front-facing*. You can construct the surface of any "reasonable" solid—a mathematician would call such a surface an orientable manifold (spheres, donuts, and teapots are orientable; Klein bottles and Möbius strips aren't)—from polygons of consistent orientation. In other words, you can use all clockwise polygons, or all counterclockwise polygons. (This is essentially the mathematical definition of *orientable*.)

Suppose you've consistently described a model of an orientable surface but that you happen to have the clockwise orientation on the outside. You can swap what OpenGL considers the back face by using the function **glFrontFace()**, supplying the desired orientation for front-facing polygons.

---

void **glFrontFace**(GLenum *mode*);

Controls how front-facing polygons are determined. By default, *mode* is GL_CCW, which corresponds to a counterclockwise orientation of the ordered vertices of a projected polygon in window coordinates. If *mode* is GL_CW, faces with a clockwise orientation are considered front-facing.

Advanced

In more technical terms, the decision of whether a face of a polygon is front- or back-facing depends on the sign of the polygon's area computed in window coordinates. One way to compute this area is

$$a = \frac{1}{2} \sum_{i=0}^{n-1} x_i y_{i \oplus 1} - x_{i \oplus 1} y_i$$

where x_i and y_i are the x and y window coordinates of the ith vertex of the n-vertex polygon, and $i \oplus 1$ is $(i+1)$ mod n. Assuming that GL_CCW has been specified, if $a>0$, the polygon corresponding to that vertex is considered to be front-facing; otherwise, it's back-facing. If GL_CW is specified and if $a<0$, then the corresponding polygon is front-facing; otherwise, it's back-facing.

In a completely enclosed surface constructed from polygons with a consistent orientation, none of the back-facing polygons are ever visible—they're always obscured by the front-facing polygons. In this situation, you can maximize drawing speed by having OpenGL discard polygons as soon as it determines that they're back-facing. Similarly, if you are inside the object, only back-facing polygons are visible. To instruct OpenGL to discard front- or back-facing polygons, use the command **glCullFace()** and enable culling with **glEnable()**.

---

void **glCullFace**(GLenum *mode*);

Indicates which polygons should be discarded (culled) before they're converted to screen coordinates. The mode is either GL_FRONT, GL_BACK, or GL_FRONT_AND_BACK to indicate front-facing, back-facing, or all polygons. To take effect, culling must be enabled using **glEnable()** with GL_CULL_FACE; it can be disabled with **glDisable()** and the same argument.

Stippling Polygons

By default, filled polygons are drawn with a solid pattern. They can also be filled with a 32-bit by 32-bit window-aligned stipple pattern, which you specify with **glPolygonStipple()**.

---

void **glPolygonStipple**(const GLubyte **mask*);

Defines the current stipple pattern for filled polygons. The argument *mask* is a pointer to a 32×32 bitmap that's interpreted as a mask of 0s and 1s. Where a 1 appears, the corresponding pixel in the polygon is drawn, and where a 0 appears, nothing is drawn. Figure 2-9 shows how a stipple pattern is constructed from the characters in *mask*. Polygon stippling is enabled and disabled by using **glEnable()** and **glDisable()** with GL_POLYGON_STIPPLE as the argument. The interpretation of the *mask* data is affected by the **glPixelStore*()** GL_UNPACK* modes. See "Controlling Pixel-Storage Modes" on page 244.

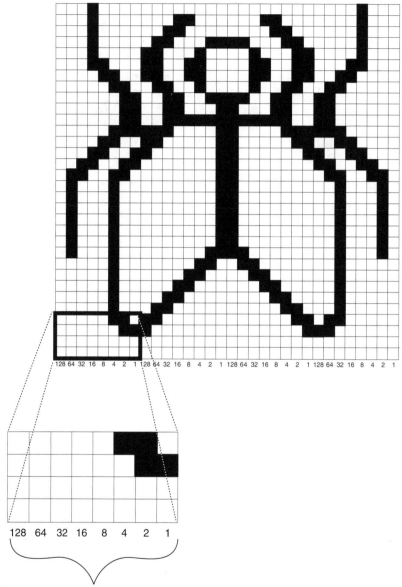

128 64 32 16 8 4 2 1 128 64 32 16 8 4 2 1 128 64 32 16 8 4 2 1 128 64 32 16 8 4 2 1

128   64   32   16   8   4   2   1

By default, for each byte the most significant bit is first.
Bit ordering can be changed by calling glPixelStore*().

Figure 2-9   Constructing a Polygon Stipple Pattern

In addition to defining the current polygon stippling pattern, you must enable stippling:

```
glEnable(GL_POLYGON_STIPPLE);
```

Use **glDisable()** with the same argument to disable polygon stippling.

Figure 2-10 shows the results of polygons drawn unstippled and then with two different stippling patterns. The program is shown in Listing 2-2. The reversal of white to black (from Figure 2-9 to Figure 2-10) occurs because the program draws in white over a black background, using the pattern in Figure 2-9 as a stencil.

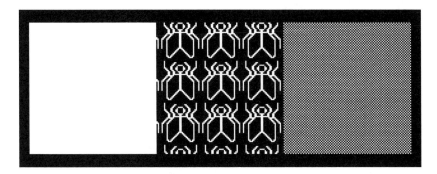

Figure 2-10   Stippled Polygons

Listing 2-2   Using Polygon Stipple Patterns: polys.c

```
#include <GL/gl.h>
#include <GL/glu.h>
#include "aux.h"

void display(void)
{
    GLubyte fly[] = {
        0x00, 0x00, 0x00, 0x00, 0x00, 0x00, 0x00, 0x00,
        0x03, 0x80, 0x01, 0xC0, 0x06, 0xC0, 0x03, 0x60,
        0x04, 0x60, 0x06, 0x20, 0x04, 0x30, 0x0C, 0x20,
        0x04, 0x18, 0x18, 0x20, 0x04, 0x0C, 0x30, 0x20,
        0x04, 0x06, 0x60, 0x20, 0x44, 0x03, 0xC0, 0x22,
        0x44, 0x01, 0x80, 0x22, 0x44, 0x01, 0x80, 0x22,
        0x44, 0x01, 0x80, 0x22, 0x44, 0x01, 0x80, 0x22,
        0x44, 0x01, 0x80, 0x22, 0x44, 0x01, 0x80, 0x22,
        0x66, 0x01, 0x80, 0x66, 0x33, 0x01, 0x80, 0xCC,
        0x19, 0x81, 0x81, 0x98, 0x0C, 0xC1, 0x83, 0x30,
```

```
                    0x07, 0xe1, 0x87, 0xe0, 0x03, 0x3f, 0xfc, 0xc0,
                    0x03, 0x31, 0x8c, 0xc0, 0x03, 0x33, 0xcc, 0xc0,
                    0x06, 0x64, 0x26, 0x60, 0x0c, 0xcc, 0x33, 0x30,
                    0x18, 0xcc, 0x33, 0x18, 0x10, 0xc4, 0x23, 0x08,
                    0x10, 0x63, 0xC6, 0x08, 0x10, 0x30, 0x0c, 0x08,
                    0x10, 0x18, 0x18, 0x08, 0x10, 0x00, 0x00, 0x08};

        GLubyte halftone[] = {
                    0xAA, 0xAA, 0xAA, 0xAA, 0x55, 0x55, 0x55, 0x55,
                    0xAA, 0xAA, 0xAA, 0xAA, 0x55, 0x55, 0x55, 0x55,
                    0xAA, 0xAA, 0xAA, 0xAA, 0x55, 0x55, 0x55, 0x55,
                    0xAA, 0xAA, 0xAA, 0xAA, 0x55, 0x55, 0x55, 0x55,
                    0xAA, 0xAA, 0xAA, 0xAA, 0x55, 0x55, 0x55, 0x55,
                    0xAA, 0xAA, 0xAA, 0xAA, 0x55, 0x55, 0x55, 0x55,
                    0xAA, 0xAA, 0xAA, 0xAA, 0x55, 0x55, 0x55, 0x55,
                    0xAA, 0xAA, 0xAA, 0xAA, 0x55, 0x55, 0x55, 0x55,
                    0xAA, 0xAA, 0xAA, 0xAA, 0x55, 0x55, 0x55, 0x55,
                    0xAA, 0xAA, 0xAA, 0xAA, 0x55, 0x55, 0x55, 0x55,
                    0xAA, 0xAA, 0xAA, 0xAA, 0x55, 0x55, 0x55, 0x55,
                    0xAA, 0xAA, 0xAA, 0xAA, 0x55, 0x55, 0x55, 0x55,
                    0xAA, 0xAA, 0xAA, 0xAA, 0x55, 0x55, 0x55, 0x55,
                    0xAA, 0xAA, 0xAA, 0xAA, 0x55, 0x55, 0x55, 0x55,
                    0xAA, 0xAA, 0xAA, 0xAA, 0x55, 0x55, 0x55, 0x55,
                    0xAA, 0xAA, 0xAA, 0xAA, 0x55, 0x55, 0x55, 0x55};

    glClear (GL_COLOR_BUFFER_BIT);

    glColor3f (1.0, 1.0, 1.0);

    glRectf (25.0, 25.0, 125.0, 125.0);
    glEnable (GL_POLYGON_STIPPLE);
    glPolygonStipple (fly);
    glRectf (125.0, 25.0, 225.0, 125.0);
    glPolygonStipple (halftone);
    glRectf (225.0, 25.0, 325.0, 125.0);
    glDisable (GL_POLYGON_STIPPLE);

    glFlush ();
}

void myinit (void)
{
    glClearColor (0.0, 0.0, 0.0, 0.0);
    glShadeModel (GL_FLAT);
}
```

```
int main(int argc, char** argv)
{
    auxInitDisplayMode (AUX_SINGLE | AUX_RGBA);
    auxInitPosition (0, 0, 350, 150);
    auxInitWindow (argv[0]);
    myinit ();
    auxMainLoop(display);
}
```

As mentioned in "Display-List Design Philosophy" on page 121, you might want to use display lists to store polygon stipple patterns to maximize efficiency.

Marking Polygon Boundary Edges

▣ Advanced

OpenGL can render only convex polygons, but many nonconvex polygons arise in practice. To draw these nonconvex polygons, you typically subdivide them into convex polygons—usually triangles, as shown in Figure 2-11—and then draw the triangles. Unfortunately, if you decompose a general polygon into triangles and draw the triangles, you can't really use **glPolygonMode()** to draw the polygon's outline, since you get all the triangle outlines inside it. To solve this problem, you can tell OpenGL whether a particular vertex precedes a boundary edge; OpenGL keeps track of this information by passing along with each vertex a bit indicating whether that vertex is followed by a boundary edge. Then, when a polygon is drawn in GL_LINE mode, the nonboundary edges aren't drawn. In Figure 2-11, the dashed lines represent added edges.

Figure 2-11   Subdividing a Nonconvex Polygon

By default, all vertices are marked as preceding a boundary edge, but you can manually control the setting of the edge flag with the command **glEdgeFlag*()**. This command is used between **glBegin()** and **glEnd()** pairs, and it affects all the vertices specified after it until the next **glEdgeFlag()** call is made. It applies only to vertices specified for polygons, triangles, and quads, not to those specified for strips of triangles or quads.

> void **glEdgeFlag**(GLboolean *flag*);
> void **glEdgeFlagv**(const GLboolean **flag*);
>
> Indicates whether a vertex should be considered as initializing a boundary edge of a polygon. If *flag* is GL_TRUE, the edge flag is set to TRUE (the default), and any vertices created are considered to precede boundary edges until this function is called again with *flag* being 0.

As an example, Listing 2-3 draws the outline shown in Figure 2-12.

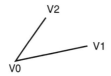

Figure 2-12   An Outlined Polygon Drawn Using Edge Flags

Listing 2-3   Marking Polygon Boundary Edges

```
glPolygonMode(GL_FRONT_AND_BACK, GL_LINE);
glBegin(GL_POLYGON);
    glEdgeFlag(GL_TRUE);
    glVertex3fv(V0);
    glEdgeFlag(GL_FALSE);
    glVertex3fv(V1);
    glEdgeFlag(GL_TRUE);
    glVertex3fv(V2);
glEnd();
```

Normal Vectors

A *normal vector* (or *normal*, for short) is a vector that points in a direction that's perpendicular to a surface. For a flat surface, one perpendicular direction suffices for every point on the surface, but for a general curved surface, the normal direction might be different at each point. With OpenGL, you can specify a normal for each vertex. Vertices might share the same normal, but you can't assign normals anywhere other than at the vertices.

An object's normal vectors define the orientation of its surface in space—in particular, its orientation relative to light sources. These vectors are used by OpenGL to determine how much light the object receives at its vertices. Lighting—a large topic by itself—is the subject of Chapter 6, and you might want to review the following information after you've read that chapter. Normal vectors are discussed briefly here because you generally define normal vectors for an object at the same time you define the object's geometry.

You use **glNormal*()** to set the current normal to the value of the argument passed in. Subsequent calls to **glVertex*()** cause the specified vertices to be assigned the current normal. Often, each vertex has a different normal, which necessitates a series of alternating calls like this:

```
glBegin (GL_POLYGON);
    glNormal3fv(n0);
    glVertex3fv(v0);
    glNormal3fv(n1);
    glVertex3fv(v1);
    glNormal3fv(n2);
    glVertex3fv(v2);
    glNormal3fv(n3);
    glVertex3fv(v3);
glEnd();
```

void **glNormal3**{bsidf}(*TYPE nx, TYPE ny, TYPE nz*);
void **glNormal3**{bsidf}**v**(const *TYPE *v);

Sets the current normal vector as specified by the arguments. The nonvector version (without the **v**) takes three arguments, which specify an (*nx, ny, nz*) vector that's taken to be the normal. Alternatively, you can use the vector version of this function (with the **v**) and supply a single array of three elements to specify the desired normal. The **b**, **s**, and **i** versions scale their parameter values linearly to the range [–1.0,1.0].

There's no magic to finding the normals for an object—most likely, you have to perform some calculations that might include taking derivatives—but there are several techniques and tricks you can use to achieve certain effects. Appendix F explains how to find normal vectors for surfaces. If you already know how to do this, if you can count on always being supplied with normal vectors, or if you don't want to use OpenGL's lighting facility, you don't need to read this appendix.

Note that at a given point on a surface, two vectors are perpendicular to the surface, and they point in opposite directions. By convention, the normal is the one that points to the outside of the surface being modeled. (If you get inside and outside reversed in your model, just change every normal vector from (x, y, z) to $(-x, -y, -z)$).

Also, keep in mind that since normal vectors indicate direction only, their length is mostly irrelevant. You can specify normals of any length, but eventually they have to be converted to having a length of 1 before lighting calculations are performed. (A vector that has a length of 1 is said to be of unit length, or *normalized*.) In general, then, you should supply normalized normal vectors. These vectors remain normalized as long as your model transformations include only rotations and translations. (Transformations are discussed in detail in Chapter 3.) If you perform irregular transformations (such as scaling or multiplying by a shear matrix), or if you specify nonunit-length normals, then you should have OpenGL automatically normalize your normal vectors after the transformations. To do this, call **glEnable()** with GL_NORMALIZE as its argument. By default, automatic normalization is disabled. Note that in some implementations of OpenGL, automatic normalization requires additional calculations that might reduce the performance of your application.

Some Hints for Building Polygonal Models of Surfaces

Following are some techniques that you might want to use as you build polygonal approximations of surfaces. You might want to review this section after you've read Chapter 6 on lighting and Chapter 4 on display lists. The lighting conditions affect how models look once they're drawn, and some of the following techniques are much more efficient when used in conjunction with display lists. As you read these techniques, keep in mind that when lighting calculations are enabled, normal vectors must be specified to get proper results.

Constructing polygonal approximations to surfaces is an art, and there is no substitute for experience. This section, however, lists a few pointers that might make it a bit easier to get started.

- Keep polygon orientations consistent. Make sure that when viewed from the outside, all the polygons on the surface are oriented in the same direction (all clockwise or all counterclockwise). Try to get this right the first time, since it's excruciatingly painful to fix the problem later.

- When you subdivide a surface, watch out for any nontriangular polygons. The three vertices of a triangle are guaranteed to lie on a plane; any polygon with four or more vertices might not. Nonplanar polygons can be viewed from some orientation such that the edges cross each other, and OpenGL might not render such polygons correctly.

- There's always a trade-off between the display speed and the quality of the image. If you subdivide a surface into a small number of polygons, it renders quickly but might have a jagged appearance; if you subdivide it into millions of tiny polygons, it probably looks good but might take a long time to render. Ideally, you can provide a parameter to the subdivision routines that indicates how fine a subdivision you want, and if the object is farther from the eye, you can use a coarser subdivision. Also, when you subdivide, use relatively large polygons where the surface is relatively flat, and small polygons in regions of high curvature.

- For high-quality images, it's a good idea to subdivide more on the silhouette edges than in the interior. If the surface is to be rotated relative to the eye, this is tougher to do, since the silhouette edges keep moving. Silhouette edges occur where the normal vectors are perpendicular to the vector from the surface to the viewpoint—that is, when their vector dot product is zero. Your subdivision algorithm might choose to subdivide more if this dot product is near zero.

- Try to avoid T-intersections in your models (see Figure 2-13). As shown, there's no guarantee that the line segments AB and BC lie on exactly the same pixels as the segment AC. Sometimes they do, and sometimes they don't, depending on the transformations and orientation. This can cause cracks to appear intermittently in the surface.

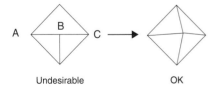

Undesirable   OK

Figure 2-13   Modifying an Undesirable T-intersection

- If you're constructing a closed surface, make sure to use exactly the same numbers for coordinates at the beginning and end of a closed loop, or you can get gaps and cracks due to numerical round-off. Here's a two-dimensional example of bad code:

```
/* don't use this code */

#define PI 3.14159265
#define EDGES 30

/* draw a circle */
for (i = 0; i < EDGES; i++) {
  glBegin(GL_LINE_STRIP);
    glVertex2f(cos((2*PI*i)/EDGES), sin((2*PI*i)/EDGES);
    glVertex2f(cos((2*PI*(i+1))/EDGES),
               sin((2*PI*(i+1))/EDGES);
  glEnd();
}
```

The edges meet exactly only if your machine manages to calculate the sine and cosine of 0 and of (2*PI*EDGES/EDGES) and gets exactly the same values. If you trust the floating-point unit on your machine to do this right, the authors have a bridge they'd like to sell you.... To correct the code, make sure that when $i ==$ EDGES–1, you use 0 for the sine and cosine, not 2*PI*EDGES/EDGES.

- Finally, note that unless tessellation is very fine, any change is likely to be visible. In some animations, these changes are more visually disturbing than the artifacts of undertessellation.

An Example: Building an Icosahedron

To illustrate some of the considerations that arise in approximating a surface, let's look at some example code sequences. This code concerns the vertices of a regular icosahedron (which is a Platonic solid composed of twenty faces that span twelve vertices, each face of which is an equilateral triangle). An icosahedron can be considered a rough approximation for a sphere. Listing 2-4 defines the vertices and triangles making up an icosahedron and then draws the icosahedron.

Listing 2-4   Drawing an Icosahedron

```
#define X .525731112119133606
#define Z .850650808352039932
```

```
static GLfloat vdata[12][3] = {
    {-X, 0.0, Z}, {X, 0.0, Z}, {-X, 0.0, -Z}, {X, 0.0, -Z},
    {0.0, Z, X}, {0.0, Z, -X}, {0.0, -Z, X}, {0.0, -Z, -X},
    {Z, X, 0.0}, {-Z, X, 0.0}, {Z, -X, 0.0}, {-Z, -X, 0.0}
};

static GLint tindices[20][3] = {
    {0,4,1}, {0,9,4}, {9,5,4}, {4,5,8}, {4,8,1},
    {8,10,1}, {8,3,10}, {5,3,8}, {5,2,3}, {2,7,3},
    {7,10,3}, {7,6,10}, {7,11,6}, {11,0,6}, {0,1,6},
    {6,1,10}, {9,0,11}, {9,11,2}, {9,2,5}, {7,2,11} };

for (i = 0; i < 20; i++) {
    /* color information here */
    glBegin(GL_TRIANGLE);
        glVertex3fv(&vdata[tindices[i][0]][0]);
        glVertex3fv(&vdata[tindices[i][1]][0]);
        glVertex3fv(&vdata[tindices[i][2]][0]);
    glEnd();
}
```

The strange numbers X and Z are chosen so that the distance from the origin to any of the vertices of the icosahedron is 1.0. The coordinates of the twelve vertices are given in the array *vdata[][]*, where the zeroth vertex is {–X, 0.0, Z}, the first is {X, 0.0, Z}, and so on. The array *tindices[][]* tells how to link the vertices to make triangles. For example, the first triangle is made from the zeroth, fourth, and first vertex. If you take the vertices for triangles in the order given, all the triangles have the same orientation.

The line that mentions color information should be replaced by a command that sets the color of the *i*th face. If no code appears here, all faces are drawn in the same color, and it'll be impossible to discern the three-dimensional quality of the object. An alternative to explicitly specifying colors is to define surface normals and use lighting, as described in the next section.

Note: In all the examples described in this section, unless the surface is to be drawn only once, you should probably save the calculated vertex and normal coordinates so that the calculations don't need to be repeated each time that the surface is drawn. This can be done using your own data structures or by constructing display lists (see Chapter 4).

Defining the Icosahedron's Normals

If the icosahedron is to be lit, you need to supply the vector normal to the surface. With the flat surfaces of an icosahedron, all three vertices defining a surface have the same normal vector. Thus, the normal needs to be specified only once for each set of three vertices. The code in Listing 2-5 can replace the "color information here" line in Listing 2-4 for drawing the icosahedron.

Listing 2-5   Supplying Normals for an Icosahedron

```
GLfloat d1[3], d2[3], norm[3];
for (j = 0; j < 3; j++) {
    d1[j] = vdata[tindices[i][0]][j] - vdata[tindices[i][1]][j];
    d2[j] = vdata[tindices[i][1]][j] - vdata[tindices[i][2]][j];
}
normcrossprod(d1, d2, norm);
glNormal3fv(norm);
```

The function **normcrossprod()** produces the normalized cross product of two vectors, as shown in Listing 2-6.

Listing 2-6   Calculating the Normalized Cross Product of Two Vectors

```
void normalize(float v[3]) {
    GLfloat d = sqrt(v[1]*v[1]+v[2]*v[2]+v[3]*v[3]);
    if (d == 0.0) {
        error("zero length vector");
        return;
    }
    v[1] /= d; v[2] /= d; v[3] /= d;
}

void normcrossprod(float v1[3], float v2[3], float out[3])
{
    GLint i, j;
    GLfloat length;

    out[0] = v1[1]*v2[2] - v1[2]*v2[1];
    out[1] = v1[2]*v2[0] - v1[0]*v2[2];
    out[2] = v1[0]*v2[1] - v1[1]*v2[0];
    normalize(out);
}
```

If you're using an icosahedron as an approximation for a shaded sphere, you'll want to use normal vectors that are perpendicular to the true surface of the sphere, rather than being perpendicular to the faces. For a sphere, the normal vectors are simple; each points in the same direction as the vector from the origin to the corresponding vertex. Since the icosahedron vertex data is for an icosahedron of radius 1, the normal and vertex data is identical. Here is the code that would draw an icosahedral approximation of a smoothly shaded sphere (assuming that lighting is enabled, as described in Chapter 6):

```
for (i = 0; i < 20; i++) {
    glBegin(GL_POLYGON);
        glNormal3fv(&vdata[tindices[i][0]][0]);
        glVertex3fv(&vdata[tindices[i][0]][0]);
        glNormal3fv(&vdata[tindices[i][1]][0]);
        glVertex3fv(&vdata[tindices[i][1]][0]);
        glNormal3fv(&vdata[tindices[i][2]][0]);
        glVertex3fv(&vdata[tindices[i][2]][0]);
    glEnd();
}
```

Improving the Model

A twenty-sided approximation to a sphere doesn't look good unless the image of the sphere on the screen is quite small, but there's an easy way to increase the accuracy of the approximation. Imagine the icosahedron inscribed in a sphere, and subdivide the triangles as shown in Figure 2-14. The newly introduced vertices lie slightly inside the sphere, so push them to the surface by normalizing them (dividing them by a factor to make them have length 1). This subdivision process can be repeated for arbitrary accuracy. The three objects shown in Figure 2-14 use twenty, eighty, and three hundred and twenty approximating triangles, respectively.

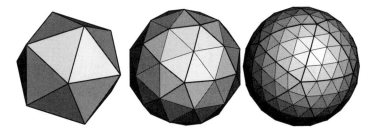

Figure 2-14   Subdividing to Improve a Polygonal Approximation to a Surface

Listing 2-7 performs a single subdivision, creating an eighty-sided spherical approximation.

Listing 2-7   Single Subdivision

```
void drawtriangle(float *v1, float *v2, float *v3)
{
    glBegin(GL_POLYGON);
        glNormal3fv(v1); vlVertex3fv(v1);
        glNormal3fv(v2); vlVertex3fv(v2);
        glNormal3fv(v3); vlVertex3fv(v3);
    glEnd();
}

void subdivide(float *v1, float *v2, float *v3)
{
    GLfloat v12[3], v23[3], v31[3];
    GLint i;

    for (i = 0; i < 3; i++) {
        v12[i] = v1[i]+v2[i];
        v23[i] = v2[i]+v3[i];
        v31[i] = v3[i]+v1[i];
    }
    normalize(v12);
    normalize(v23);
    normalize(v31);
    drawtriangle(v1, v12, v31);
    drawtriangle(v2, v23, v12);
    drawtriangle(v3, v31, v23);
    drawtriangle(v12, v23, v31);
}

for (i = 0; i < 20; i++) {
    subdivide(&vdata[tindices[i][0]][0],
              &vdata[tindices[i][1]][0],
              &vdata[tindices[i][2]][0]);
}
```

Listing 2-8 is a slight modification of Listing 2-7 that recursively subdivides the triangles to the proper depth. If the depth value is 0, no subdivisions are performed, and the triangle is drawn as is. If the depth is 1, a single subdivison is performed, and so on.

Listing 2-8   Recursive Subdivision

```
void subdivide(float *v1, float *v2, float *v3, long depth)
{
    GLfloat v12[3], v23[3], v31[3];
    GLint i;

    if (depth == 0) {
        drawtriangle(v1, v2, v3);
        return;
    }
    for (i = 0; i < 3; i++) {
        v12[i] = v1[i]+v2[i];
        v23[i] = v2[i]+v3[i];
        v31[i] = v3[i]+v1[i];
    }
    normalize(v12);
    normalize(v23);
    normalize(v31);
    subdivide(v1, v12, v31, depth-1);
    subdivide(v2, v23, v12, depth-1);
    subdivide(v3, v31, v23, depth-1);
    subdivide(v12, v23, v31, depth-1);
}
```

Generalized Subdivision

A recursive subdivision technique such as the one described in Listing 2-8 can be used for other types of surfaces. Typically, the recursion ends either if a certain depth is reached, or if some condition on the curvature is satisfied (highly curved parts of surfaces look better with more subdivision).

To look at a more general solution to the problem of subdivision, consider an arbitrary surface parameterized by two variables *u[0]* and *u[1]*. Suppose that two routines are provided:

```
void surf(GLfloat u[2], GLfloat vertex[3], GLfloat normal[3]);
float curv(GLfloat u[2]);
```

If **surf()** is passed *u[]*, the corresponding three-dimensional vertex and normal vectors (of length 1) are returned. If *u[]* is passed to **curv()**, the curvature of the surface at that point is calculated and returned. (See an introductory textbook on differential geometry for more information about measuring surface curvature.)

Listing 2-9 shows the recursive routine that subdivides a triangle either until the maximum depth is reached or until the maximum curvature at the three vertices is less than some cutoff.

Listing 2-9 Generalized Subdivision

```
void subdivide(float u1[2], float u2[2], float u3[2],
               float cutoff, long depth)
{
   GLfloat v1[3], v2[3], v3[3], n1[3], n2[3], n3[3];
   GLfloat u12[2], u23[2], u32[2];
   GLint i;

   if (depth == maxdepth || (curv(u1) < cutoff &&
       curv(u2) < cutoff && curv(u3) < cutoff)) {
       surf(u1, v1, n1); surf(u2, v2, n2); surf(u3, v3, n3);
       glBegin(GL_POLYGON);
           glNormal3fv(n1); glVertex3fv(v1);
           glNormal3fv(n2); glVertex3fv(v2);
           glNormal3fv(n3); glVertex3fv(v3);
       glEnd();
       return;
   }
   for (i = 0; i < 2; i++) {
       u12[i] = (u1[i] + u2[i])/2.0;
       u23[i] = (u2[i] + u3[i])/2.0;
       u31[i] = (u3[i] + u1[i])/2.0;
   }
   subdivide(u1, u12, u31, cutoff, depth+1);
   subdivide(u2, u23, u12, cutoff, depth+1);
   subdivide(u3, u31, u23, cutoff, depth+1);
   subdivide(u12, u23, u31, cutoff, depth+1);
}
```

Chapter 3

Viewing

Chapter Objectives

After reading this chapter, you'll be able to do the following:

- View a geometric model in any orientation by transforming it in three-dimensional space

- Control the location in three-dimensional space from which the model is viewed

- Clip undesired portions of the model out of the scene that's to be viewed

- Manipulate the appropriate matrix stacks that control model transformation for viewing and project the model onto the screen

- Combine multiple transformations to mimic sophisticated systems in motion, such as a solar system or an articulated robot arm

Chapter 2 explained how to instruct OpenGL to draw the geometric models you want displayed in your scene. Now you must decide how you want to position the models in the scene, and you must choose a vantage point from which to view the scene. You can use the default positioning and vantage point, but most likely you want to specify them.

Look at the image on the cover of this book. The program that produced that image contained a single geometric description of a building block. Each block was carefully positioned in the scene: Some blocks were scattered on the floor, some were stacked on top of each other on the table, and some were assembled to make the globe. Also, a particular viewpoint had to be chosen. Obviously, we wanted to look at the corner of the room containing the globe. But how far away from the scene—and where exactly—should the viewer be? We wanted to make sure that the final image of the scene contained a good view out the window, that a portion of the floor was visible, and that all the objects in the scene were not only visible but presented in an interesting arrangement. This chapter explains how to use OpenGL to accomplish these tasks: how to position and orient models in three-dimensional space and how to establish the location—also in three-dimensional space—of the viewpoint. All of these factors help determine exactly what image appears on the sceen.

You want to remember that the point of computer graphics is to create a two-dimensional image of three-dimensional objects (it has to be two-dimensional because it's drawn on the screen), but you need to think in three-dimensional coordinates while making many of the decisions that determine what gets drawn on the screen. A common mistake people make when creating three-dimensional graphics is to start thinking too soon that the final image appears on a flat, two-dimensional screen. Avoid thinking about which pixels need to be drawn, and instead try to visualize three-dimensional space. Create your models in some three-dimensional universe that lies deep inside your computer, and let the computer do its job of calculating which pixels to color.

A series of three computer operations convert an object's three-dimensional coordinates to pixel positions on the screen:

- Transformations, which are represented by matrix multiplication, include modeling, viewing, and projection operations. Such operations include rotation, translation, scaling, reflecting, orthographic projection, and perspective projection. Generally, you use a combination of several transformations to draw a scene.

- Since the scene is rendered on a rectangular window, objects (or parts of objects) that lie outside the window must be clipped. In three-dimensional computer graphics, clipping occurs by throwing out objects on one side of a clipping plane.

- Finally, a correspondence must be established between the transformed coordinates and screen pixels. This is known as a *viewport* transformation.

This chapter describes all of these operations, and how to control them, in the following major sections:

- **"Overview: The Camera Analogy"** gives an overview of the transformation process by describing the analogy of taking a photograph with a camera, presents a simple example program that transforms an object, and briefly describes the basic OpenGL transformation commands.

- **"Viewing and Modeling Transformations"** explains in detail how to specify and to imagine the effect of viewing and modeling transformations. These transformations orient the model and the camera relative to each other to obtain the desired final image.

- **"Projection Transformations"** describes how to specify the shape and orientation of the *viewing volume*. The viewing volume determines how a scene is projected onto the screen (with a perspective or orthographic projection) and which objects or parts of objects are clipped out of the scene.

- **"Viewport Transformation"** explains how to control the conversion of three-dimensional model coordinates to screen coordinates.

- **"Troubleshooting Transformations"** presents some tips for discovering why you might not be getting the desired effect from your modeling, viewing, projection, and viewport transformations.

- **"Manipulating the Matrix Stacks"** discusses how to save and restore certain transformations. This is particularly useful when you're drawing complicated objects that are built up from simpler ones.

- **"Additional Clipping Planes"** describes how to specify additional clipping planes beyond those defined by the viewing volume.

- **"Examples of Composing Several Transformations"** walks you through a couple of more complicated uses for transformations.

Overview: The Camera Analogy

The transformation process to produce the desired scene for viewing is analogous to taking a photograph with a camera. As shown in Figure 3-1, the steps with a camera (or a computer) might be the following:

1. Setting up your tripod and pointing the camera at the scene (viewing transformation).

2. Arranging the scene to be photographed into the desired composition (modeling transformation).

3. Choosing a camera lens or adjusting the zoom (projection transformation).

4. Determining how large you want the final photograph to be—for example, you might want it enlarged (viewport transformation).

After these steps are performed, the picture can be snapped, or the scene can be drawn.

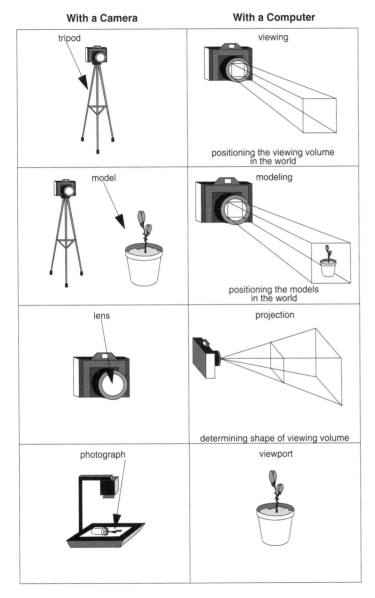

With a Camera

With a Computer

tripod

viewing

positioning the viewing volume
in the world

model

modeling

positioning the models
in the world

lens

projection

determining shape of viewing volume

photograph

viewport

Figure 3-1   The Camera Analogy

Note that these steps correspond to the order in which you specify the
desired transformations in your program, not necessarily the order in
which the relevant mathematical operations are performed on an object's

vertices. The viewing transformations must precede the modeling transformations in your code, but you can specify the projection and viewport transformations at any point before drawing occurs. Figure 3-2 shows the order in which these operations occur on your computer.

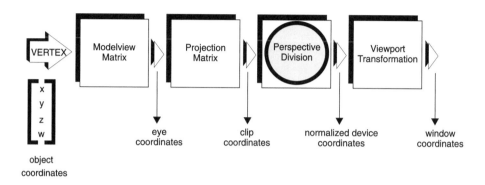

Figure 3-2   Stages of Vertex Transformation

To specify viewing, modeling, and projection transformations, you construct a 4×4 matrix **M**, which is then multiplied by the coordinates of each vertex **v** in the scene to accomplish the transformation

v′=Mv

(Remember that vertices always have four coordinates (x ,y, z, w), though in most cases w is 1 and for two-dimensional data z is 0.) Note that viewing and modeling transformations are automatically applied to surface normal vectors, in addition to vertices. (Normal vectors are used only in eye coordinates.) This ensures that the normal vector's relationship to the vertex data is properly preserved.

The viewing and modeling transformations you specify are combined to form the modelview matrix, which is applied to the incoming *object coordinates* to yield *eye coordinates*. Next, if you've specified arbitrary clipping planes to remove certain objects from the scene or to provide cutaway views of objects, these clipping planes are applied.

After that, OpenGL applies the projection matrix to yield *clip coordinates*. This transformation defines a *viewing volume*; objects outside this volume are clipped so that they're not drawn in the final scene. After this point, the perspective division is performed by dividing coordinate values by w, to produce *normalized device coordinates*. (See Appendix G for more information about the meaning of the w coordinate and how it affects matrix transformations.) Finally, the transformed coordinates are converted to *window coordinates* by applying the viewport transformation. You can manipulate the dimensions of the viewport to cause the final image to be enlarged, shrunk, or stretched.

You might correctly suppose that the x and y coordinates are sufficient to determine which pixels need to be drawn on the screen. However, all the transformations are performed on the z coordinates as well. This way, at the end of this transformation process, the z values correctly reflect the depth of a given vertex (measured in distance away from the screen). One use for this depth value is to eliminate unnecessary drawing. For example, suppose two vertices have the same x and y values but different z values. OpenGL can use this information to determine which surfaces are obscured by other surfaces and can then avoid drawing the hidden surfaces. (See Chapter 10 for more information about this technique, which is called *hidden-surface removal*.)

As you've probably guessed by now, you need to know a few things about matrix mathematics to get the most out of this chapter. If you want to brush up on your knowledge in this area, you might consult a textbook on linear algebra.

A Simple Example: Drawing a Cube

Listing 3-1 draws a cube that's scaled by a modeling transformation (see Figure 3-3). The viewing transformation used is a simple translation down the *z*-axis. A projection transformation and a viewport transformation are also specified. The rest of this section walks you through Listing 3-1 and briefly explains the transformation commands it uses. The succeeding sections contain the complete, detailed discussion of all OpenGL's transformation commands.

Figure 3-3   A Transformed Cube

Listing 3-1   A Transformed Cube: cube.c

```c
#include <GL/gl.h>
#include <GL/glu.h>
#include "aux.h"

void display (void)
{
    glClear(GL_COLOR_BUFFER_BIT);
    glColor3f (1.0, 1.0, 1.0);
    glLoadIdentity ();               /* clear the matrix */
    glTranslatef (0.0, 0.0, -5.0); /* viewing transformation */
    glScalef (1.0, 2.0, 1.0);      /* modeling transformation */
    auxWireCube(1.0);     /*  draw the cube */
    glFlush();
}

void myinit (void)
{
    glShadeModel (GL_FLAT);
}

void myReshape(GLsizei w, GLsizei h)
{
    glMatrixMode (GL_PROJECTION);    /* prepare for and then */
    glLoadIdentity ();               /* define the projection */
    glFrustum (-1.0, 1.0, -1.0, 1.0, /* transformation */
                1.5, 20.0);
    glMatrixMode (GL_MODELVIEW);  /* back to modelview matrix */
    glViewport (0, 0, w, h);      /* define the viewport */
}


int main(int argc, char** argv)
{
    auxInitDisplayMode (AUX_SINGLE | AUX_RGBA);
    auxInitPosition (0, 0, 500, 500);
    auxInitWindow (argv[0]);
    myinit ();
    auxReshapeFunc (myReshape);
    auxMainLoop(display);
}
```

The Viewing Transformation

Recall that the viewing transformation is analogous to positioning and aiming a camera. In this code example, before the viewing transformation can be specified, the current matrix is set to the identity matrix with **glLoadIdentity()**. This step is necessary since most of the transformation commands multiply the current matrix by the specified matrix and then set the result to be the current matrix. If you don't clear the current matrix by loading it with the identity matrix, you continue to combine previous transformation matrices with the new one you supply. In some cases, you do want to perform such combinations, but you also need to clear the matrix sometimes.

Once the matrix is initialized, the viewing transformation is specified with **glTranslatef()**. The arguments for this command indicate how the camera should be translated (moved) in the *x*, *y*, and *z* directions. The arguments used here move the camera 5 units in the negative *z* direction. By default, the camera as well as any objects in the scene are originally situated at the origin; also, the camera initially points down the negative *z*-axis. Thus, the particular viewing transformation used here has the effect of pulling the camera away from where the cube is, but it leaves the camera pointing at the object. If the camera needed to be pointed in another direction, you could have used the **glRotatef()** command to change its orientation. Viewing transformations are discussed in detail in "Viewing and Modeling Transformations" on page 76.

The Modeling Transformation

You use the modeling transformation to position and orient the model. For example, you can rotate, translate, or scale the model—or perform some combination of these operations. Rotating and translating are performed using the commands already mentioned—**glRotatef()** and **glTranslatef()**. In this example, however, the modeling transformation is invoked with **glScalef()**. The arguments for this command specify how scaling should occur along the three axes. If all the arguments are 1.0, this command has no effect; in Listing 3-1, the cube is drawn twice as large in the *y* direction. Thus, if one corner of the cube had originally been at (3.0, 3.0, 3.0), that corner would wind up being drawn at (3.0, 6.0, 3.0). The effect of this modeling transformation is to transform the cube so that it isn't a cube but a rectangular box.

Note that instead of pulling the camera back away from the cube (with a viewing transformation) so that it could be viewed, you could have moved the cube away from the camera (with a modeling transformation). This duality in the nature of viewing and modeling transformations is why you need to think about the effect of both types of transformations simultaneously. It doesn't make sense to try to separate the effects, but sometimes it's easier to think about them one way rather than the other. This is also why modeling and viewing transformations are combined into the *modelview matrix* before the transformations are applied. "Viewing and Modeling Transformations" on page 76 explains in more detail how to think about modeling and viewing transformations and how to specify them so that you get the result you want.

Also note that the modeling and viewing transformations are included in the **display**() routine, along with the call that's used to draw the cube, **auxWireCube**(). This way, **display**() can be used repeatedly to draw the contents of the window if, for example, the window is moved or uncovered, and you've ensured that each time, the cube is drawn in the desired way, with the appropriate transformations. The potential repeated use of **display**() underscores the need to load the identity matrix before performing the viewing and modeling transformations, especially when other transformations might be performed between calls to **display**().

The Projection Transformation

Specifying the projection transformation is like choosing a lens for a camera. You can think of this transformation as determining what the field of view or viewing volume is and therefore what objects are inside it and to some extent how they look. This is equivalent to choosing among wide-angle, normal, and telephoto lenses, for example. With a wide-angle lens, you can include a wider scene in the final photograph than with a telephoto lens, but a telephoto lens allows you to photograph objects as though they're closer to you than they actually are. In computer graphics, you don't have to pay $10,000 for a 2000-millimeter telephoto lens; once you've bought your graphics workstation, all you need to do is use a smaller number for your field of view.

In addition to the field-of-view considerations, the projection transformation determines how objects are *projected* onto the screen, as its name suggests. Two basic types of projections are provided for you by OpenGL, along with several corresponding commands for describing the relevant parameters in different ways. One type is the *perspective* projection, which matches how you see things in daily life. Perspective makes objects that are farther away appear smaller; for example, it makes railroad tracks appear to converge in the distance. If you're trying to make realistic pictures, you'll want to choose perspective projection, which is specified with the **glFrustum**() command in this code example.

The other type of projection is *orthographic*, which maps objects directly onto the screen without affecting their relative size. Orthographic projection is used in architectural and computer-aided design applications where the final image needs to reflect the measurements of objects rather than how they might look. Architects create perspective drawings to show how particular buildings or interior spaces look when viewed from various vantage points; the need for orthographic projection arises when blueprint plans or elevations are generated, which are used in the construction of buildings. "Projection Transformations" on page 90 discusses the ways to specify both kinds of projection transformations in more detail.

Before **glFrustum()** can be called to set the projection transformation, some preparation needs to happen. As shown in the **myReshape()** routine in Listing 3-1, the command called **glMatrixMode()** is used first, with the argument GL_PROJECTION. This indicates that the current matrix specifies the projection transformation; the following transformation calls then affect the *projection matrix*. As you can see, a few lines later **glMatrixMode()** is called again, this time with GL_MODELVIEW as the argument. This indicates that succeeding transformations now affect the modelview matrix instead of the projection matrix. See "Manipulating the Matrix Stacks" on page 102 for more information about how to control the projection and modelview matrices.

Note that **glLoadIdentity()** is used to initialize the current projection matrix so that only the specified projection transformation has an effect. Now **glFrustum()** can be called, with arguments that define the parameters of the projection transformation. In this example, both the projection transformation and the viewport transformation are contained in the **myReshape()** routine, which is called when the window is first created and whenever the window is moved or reshaped. This makes sense, since both projecting and applying the viewport relate directly to the screen, and specifically to the size of the window on the screen.

The Viewport Transformation

Together, the projection transformation and the viewport transformation determine how a scene gets mapped onto the computer screen. The projection transformation specifies the mechanics of how the mapping should occur, and the viewport indicates the shape of the available screen area into which the scene is mapped. Since the viewport specifies the region the image occupies on the computer screen, you can think of the viewport transformation as defining the size and location of the final processed photograph—whether it should be enlarged or shrunk, for example.

The arguments to **glViewport()** describe the origin of the available screen space within the window—(0, 0) in this example—and the width and height of the available screen area, all measured in pixels on the screen. This is why this command needs to be called within **myReshape()**—if the window changes size, the viewport needs to change accordingly. Note that the width and height are specified using the actual width and height of the window; often, you want to specify the viewport this way rather than giving an absolute size. See "Viewport Transformation" on page 96 for more information about how to define the viewport.

Drawing the Scene

Once all the necessary transformations have been specified, you can draw the scene (that is, take the photograph). As the scene is drawn, OpenGL transforms each vertex of every object in the scene by the modeling and viewing transformations. Each vertex is then transformed as specified by the projection transformation and clipped if it lies outside the viewing volume described by the projection transformation. Finally, the remaining transformed vertices are divided by *w* and mapped onto the viewport.

General-Purpose Transformation Commands

This section discusses some OpenGL commands that you might find useful as you specify desired transformations. You've already seen a couple of these commands, **glMatrixMode()** and **glLoadIdentity()**. The other two commands described here—**glLoadMatrix*()** and **glMultMatrix*()**—allow you to specify any transformation matrix directly and then to multiply the current matrix by that specified matrix. More specific transformation commands—such as **glTranslate*()** and **glScale*()**—are described in later sections.

As described in the preceding section, you need to state whether you want to modify the modelview or projection matrix before supplying a transformation command. You do this with **glMatrixMode()**. When you use nested sets of OpenGL commands that might be called repeatedly, remember to reset the matrix mode correctly. (The **glMatrixMode()** command can also be used to indicate the texture matrix; texturing is discussed in detail in Chapter 9.)

void **glMatrixMode**(GLenum *mode*);

Specifies whether the modelview, projection, or texture matrix will be modified, using the argument GL_MODELVIEW, GL_PROJECTION, or GL_TEXTURE for *mode*. Subsequent transformation commands affect the specified matrix. Note that only one matrix can be modified at a time. By default, the modelview matrix is the one that's modifiable, and all three matrices contain the identity matrix.

You use the **glLoadIdentity**() command to clear the currently modifiable matrix for future transformation commands, since these commands modify the current matrix. Typically, you always call this command before specifying projection or viewing transformations, but you might also call it before specifying a modeling transformation.

void **glLoadIdentity**(void);

Sets the currently modifiable matrix to the 4×4 identity matrix.

If you want to explicitly specify a particular matrix to be loaded as the current matrix, use **glLoadMatrix***(). Similarly, use **glMultMatrix***() to multiply the current matrix by the matrix passed in as an argument. The argument for both these commands is a vector of sixteen values (m_1, m_2, ... , m_{16}) that specifies a matrix **M** as follows:

$$\mathbf{M} = \begin{bmatrix} m_1 & m_5 & m_9 & m_{13} \\ m_2 & m_6 & m_{10} & m_{14} \\ m_3 & m_7 & m_{11} & m_{15} \\ m_4 & m_8 & m_{12} & m_{16} \end{bmatrix}$$

Remember that you might be able to maximize efficiency by using display lists to store frequently used matrices (and their inverses) rather than recomputing them; see "Display-List Design Philosophy" on page 121. (OpenGL implementations often must compute the inverse of the modelview matrix so that normals and clipping planes can be correctly transformed to eye coordinates.)

Caution: If you're programming in C, and you declare a matrix as $m[4][4]$, then the element *m[i][j]* is in the *i*th column and *j*th row of the OpenGL transformation matrix. This is the reverse of the standard C convention in which *m[i][j]* is in row *i* and column *j*. To avoid confusion, you should declare your matrices as $m[16]$.

---

void **glLoadMatrix**{fd}(const *TYPE* *m);

Sets the sixteen values of the current matrix to those specified by *m*.

---

void **glMultMatrix**{fd}(const *TYPE* *m);

Multiplies the matrix specified by the sixteen values pointed to by *m* by the current matrix and stores the result as the current matrix.

Note: All matrix multiplication with OpenGL occurs as follows: Suppose the current matrix is **C** and the matrix specified with **glMultMatrix*()** or any of the transformation commands is **M**. After multiplication, the final matrix is always **CM**. Since matrix multiplication isn't generally commutative, the order makes a difference.

Viewing and Modeling Transformations

As noted in "A Simple Example: Drawing a Cube" on page 69, viewing and modeling transformations are inextricably related in OpenGL and are in fact combined into a single modelview matrix. One of the toughest problems newcomers to computer graphics face is understanding the effects of combined three-dimensional transformations. As you've already seen, there are alternative ways to think about transformations—do you want to move the camera in one direction, or move the object in the opposite direction? Each way of thinking about transformations has advantages and disadvantages, but in some cases one way more naturally matches the effect of the intended transformation. If you can find a natural approach for your particular application, it's easier to visualize the necessary transformations and then write the corresponding code to specify the matrix manipulations. The first part of this section discusses how to think about transformations; later, specific commands are presented. For now, we use only the matrix-manipulation commands you've already seen. Finally, keep in mind that you must call **glMatrixMode()** with GL_MODELVIEW as its argument prior to performing modeling or viewing transformations.

Thinking about Transformations

Let's start with a simple case of two transformations: a 45-degree counterclockwise rotation about the origin around the *z*-axis, and a translation down the *x*-axis. Suppose that the object you're drawing is small compared to the translation (so that you can see the effect of the translation), and that it's originally located at the origin. If you rotate the object first and then translate it, the rotated object appears on the *x*-axis. If you translate it down the *x*-axis first, however, and then rotate about the origin, the object is on the line *y=x*, as shown in Figure 3-4. In general, the order of transformations is critical. If you do transformation A and then transformation B, you almost certainly get something different than if you do them in the opposite order.

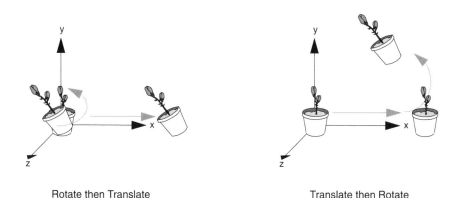

Rotate then Translate   Translate then Rotate

Figure 3-4   Rotating First or Translating First

Now let's talk about the order in which you specify a series of transformations. All viewing and modeling transformations are represented as 4×4 matrices. Each successive **glMultMatrix*()** or transformation command multiplies a new 4×4 matrix **M** by the current modelview matrix **C** to yield **CM**. Finally, vertices **v** are multiplied by the current modelview matrix. This process means that the last transformation command called in your program is actually the first one applied to the vertices: **CMv**. Thus, one way of looking at it is to say that you have to specify the matrices in the reverse order. Like many other things, however, once you've gotten used to thinking about this correctly, backward will seem like forward.

Consider the following code sequence, which draws a single point using three transformations:

```
glMatrixMode(GL_MODELVIEW);
glLoadIdentity();
glMultMatrixf(N);        /* apply transformation N */
glMultMatrixf(M);        /* apply transformation M */
glMultMatrixf(L);        /* apply transformation L */
glBegin(GL_POINTS);
glVertex3f(v);           /* draw transformed vertex v */
glEnd();
```

With this code, the modelview matrix successively contains **I**, **N**, **NM**, and finally **NML**, where **I** represents the identity matrix. The transformed vertex is **NMLv**. Thus, the vertex transformation is **N(M(Lv))**—that is, **v** is multiplied first by **L**, the resulting **Lv** is multiplied by **M**, and the resulting **MLv** is multiplied by **N**. Notice that the transformations to vertex **v** effectively occur in the opposite order than they were specified. (Actually, only a single multiplication of a vertex by the modelview matrix occurs; in this example, the **N**, **M**, and **L** matrices are already multiplied into a single matrix before it's applied to **v**.)

Thus, if you like to think in terms of a grand, fixed coordinate system—in which matrix multiplications affect the position, orientation, and scaling of your model—you have to think of the multiplications as occurring in the opposite order from how they appear in the code. Using the simple example discussed in Figure 3-4 (a rotation about the origin and a translation along the *x*-axis), if you want the object to appear on the axis after the operations, the rotation must occur first, followed by the translation. To do this, the code looks something like this (where **R** is the rotation matrix and **T** is the translation matrix):

```
glMatrixMode(GL_MODELVIEW);
glLoadIdentity();
glMultMatrixf(T);        /* translation */
glMultMatrixf(R);        /* rotation */
draw_the_object();
```

Another way to view matrix multiplications is to forget about a grand, fixed coordinate system in which your model is transformed and instead imagine that a local coordinate system is tied to the object you're drawing. All operations occur relative to this changing coordinate system. With this approach, the matrix multiplications now appear in the natural order in the code. (Regardless of which analogy you're using, the code is the same, but how you think about it differs.) To see this in the translation-rotation example, begin by visualizing the object with a coordinate system tied to it. The translation operation moves the object and its coordinate system down the *x*-axis. Then, the rotation occurs about the (now-translated) origin, so the object rotates in place in its position on the axis.

This approach is what you should use for applications such as articulated robot arms, where there are joints at the shoulder, elbow, and wrist, and on each of the fingers. To figure out where the tips of the fingers go relative to the body, you'd like to start at the shoulder, go down to the wrist, and so on, applying the appropriate rotations and translations at each joint. Thinking about it in reverse would be far more confusing.

This second approach can be problematic, however, in cases where scaling occurs, and especially so when the scaling is nonuniform (scaling different amounts along the different axes). After uniform scaling, translations move a vertex by a multiple of what they did before, since the coordinate system is stretched. Nonuniform scaling mixed with rotations may make the axes of the local coordinate system nonperpendicular.

As mentioned earlier, you normally issue viewing transformation commands in your program before any modeling transformations. This way, a vertex in a model is first transformed into the desired orientation and then transformed by the viewing operation. Since the matrix multiplications must be specified in reverse order, the viewing commands need to come first. Note, however, that you don't need to specify either viewing or modeling transformations if you're satisfied with the default conditions. If there's no viewing transformation, the "camera" is left in the default position at the origin, pointed toward the negative *z*-axis; if there's no modeling transformation, the model isn't moved, and it retains its specified position, orientation, and size.

Since the commands for performing modeling transformations can be used to perform viewing transformations, modeling transformations are *discussed* first, even if viewing transformations are actually *issued* first. This order for discussion also matches the way many programmers think when planning their code: Often, they write all the code necessary to compose the scene, which involves transformations to position and orient objects correctly relative to each other. Then, they decide where they want the viewpoint to be relative to the scene they've composed, and they write the viewing transformations accordingly.

Modeling Transformations

The three OpenGL routines for modeling transformations are
glTranslate*(), **glRotate*()**, and **glScale*()**. As you might suspect, these
routines transform an object (or coordinate system, if you're thinking of it
that way) by moving, rotating, stretching, or shrinking it. All three
commands are equivalent to producing an appropriate translation,
rotation, or scaling matrix, and then calling **glMultMatrix*()** with that
matrix as the argument. However, these three routines might be faster
than using **glMultMatrix*()**. OpenGL automatically computes the
matrices for you; if you're interested in the details, see Appendix G.

In the command summaries that follow, each matrix multiplication is
described in terms of what it does to the vertices of a geometric object
using the fixed coordinate system approach, and in terms of what it does
to the local coordinate system that's attached to an object.

Translate

---
void **glTranslate**{fd}(*TYPE x*, *TYPE y*, *TYPE z*);

Multiplies the current matrix by a matrix that moves (translates) an
object by the given *x*, *y*, and *z* values (or moves the local coordinate
system by the same amounts).

Figure 3-5 shows the effect of **glTranslatef()**.

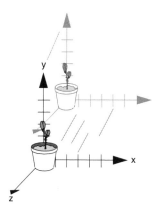

Figure 3-5   Translating an Object

Note that using (0.0, 0.0, 0.0) as the argument for **glTranslate*()** is the identity operation—that is, it has no effect on an object or its local coordinate system.

Rotate

---

void **glRotate**{fd}(TYPE *angle*, TYPE *x*, TYPE *y*, TYPE *z*);

Multiplies the current matrix by a matrix that rotates an object (or the local coordinate system) in a counterclockwise direction about the ray from the origin through the point (*x, y, z*). The *angle* parameter specifies the angle of rotation in degrees.

The effect of **glRotatef**(45.0, 0.0, 0.0, 1.0), which is a rotation of 45 degrees about the *z*-axis, is shown in Figure 3-6.

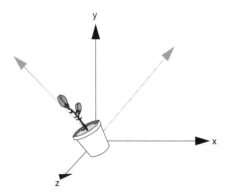

Figure 3-6   Rotating an Object

Note that an object that lies farther from the axis of rotation is more dramatically rotated (has a larger orbit) than an object drawn near the axis. Also, if the *angle* argument is zero, the **glRotate*()** command has no effect.

Scale

---

void **glScale**{fd}(*TYPE x*, *TYPE y*, *TYPE z*);

Multiplies the current matrix by a matrix that stretches, shrinks, or reflects an object along the axes. Each *x*, *y*, and *z* coordinate of every point in the object is multiplied by the corresponding argument *x*, *y*, or *z*. With the local coordinate system approach, the local coordinate axes are stretched by the *x*, *y*, and *z* factors, and the associated object is stretched with them.

Figure 3-7 shows the effect of **glScalef**(2.0, -0.5, 1.0).

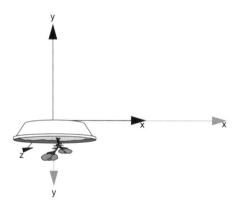

Figure 3-7   Scaling and Reflecting an Object

glScale*() is the only one of the three modeling transformations that changes the apparent size of an object: Scaling with values greater than 1.0 stretches an object, and using values less than 1.0 shrinks it. Scaling with a −1.0 value reflects an object across an axis. The identity values for scaling are (1.0, 1.0, 1.0). In general, you should limit your use of **glScale*()** to those cases where it is necessary. Using **glScale*()** decreases the performance of lighting calculations, because the normal vectors have to be renormalized after transformation.

Note: A scale value of zero collapses all object coordinates along that axis to zero. It's usually not a good idea to do this, because such an operation cannot be undone. Mathematically speaking, the matrix cannot be inverted, and inverse matrices are required for certain lighting operations (see Chapter 6). Sometimes collapsing coordinates does make sense, however; the calculation of shadows on a planar surface is a typical application (see "Shadows" on page 401). In general, if a coordinate system is to be collapsed, the projection matrix should be used rather than the modelview matrix.

A Modeling Transformation Code Example

Listing 3-2 is a portion of a program that renders a triangle four times, as shown in Figure 3-8:

- A solid wireframe triangle is drawn with no modeling transformation.

- The same triangle is drawn again, but with a dashed line stipple and translated.

- A triangle is drawn with a long dashed line stipple, with its height (y-axis) halved and its width (x-axis) doubled.

- A rotated, scaled triangle, made of dotted lines, is drawn.

Figure 3-8   Modeling Transformation Example

Listing 3-2   Using Modeling Transformations: model.c

```
glLoadIdentity();
glColor3f(1.0, 1.0, 1.0);
draw_triangle();                      /* solid lines */

glEnable(GL_LINE_STIPPLE);            /* dashed lines */
glLineStipple(1, 0xF0F0);
glLoadIdentity();
glTranslatef(-20.0, 0.0, 0.0);
draw_triangle();

glLineStipple(1, 0xF00F);             /*long dashed lines */
glLoadIdentity();
glScalef(1.5, 0.5, 1.0);
draw_triangle();
```

```
glLineStipple(1, 0x8888);           /* dotted lines */
glLoadIdentity();
glRotatef (90.0, 0.0, 0.0, 1.0);
draw_triangle ();
glDisable (GL_LINE_STIPPLE);
```

Note the use of **glLoadIdentity()** to isolate the effects of modeling transformations; initializing the matrix values prevents successive transformations from having a cumulative effect. Even though using **glLoadIdentity()** repeatedly has the desired effect, it might be inefficient, depending on your particular OpenGL implementation. See "Manipulating the Matrix Stacks" on page 102 for a better way to isolate transformations.

Note: Sometimes, programmers who want a continuously rotating object attempt to achieve this by repeatedly applying a rotation matrix that has small values. The problem with this technique is that because of round-off errors, the product of thousands of tiny rotations gradually drifts away from the value you really want (it might even become something that isn't a rotation). Instead of using this technique, increment the angle and issue a new rotation command with the new angle at each update step.

Viewing Transformations

A viewing transformation changes the position and orientation of the viewpoint. If you recall the camera analogy, the viewing transformation positions the camera tripod, pointing the camera toward the model. Just as you move the camera to some position and rotate it until it points in the desired direction, viewing transformations are generally composed of translations and rotations. Also remember that, to achieve a certain scene composition in the final image or photograph, either you can move the camera, or you can move all the objects in the opposite direction. Thus, a modeling transformation that rotates an object counterclockwise is equivalent to a viewing transformation that rotates the camera clockwise, for example. Finally, keep in mind that the viewing transformation commands must be called before any modeling transformations are performed, so that the modeling transformations take effect on the objects first.

You can accomplish a viewing transformation in any of several ways, as described below. You can also choose to use the default location and orientation of the viewpoint, which is at the origin, looking down the negative z-axis.

- Use one or more modeling transformation commands (that is, **glTranslate*()** and **glRotate*()**). You can think of the effect of these transformations as moving the camera position or as moving all the objects in the world, relative to a stationary camera.

- Use the Utility Library routine **gluLookAt()** to define a line of sight. This routine encapsulates a series of rotation and translation commands.

- Create your own utility routine that encapsulates rotations and translations. Some applications might require custom routines that allow you to specify the viewing transformation in a convenient way. For example, you might want to specify the roll, pitch, and heading rotation angles of a plane in flight, or you might want to specify a transformation in terms of polar coordinates for a camera that's orbiting around an object.

Using glTranslate*() and glRotate*()

When you use modeling transformation commands to emulate viewing transformations, you're trying to move the viewpoint in a desired way while keeping the objects in the world stationary. Since the viewpoint is initially located at the origin and since objects are often most easily constructed there as well (see Figure 3-9), in general you have to perform some transformation so that the objects can be viewed. Note that, as shown in the figure, the camera initially points down the negative z-axis. (You're seeing the back of the camera.)

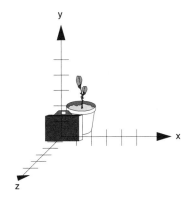

Figure 3-9　　Object and Viewpoint at the Origin

In the simplest case, you can move the viewpoint backward, away from the objects; this has the same effect as moving the objects forward, or away from the viewpoint. Remember that by default forward is down the negative *z*-axis; if you rotate the viewpoint, forward has a different meaning. So, to put 5 units of distance between the viewpoint and the objects by moving the viewpoint, as shown in Figure 3-10, use

```
glTranslatef(0.0, 0.0, -5.0);
```

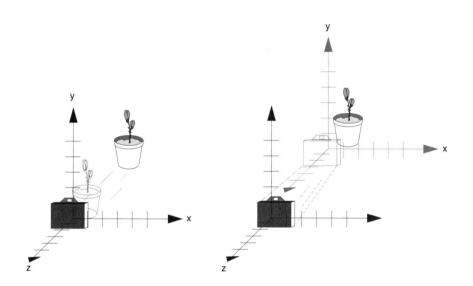

Figure 3-10 Separating the Viewpoint and the Object

Now suppose you want to view the objects from the side. Should you issue a rotate command before or after the translate command? If you're thinking in terms of a grand, fixed coordinate system, first imagine both the object and the camera at the origin. You could rotate the object first and then move it away from the camera so that the desired side is visible. Since you know that with the fixed coordinate system approach, commands have to be issued in the opposite order in which they should take effect, you know that you need to write the translate command first in your code and follow it with the rotate command.

Now let's use the local coordinate system approach. In this case, think about moving the object and its local coordinate system away from the origin; then, the rotate command is carried out using the now-translated coordinate system. With this approach, commands are issued in the order in which they're applied, so once again the translate command comes first. Thus, the sequence of transformation commands to produce the desired result is

```
glTranslatef(0.0, 0.0, -5.0);
glRotatef(90.0, 0.0, 1.0, 0.0);
```

If you're having trouble keeping track of the effect of successive matrix multiplications, try using both the fixed and local coordinate system approaches and see whether one makes more sense to you. Note that with the fixed coordinate system, rotations always occur about the grand origin, whereas with the local coordinate system, rotations occur about the origin of the local system. You might also try using the **gluLookAt()** utility routine described in the next section.

Using the gluLookAt() Utility Routine

Often, programmers construct a scene around the origin or some other convenient location, then they want to look at it from an arbitrary point to get a good view of it. As its name suggests, the **gluLookAt()** utility routine is designed for just this purpose. It takes three sets of arguments, which specify the location of the viewpoint, define a reference point toward which the camera is aimed, and indicate which direction is up. Choose the viewpoint to yield the desired view of the scene. The reference point is typically somewhere in the middle of the scene: If you've built your scene at the origin, the reference point is probably the origin. It might be a little trickier to specify the correct up-vector. Again, if you've built some real-world scene at or around the origin, and if you've been taking the positive y-axis to point upward, then that's your up-vector for **gluLookAt()**. However, if you're designing a flight simulator, up is the direction perpendicular to the plane's wings, from the plane toward the sky when the plane is right-side up on the ground.

The **gluLookAt()** routine is particularly useful when you want to pan across a landscape, for instance. With a viewing volume that's symmetric in both x and y, the (*eyex, eyey, eyez*) point specified is always in the center of the image on the screen, so you can use a series of commands to move this point slightly, thereby panning across the scene.

> void **gluLookAt**(GLdouble *eyex*, GLdouble *eyey*, GLdouble *eyez*,
> GLdouble *centerx*, GLdouble *centery*,
> GLdouble *centerz*, GLdouble *upx*,
> GLdouble *upy*, GLdouble *upz*);
>
> Defines a viewing matrix and multiplies it to the right of the current matrix. The desired viewpoint is specified by *eyex*, *eyey*, and *eyez*. The *centerx*, *centery*, and *centerz* arguments specify any point along the desired line of sight, but typically they're some point in the center of the scene being looked at. The *upx*, *upy*, and *upz* arguments indicate which direction is up (that is, the direction from the bottom to the top of the viewing volume).

Note that **gluLookAt()** is part of the Utility Library rather than the basic OpenGL library. This isn't because it's not useful, but because it encapsulates several basic OpenGL commands—specifically, **glTranslate*()** and **glRotate*()**. To see this, imagine a camera located at an arbitrary viewpoint and oriented according to a line of sight, both as specified with **gluLookAt()**, and a scene located at the origin. To "undo" what **gluLookAt()** does, you need to transform the camera so that it sits at the origin and points down the negative *z*-axis, the default position. A simple translate moves the camera to the origin. You can easily imagine a series of rotations about each of the three axes of a fixed coordinate system that would orient the camera so that it pointed toward negative *z* values. Since OpenGL allows rotation about an arbitrary axis, you can accomplish any desired rotation of the camera with a single **glRotate*()** command.

| Advanced |

To transform any arbitrary vector so that it's coincident with another arbitrary vector (for instance, the negative *z*-axis), you need to do a little mathematics. The axis about which you want to rotate is given by the cross product of the two normalized vectors. To find the angle of rotation, normalize the initial two vectors. The cosine of the desired angle between the vectors is equal to the dot product of the normalized vectors. To disambiguate between the two possible angles identified by the cosine (*x* degrees and *x*+180 degrees), recall that the length of the cross product of the normalized vectors equals the sine of the angle of rotation. (See Appendix F for definitions of cross and dot products.)

Creating a Custom Utility Routine

Advanced

For some specialized applications, you might want to define your own transformation routine. Since this is rarely done and in any case is a fairly advanced topic, it's left mostly as an exercise for the reader. The following exercises suggest two custom viewing transformations that might be useful.

Try This:

Try This

- Suppose you're writing a flight simulator and you'd like to display the world from the point of view of the pilot of a plane. The world is described in a coordinate system with the origin on the runway and the plane at coordinates (x, y, z). Suppose further that the plane has some *roll*, *pitch*, and *heading* (these are rotation angles of the plane relative to its center of gravity).

  Show that the following routine could serve as the viewing transformation:

  ```
  void pilotView{GLdouble planex, GLdouble planey,
                 GLdouble planez, GLdouble roll,
                 GLdouble pitch, GLdouble heading)
  {
     glRotated(roll, 0.0, 0.0, 1.0);
     glRotated(pitch, 0.0, 1.0, 0.0);
     glRotated(heading, 1.0, 0.0, 0.0);
     glTranslated(-planex, -planey, -planez);
  }
  ```

- Suppose your application involves orbiting the camera around an object that's centered at the origin. In this case, you'd like to specify the viewing transformation by using polar coordinates. Let the *distance* variable define the radius of the orbit, or how far the camera is from the origin. (Initially, the camera is moved *distance* units along the positive *z*-axis.) The *azimuth* describes the angle of rotation of the camera about the object in the *x-y* plane, measured from the positive *y*-axis. Similarly, *elevation* is the angle of rotation of the camera in the *y-z* plane, measured from the positive *z*-axis. Finally, *twist* represents the rotation of the viewing volume around its line of sight.

Show that the following routine could serve as the viewing transformation:

```
void polarView{GLdouble distance, GLdouble twist,
               GLdouble elevation, GLdouble azimuth)
{
   glTranslated(0.0, 0.0, -distance);
   glRotated(-twist, 0.0, 0.0, 1.0);
   glRotated(-elevation, 1.0, 0.0, 0.0);
   glRotated(azimuth, 0.0, 0.0, 1.0);
}
```

Projection Transformations

The previous section described how to compose the desired modelview matrix so that the correct modeling and viewing transformations are applied. This section explains how to define the desired projection matrix, which is also used to transform the vertices in your scene. Before you issue any of the transformation commands described in this section, remember to call

```
glMatrixMode(GL_PROJECTION);
glLoadIdentity();
```

so that the commands affect the projection matrix rather than the modelview matrix, and so that you avoid compound projection transformations. Since each projection transformation command completely describes a particular transformation, typically you don't want to combine a projection transformation with another transformation.

The purpose of the projection transformation is to define a *viewing volume*, which is used in two ways. The viewing volume determines how an object is projected onto the screen (that is, by using a perspective or an orthographic projection), and it defines which objects or portions of objects are clipped out of the final image. You can think of the viewpoint we've been talking about as existing at one end of the viewing volume. At this point, you might want to reread "A Simple Example: Drawing a Cube" on page 69 for its overview of all the transformations, including projection transformations.

Perspective Projection

The most unmistakable characteristic of perspective projection is foreshortening: the farther an object is from the camera, the smaller it appears in the final image. This occurs because the viewing volume for a perspective projection is a frustum of a pyramid (a truncated pyramid whose top has been cut off by a plane parallel to its base). Objects that fall within the viewing volume are projected toward the apex of the pyramid, where the camera or viewpoint is. Objects that are closer to the viewpoint appear larger because they occupy a proportionally larger amount of the viewing volume than those that are farther away, in the larger part of the frustum. This method of projection is commonly used for animation, visual simulation, and any other applications that strive for some degree of realism because it's similar to how our eye (or a camera) works.

The command to define a frustum, **glFrustum()**, calculates a matrix that accomplishes perspective projection and multiplies the current projection matrix (typically the identity matrix) by it. Recall that the viewing volume is used to clip objects that lie outside of it; the four sides of the frustum, its top, and its base correspond to the six clipping planes of the viewing volume, as shown in Figure 3-11. Objects or parts of objects outside these planes are clipped from the final image. Note that **glFrustum()** doesn't require you to define a symmetric viewing volume.

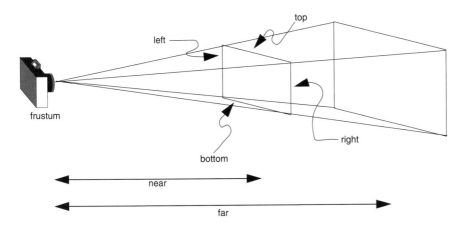

Figure 3-11   The Perspective Viewing Volume Specified by glFrustum()

> void **glFrustum**(GLdouble *left*, GLdouble *right*, GLdouble *bottom*,
> GLdouble *top*, GLdouble *near*, GLdouble *far*);
>
> Creates a matrix for a perspective-view frustum and multiplies the current matrix by it. The frustum's viewing volume is defined by the parameters: (*left, bottom, –near*) and (*right, top, –near*) specify the (*x, y, z*) coordinates of the lower left and upper right corners of the near clipping plane; *near* and *far* give the distances from the viewpoint to the near and far clipping planes. They should always be positive.

The frustum has a default orientation in three-dimensional space. You can perform rotations or translations on the projection matrix to alter this orientation, but this is tricky and nearly always avoidable.

Also, the frustum doesn't have to be symmetrical, and its axis isn't necessarily aligned with the *z*-axis. For example, you can use **glFrustum()** to draw a picture as if you were looking through a rectangular window of a house, where the window was above and to the right of you. Photographers use such a viewing volume to create false perspectives. You might use it to have the hardware calculate images at much higher than normal resolutions, perhaps for use on a printer. For example, if you want an image that has twice the resolution of your screen, draw the same picture four times, each time using the frustum to cover the entire screen with one-quarter of the image. After each quarter of the image is rendered, you can read the pixels back to collect the data for the higher-resolution image. (See Chapter 8 for more information about reading pixel data.)

Although it's easy to understand conceptually, **glFrustum()** isn't intuitive to use. Instead, you might try the Utility Library routine **gluPerspective()**. This routine creates a viewing volume of the same shape as **glFrustum()** does, but you specify it in a different way. Rather than specifying corners of the near clipping plane, you specify the angle of the field of view in the *x-z* plane and the aspect ratio of the width to height (*x/y*). (For a square portion of the screen, the aspect ratio is 1.0.) These two parameters are enough to determine an untruncated pyramid along the line of sight, as shown in Figure 3-12. You also specify the distance between the viewpoint and the near and far clipping planes, thereby truncating the pyramid. Note that **gluPerspective()** is limited to creating frustums that are symmetric in both the *x*- and *y*-axes along the line of sight, but this is usually what you want.

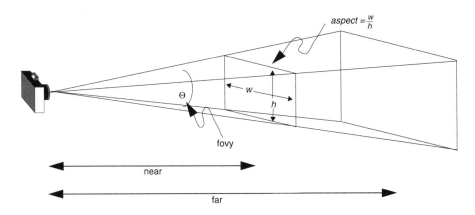

$$aspect = \frac{w}{h}$$

Θ

fovy

near

far

Figure 3-12 The Perspective Viewing Volume Specified by gluPerspective()

---

void **gluPerspective**(GLdouble *fovy*, GLdouble *aspect*, GLdouble *zNear*,
GLdouble *zFar*);

Creates a matrix for a symmetric perspective-view frustum and
multiplies the current matrix by it. The *fovy* argument is the angle of the
field of view in the *x-z* plane; its value must be in the range [0.0,180.0].
The *aspect* ratio is the width of the frustum divided by its height. The
zNear and *zFar* values are the distances between the viewpoint and the
clipping planes, along the negative *z*-axis. They should always be
positive.

Just as with **glFrustum**(), you can apply rotations or translations to change
the default orientation of the viewing volume created by **gluPerspective**().
With no such transformations, the viewpoint remains at the origin, and
the line of sight points down the negative *z*-axis.

With **gluPerspective**(), you need to pick appropriate values for the field of
view, or the image may look distorted. For example, suppose you're
drawing to the entire screen, which happens to be 11 inches high. If you
choose a field of view of 90 degrees, your eye has to be about 7.8 inches
from the screen for the image to appear undistorted. (This is the distance
that makes the screen subtend 90 degrees.) If your eye is farther from the
screen, as it usually is, the perspective doesn't look right. If your drawing
area occupies less than the full screen, your eye has to be even closer. To
get a perfect field of view, figure out how far your eye normally is from the

screen and how big the window is, and calculate the angle the window subtends at that size and distance. It's probably smaller than you would guess. Another way to think about it is that a 94-degree field of view with a 35-millimeter camera requires a 20-millimeter lens, which is a very wide-angle lens. "Troubleshooting Transformations" on page 99 gives more details on how to calculate the desired field of view.

The preceding paragraph mentions inches and millimeters—do these really have anything to do with OpenGL? The answer is, in a word, no. The projection and other transformations are inherently unitless. If you want to think of the near and far clipping planes as located at 1.0 and 20.0 meters, inches, kilometers, or leagues, it's up to you. The only rule is that you have to use a consistent unit of measurement. Then the resulting image is drawn to scale.

Orthographic Projection

With an orthographic projection, the viewing volume is a rectangular parallelepiped, or more informally, a box (see Figure 3-13). Unlike perspective projection, the size of the viewing volume doesn't change from one end to the other, so distance from the camera doesn't affect how large an object appears. This type of projection is used for applications such as creating architectural blueprints and computer-aided design, where it's crucial to maintain the actual sizes of objects and angles between them as they're projected.

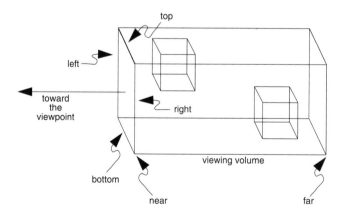

Figure 3-13   The Orthographic Viewing Volume

The command **glOrtho()** creates an orthographic parallel viewing volume. As with **glFrustum()**, you specify the corners of the near clipping plane and the distance to the far clipping plane.

void **glOrtho**(GLdouble *left*, GLdouble *right*, GLdouble *bottom*,
GLdouble *top*, GLdouble *near*, GLdouble *far*);

Creates a matrix for an orthographic parallel viewing volume and multiplies the current matrix by it. The near clipping plane is a rectangle with the lower left corner at (*left, bottom, –near*) and the upper right corner at (*right, top, –near*). The far clipping plane is a rectangle with corners at (*left, bottom, –far*) and (*right, top, –far*). Both *near* and *far* can be positive or negative.

With no other transformations, the direction of projection is parallel to the z-axis, and the viewpoint faces toward the negative z-axis. Note that this means that the values passed in for *far* and *near* are used as negative z values if these planes are in front of the viewpoint, and positive if they're behind the viewpoint.

For the special case of projecting a two-dimensional image onto a two-dimensional screen, use the Utility Library routine **gluOrtho2D()**. This routine is identical to the three-dimensional version, **glOrtho()**, except that all the z coordinates for objects in the scene are assumed to lie between –1.0 and 1.0. If you're drawing two-dimensional objects using the two-dimensional vertex commands, all the z coordinates are zero; thus, none of the objects are clipped because of their z values.

void **gluOrtho2D**(GLdouble *left*, GLdouble *right*, GLdouble *bottom*,
GLdouble *top*);

Creates a matrix for projecting two-dimensional coordinates onto the screen and multiplies the current projection matrix by it. The clipping plane is a rectangle with the lower left corner at (*left, bottom*) and the upper right corner at (*right, top*).

Viewing Volume Clipping

After the vertices of the objects in the scene have been transformed by the modelview and projection matrices, any vertices that lie outside the viewing volume are clipped. The six clipping planes used are those that define the sides and ends of the viewing volume. You can specify additional clipping planes and locate them wherever you choose; this relatively advanced topic is discussed in "Additional Clipping Planes" on page 106. Keep in mind that OpenGL reconstructs the edges of polygons that get clipped.

Viewport Transformation

Recalling the camera analogy, the viewport transformation corresponds to the stage where the size of the developed photograph is chosen. Do you want a wallet-size or a poster-size photograph? Since this is computer graphics, the viewport is the rectangular region of the window where the image is drawn. Figure 3-14 shows a viewport that occupies most of the screen. The viewport is measured in window coordinates, which reflect the position of pixels on the screen relative to the lower left corner of the window. Keep in mind that all vertices have been transformed by the modelview and projection matrices by this point, and vertices outside the viewing volume have been clipped.

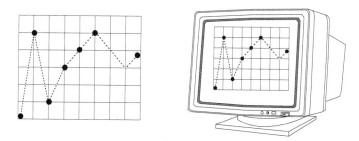

Figure 3-14   A Viewport Rectangle

Defining the Viewport

The window manager, not OpenGL, is responsible for opening a window on the screen. However, by default the viewport is set to the entire pixel rectangle of the window that's opened. You use the **glViewport()** command to choose a smaller drawing region; for example, you can subdivide the window to create a split-screen effect for multiple views in the same window.

---

void **glViewport**(GLint *x*, GLint *y*, GLsizei *width*, GLsizei *height*);

Defines a pixel rectangle in the window into which the final image is mapped. The (*x*, *y*) parameter specifies the lower left corner of the viewport, and *width* and *height* are the size of the viewport rectangle. By default, the initial viewport values are (*0, 0, winWidth, winHeight*), where *winWidth* and *winHeight* are the size of the window.

The aspect ratio of a viewport should generally equal the aspect ratio of the viewing volume. If the two ratios are different, the projected image will be distorted as it's mapped to the viewport, as shown in Figure 3-15. Note that subsequent changes to the size of the window don't explicitly affect the viewport. Your application should detect window resize events and modify the viewport appropriately.

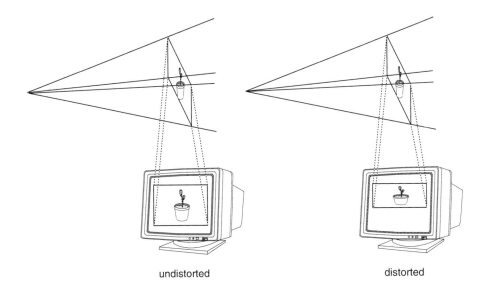

undistorted   distorted

Figure 3-15   Mapping the Viewing Volume to the Viewport

For example, this sequence maps a square image onto a square viewport:

```
gluPerspective(myFovy, 1.0, myNear, myFar);
glViewport(0, 0, 400, 400);
```

However, the following sequence projects a nonequilateral rectangular image onto a square viewport. The image appears compressed along the *x*-axis, as shown in Figure 3-15.

```
gluPerspective(myFovy, 2.0, myNear, myFar);
glViewport (0, 0, 400, 400);
```

To avoid the distortion, this line could be used:

```
glViewport(0, 0, 400, 200);
```

Try This

- Modify an existing program so that an object is drawn twice, in different viewports. You might draw the object with different projection and/or viewing transformations for each viewport. To create two side-by-side viewports, you might issue these commands, along with the appropriate modeling, viewing, and projection transformations:

```
glViewport (0, 0, sizex/2, sizey);
              .
              .
              .
glViewport (sizex/2, 0, sizex/2, sizey);
```

The Transformed z Coordinate

The *z* or depth coordinate is encoded and then stored during the viewport transformation. You can scale *z* values to lie within a desired range with the **glDepthRange()** command. (Chapter 10 discusses the depth buffer and the corresponding uses for the *z* coordinate.) Unlike *x* and *y* window coordinates, *z* window coordinates are treated by OpenGL as though they always range from 0.0 to 1.0.

void **glDepthRange**(GLclampd *near*, GLclampd *far*);

Defines an encoding for z coordinates that's performed during the viewport transformation. The *near* and *far* values represent adjustments to the minimum and maximum values that can be stored in the depth buffer. By default, they're 0.0 and 1.0, respectively, which work for most applications. These parameters are clamped to lie within [0,1].

Troubleshooting Transformations

It's pretty easy to get a camera pointed in the right direction, but in computer graphics, you have to specify position and direction with coordinates and angles. As we can attest, it's all too easy to achieve the well-known black-screen effect. Although any number of things can go wrong, often you get this effect—which results in absolutely nothing being drawn in the window you open on the screen—from incorrectly aiming the "camera" and taking a picture with the model behind you. A similar problem arises if you don't choose a field of view that's wide enough to view your objects but narrow enough so they appear reasonably large.

If you find yourself exerting great programming effort only to create a black window, try these diagnostic steps:

1. Check the obvious possibilities. Make sure your system is plugged in. Make sure you're drawing your objects with a color that's different from the color with which you're clearing the screen. Make sure that whatever states you're using (such as lighting, texturing, alpha blending, logical operations, or antialiasing) are correctly turned on or off, as desired.

2. Remember that with the projection commands, the near and far coordinates measure distance from the viewpoint and that (by default) you're looking down the negative z axis. Thus, if the near value is 1.0 and the far 3.0, objects must have z coordinates between −1.0 and −3.0 in order to be visible. To ensure that you haven't clipped everything out of your scene, temporarily set the near and far clipping planes to some absurdly inclusive values, such as 0.001 and 1000000.0. This might negatively affect performance for such operations as depth-buffering and fog, but it might uncover inadvertently clipped objects.

3. Determine where the viewpoint is, in which direction you're looking, and where your objects are. It might help to create a real three-dimensional space—using your hands, for instance—to figure these things out.

4. Make sure you know where you're rotating about. You might be rotating about some arbitrary location unless you translated back to the origin first. It's OK to rotate about any point unless you're expecting to rotate about the origin.

5. Check your aim. Use **gluLookAt()** to aim the viewing volume at your objects. Or draw your objects at or near the origin, and use **glTranslate*()** as a viewing transformation to move the camera far enough in the *z* direction only, so that the objects fall within the viewing volume. Once you've managed to make your objects visible, try to incrementally change the viewing volume to achieve the exact result you want, as described below.

Even after you've aimed the camera in the correct direction and you can see your objects, they might appear too small or too large. If you're using **gluPerspective()**, you might need to alter the angle defining the field of view by changing the value of the first parameter for this command. You can use trigonometry to calculate the desired field of view given the size of the object and its distance from the viewpoint: The tangent of half the desired angle is half the size of the object divided by the distance to the object (see Figure 3-16). Thus, you can use an arctangent routine to compute half the desired angle. Listing 3-3 assumes such a routine, **atan2()**, which calculates the arctangent given the length of the opposite and adjacent sides of a right triangle. This result then needs to be converted from radians to degrees.

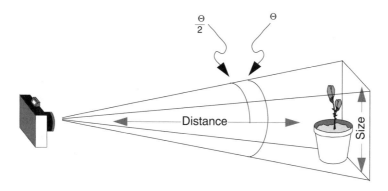

Figure 3-16   Using Trigonometry to Calculate the Field of View

Listing 3-3   Calculating Field of View

```
#define PI 3.1415926535

double calculateAngle(double size, double distance)
{
    double radtheta, degtheta;

    radtheta = 2.0 * atan2 (size/2.0, distance);
    degtheta = (180.0 * radtheta) / PI;
    return (degtheta);
}
```

Of course, typically you don't know the exact size of an object, and the distance can only be determined between the viewpoint and a single point in your scene. To obtain a fairly good approximate value, find the bounding box for your scene by determining the maximum and minimum x, y, and z coordinates of all the objects in your scene. Then calculate the radius of a bounding sphere for that box, and use the center of the sphere to determine the distance and the radius to determine the size.

For example, suppose all the coordinates in your object satisfy the equations $-1 \le x \le 3$, $5 \le y \le 7$, and $-5 \le z \le 5$. Then, the center of the bounding box is $(1, 6, 0)$, and the radius of a bounding sphere is the distance from the center of the box to any corner—say $(3, 7, 5)$—or:

$$\sqrt{(3-1)^2 + (7-6)^2 + (5-0)^2} = \sqrt{30} = 5.477$$

If the viewpoint is at $(8, 9, 10)$, the distance between it and the center is

$$\sqrt{(8-1)^2 + (9-6)^2 + (10-0)^2} = \sqrt{158} = 12.570$$

The tangent of the half angle is 5.477 divided by 12.570, or 0.4357, so the half angle is 23.54 degrees.

Remember that the field-of-view angle affects the optimal position for the viewpoint, if you're trying to achieve a realistic image. For example, if your calculations indicate that you need a 179-degree field of view, the viewpoint must be a fraction of an inch from the screen to achieve realism. If your calculated field of view is too large, you might need to move the viewpoint farther away from the object.

Manipulating the Matrix Stacks

The modelview and projection matrices you've been creating, loading, and multiplying have only been the visible tips of their respective icebergs: Each of these matrices is actually the topmost member of a stack of matrices (see Figure 3-17).

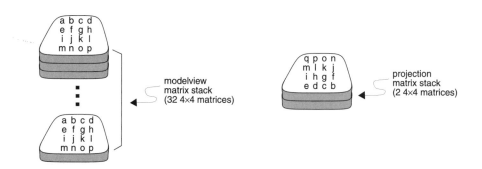

Figure 3-17   Modelview and Projection Matrix Stacks

A stack of matrices is useful for constructing hierarchical models, in which complicated objects are constructed from simpler ones. For example, suppose you're drawing an automobile that has four wheels, each of which is attached to the car with five bolts. You have a single routine to draw a wheel and another to draw a bolt, since all the wheels and all the bolts look the same. These routines draw a wheel or a bolt in some convenient position and orientation, say centered at the origin with its axis coincident with the z axis. When you draw the car, including the wheels and bolts, you want to call the wheel-drawing routine four times with different transformations in effect each time to position the wheels correctly. As you draw each wheel, you want to draw the bolts five times, each time translated appropriately relative to the wheel.

Suppose for a minute that all you have to do is draw the car body and the wheels. The English description of what you want to do might be something like this:

> Draw the car body. Remember where you are, and translate to the right front wheel. Draw the wheel and throw away the last translation so your current position is back at the origin of the car body. Remember where you are, and translate to the left front wheel....

Similarly, for each wheel, you want to draw the wheel, remember where you are, and successively translate to each of the positions that bolts are drawn, throwing away the transformations after each bolt is drawn.

Since the transformations are stored as matrices, a matrix stack provides an ideal mechanism for doing this sort of successive remembering, translating, and throwing away. All the matrix operations that have been described so far (**glLoadMatrix()**, **glMultMatrix()**, **glLoadIdentity()**, and the commands that create specific transformation matrices) deal with the current matrix, or the top matrix on the stack. You can control which matrix is on top with the commands that perform stack operations: **glPushMatrix()**, which copies the current matrix and adds the copy to the top of the stack, and **glPopMatrix()**, which discards the top matrix on the stack, as shown in Figure 3-18. (Remember that the current matrix is always the matrix on the top.) In effect, **glPushMatrix()** means "remember where you are" and **glPopMatrix()** means "go back to where you were."

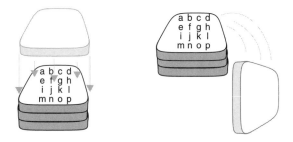

Figure 3-18 Pushing and Popping the Matrix Stack

---

void **glPushMatrix**(void);

Pushes all matrices in the current stack down one level. The current stack is determined by **glMatrixMode()**. The topmost matrix is copied, so its contents are duplicated in both the top and second-from-the-top matrix. If too many matrices are pushed, an error is generated.

Pops the top matrix off the stack. What was the second-from-the-top matrix becomes the top matrix. The current stack is determined by **glMatrixMode()**. The contents of the topmost matrix are destroyed. If the stack contains a single matrix, calling **glPopMatrix()** generates an error.

Listing 3-4 draws an automobile, assuming the existence of routines that draw the car body, a wheel, and a bolt.

Listing 3-4   Pushing and Popping the Matrix

```
draw_wheel_and_bolts()
{
    long i;

    draw_wheel();
    for(i=0;i<5;i++){
        glPushMatrix();
            glRotatef(72.0*i,0.0,0.0,1.0);
            glTranslatef(3.0,0.0,0.0);
            draw_bolt();
        glPopMatrix();
    }
}

draw_body_and_wheel_and_bolts()
{
    draw_car_body();
    glPushMatrix();
        glTranslatef(40,0,30);  /*move to first wheel position*/
        draw_wheel_and_bolts();
    glPopMatrix();
    glPushMatrix();
        glTranslatef(40,0,-30); /*move to 2nd wheel position*/
        draw_wheel_and_bolts();
    glPopMatrix();
    ...                         /*draw last two wheels similarly*/
}
```

This code assumes the wheel and bolt axes are coincident with the *z*-axis, that the bolts are evenly spaced every 72 degrees, 3 units (maybe inches) from the center of the wheel, and that the front wheels are 40 units in front of and 30 units to the right and left of the car's origin.

A stack is more efficient than an individual matrix, especially if the stack is implemented in hardware. When you push a matrix, you don't need to copy the current data back to the main process, and the hardware may be able to copy more than one element of the matrix at a time. Sometimes you might want to keep an identity matrix at the bottom of the stack so that you don't need to call **glLoadIdentity**() repeatedly.

The Modelview Matrix Stack

As you've seen earlier in this chapter, the modelview matrix contains the cumulative product of multiplying viewing and modeling transformation matrices. Each viewing or modeling transformation creates a new matrix that multiplies the current modelview matrix; the result, which becomes the new current matrix, represents the composite transformation. The modelview matrix stack contains at least thirty-two 4×4 matrices; initially, the topmost matrix is the identity matrix. Some implementations of OpenGL may support more than thirty-two matrices on the stack. You can use the query command **glGetIntegerv**() with the argument GL_MAX_MODELVIEW_STACK_DEPTH to find the maximum allowable number of matrices.

The Projection Matrix Stack

The projection matrix contains a matrix for the projection transformation, which describes the viewing volume. Generally, you don't want to compose projection matrices, so you issue **glLoadIdentity**() before performing a projection transformation. Also for this reason, the projection matrix stack need be only two levels deep; some OpenGL implementations may allow more than two 4×4 matrices. (You can use **glGetIntegerv**() with GL_MAX_PROJECTION_STACK_DEPTH as the argument to find the stack depth.)

One use for a second matrix in the stack would be an application that needs to display a help window with text in it, in addition to its normal window showing a three-dimensional scene. Since text is most easily drawn with an orthographic projection, you could change temporarily to an orthographic projection, display the help, and then return to your previous projection:

```
glMatrixMode(GL_PROJECTION);
glPushMatrix();                /*save the current projection*/
    glLoadIdentity();
    glOrtho(...);              /*set up for displaying help*/
    display_the_help();
glPopMatrix();
```

Note that you'd probably have to also change the modelview matrix appropriately.

If you know enough mathematics, you can create custom projection matrices that perform arbitrary projective transformations. For example, the OpenGL and its Utility Library have no built-in mechanism for two-point perspective. If you were trying to emulate the drawings in drafting texts, you might need such a projection matrix.

Additional Clipping Planes

In addition to the six clipping planes of the viewing volume (left, right, bottom, top, near, and far), you can define up to six additional clipping planes to further restrict the viewing volume, as shown in Figure 3-19. This is useful for removing extraneous objects in a scene—for example, if you want to display a cutaway view of an object.

Each plane is specified by the coefficients of its equation: $Ax+By+Cz+D = 0$. The clipping planes are automatically transformed appropriately by modeling and viewing transformations. The clipping volume becomes the intersection of the viewing volume and all half-spaces defined by the additional clipping planes. Remember that polygons that get clipped automatically have their edges reconstructed appropriately by OpenGL.

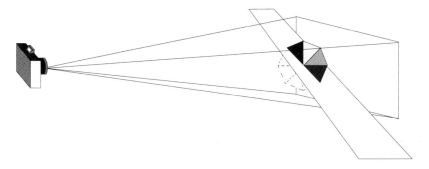

Figure 3-19   Additional Clipping Planes and the Viewing Volume

---

void **glClipPlane**(GLenum *plane*, const GLdouble **equation*);

Defines a clipping plane. The *equation* argument points to the four coefficients of the plane equation, $Ax+By+Cz+D = 0$. All points with eye coordinates (x_e, y_e, z_e, w_e) that satisfy $(A\ B\ C\ D)\mathbf{M}^{-1} (x_e\ y_e\ z_e\ w_e)^T >= 0$ lie in the half-space defined by the plane, where $\mathbf{M}$ is the current modelview matrix at the time **glClipPlane**() is called. All points not in this half-space are clipped away. The *plane* argument is GL_CLIP_PLANE*i*, where *i* is an integer between 0 and 5, specifying which of the six clipping planes to define.

Note: Clipping performed as a result of **glClipPlane**() is done in eye coordinates, not in clip coordinates. This difference is noticeable if the projection matrix is singular (that is, a real projection matrix that flattens three-dimensional coordinates to two-dimensional ones). Clipping performed in eye coordinates continues to take place in three dimensions even when the projection matrix is singular.

You need to enable each additional clipping plane you define:

```
glEnable(GL_CLIP_PLANEi);
```

You can disable a plane with

```
glDisable(GL_CLIP_PLANEi);
```

Some implementations may allow more than six clipping planes. You can use **glGetIntegerv**() with GL_MAX_CLIP_PLANES to find how many clipping planes are supported.

A Clipping Plane Code Example

Listing 3-5 renders a wireframe sphere with two clipping planes that slice away three-quarters of the original sphere, as shown in Figure 3-20.

Figure 3-20   A Clipped Wireframe Sphere

Listing 3-5   A Wireframe Sphere with Two Clipping Planes: clip.c

```
#include <GL/gl.h>
#include <GL/glu.h>
#include "aux.h"

void display(void)
{
    GLdouble eqn[4] = {0.0, 1.0, 0.0, 0.0};     /* y < 0 */
    GLdouble eqn2[4] = {1.0, 0.0, 0.0, 0.0};    /* x < 0 */

    glClear(GL_COLOR_BUFFER_BIT);

    glColor3f (1.0, 1.0, 1.0);
    glPushMatrix();
    glTranslatef (0.0, 0.0, -5.0);

    glClipPlane (GL_CLIP_PLANE0, eqn);
    glEnable (GL_CLIP_PLANE0);
    glClipPlane (GL_CLIP_PLANE1, eqn2);
    glEnable (GL_CLIP_PLANE1);

    glRotatef (90.0, 1.0, 0.0, 0.0);
    auxWireSphere(1.0);
    glPopMatrix();
    glFlush();
}

void myinit (void)
{
    glShadeModel (GL_FLAT);
}
```

```
void myReshape(GLsizei w, GLsizei h)
{
    glViewport(0, 0, w, h);
    glMatrixMode(GL_PROJECTION);
    glLoadIdentity();
    gluPerspective(60.0, (GLfloat) w/(GLfloat) h, 1.0, 20.0);
    glMatrixMode(GL_MODELVIEW);
}


int main(int argc, char** argv)
{
    auxInitDisplayMode (AUX_SINGLE | AUX_RGBA);
    auxInitPosition (0, 0, 500, 500);
    auxInitWindow (argv[0]);
    myinit ();
    auxReshapeFunc (myReshape);
    auxMainLoop(display);
}
```

Try This

- Try changing the coefficients that describe the clipping planes in Listing 3-5.

- Try calling a modeling transformation, such as **glRotate*()**, to affect **glClipPlane()**. Make the clipping plane move independently of the objects in the scene.

Examples of Composing Several Transformations

This section demonstrates how to combine several transformations to achieve a particular result. The two examples discussed are a solar system, in which objects need to rotate on their axes as well as in orbit around each other, and a robot arm, which has several joints that effectively transform coordinate systems as they move relative to each other.

Building a Solar System

The program described in this section draws a simple solar system with a planet and a sun, both using the same sphere-drawing routine. To write this program, you need to use **glRotate*()** for the revolution of the planet around the sun and for the rotation of the planet around its own axis. You also need **glTranslate*()** to move the planet out to its orbit, away from the origin of the solar system. Remember that you can specify the desired size of the two spheres by supplying the appropriate arguments for the **auxSphere()** routine.

To draw the solar system, you first want to set up a projection and a viewing transformation. For this example, **gluPerspective()** and **gluLookAt()** are used.

Drawing the sun is straightforward, since it should be located at the origin of the grand, fixed coordinate system, which is where the sphere routine places it. Thus, drawing the sun doesn't require translation; you can use **glRotate*()** to make the sun rotate about an arbitrary axis. To draw a planet rotating around the sun, as shown in Figure 3-21, requires several modeling transformations. The planet needs to rotate about its own axis once a day. And once a year, the planet completes one revolution around the sun.

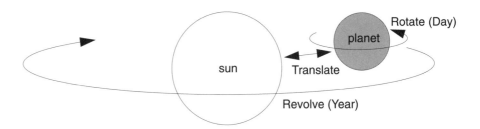

Figure 3-21   Planet and Sun

To determine the order of modeling transformations, visualize what happens to the local coordinate system. An initial **glRotate*()** rotates the local coordinate system that initially coincides with the grand coordinate system. Next, **glTranslate*()** moves the local coordinate system to a position on the planet's orbit; the distance moved should equal the radius of the orbit. Thus, the initial **glRotate*()** actually determines where along the orbit the planet is (or what time of year it is).

A second **glRotate*()** rotates the local coordinate system around the local axes, thus determining the time of day for the planet. Once you've issued all these transformation commands, the planet can be drawn.

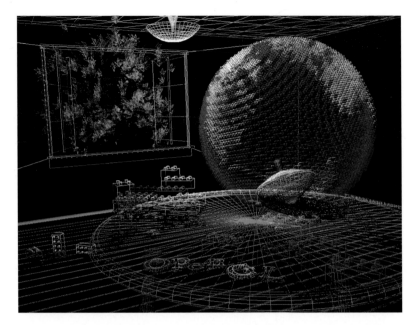

Plate 1. The scene from the cover of this book, with the objects rendered as wireframe models. See Chapter 2.

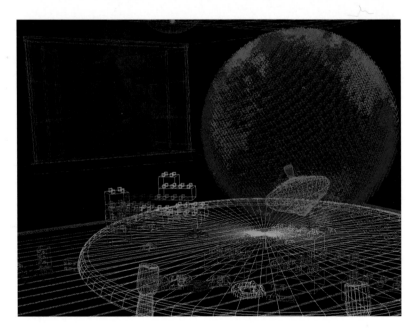

Plate 2. The same scene using fog for depth-cueing (lines further from the eye are dimmer). See Chapter 7.

Plate 3. The same scene with antialiased lines that smooth the jagged edges. See Chapter 7.

Plate 4. The scene drawn with flat-shaded polygons (a single color for each filled polygon). See Chapter 5.

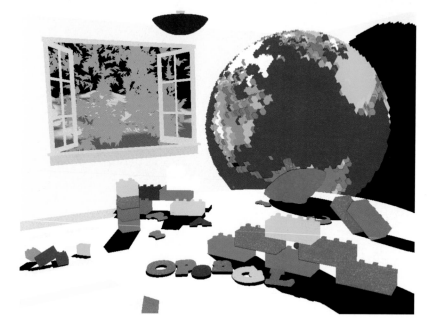

Plate 5. The scene rendered with lighting and smooth-shaded polygons. See Chapters 5 and 6.

Plate 6. The scene with texture maps and shadows added. See Chapters 9 and 13.

Plate 7. The scene drawn with one of the objects motion-blurred. The accumulation buffer is used to compose the sequence of images needed to blur the moving object. See Chapter 10.

Plate 8. A close-up shot—the scene is rendered from a new viewpoint. See Chapter 3.

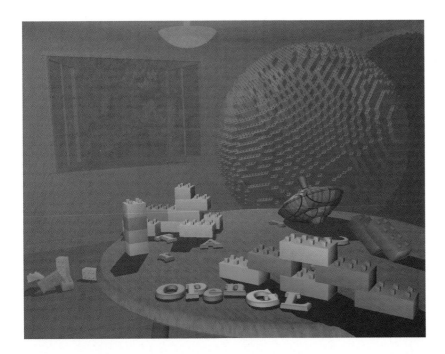

Plate 9. The scene drawn using atmospheric effects (fog) to simulate a smoke-filled room. See Chapter 7.

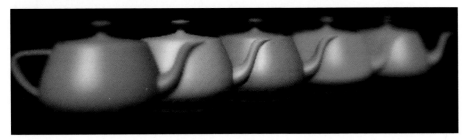

Plate 10. Teapots drawn with jittered viewing volumes into the accumulation buffer for a depth-of-field effect. The gold teapot is in sharpest focus. See Chapter 10.

Plate 11. A smooth-shaded triangle. The three vertices at the corners are drawn in red, green, and blue; the rest of the triangle is smoothly shaded between these three colors. See Chapter 5.

Plate 12. The color cube. On the left, the red, green, and blue axes are shown; on the right, the axes denote yellow, cyan, and magenta. See Chapter 5.

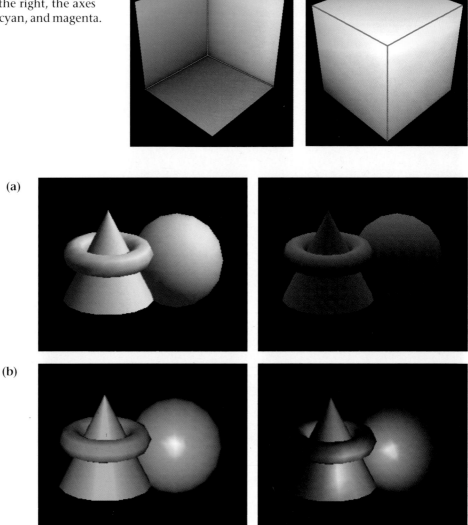

(a)

(b)

Plate 13. Objects drawn with gray material parameters and colored light sources. **(a)** The scene on the left has pale blue ambient light and a white diffuse light source. The scene on the right has a pale blue diffuse light source and almost no ambient light. **(b)** On the left, an infinite light source is used; on the right, a local light source is used. With the infinite light source, the highlight (specular reflection) is centered on both the cone and the sphere because the angle between the object and the line of sight is ignored. With a local light source, the angle is taken into account, so the highlights are located appropriately on both objects. See Chapter 6.

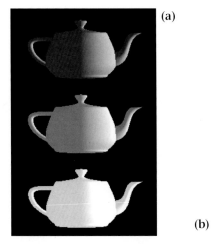

(a)

(b)

Plate 15. A lighted sphere drawn using color index mode. See Chapter 6.

Plate 14. Gray teapots drawn with different lighting conditions. **(a)** Each of the three teapots is drawn with increasing ambient light. **(b)** The teapots are clipped to expose their interiors. The top teapot uses one-sided lighting, the middle one uses two-sided lighting with the same material for both front and back faces, and the bottom teapot uses two-sided lighting and different materials for the front and back faces. See Chapter 6.

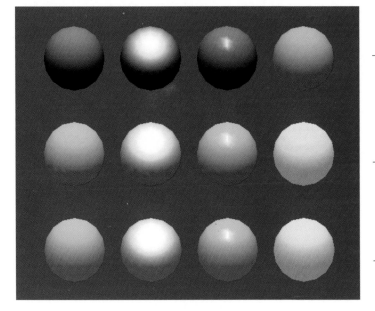

— No ambient reflection.

— Grey ambient reflection.

— Blue ambient reflection.

Plate 16. Twelve spheres, each with different material parameters. The row properties are as labeled above. The first column uses a blue diffuse material color with no specular properties. The second column adds white specular reflection with a low shininess exponent. The third column uses a high shininess exponent and thus has a more concentrated highlight. The fourth column uses the blue diffuse color and, instead of specular reflection, adds an emissive component. See Chapter 6.

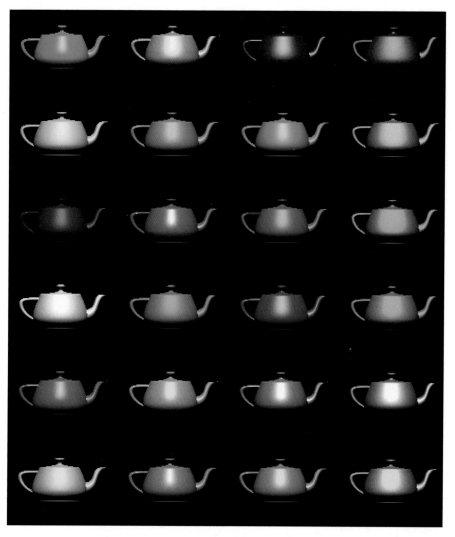

Plate 17. Lighted, smooth-shaded teapots drawn with different material properties that approximate real materials. The first column has materials that resemble (from top to bottom) emerald, jade, obsidian, pearl, ruby, and turquoise. The second column resembles brass, bronze, chrome, copper, gold, and silver. The third column represents various colors of plastic: black, cyan, green, red, white, and yellow. The fourth column is drawn with similar colors of rubber. See Chapter 6.

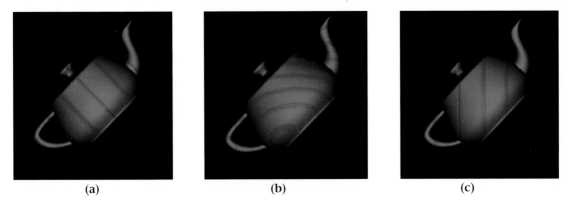

(a)　　　　**(b)**　　　　**(c)**

Plate 18. Lighted, green teapots drawn using automatic texture-coordinate generation and a red contour texture map. **(a)** The texture contour stripes are parallel to the plane x = 0, relative to the transformed object (that is, using GL_OBJECT_LINEAR). As the object moves, the texture appears to be attached to it. **(b)** A different planar equation (x + y + z = 0) is used, so the stripes have a different orientation. **(c)** The texture coordinates are calculated relative to eye coordinates and hence aren't fixed to the object (GL_EYE_LINEAR). As the object moves, it appears to "swim" through the texture. See Chapter 9.

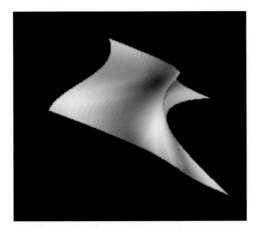

Plate 19. A texture-mapped Bezier surface mesh created using evaluators. See Chapters 9 and 11.

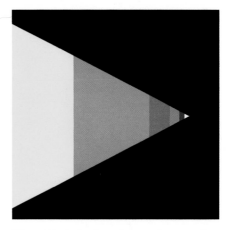

Plate 20. A single polygon drawn using a set of mipmapped textures. In this case, each texture is simply a different color. The polygon is actually a rectangle oriented so that it recedes into the distance, appearing to become progressively smaller. As the visible area of the polygon becomes smaller, correspondingly smaller mipmaps are used. See Chapter 9.

Plate 21. An environment-mapped object. On the left is the original texture, a processed photograph of a coffee shop in Palo Alto, taken with a very wide-angle lens. Below is a goblet with the environment map applied; because of the mapping, the goblet appears to reflect the coffee shop off its surface. See Chapter 9.

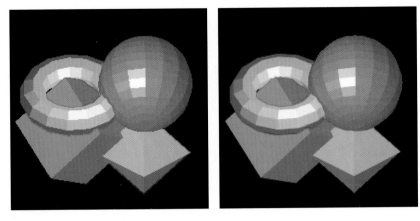

Plate 22. A scene with several flat-shaded objects. On the left, the scene is aliased. On the right, the accumulation buffer is used for scene antialiasing: the scene is rendered several times, each time jittered less than one pixel, and the images are accumulated and then averaged. See Chapter 10.

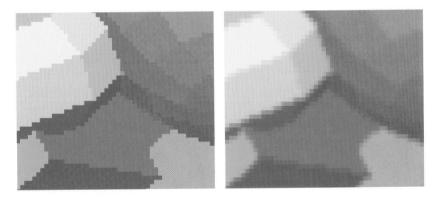

Plate 23. A magnification of the previous scenes. The left image shows the aliased, jagged edges. In the right image, the edges are blurred, or antialiased, and hence less jagged. See Chapter 10.

Plate 24. A scene drawn with texture-mapping, lighting, and shadows. The paintings, floor, ceiling, and benches are texture mapped. Note the use of spotlights and shadows. See Chapters 6, 9, and 13.

Plate 25. A lighted, smooth-shaded model on a texture-mapped surface. See Chapters 5, 6, and 9.

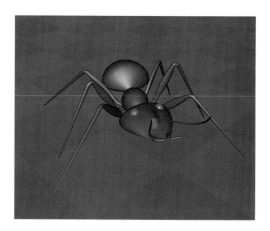

Plate 26. A dramatically lit and shadowed scene, with most of the surfaces textured. The iris is a polygonal model. See Chapters 2, 6, 9, and 13.

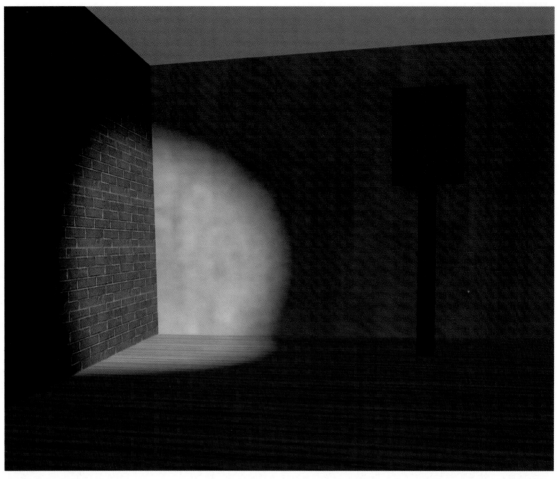

Plate 27. Sophisticated use of texturing. All surfaces are texture-mapped. In addition, the attenuated spotlight effect is created using a projected texture. See Chapters 9 and 13.

Plate 28. Lit, smooth-shaded three-dimensional font. The font is created by extruding a two-dimensional shape along a specified axis. See Chapters 2, 5, and 6.

Plates 29 and 30. Two scenes snapped from a visual simulation program. The hills are composed of just a few polygons, but all the polygons are texture-mapped. Similarly, the buildings are composed of only a few textured rectangular walls. See Chapters 2, 3, and 9.

Plate 31. Another scene from a different visual simulation program. The hills are textured, and the scene is rendered with fog. The airplanes, obviously, are polygonal. See Chapters 2, 3, 7, and 9.

In summary, these are the OpenGL commands to draw the sun and planet; the full program is shown in Listing 3-6.

```
glPushMatrix();
    auxWireSphere(1.0);                        /* draw sun */
    glRotatef ((GLfloat) year, 0.0, 1.0, 0.0);
    glTranslatef (2.0, 0.0, 0.0);
    glRotatef ((GLfloat) day, 0.0, 1.0, 0.0);
    auxWireSphere(0.2);                 /* draw smaller planet */
glPopMatrix();
```

Listing 3-6   A Planetary System: planet.c

```c
#include <GL/gl.h>
#include <GL/glu.h>
#include "aux.h"

static int year = 0, day = 0;

void dayAdd (void)
{
    day = (day + 10) % 360;
}

void daySubtract (void)
{
    day = (day - 10) % 360;
}

void yearAdd (void)
{
    year = (year + 5) % 360;
}

void yearSubtract (void)
{
    year = (year - 5) % 360;
}

void display(void)
{
    glClear(GL_COLOR_BUFFER_BIT);

    glColor3f (1.0, 1.0, 1.0);
    glPushMatrix();
        auxWireSphere(1.0);            /* draw sun */
        glRotatef((GLfloat) year, 0.0, 1.0, 0.0);
```

```
            glTranslatef (2.0, 0.0, 0.0);
            glRotatef((GLfloat) day, 0.0, 1.0, 0.0);
            auxWireSphere(0.2);          /* draw smaller planet */
        glPopMatrix();
        glFlush();
}

void myinit(void)
{
    glShadeModel(GL_FLAT);
}

void myReshape(GLsizei w, GLsizei h)
{
    glViewport(0, 0, w, h);
    glMatrixMode(GL_PROJECTION);
    glLoadIdentity();
    gluPerspective(60.0, (GLfloat) w/(GLfloat) h, 1.0, 20.0);
    glMatrixMode(GL_MODELVIEW);
    glLoadIdentity();
    glTranslatef (0.0, 0.0, -5.0);
}


int main(int argc, char** argv)
{
    auxInitDisplayMode(AUX_SINGLE | AUX_RGBA);
    auxInitPosition(0, 0, 500, 500);
    auxInitWindow(argv[0]);
    myinit();
    auxKeyFunc(AUX_LEFT, yearSubtract);
    auxKeyFunc(AUX_RIGHT, yearAdd);
    auxKeyFunc(AUX_UP, dayAdd);
    auxKeyFunc(AUX_DOWN, daySubtract);
    auxReshapeFunc(myReshape);
    auxMainLoop(display);
}
```

Try This

- Try adding a moon to the planet. Or try several moons and additional planets. Hint: Use **glPushMatrix()** and **glPopMatrix()** to save and restore the position and orientation of the coordinate system at appropriate moments. If you're going to draw several moons around a planet, you need to save the coordinate system prior to positioning each moon and restore the coordinate system after each moon is drawn.

- Try tilting the planet's axis.

Building an Articulated Robot Arm

This section discusses a program that creates an articulated robot arm with two or more segments. The arm should be connected with pivot points at the shoulder, elbow, or other joints. Figure 3-22 shows a single joint of such an arm.

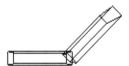

Figure 3-22   A Robot Arm

You can use a scaled box as a segment of the robot arm, but first you must call the appropriate modeling transformations to orient each segment. Since the origin of the local coordinate system is initially at the center of the box, you need to move the local coordinate system to one edge of the box. Otherwise, the box rotates about its center rather than the pivot point.

After you call **glTranslate*()** to establish the pivot point and **glRotate*()** to pivot the box, translate back to the center of the box and then draw the box. Here's what your code might look like for this first segment of the arm (the entire program is shown in Listing 3-7):

```
glTranslatef (-1.0, 0.0, 0.0);
glRotatef ((GLfloat) shoulder_angle, 0.0, 0.0, 1.0);
glTranslatef (1.0, 0.0, 0.0);
auxWireBox(2.0, 0.4, 1.0);
```

To build a second segment, you need to move the local coordinate system to the next pivot point. Since the coordinate system has previously been rotated, the *x*-axis is already oriented along the length of the rotated arm. Therefore, translating along the *x*-axis moves the local coordinate system to the next pivot point. Once it's at that pivot point, you can use the same code to draw the second segment as you used for the first one. This can be continued for an indefinite number of segments (shoulder, elbow, wrist, fingers).

```
glTranslatef (1.0, 0.0, 0.0);
glRotatef ((GLfloat) elbow_angle, 0.0, 0.0, 1.0);
glTranslatef (1.0, 0.0, 0.0);
auxWireBox(2.0, 0.4, 1.0);
```

Listing 3-7 A Robot Arm: robot.c

```
#include <GL/gl.h>
#include <GL/glu.h>
#include "aux.h"

static int shoulder = 0, elbow = 0;

void elbowAdd (void)
{
    elbow = (elbow + 5) % 360;
}

void elbowSubtract (void)
{
    elbow = (elbow - 5) % 360;
}

void shoulderAdd (void)
{
    shoulder = (shoulder + 5) % 360;
}

void shoulderSubtract (void)
{
    shoulder = (shoulder - 5) % 360;
}

void display(void)
{
    glClear(GL_COLOR_BUFFER_BIT);
    glColor3f (1.0, 1.0, 1.0);
```

```
    glPushMatrix();
        glTranslatef (-1.0, 0.0, 0.0);
        glRotatef ((GLfloat) shoulder, 0.0, 0.0, 1.0);
        glTranslatef (1.0, 0.0, 0.0);
        auxWireBox(2.0, 0.4, 1.0);        /* shoulder */

        glTranslatef (1.0, 0.0, 0.0);
        glRotatef ((GLfloat) elbow, 0.0, 0.0, 1.0);
        glTranslatef (1.0, 0.0, 0.0);
        auxWireBox(2.0, 0.4, 1.0);        /* elbow */

    glPopMatrix();
    glFlush();
}

void myinit (void)
{
    glShadeModel (GL_FLAT);
}

void myReshape(GLsizei w, GLsizei h)
{
    glViewport(0, 0, w, h);
    glMatrixMode(GL_PROJECTION);
    glLoadIdentity();
    gluPerspective(65.0, (GLfloat) w/(GLfloat) h, 1.0, 20.0);
    glMatrixMode(GL_MODELVIEW);
    glLoadIdentity();
    glTranslatef(0.0, 0.0, -5.0);
}


int main(int argc, char** argv)
{
    auxInitDisplayMode (AUX_SINGLE | AUX_RGBA);
    auxInitPosition (0, 0, 400, 400);
    auxInitWindow (argv[0]);
    myinit ();
    auxKeyFunc (AUX_LEFT, shoulderSubtract);
    auxKeyFunc (AUX_RIGHT, shoulderAdd);
    auxKeyFunc (AUX_UP, elbowAdd);
    auxKeyFunc (AUX_DOWN, elbowSubtract);
    auxReshapeFunc (myReshape);
    auxMainLoop(display);
}
```

Examples of Composing Several Transformations   **115**

Try This

- Modify Listing 3-7 to add additional segments onto the robot arm.

- Modify Listing 3-7 to add additional segments at the same position. For example, give the robot arm several "fingers" at the wrist, as shown in Figure 3-23. Hint: Use **glPushMatrix()** and **glPopMatrix()** to save and restore the position and orientation of the coordinate system at the wrist. If you're going to draw fingers at the wrist, you need to save the current matrix prior to positioning each finger and restore the current matrix after each finger is drawn.

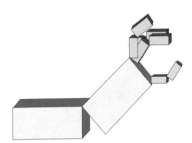

Figure 3-23   Robot Arm with Fingers

Chapter 4

Display Lists

Chapter Objectives

After reading this chapter, you'll be able to do the following:

● Understand how clients and servers work together in a networked OpenGL system

● Understand how display lists can be used along with commands in immediate mode to improve performance

● Maximize performance by knowing how and when to use display lists

A *display list* is a group of OpenGL commands that have been stored for later execution. When a display list is invoked, the commands in it are executed in the order in which they were issued. Most OpenGL commands can be either stored in a display list or issued in *immediate mode*, which causes them to be executed immediately. You can freely mix immediate-mode programming and display lists within a single program. The programming examples you've seen so far have used immediate mode. This chapter discusses what display lists are and how best to use them. It has the following major sections:

- **"An Example of Using a Display List"** gives a brief example, showing the basic commands for using display lists.

- **"Display-List Design Philosophy"** explains when to use display lists.

- **"Creating and Executing a Display List"** discusses in detail the commands for creating and executing display lists.

- **"Managing Display Lists and Their Indices"** explains how to let OpenGL generate display-list indices for you automatically.

- **"Executing Multiple Display Lists"** shows how to execute several display lists in succession, using a small character set as an example.

- **"Encapsulating Mode Changes"** tells you how to use display lists to switch efficiently among different modes.

An Example of Using a Display List

A display list is a convenient and efficient way to name and organize a set of OpenGL commands. For example, suppose you want to draw a circle with 100 line segments. Without using display lists, you might write immediate-mode code like this:

```
drawCircle()
{
    GLint i;
    GLfloat cosine, sine;

    glBegin(GL_POLYGON);
        for(i=0;i<100;i++){
            cosine=cos(i*2*PI/100.0);
            sine=sin(i*2*PI/100.0);
            glVertex2f(cosine,sine);
        }
    glEnd();
}
```

This method is terribly inefficient because the trigonometry has to be performed each time the circle is rendered. Instead, you could save the coordinates in a table, and then pull the coordinates out of the table as needed:

```
drawCircle()
{
    GLint i;
    GLfloat cosine, sine;
    static GLfloat circoords[100][2];
    static GLint inited=0;

    if(inited==0){
        inited=1;
        for(i=0;i<100;i++){
            circcoords[i][0]=cos(i*2*PI/100.0);
            circcoords[i][1]=sin(i*2*PI/100.0);
        }
    }
    glBegin(GL_POLYGON);
        for(i=0;i<100;i++)
            glVertex2fv(&circcoords[i][0]);
    glEnd();
}
```

Even with this improved method, you still incur a slight penalty from incrementing and testing the variable *i*. What you really want to do is draw the circle once and have OpenGL remember how to draw it for later use. This is exactly what a display list is for, as shown in Listing 4-1.

Listing 4-1   Creating a Display List

```
#define MY_CIRCLE_LIST 1

buildCircle()
{
    GLint i;
    GLfloat cosine, sine;

    glNewList(MY_CIRCLE_LIST, GL_COMPILE);
        glBegin(GL_POLYGON);
            for(i=0;i<100;i++){
                cosine=cos(i*2*PI/100.0);
                sine=sin(i*2*PI/100.0);
                glVertex2f(cosine,sine);
            }
        glEnd();
    glEndList();
}
```

Note that the code for drawing a circle is bracketed by **glNewList()** and **glEndList()**. As you might have guessed, these commands define a display list. The argument MY_CIRCLE_LIST for **glNewList()** is an integer index that uniquely identifies this display list. You can execute the display list later with this **glCallList()** command:

```
glCallList(MY_CIRCLE_LIST);
```

A display list contains only OpenGL calls. Other calls—in Listing 4-1, the C functions **cos()** and **sin()**—aren't stored in the display list. Instead, the coordinates and other variables (such as array contents) are evaluated and copied into the display list with the values they have when the list is compiled. After such a list has been compiled, these values can't be changed. You can delete a display list and create a new one, but you can't edit an existing display list.

Display-List Design Philosophy

OpenGL display lists are designed to optimize performance, particularly over networks, but never at the expense of performance on a local machine. A display list resides with the OpenGL server state, which in a networked environment might be on a different machine than the host (or client state). "What Is OpenGL?" on page 2 discusses OpenGL's client-server model.

To optimize performance, an OpenGL display list is a cache of commands rather than a dynamic database. In other words, once a display list is created, it can't be modified. If a display list were modifiable, performance could be reduced by the overhead required to search through the display list and to perform memory management. As portions of a modifiable display list were changed, memory allocation and deallocation might lead to memory fragmentation. Using display lists is typically at least as fast as using immediate mode. Display lists can substantially increase performance—particularly when you issue OpenGL routines across networks, since display lists reside with the server and network traffic is minimized.

Even locally, a display list might be more efficient since it can be processed as it's created into a form that's more compatible with the graphics hardware. The particular commands that are so optimized may vary from implementation to implementation. For example, a command as simple as **glRotate*()** might show a significant improvement if it's in a display list, since the calculations to produce the rotation matrix aren't trivial (they can involve square roots and trigonometric functions). In the display list, however, only the final rotation matrix needs to be stored, so a display-list rotation command can be executed as fast as the hardware can execute **glMultMatrix()**. A sophisticated OpenGL implementation might even concatenate adjacent transformation commands into a single matrix multiplication.

Although you're not guaranteed that your OpenGL implementation optimizes display lists for any particular uses, you know that execution of display lists isn't slower than executing the commands contained within them. There is some overhead, however, involved in jumping to a display list. If a particular list is small, this overhead could exceed any execution advantage. The most likely possibilities for optimization are listed below, with references to the chapters where the topics are discussed.

* Matrix operations (Chapter 3). Most matrix operations require OpenGL to compute inverses. Both the computed matrix and its inverse might be stored by a particular OpenGL implementation in a display list.

- Raster bitmaps and images (Chapter 4). The format in which you specify raster data isn't likely to be one that's ideal for the hardware. When a display list is compiled, OpenGL might transform the data into the representation preferred by the hardware. This can have a significant effect on the speed of raster character drawing, since character strings usually consist of a series of small bitmaps.

- Lights, material properties, and lighting models (Chapter 6). When you draw a scene with complex lighting conditions, you might change the materials for each item in the scene. Setting the materials can be slow, since it might involve significant calculations. If you put the material definitions in display lists, these calculations don't have to be done each time you switch materials, since only the results of the calculations need to be stored; as a result, rendering lit scenes might be faster. See "Encapsulating Mode Changes" on page 137 for more details on using display lists to change such values as lighting conditions.

- Textures (Chapter 9). You might be able to maximize efficiency when defining textures by compiling them into a display list, since the hardware texture format might differ from the OpenGL format, and the conversion can be done at display-list compile time rather than during display.

- Polygon stipple patterns (Chapter 2).

Some of the commands to specify the properties listed here are context-sensitive, so you need to take this into account to ensure optimum performance. Most situations where this makes a difference involve pixel-transfer functions, lighting models, and texturing. Since all these topics haven't been introduced yet—they're covered in later chapters—the following example is a bit contrived. Although the specifics of this example are very unlikely, it illustrates an important principle that's discussed again in later chapters.

Imagine an implementation of OpenGL that's optimized to perform matrix transformations on vertices before storing them in a display list. If this were true, the time needed to perform the transformations would occur before rather than during display. Now suppose your code looked something like this:

```
glLoadMatrix(M);
glNewList(1, GL_COMPILE);
draw_some_geometric_objects();
glEndList();
```

The vertices in the objects would be compiled into the display list after having been transformed by matrix **M**. Suppose you invoke the display list as follows:

```
glLoadMatrix(N);
glCallList(1);
```

In this case, the geometric objects should be drawn using matrix **N**, but the data in the display list has been transformed by matrix **M** before it was stored. Thus, the display list has to save two copies of the original data (both the untransformed and the transformed vertices), thereby wasting memory. In addition, the vertices undergo two transformations when perhaps one would have sufficed. If instead you had defined the display list as follows:

```
glNewList(1, GL_COMPILE);
glLoadMatrix(M);
draw_some_geometry();
glEndList();
```

then no extra data would have to be stored, and full optimization would be possible. Of course, in this second case, you'd want to be sure that matrix **M** was really the transformation matrix you wanted.

Remember that display lists have some disadvantages. The **buildCircle()** example in Listing 4-1 requires storage for at least 200 floating-point numbers, whereas the object code for the original **drawCircle()** routine (in immediate mode) is probably a lot smaller than that. Another disadvantage is the immutability of the contents of a display list. To optimize performance, an OpenGL display list can't be changed, and its contents can't be read.

Creating and Executing a Display List

As you've already seen, **glNewList()** and **glEndList()** are used to begin and end the definition of a display list, which is then invoked by supplying its identifying index with **glCallList()**. In Listing 4-2, a display list is created in the **makeList()** routine. This display list contains OpenGL commands to draw a red triangle. Then, in the **display()** routine, the display list is executed ten times. In addition, a line is drawn in immediate mode. Note that the display list allocates memory to store the commands and the values of any necessary variables.

Listing 4-2   Using a Display List: list.c

```c
#include <GL/gl.h>
#include <GL/glu.h>
#include "aux.h"

GLuint listName = 1;

void myinit (void)
{
glNewList (listName, GL_COMPILE);
        glColor3f(1.0, 0.0, 0.0);
        glBegin (GL_TRIANGLES);
            glVertex2f (0.0, 0.0);
            glVertex2f (1.0, 0.0);
            glVertex2f (0.0, 1.0);
        glEnd ();
        glTranslatef (1.5, 0.0, 0.0);
    glEndList ();
    glShadeModel (GL_FLAT);
}

void drawLine (void)
{
    glBegin (GL_LINES);
        glVertex2f (0.0, 0.5);
        glVertex2f (15.0, 0.5);
    glEnd ();
}

void display(void)
{
    GLuint i;

    glClear (GL_COLOR_BUFFER_BIT);
    glColor3f(0.0, 1.0, 0.0);
    for (i = 0; i < 10; i++)
        glCallList (listName);
    drawLine ();
    glFlush ();
}

void myReshape(GLsizei w, GLsizei h)
{
    glViewport(0, 0, w, h);
    glMatrixMode(GL_PROJECTION);
    glLoadIdentity();
```

```
    if (w <= h)
        gluOrtho2D (0.0, 2.0, -0.5 * (GLfloat) h/(GLfloat) w,
                1.5 * (GLfloat) h/(GLfloat) w);
    else
        gluOrtho2D (0.0, 2.0 * (GLfloat) w/(GLfloat) h, -0.5,
                1.5);
    glMatrixMode(GL_MODELVIEW);
    glLoadIdentity();
}


int main(int argc, char** argv)
{
    auxInitDisplayMode (AUX_SINGLE | AUX_RGBA);
    auxInitPosition (0, 0, 400, 50);
    auxInitWindow (argv[0]);
    myinit ();
    auxReshapeFunc (myReshape);
    auxMainLoop(display);
}
```

The **glTranslatef()** routine in the display list alters the position of the next object to be drawn. Without it, calling the display list twice would just draw the triangle on top of itself. The **drawLine()** routine, which is called in immediate mode, is also affected by the ten **glTranslatef()** calls that precede it. Thus, if you call transformation commands within a display list, don't forget to take the effect of those commands into account later in your program.

Only one display list can be created at a time. In other words, you must eventually follow **glNewList()** with **glEndList()** to end the creation of a display list before starting another one. As you might expect, calling **glEndList()** without having started a display list generates the error GL_INVALID_OPERATION.

---

void **glNewList** (GLuint *list*, GLenum *mode*);

Specifies the start of a display list. OpenGL routines that are called subsequently (until **glEndList**() is called to end the display list) are stored in a display list, except for a few restricted OpenGL routines that can't be stored. (Those restricted routines are executed immediately, during the creation of the display list.) The *list* parameter is a unique positive integer that identifies the display list. The possible values for the *mode* parameter are GL_COMPILE and GL_COMPILE_AND_EXECUTE. Use GL_COMPILE if you don't want the following OpenGL commands executed as they're placed in the display list; to cause the commands to be executed immediately as well as placed in the display list for later use, specify GL_COMPILE_AND_EXECUTE.

---

void **glEndList** (void);

Marks the end of a display list.

What's Stored in a Display List

When you're building a display list, only the values for expressions are stored in the list. Thus, if values in an array are subsequently changed, for example, the display-list values don't change. In the following code fragment, the display list contains a command to set the current color to black (0.0, 0.0, 0.0). The subsequent change of the value of the *color_vector* array to red (1.0, 0.0, 0.0) has no effect on the display list because the display list contains the values that were in effect when it was created.

```
GLfloat color_vector[3]={0.0,0.0,0.0};
glNewList(1,GL_COMPILE);
    glColor3fv(color_vector);
glEndList();
color_vector[0]=1.0;
```

Not all OpenGL commands can be stored and executed from within a display list. Generally, commands that pass parameters by reference or that return a value can't be stored in a display list, since the list might be called outside the scope of where the parameters are originally defined. If such commands are called when making a display list, they're executed immediately and aren't stored in the display list. Here are the OpenGL commands that aren't stored in a display list (also, note that **glNewList()** generates an error if it's called while you're creating a display list). Some of these commands haven't been described yet; you can look in the index to see where they're discussed.

glDeleteLists()	glIsEnabled()
glFeedbackBuffer()	glIsList()
glFinish()	glPixelStore()
glFlush()	glReadPixels()
glGenLists()	glRenderMode()
glGet*()	glSelectBuffer()

To understand more clearly why these commands can't be stored in a display list, remember that when you're using OpenGL across a network, the client may be on one machine and the server on another. After a display list is created, it resides with the server, so the server can't rely on the client for any information related to the display list. If querying commands, such as **glGet*()** or **glIs*()**, were allowed in a display list, the calling program would be surprised at random times by data returned over the network. Without parsing the display list as it was sent, the calling program wouldn't know where to put the data. Thus, any command that returns a value can't be stored in a display list. Other routines—such as **glFlush()** and **glFinish()**—can't be stored in a display list because they depend on information about the client state. Finally, commands that change a state value maintained by the client can't be stored in a display list.

Executing a Display List

After you've created a display list, you can execute it by calling **glCallList()**. Naturally, you can execute the same display list many times, and you can mix calls to execute display lists with calls to perform immediate-mode graphics, as you've already seen.

---

void **glCallList** (GLuint *list*);

This routine executes the display list specified by *list*. The commands in the display list are executed in the order they were saved, just as if they were issued without using a display list. If *list* hasn't been defined, nothing happens.

Since a display list can contain calls that change the value of OpenGL state variables, these values change as the display list is executed, just as if the commands were called in immediate mode. The changes to OpenGL state persist after execution of the display list is completed. In Listing 4-2, the changes to the current color and current matrix made during the execution of the display list remain in effect after it's been called, as shown in Listing 4-3.

Listing 4-3   Persistence of State Changes after Execution of a Display List

```
glNewList(listIndex,GL_COMPILE);
    glColor3f(1.0, 0.0, 0.0);
    glBegin(GL_POLYGON);
        glVertex2f(0.0,0.0);
        glVertex2f(1.0,0.0);
        glVertex2f(0.0,1.0);
    glEnd();
    glTranslatef(1.5,0.0,0.0);
glEndList();
```

Sometimes you want state changes to persist, but other times you want to save the values of state variables before executing a display list and then restore these values after the list has executed. Use **glPushAttrib()** to save a group of state variables and **glPopAttrib()** to restore the values when you're ready for them. (See Appendix B for more information about these commands.) To save and restore the current matrix, use **glPushMatrix()** and **glPopMatrix()** as described in "Manipulating the Matrix Stacks" on page 102. To restore the state variables in Listing 4-3, you might use the code shown in Listing 4-4.

Listing 4-4   Restoring State Variables within a Display List

```
glNewList(listIndex,GL_COMPILE);
    glPushMatrix();
    glPushAttrib(GL_CURRENT_BIT);
        glColor3f(1.0, 0.0, 0.0);
```

```
    glBegin(GL_POLYGON);
        glVertex2f(0.0,0.0);
        glVertex2f(1.0,0.0);
        glVertex2f(0.0,1.0);
    glEnd();
    glTranslatef(1.5,0.0,0.0);
    glPopAttrib();
    glPopMatrix();
glEndList();
```

Thus, if you used this kind of a display list that restores values, the code in Listing 4-5 would draw a green, untranslated line. With the display list in Listing 4-3 that doesn't save and restore values, the line drawn would be red, and its position would be translated.

Listing 4-5   Using a Display List That Restores State Variables

```
void display(void)
{
    GLint i;

    glClear (GL_COLOR_BUFFER_BIT);
    glColor3f(0.0, 1.0, 0.0);
    for (i = 0; i < 10; i++)
      glCallList (listIndex);
    drawLine ();
    glFlush ();
}
```

You can call **glCallList()** from anywhere within a program, as long as its OpenGL context is still active. A display list can be created in one routine and executed in a different one, since its index uniquely identifies it. Also, there is no facility to save the contents of a display list into a data file, nor a facility to create a display list from a file. In this sense, a display list is designed for temporary use. Also, a display list is destroyed when its OpenGL context is destroyed.

Hierarchical Display Lists

You can create a *hierarchical display list*, which is a display list that executes another display list, by calling **glCallList()** between a **glNewList()** and **glEndList()** pair. A hierarchical display list is useful for an object that's made of components, especially if some of those components are used more than once. For example, this is a display list that renders a bicycle by calling other display lists to render parts of the bicycle:

```
glNewList(listIndex,GL_COMPILE);
    glCallList(handlebars);
    glCallList(frame);
    glTranslatef(1.0,0.0,0.0);
    glCallList(wheel);
    glTranslatef(3.0,0.0,0.0);
    glCallList(wheel);
glEndList();
```

To avoid infinite recursion, there's a limit on the nesting level of display lists; the limit is at least 64, but it might be higher, depending on the implementation. To determine the nesting limit for your implementation of OpenGL, call

```
glGetIntegerv(GL_MAX_LIST_NESTING, GLint *data);
```

OpenGL allows you to create a display list that calls another list that hasn't been created yet. Nothing happens when the first list calls the second, undefined one.

You can use a hierarchical display list to approximate an editable display list by wrapping a list around several lower-level lists. For example, to put a polygon in a display list while allowing yourself to be able to easily edit its vertices, you could use the code in Listing 4-6.

Listing 4-6   Using a Hierarchical Display List

```
glNewList(1,GL_COMPILE);
    glVertex3f(v1);
glEndList();
glNewList(2,GL_COMPILE);
    glVertex3f(v2);
glEndList();
glNewList(3,GL_COMPILE);
    glVertex3f(v3);
glEndList();

glNewList(4,GL_COMPILE);
    glBegin(GL_POLYGON);
        glCallList(1);
        glCallList(2);
        glCallList(3);
    glEnd();
glEndList();
```

To render the polygon, call display list number 4. To edit a vertex, you need only recreate the single display list corresponding to that vertex.

Since an index number uniquely identifies a display list, creating one with the same index as an existing one automatically deletes the old one. Keep in mind that this technique doesn't necessarily provide optimal memory usage or peak performance, but it's acceptable and useful in some cases.

Managing Display Lists and Their Indices

So far, we've used an arbitrary positive integer as a display-list index. This could be dangerous in practice because you might accidentally choose an index that's already in use, thereby overwriting an existing display list. To avoid accidental deletions, use **glGenLists()** to generate an unused index and **glIsList()** to determine whether a specific index is in use. You can explicitly delete a specific display list or a range of lists with **glDeleteLists()**.

GLuint **glGenLists**(GLsizei *range*);

Allocates *range* number of contiguous, previously unallocated display-list indices. The integer returned is the index that marks the beginning of a contiguous block of empty display-list indices. The returned indices are all marked as empty and used, so subsequent calls to **glGenLists()** don't return these indices until they're deleted. Zero is returned if the requested number of indices isn't available, or if *range* is zero.

GLboolean **glIsList**(GLuint *list*);

Returns TRUE if *list* is already used for a display list and FALSE otherwise.

In the following example, a single index is requested, and if it proves to be available, it's used to create a new display list:

```
listIndex=glGenLists(1);
if(listIndex!=0) {
    glNewList(listIndex,GL_COMPILE);
        . . .
    glEndList();
}
```

The command **glDeleteLists()** deletes a contiguous group of display lists, thereby making their indices available again.

void **glDeleteLists**(GLuint *list*, GLsizei *range*);

Deletes *range* display lists, starting at the index specified by *list*. An attempt to delete a list that has never been created is ignored.

Executing Multiple Display Lists

OpenGL provides an efficient mechanism to execute several display lists in succession. This mechanism requires that you put the display-list indices in an array and call **glCallLists**(). An obvious use for such a mechanism occurs when display-list indices correspond to meaningful values. For example, if you're creating a font, each display-list index might correspond to the ASCII value of a character in that font. To have several such fonts, you would need to establish a different initial display-list index for each font. You can specify this initial index by using **glListBase**() before calling **glCallLists**().

void **glListBase**(GLuint *base*);

Specifies the offset that's added to the display-list indices in **glCallLists**() to obtain the final display-list indices. The default display-list base is 0. The list base has no effect on **glCallList**(), which executes only one display list, or on **glNewList**().

void **glCallLists**(GLsizei *n*, GLenum *type*, const GLvoid **lists*);

Executes *n* display lists. The indices of the lists to be executed are computed by adding the offset indicated by the current display-list base (specified with **glListBase**()) to the signed integer values in the array pointed to by *lists*.

The *type* parameter indicates the data type and the "stride" (or size) of each element in the array of indices. It's usually one of these constants: GL_BYTE, GL_UNSIGNED_BYTE, GL_SHORT, GL_UNSIGNED_SHORT, GL_INT, GL_UNSIGNED_INT, or GL_FLOAT. It can also be GL_2_BYTES, GL_3_BYTES, or GL_4_BYTES, in which case sequences of two, three, or four bytes are shifted and added together, byte by byte, to calculate the display-list offset, using this algorithm:

```
/* b = 2, 3, or 4; bytes are numbered 0, 1, 2, 3 in array */
 offset = 0;
 for (i = 0; i < b; i++) {
 offset = offset << 8;
 offset += byte[i];
 }
index = offset + listbase;
```

This means that for multiple-byte data, as bytes are taken from the array in order, the highest-order data comes first.

As an example of the use of multiple display lists, look at the program fragments in Listing 4-7 taken from the full program in Listing 4-8. This program draws characters with a stroked font (a set of letters made from line segments). The routine **initStrokedFont**() sets up the display-list indices for each letter so they correspond with their ASCII values.

Listing 4-7   Defining Multiple Display Lists

```
void initStrokedFont(void)
{
    GLuint base;

    base = glGenLists (128);
    glListBase(base);
    glNewList(base+'A', GL_COMPILE);
        drawLetter(Adata); glEndList();
    glNewList(base+'E', GL_COMPILE);
        drawLetter(Edata); glEndList();
    glNewList(base+'P', GL_COMPILE);
        drawLetter(Pdata); glEndList();
    glNewList(base+'R', GL_COMPILE);
        drawLetter(Rdata); glEndList();
    glNewList(base+'S', GL_COMPILE);
        drawLetter(Sdata); glEndList();
    glNewList(base+' ', GL_COMPILE);      /* space character */
        glTranslatef(8.0, 0.0, 0.0); glEndList();
}
```

The **glGenLists**() command allocates 128 contiguous display-list indices. The first of the contiguous indices becomes the display-list base. A display list is made for each letter; each display-list index is the sum of the base and the ASCII value of that letter. In this example, only a few letters and the space character are created.

After the display lists have been created, **glCallLists()** can be called to execute the display lists. For example, you can pass a character string to the subroutine **printStrokedString()**:

```
void printStrokedString(GLbyte *s)
{
    GLint len = strlen(s);
    glCallLists(len, GL_BYTE, s);
}
```

The ASCII value for each letter in the string is used as the offset into the display-list indices. The current list base is added to the ASCII value of each letter to determine the final display-list index to be executed. The output produced by Listing 4-8 is shown in Figure 4-1.

Figure 4-1   Example of a Stroked Font That Defines the Characters A, E, P, R, S

Listing 4-8   Using Multiple Display Lists to Define a Stroked Font: stroke.c

```
#include <GL/gl.h>
#include <GL/glu.h>
#include "aux.h"

#define PT 1
#define STROKE 2
#define END 3

typedef struct charpoint {
    GLfloat    x, y;
    int        type;
} CP;

CP Adata[] = {
    { 0, 0, PT}, {0, 9, PT}, {1, 10, PT}, {4, 10, PT},
    {5, 9, PT}, {5, 0, STROKE}, {0, 5, PT}, {5, 5, END}
};
```

```
CP Edata[] = {
    {5, 0, PT}, {0, 0, PT}, {0, 10, PT}, {5, 10, STROKE},
    {0, 5, PT}, {4, 5, END}
};

CP Pdata[] = {
    {0, 0, PT}, {0, 10, PT},  {4, 10, PT}, {5, 9, PT},
    {5, 6, PT}, {4, 5, PT}, {0, 5, END}
};

CP Rdata[] = {
    {0, 0, PT}, {0, 10, PT},  {4, 10, PT}, {5, 9, PT},
    {5, 6, PT}, {4, 5, PT}, {0, 5, STROKE}, {3, 5, PT},
    {5, 0, END}
};

CP Sdata[] = {
    {0, 1, PT}, {1, 0, PT}, {4, 0, PT}, {5, 1, PT}, {5, 4, PT},
    {4, 5, PT}, {1, 5, PT}, {0, 6, PT}, {0, 9, PT}, {1, 10, PT},
    {4, 10, PT}, {5, 9, END}
};

void drawLetter(CP *l)
{
    glBegin(GL_LINE_STRIP);
    while (1) {
        switch (l->type) {
            case PT:
                glVertex2fv(&l->x);
                break;
            case STROKE:
                glVertex2fv(&l->x);
                glEnd();
                glBegin(GL_LINE_STRIP);
                break;
            case END:
                glVertex2fv(&l->x);
                glEnd();
                glTranslatef(8.0, 0.0, 0.0);
                return;
        }
        l++;
    }
}
```

```
void myinit (void)
{
    GLuint base;

    glShadeModel (GL_FLAT);

    base = glGenLists (128);
    glListBase(base);
    glNewList(base+'A', GL_COMPILE); drawLetter(Adata);
        glEndList();
    glNewList(base+'E', GL_COMPILE); drawLetter(Edata);
        glEndList();
    glNewList(base+'P', GL_COMPILE); drawLetter(Pdata);
        glEndList();
    glNewList(base+'R', GL_COMPILE); drawLetter(Rdata);
        glEndList();
    glNewList(base+'S', GL_COMPILE); drawLetter(Sdata);
        glEndList();
    glNewList(base+' ', GL_COMPILE);
        glTranslatef(8.0, 0.0, 0.0); glEndList();
}

char *test1 = "A SPARE SERAPE APPEARS AS";
char *test2 = "APES PREPARE RARE PEPPERS";

void printStrokedString(char *s)
{
    GLsizei len = strlen(s);
    glCallLists(len, GL_BYTE, (GLbyte *)s);
}

void display(void)
{
    glClear(GL_COLOR_BUFFER_BIT);
    glColor3f(1.0, 1.0, 1.0);
    glPushMatrix();
    glScalef(2.0, 2.0, 2.0);
    glTranslatef(10.0, 30.0, 0.0);
    printStrokedString(test1);
    glPopMatrix();
    glPushMatrix();
    glScalef(2.0, 2.0, 2.0);
    glTranslatef(10.0, 13.0, 0.0);
    printStrokedString(test2);
    glPopMatrix();
    glFlush();
}
```

```
int main(int argc, char** argv)
{
    auxInitDisplayMode (AUX_SINGLE | AUX_RGBA);
    auxInitPosition (0, 0, 440, 120);
    auxInitWindow (argv[0]);
    myinit ();
    auxMainLoop(display);
}
```

Encapsulating Mode Changes

You can use display lists to organize and store groups of commands to change various modes or set various parameters. When you want to switch from one group of settings to another, using display lists might be more efficient than making the calls directly, since the settings might be cached in a format that matches the requirements of your graphics system.

Display lists are likely to be more efficient when you're switching between multiple texture maps, for example. (Texture mapping is described in Chapter 9.) Suppose you have two different textures that are fairly large, as textures tend to be, but that both of them fit into texture memory. Without display lists, you would have to load the data for the first texture, use it to draw some objects, wait for the second texture to be loaded into memory, and then use it for drawing. When you want to switch back to the first texture, it would have to be loaded into memory again rather than being plucked out of texture memory. There's no way for OpenGL to know that it's already been stored without the display-list mechanism to provide a "handle" to identify it. With display lists, both textures can be loaded into texture memory once and then used as often as necessary without having to be reloaded.

Another case where display lists are likely to be more efficient than immediate mode is for switching among various lighting, lighting-model, and material-parameter settings. (These topics are discussed in Chapter 6.) You might also use display lists for stipple patterns, fog parameters, and clipping-plane equations. In general, you're guaranteed that executing display lists is at least as fast as making the relevant calls directly, but remember that some overhead is involved in jumping to a display list.

Listing 4-9 shows how to use display lists to switch among three different line stipples. First, you call **glGenLists()** to allocate a display list for each stipple pattern and create a display list for each pattern. Then, you use **glCallList()** to switch from one stipple pattern to another.

Listing 4-9 Using Display Lists for Mode Changes

```
GLuint offset;
offset = glGenLists (3);

glNewList (offset, GL_COMPILE);
    glDisable (GL_LINE_STIPPLE);
glEndList ();

glNewList (offset+1, GL_COMPILE);
    glEnable (GL_LINE_STIPPLE);
    glLineStipple (1, 0x0F0F);
glEndList ();

glNewList (offset+2, GL_COMPILE);
    glEnable (GL_LINE_STIPPLE);
    glLineStipple (1, 0x1111);
glEndList ();


#define drawOneLine(x1,y1,x2,y2) glBegin(GL_LINES); \
    glVertex2f ((x1),(y1)); glVertex2f ((x2),(y2)); glEnd();

glCallList (offset);
drawOneLine (50.0, 125.0, 350.0, 125.0);

glCallList (offset+1);
drawOneLine (50.0, 100.0, 350.0, 100.0);

glCallList (offset+2);
drawOneLine (50.0, 75.0, 350.0, 75.0);
```

Chapter 5

Color

Chapter Objectives

After reading this chapter, you'll be able to do the following:

- Decide between using RGBA or color-index mode for your application

- Specify desired colors for drawing objects

- Use smooth shading to draw a single polygon with more than one color

The goal of almost all OpenGL applications is to draw color pictures in a window on the screen. The window is a rectangular array of pixels, each of which contains and displays its own color. Thus, in a sense, the point of all the calculations performed by an OpenGL implementation—calculations that take into account OpenGL commands, state information, and values of parameters—is to determine the final color of every pixel that's to be drawn in the window. This chapter explains the commands for specifying colors and how OpenGL interprets them in the following major sections:

- "Color Perception" discusses how the eye perceives color.

- "Computer Color" describes the relationship between pixels on a computer monitor and their colors; it also defines the two display modes, RGBA and color index.

- "RGBA versus Color-Index Mode" explains how the two display modes use graphics hardware and how to decide which mode to use.

- "Specifying a Color and a Shading Model" describes the OpenGL commands you use to specify the desired color or shading model.

Color Perception

Physically, light is composed of photons—tiny particles of light, each traveling along its own path, and each vibrating at its own frequency (or wavelength, or energy—any one of frequency, wavelength, or energy determines the others). A photon is completely characterized by its position, direction, and frequency/wavelength/energy. Photons with wavelengths ranging from about 390 nanometers (nm) (violet) and 720 nm (red) cover the colors of the visible spectrum, forming the colors of a rainbow (violet, indigo, blue, green, yellow, orange, red). However, your eyes perceive lots of colors that aren't in the rainbow—white, black, brown, and pink, for example. How does this happen?

What your eye actually sees is a mixture of photons of different frequencies. Real light sources are characterized by the distribution of photon frequencies they emit. Ideal white light consists of an equal amount of light of all frequencies. Laser light is usually very pure, and all photons have almost identical frequencies (and direction and phase, as well). Light from a sodium-vapor lamp has more light in the yellow frequency. Light from most stars in space has a distribution that depends heavily on their temperatures (black-body radiation). The frequency distribution of light from most sources in your immediate environment is more complicated.

The human eye perceives color when certain cells in the retina (called *cone cells*, or just *cones*) become excited after being struck by photons. The three different kinds of cone cells respond best to three different wavelengths of light: one type of cone cell responds best to red light, one type to green, and the other to blue. (A person who is color-blind is usually missing one or more types of cone cells.) When a given mixture of photons enters the eye, the cone cells in the retina register different degrees of excitation depending on their types, and if a different mixture of photons comes in that happens to excite the three types of cone cells to the same degrees, its color is indistinguishable from that of the first mixture.

Since each color is recorded by the eye as the levels of excitation of the cone cells by the incoming photons, the eye can perceive colors that aren't in the spectrum produced by a prism or rainbow. For example, if you send a mixture of red and blue photons so that both the red and blue cones in the retina are excited, your eye sees it as magenta, which isn't in the spectrum. Other combinations give browns, turquoises, and mauves, none of which appear in the color spectrum.

A computer-graphics monitor emulates visible colors by lighting pixels with a combination of red, green, and blue light in proportions that excite the red-, green-, and blue-sensitive cones in the retina in such a way that it matches the excitation levels generated by the photon mix it's trying to emulate. If humans had more types of cone cells, some that were yellow-sensitive for example, color monitors would probably have a yellow gun as well, and we'd use RGBY (red, green, blue, yellow) quadruples to specify colors. And if everyone were color-blind in the same way, this chapter would be simpler.

To display a particular color, the monitor sends the right amounts of red, green, and blue light to appropriately stimulate the different types of cone cells in your eye. A color monitor can send different proportions of red, green, and blue to each of the pixels, and the eye sees a million or so pinpoints of light, each with its own color.

This section considers only how the eye perceives combinations of photons that enter it. The situation for light bouncing off of materials and entering the eye is even more complex—white light bouncing off a red ball will appear red, or yellow light shining through blue glass appears almost black, for example. These effects are discussed in "Real-World and OpenGL Lighting" on page 159.

Computer Color

On a color computer screen, the hardware causes each pixel on the screen to emit different amounts of red, green, and blue light. These are called the R, G, and B values. They're often packed together (sometimes with a fourth value, called alpha, or A), and the packed value is called the RGB (or RGBA) value. (See "Blending" on page 196 for an explanation of the alpha values.) The color information at each pixel can be stored either in *RGBA mode*, in which the R, G, B, and possibly A values are kept for each pixel, or in *color-index mode*, in which a single number (called the color index) is stored for each pixel. Each color index indicates an entry in a table that defines a particular set of R, G, and B values. Such a table is called a *color map*.

In color-index mode, you might want to alter the values in the color map. Since color maps are controlled by the window system, there are no OpenGL commands to do this. All the examples in this book initialize the color-display mode at the time the window is opened by using routines from the auxiliary library, which is described in detail in Appendix E.

Different graphics hardware varies greatly in both the size of the pixel array and the number of colors that can be displayed at each pixel. On a given graphics system, every pixel has the same amount of memory for storing its color, and all the memory for all the pixels is called the *color buffer*. The size of a buffer is usually measured in bits, so an 8-bit buffer could store 8 bits of data (256 possible different colors) for each pixel. The size of the possible buffers varies from machine to machine. (See Chapter 10 for more information.)

The R, G, and B values can range from 0.0 (none) to 1.0 (full intensity). For example, R = 0.0, G = 0.0, and B = 1.0 represents the brightest possible blue. If R, G, and B are all 0.0, the pixel is black; if all are 1.0, the pixel is drawn in the brightest white that can be displayed on the screen. Blending green and blue creates shades of cyan. Blue and red combine for magenta. Red and green create yellow. To help you create the colors you want from the R, G, and B components, look at the color cube shown in Plate 12. The axes of this cube represent intensities of red, blue, and green. A black-and-white version of the cube is shown in Figure 5-1.

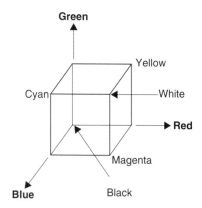

Figure 5-1   The Color Cube in Black and White

The commands to specify a color for an object (in this case, a point) can be as simple as this:

```
glColor3f (1.0, 0.0, 0.0);   /* the current RGB color is red: */
                             /* full red, no green, no blue. */
glBegin (GL_POINTS);
    glVertex3fv (point_array);
glEnd ();
```

In certain modes (for example, if lighting or texturing calculations are performed), the assigned color might go through other operations before arriving in the framebuffer as a value representing a color for a pixel. In fact, the color of a pixel is determined by a lengthy sequence of operations.

Early in a program's execution, the color-display mode is set to either RGBA mode or color-index mode. Once the color-display mode is initialized, it can't be changed. As the program executes, a color (either a color index or an RGBA value) is determined on a per-vertex basis for each geometric primitive. Either a color you've explicitly specified for a vertex is used or, if lighting is enabled, the transformation matrices interact with the surface normals and other material properties to determine the vertex's color. In other words, a red ball with a blue light shining on it looks different from the same ball with no light on it. (See Chapter 6 for details.) After the relevant lighting calculations are performed, the chosen shading model is applied. As explained in "Specifying a Color and a Shading Model" on page 150, you can choose flat or smooth shading, each of which has different effects on the eventual color of a pixel.

Next, the primitives are *rasterized*, or converted to a two-dimensional image. Rasterizing involves determining which squares of an integer grid in window coordinates are occupied by the primitive and then assigning color and other values to each such square. A grid square along with its associated values of color, *z* (depth), and texture coordinates is called a *fragment*. Pixels are elements of the framebuffer; a fragment comes from a primitive and is combined with its corresponding pixel to yield a new pixel. Once a fragment is constructed, texturing, fog, and antialiasing are applied—if they're enabled—to the fragments. After that, any specified alpha blending, dithering, and bitwise logical operations are carried out using the fragment and the pixel already stored in the framebuffer. Finally, the fragment's color value (either color index or RGBA) is written into the pixel and displayed in the window using the window's color-display mode.

RGBA versus Color-Index Mode

In either color-index or RGBA mode, a certain amount of color data is stored at each pixel. This amount is determined by the number of bitplanes in the framebuffer. A bitplane contains one bit of data for each pixel. If there are eight color bitplanes, there are 8 color bits per pixel, and hence 2^8 = 256 different values or colors that can be stored at the pixel.

Bitplanes are often divided evenly into storage for R, G, and B components (that is, a 24-bitplane system devotes 8 bits each to red, green, and blue), but this isn't always true. To find out the number of bitplanes available on your system for red, green, blue, alpha, or color-index values, use **glGetIntegerv()** with GL_RED_BITS, GL_GREEN_BITS, GL_BLUE_BITS, GL_ALPHA_BITS, and GL_INDEX_BITS.

Note: Color intensities on most computer screens aren't perceived as linear by the human eye. Consider colors consisting of just a red component, with green and blue set to zero. As the intensity varies from 0.0 (off) to 1.0 (full on), the number of electrons striking the pixels increases, but the question is, does 0.5 look like halfway between 0.0 and 1.0? To test this, write a program that draws alternate pixels in a checkerboard pattern to intensities 0.0 and 1.0, and compare it with a region drawn solidly in color 0.5. OpenGL assumes they're the same. If they're not, you need to use whatever correction mechanism is provided on your particular system. For example, many systems have a table to adjust intensities so that 0.5 appears to be halfway between 0.0 and 1.0. The mapping usually used is an exponential one, with the exponent referred to as gamma (hence the term *gamma correction*). Using the same gamma for the red, green, and blue components gives pretty good results, but three different gamma values might give slightly better results. For more details on this topic, see Foley, van Dam, et al.

RGBA Display Mode

In RGBA mode, the hardware sets aside a certain number of bitplanes for each of the R, G, B, and A components (not necessarily the same number for each component). See Figure 5-2. The R, G, and B values are typically stored as integers rather than floating-point numbers, and they're scaled to the number of available bits for storage and retrieval. For example, if a system has 8 bits available for the R component, integers between 0 and 255 can be stored; thus, 0, 1, 2, ..., 255 in the bitplanes would correspond to R values of 0/255 = 0.0, 1/255, 2/255, ..., 255/255 = 1.0. Regardless of the number of bitplanes, 0.0 specifies the minimum intensity, and 1.0 specifies the maximum intensity.

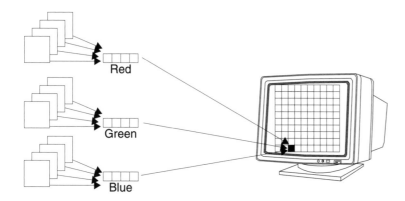

Figure 5-2   RGB Values from the Bitplanes

Note: The alpha value (the A in RGBA) has no direct effect on the color displayed on the screen. It can be used for many things, including blending and transparency, and it can have an effect on the values of R, G, and B that are written. See "Blending" on page 196 for more information about alpha values.

The number of distinct colors that can be displayed at a single pixel depends on the number of bitplanes and the capacity of the hardware to interpret those bitplanes. The number of distinct colors can't exceed 2^n, where n is the number of bitplanes. Thus, a machine with 24 bitplanes for RGB can display up to 16.77 million distinct colors.

▨ Advanced

Dithering

Some graphics hardware uses *dithering* to increase the number of displayable colors at the expense of spatial resolution. Dithering is the technique of using combinations of some colors to create the effect of other colors. To illustrate how dithering works, suppose your system has only one bit each for R, G, and B, so it can display only eight colors: black, white, red, blue, green, yellow, cyan, and magenta. To display a pink region, the hardware can fill the region in a checkerboard manner, alternating red and white pixels. If your eye is far enough back from the screen that it can't distinguish individual pixels, the region appears pink— the average of red and white. Redder pinks can be achieved by filling a higher proportion of the pixels with red, whiter pinks would use more white pixels, and so on.

With this technique, there are no pink pixels. The only way to achieve the effect of "pinkness" is to cover a region consisting of multiple pixels—you can't dither a single pixel. If you specify an RGB value for an unavailable color and fill a polygon, the hardware fills the pixels in the interior of the polygon with a mixture of nearby colors whose average appears to your eye to be the color you want. (Remember, though, that if you're reading pixel information out of the framebuffer, you get the actual red and white pixel values, since there aren't any pink ones. See Chapter 8 for more information about reading pixel values.)

Figure 5-3 illustrates some simple dithering of black and white pixels to make shades of gray. From left to right, the 4×4 patterns at the top represent dithering patterns for 50 percent, 19 percent, and 69 percent gray. Under each pattern, you can see repeated reduced copies of each pattern, but these black and white squares are still bigger than most pixels. If you look at them from across the room, you can see that they blur together and appear as three levels of gray.

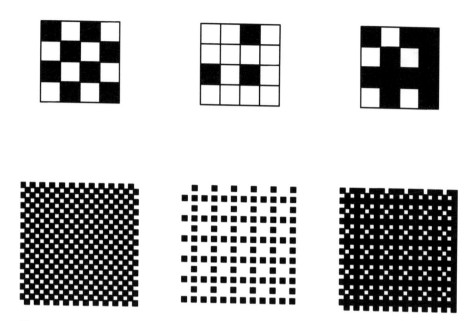

Figure 5-3   Dithering Black and White to Create Gray

With about 8 bits each of R, G, and B, you can get a fairly high-quality image without dithering. Just because your machine has twenty-four color bitplanes, however, doesn't mean that dithering won't occur. For example, if you are running in double-buffer mode, the bitplanes might be divided into two sets of twelve, so there are really only 4 bits each per R, G, and B component. Without dithering, 4-bit-per-component color can give less than satisfactory results in many situations.

You enable or disable dithering by passing GL_DITHER to **glEnable()** or **glDisable()**.

Color-Index Display Mode

With color-index mode, OpenGL uses a color map (or *lookup table*), which is similar to using a palette to mix paints to prepare for a paint-by-number scene. A painter's palette provides spaces to mix paints together; similarly, a computer's color map provides indices where the primary red, green, and blue values can be mixed, as shown in Figure 5-4.

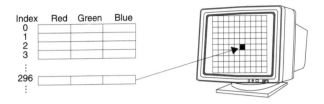

Figure 5-4   A Color Map

A painter filling in a paint-by-number scene chooses a color from the color palette and fills the corresponding numbered regions with that color. A computer stores the color index in the bitplanes for each pixel. Then those bitplane values reference the color map, and the screen is painted with the corresponding red, green, and blue values from the color map, as shown in Figure 5-5.

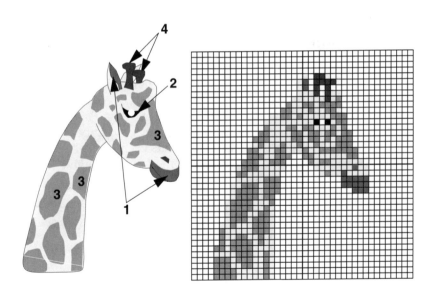

Figure 5-5   Using a Color Map to Paint a Picture

In color-index mode, the number of simultaneously available colors is limited by the size of the color map and the number of bitplanes available. The size of the color map is determined by the amount of hardware dedicated to it. Typical sizes range from 256 (2^8) to 4096 (2^{12}). The size of the color map is a power of 2, indexed by the number of bitplanes available in color-index mode. If there are 2^n indices in the color map and m available bitplanes, the number of usable entries is the smaller of 2^n and 2^m.

With RGBA mode, each pixel's color is independent of other pixels. However, in color-index mode, each pixel with the same index stored in its bitplanes shares the same color-map location. If the contents of an entry in the color map change, then all pixels of that color index change their color.

Choosing between RGBA and Color-Index Mode

You should base your decision to use RGBA or color-index mode on what hardware is available and on what your application needs. For most systems, more colors can be simultaneously represented with RGBA mode than with color-index mode. Also, for several effects, such as shading, lighting, texture mapping, and fog, RGBA provides more flexibility than color-index mode.

You might prefer to use color-index mode in the following cases:

- If you're porting an existing application that makes significant use of color-index mode, it might be easiest to not change to RGBA mode.

- If you have only a small number n of bitplanes available and if you need fewer than 2^n different colors, you should consider color-index mode.

- If you have a limited number of bitplanes available, RGBA mode might produce noticeably coarse shading. Color-index mode might work better if you have limited shading requirements (only shades of gray, for example).

- Color-index mode can be useful for various tricks, such as color-map animation and drawing in layers. See Chapter 13 for more information.

In general, use RGBA mode: It works with texture mapping and works better with lighting, shading, fog, antialiasing, and blending.

Specifying a Color and a Shading Model

OpenGL maintains a current color (in RGBA mode) and a current color index (in color-index mode). Unless you're using a more complicated coloring model such as lighting or texture mapping, each object is drawn using the current color (or color index). Look at the following pseudocode sequence:

```
set_color(RED);
draw_item(A);
draw_item(B);
set_color(GREEN);
set_color(BLUE);
draw_item(C);
```

Items A and B are drawn in red, and item C is drawn in blue. The fourth line, which sets the current color to green, has no effect (except to waste a bit of time). With no lighting or texturing, when the current color is set, all items drawn afterward are drawn in that color until the current color is changed to something else.

Specifying a Color in RGBA Mode

In RGBA mode, use the **glColor*()** command to select a current color.

---

void **glColor3**{b s i f d ub us ui} (*TYPE r*, *TYPE g*, *TYPE b*);
void **glColor4**{b s i f d ub us ui} (*TYPE r*, *TYPE g*, *TYPE b*, *TYPE a*);
void **glColor3**{b s i f d ub us ui}**v** (const *TYPE *v*);
void **glColor4**{b s i f d ub us ui}**v** (const *TYPE *v*);

Sets the current red, green, blue, and alpha values. This command can have up to three suffixes, which differentiate variations of the parameters accepted. The first suffix is either 3 or 4, to indicate whether you supply an alpha value in addition to the red, green, and blue values. If you don't supply an alpha value, it's automatically set to 1.0. The second suffix indicates the data type for parameters: byte, short, integer, float, double, unsigned byte, unsigned short, or unsigned integer. The third suffix is an optional **v**, which indicates that the argument is a pointer to an array of values of the given data type.

For the versions of **glColor*()** that accept floating-point data types, the values should typically range between 0.0 and 1.0, the minimum and maximum values that can be stored in the framebuffer. (Values ouside the range [0,1] are clamped to the range [0,1] when used directly, but aren't clamped when used to modify lighting material parameters.) Unsigned-integer color components, when specified, are linearly mapped to floating-point values such that the largest representable value maps to 1.0 (full intensity), and zero maps to 0.0 (zero intensity). Signed-integer color components, when specified, are linearly mapped to floating-point values such that the most positive representable value maps to 1.0, and the most negative representable value maps to −1.0 (see Table 5-1). Floating-point values are mapped directly. Neither floating-point nor signed-integer values are clamped to the range [0,1] before updating the current color. However, color components are clamped to this range before they are interpolated or written into a color buffer.

Suffix	Data Type	Minimum Value	Min Value Maps to	Maximum Value	Max Value Maps to
b	1-byte integer	−128	−1.0	127	1.0
s	2-byte integer	−32,768	−1.0	32,767	1.0
i	4-byte integer	−2,147,483,648	−1.0	2,147,483,647	1.0
ub	unsigned 1-byte integer	0	0.0	255	1.0
us	unsigned 2-byte integer	0	0.0	65,535	1.0
ui	unsigned 4-byte integer	0	0.0	4,294,967,295	1.0

Table 5-1   Converting Color Values to Floating-Point Numbers

Specifying a Color in Color-Index Mode

In color-index mode, use the **glIndex*()** command to select a single-valued color index as the current color index.

> void **glIndex**{sifd}(TYPE *c*);
> void **glIndex**{sifd}**v**(const TYPE ***c*);
>
> Sets the current color index. The first suffix for this command indicates the data type for parameters: short, integer, float, or double. The second, optional suffix is **v**, which indicates that the argument is an array of values of the given data type (the array contains only one value).

The current index is stored as a floating-point value. Integer values are converted directly to floating-point values, with no special mapping. Index values outside the representable range of the color-index buffer aren't clamped. However, before an index is dithered (if enabled) and written to the framebuffer, it's converted to fixed-point format. Any bits in the integer portion of the resulting fixed-point value that don't correspond to bits in the framebuffer are masked out.

Specifying a Shading Model

A line or a filled polygon primitive can be drawn with a single color (flat shading) or with many different colors (smooth shading, also called *Gouraud shading*). You specify the desired shading technique with **glShadeModel()**.

> void **glShadeModel** (GLenum *mode*);
>
> Sets the shading model. The mode parameter can be either GL_SMOOTH (the default) or GL_FLAT.

With flat shading, the color of one vertex of a primitive is duplicated across all the primitive's vertices. With smooth shading, the color at each vertex is treated individually. For a line primitive, the colors along the line segment are interpolated between the vertex colors. For a polygon primitive, the colors for the interior of the polygon are interpolated between the vertex colors. Listing 5-1 draws a smooth-shaded triangle, as shown in Plate 11.

Listing 5-1   Drawing a Smooth-Shaded Triangle: smooth.c

```c
#include <GL/gl.h>
#include <GL/glu.h>
#include "aux.h"

void myinit (void)
{
    glShadeModel (GL_SMOOTH);    /* GL_SMOOTH is the default */
}

void triangle(void)
{
    glBegin (GL_TRIANGLES);
        glColor3f (1.0, 0.0, 0.0);
        glVertex2f (5.0, 5.0);
        glColor3f (0.0, 1.0, 0.0);
        glVertex2f (25.0, 5.0);
        glColor3f (0.0, 0.0, 1.0);
        glVertex2f (5.0, 25.0);
    glEnd ();
}

void display(void)
{
    glClear (GL_COLOR_BUFFER_BIT);
    triangle ();
    glFlush ();
}

void myReshape(GLsizei w, GLsizei h)
{
    glViewport(0, 0, w, h);
    glMatrixMode(GL_PROJECTION);
    glLoadIdentity();
    if (w <= h)
        gluOrtho2D (0.0, 30.0, 0.0,
            30.0 * (GLfloat) h/(GLfloat) w);
    else
        gluOrtho2D (0.0, 30.0 * (GLfloat) w/(GLfloat) h, 0.0,
            30.0);
    glMatrixMode(GL_MODELVIEW);
}
```

```
int main(int argc, char** argv)
{
    auxInitDisplayMode (AUX_SINGLE | AUX_RGBA);
    auxInitPosition (0, 0, 500, 500);
    auxInitWindow (argv[0]);
    myinit();
    auxReshapeFunc (myReshape);
    auxMainLoop(display);
}
```

With smooth shading, neighboring pixels have slightly different color values. In RGBA mode, adjacent pixels with slightly different values look similar, so the color changes across a polygon appear gradual. In color-index mode, adjacent pixels may reference different locations in the color-index table, which may not have similar colors at all. Adjacent color-index entries may contain wildly different colors, so a smooth-shaded polygon in color-index mode can look psychedelic.

To avoid this problem, you have to create a *color ramp* of smoothly changing colors among a contiguous set of indices in the color map. Remember that loading colors into a color map is performed through your window system rather than OpenGL. For the moment, however, assume you have an **auxSetOneColor()** routine that loads a single index in the color map with specified red, green, and blue values. The first argument for this routine is the index, and the others are the red, green, and blue values. To load thirty-two contiguous color indices (from color index 16 to 47) with slightly differing shades of yellow, you might call

```
for(i=0; i<32; i++){
    auxSetOneColor(16+i, 1.0*(i/32.0), 1.0*(i/32.0), 0.0);
}
```

Now, if you render smooth-shaded polygons that use only the colors from index 16 to 47, those polygons have gradually differing shades of yellow.

With flat shading, the color of a single vertex defines the color of an entire primitive. For a line segment, the color of the line is the current color when the second (ending) vertex is specified. For a polygon, the color used is the one that's in effect when a particular vertex is specified, as shown in Table 5-2. The table counts vertices and polygons starting from 1. OpenGL follows these rules consistently, but the best way to avoid uncertainty about how a flat-shaded primitive will be drawn is to specify only one color for the primitive.

Type of Polygon	Vertex Used to Select the Color for the ith Polygon
single polygon	1
triangle strip	i+2
triangle fan	i+2
independent triangle	3i
quad strip	2i+2
independent quad	4i

Table 5-2   How OpenGL Selects a Color for the ith Flat-Shaded Polygon

Chapter 6

Lighting

Chapter Objectives

After reading this chapter, you'll be able to do the following:

- Understand how real-world lighting conditions are approximated by OpenGL

- Render illuminated objects by defining the desired light sources and lighting model

- Define the material properties of the objects being illuminated

- Manipulate the matrix stack to control the position of light sources

As you saw in Chapter 5, OpenGL computes the color of each pixel in a final, displayed scene that's held in the framebuffer. Part of this computation depends on what lighting is used in the scene and on how objects in the scene reflect or absorb that light. As an example of this, recall that the ocean has a different color on a bright, sunny day than it does on a gray, cloudy day. The presence of sunlight or clouds determines whether you see the ocean as bright turquoise or murky gray-green. In fact, most objects don't even look three-dimensional until they're lit. Figure 6-1 shows two versions of the exact same scene (a single sphere), one with lighting and one without.

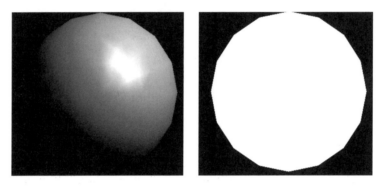

Figure 6-1   A Lit and an Unlit Sphere

As you can see, an unlit sphere looks no different from a two-dimensional disk. This demonstrates how critical the interaction between objects and light is in creating a three-dimensional scene.

With OpenGL, you can manipulate the lighting and objects in a scene to create many different kinds of effects. This chapter explains how to control the lighting in a scene. It discusses OpenGL's conceptual model of lighting, and it describes in detail how to set the numerous illumination parameters to achieve certain effects. Toward the end of the chapter, the mathematical computations that determine how lighting affects color are presented.

This chapter contains the following major sections:

- **"Real-World and OpenGL Lighting"** explains in general terms how light behaves in the world and how OpenGL models this behavior.

- **"A Simple Example: Rendering a Lit Sphere"** introduces OpenGL's lighting facility by presenting a short program that renders a lit sphere.

- **"Creating Light Sources"** explains how to define and position light sources.

- **"Selecting a Lighting Model"** discusses the elements of a lighting model and how to specify them.

- **"Defining Material Properties"** explains how to describe the properties of objects so that they interact with light in a desired way.

- **"The Mathematics of Lighting"** presents the mathematical calculations used by OpenGL to determine the effect of lights in a scene.

- **"Lighting in Color-Index Mode"** discusses the differences between using RGBA mode and color-index mode for lighting.

Real-World and OpenGL Lighting

When you look at a physical surface, your eye's perception of the color depends on the distribution of photon energies that arrive and trigger your cone cells, as described in "Color Perception" on page 140. Those photons come from a light source or combination of sources, some of which are absorbed and some of which are reflected by the surface. In addition, different surfaces may have very different properties—some are shiny, and preferentially reflect light in certain directions, while others scatter incoming light equally in all directions. Most surfaces are somewhere in between.

OpenGL approximates light and lighting as if light can be broken into red, green, and blue components. Thus, the color of light sources is characterized by the amount of red, green, and blue light they emit, and the material of surfaces is characterized by the percentage of the incoming red, green, and blue components that are reflected in various directions. The OpenGL lighting equations are just an approximation, but one that works fairly well and can be computed relatively quickly. If you desire a more accurate (or just different) lighting model, you have to do your own calculations in software. Such software can be enormously complex, as a few hours of reading any optics textbook should convince you.

In the OpenGL lighting model, the light in a scene comes from several light sources that can individually be turned on and off. Some light comes from a particular direction or position, and some light is generally scattered about the scene. For example, when you turn on a light bulb in a room, most of the light comes from the bulb, but some light comes after bouncing off one, two, three, or more walls. This bounced light (called *ambient*) is assumed to be so scattered that there is no way to tell its original direction, but it disappears if a particular light source is turned off.

Finally, there might be a general ambient light in the scene that comes from no particular source, as if it had been scattered so many times that its original source is impossible to determine.

In the OpenGL model, the light sources have an effect only when there are surfaces that absorb and reflect light. Each surface is assumed to be composed of a material with various properties. A material might emit its own light (like headlights on an automobile), it might scatter some incoming light in all directions, and it might reflect some portion of the incoming light in a preferential direction like a mirror or shiny surface.

The OpenGL lighting model considers the lighting to be divided into four independent components: emitted, ambient, diffuse, and specular. All four components are computed independently, and then added together.

Emitted, Ambient, Diffuse, and Specular Light

Emitted light is the simplest—it originates from an object and is unaffected by any light sources.

The *ambient* component is the light from that source that's been scattered so much by the environment that its direction is impossible to determine—it seems to come from all directions. Backlighting in a room has a large ambient component, since most of the light that reaches your eye has bounced off many surfaces first. A spotlight outdoors has a tiny ambient component; most of the light travels in the same direction, and since you're outdoors, very little of the light reaches your eye after bouncing off other objects. When ambient light strikes a surface, it's scattered equally in all directions.

Diffuse light comes from one direction, so it's brighter if it comes squarely down on a surface than if it barely glances off the surface. Once it hits a surface, however, it's scattered equally in all directions, so it appears equally bright, no matter where the eye is located. Any light coming from a particular position or direction probably has a diffuse component.

Finally, *specular* light comes from a particular direction, and it tends to bounce off the surface in a preferred direction. A well-collimated laser beam bouncing off a high-quality mirror produces almost 100 percent specular reflection. Shiny metal or plastic has a high specular component, and chalk or carpet has almost none. You can think of specularity as shininess.

Although a light source delivers a single distribution of frequencies, the ambient, diffuse, and specular components might be different. For example, if you have a white light in a room with red walls, the scattered light tends to be red, although the light directly striking objects is white. OpenGL allows you to set the red, green, and blue values for each component of light independently.

Material Colors

The OpenGL lighting model makes the approximation that a material's color depends on the percentages of the incoming red, green, and blue light it reflects. For example, a perfectly red ball reflects all the incoming red light and absorbs all the green and blue light that strikes it. If you view such a ball in white light (composed of equal amounts of red, green, and blue light), all the red is reflected, and you see a red ball. If the ball is viewed in pure red light, it also appears to be red. If, however, the red ball is viewed in pure green light, it appears black (all the green is absorbed, and there's no incoming red, so no light is reflected).

Like lights, materials have different ambient, diffuse, and specular colors, which determine the ambient, diffuse, and specular reflectances of the material. A material's ambient reflectance is combined with the ambient component of each incoming light source, the diffuse reflectance with the light's diffuse component, and similarly for the specular reflectance and component. Ambient and diffuse reflectances define the color of the material and are typically similar if not identical. Specular reflectance is usually white or gray, so that specular highlights end up being the color of the light source's specular intensity. If you think of a white light shining on a shiny red plastic sphere, most of the sphere appears red, but the shiny highlight is white.

RGB Values for Lights and Materials

The color components specified for lights mean something different than for materials. For a light, the numbers correspond to a percentage of full intensity for each color. If the R, G, and B values for a light's color are all 1.0, the light is the brightest possible white. If the values are 0.5, the color is still white, but only at half intensity, so it appears gray. If R=G=1 and B=0 (full red and green with no blue), the light appears yellow.

For materials, the numbers correspond to the reflected proportions of those colors. So if R=1, G=0.5, and B=0 for a material, that material reflects all the incoming red light, half the incoming green, and none of the incoming blue light. In other words, if an OpenGL light has components (LR, LG, LB), and a material has corresponding components (MR, MG, MB), then, ignoring all other reflectivity effects, the light that arrives at the eye is given by (LR*MR, LG*MG, LB*MB).

Similarly, if you have two lights, which send (R1, G1, B1) and (R2, G2, B2) to the eye, OpenGL adds the components, giving (R1+R2, G1+G2, B1+B2). If any of the sums are greater than 1 (corresponding to a color brighter than the equipment can display), the component is clamped to 1.

A Simple Example: Rendering a Lit Sphere

These are the steps required to add lighting to your scene:

1. Define normal vectors for each vertex of all the objects. These normals determine the orientation of the object relative to the light sources.

2. Create, select, and position one or more light sources.

3. Create and select a *lighting model*, which defines the level of global ambient light and the effective location of the viewpoint (for the purposes of lighting calculations).

4. Define material properties for the objects in the scene.

Listing 6-1 accomplishes these tasks. It displays a sphere illuminated by a single light source, as shown earlier in Figure 6-1.

Listing 6-1   Drawing a Lit Sphere:

```
#include <GL/gl.h>
#include <GL/glu.h>
#include "aux.h"

void myinit(void)
{
    GLfloat mat_specular[] = { 1.0, 1.0, 1.0, 1.0 };
    GLfloat mat_shininess[] = { 50.0 };
    GLfloat light_position[] = { 1.0, 1.0, 1.0, 0.0 };

    glMaterialfv(GL_FRONT, GL_SPECULAR, mat_specular);
    glMaterialfv(GL_FRONT, GL_SHININESS, mat_shininess);
    glLightfv(GL_LIGHT0, GL_POSITION, light_position);
```

```
    glEnable(GL_LIGHTING);
    glEnable(GL_LIGHT0);
    glDepthFunc(GL_LEQUAL);
    glEnable(GL_DEPTH_TEST);
}

void display(void)
{
    glClear(GL_COLOR_BUFFER_BIT | GL_DEPTH_BUFFER_BIT);
    auxSolidSphere(1.0);
    glFlush();
}

void myReshape(GLsizei w, GLsizei h)
{
    glViewport(0, 0, w, h);
    glMatrixMode(GL_PROJECTION);
    glLoadIdentity();
    if (w <= h)
        glOrtho (-1.5, 1.5, -1.5*(GLfloat)h/(GLfloat)w,
            1.5*(GLfloat)h/(GLfloat)w, -10.0, 10.0);
    else
        glOrtho (-1.5*(GLfloat)w/(GLfloat)h,
            1.5*(GLfloat)w/(GLfloat)h, -1.5, 1.5, -10.0, 10.0);
    glMatrixMode(GL_MODELVIEW);
    glLoadIdentity();
}

int main(int argc, char** argv)
{
    auxInitDisplayMode (AUX_SINGLE | AUX_RGBA | AUX_DEPTH);
    auxInitPosition (0, 0, 500, 500);
    auxInitWindow (argv[0]);
    myinit();
    auxReshapeFunc (myReshape);
    auxMainLoop(display);
}
```

The lighting-related calls are in the **myinit()** command; they're discussed briefly in the following paragraphs and in more detail later in the chapter. One thing to note about Listing 6-1 is that it uses RGBA color mode, not color-index mode. OpenGL's lighting calculation is different for the two modes, and in fact the lighting capabilities are more limited in color-index mode. Thus, RGBA is the preferred mode when doing lighting, and all the examples in this chapter use it. See "Lighting in Color-Index Mode" on page 192 for more information about lighting in color-index mode.

A Simple Example: Rendering a Lit Sphere   **163**

Define Normal Vectors for Each Vertex of All the Objects

An object's normals determine its orientation relative to the light sources. For each vertex, OpenGL uses the assigned normal to determine how much light that particular vertex receives from each light source. In this example, the normals for the sphere are defined as part of the **auxSolidSphere**() routine. See "Normal Vectors" on page 52 for more details on how to define normals.

Create, Position, and Enable One or More Light Sources

Listing 6-1 uses only one, white light source; its location is specified by the **glLightfv**() call. This example uses the default color for light zero (GL_LIGHT0), which is white; if you had wanted a differently colored light, you'd use **glLight*** () to indicate this. You can include at least eight different light sources in your scene of various colors; the default color of these other lights is black. (The particular implementation of OpenGL you're using might allow more than eight.) You can also locate the lights wherever you desire—you can position them near the scene, as a desk lamp would be, or an infinite distance away, like the sun. In addition, you can control whether a light produces a narrow, focused beam or a wider beam. Remember that each light source adds significantly to the calculations needed to render the scene, so performance is affected by the number of lights in the scene. See "Creating Light Sources" on page 165 for more information about how to create lights with the desired characteristics.

After you've defined the characteristics of the lights you want, you have to turn them on with the **glEnable**() command. You also need to call this command with GL_LIGHTING as a parameter to prepare OpenGL to perform lighting calculations. See "Enabling Lighting" on page 179 for more information about how to do this.

Select a Lighting Model

As you might expect, the **glLightModel*** () command describes the parameters of a lighting model. In Listing 6-1, the only element of the lighting model that's defined explicitly is the global ambient light. The lighting model also defines whether the viewer of the scene should be considered to be an infinite distance away or local to the scene, and whether lighting calculations should be performed differently for the front and back surfaces of objects in the scene. Listing 6-1 uses the default settings for these two aspects of the model—an infinite viewer and one-sided lighting. Using a local viewer adds significantly to the complexity of the calculations that must be performed because OpenGL must calculate the angle between the viewpoint and each object. With an infinite viewer, however, the angle is ignored, and the results are slightly less realistic. Further, since in this example, the back surface of the sphere is never seen (it's the inside of the sphere), one-sided lighting is sufficient. The section "Selecting a Lighting Model" on page 177 describes the elements of an OpenGL lighting model in more detail.

Define Material Properties for the Objects in the Scene

An object's material properties determine how it reflects light and therefore what material it seems to be made of. Because the interaction between an object's material surface and incident light is complex, specifying material properties so that an object has a certain desired appearance is an art. You can specify a material's ambient, diffuse, and specular colors and how shiny it is. In this example, only these last two material properties—the specular material color and shininess—are explicitly specified (with the **glMaterialfv()** calls). "Defining Material Properties" on page 179 describes and gives examples of all the material-property parameters.

Some Important Notes

As you write your own lighting program, remember that you can use the default values for some lighting parameters; others need to be changed. Also, don't forget to enable whatever lights you define and to enable lighting calculations. Finally, remember that you might be able to use display lists to maximize efficiency as you change lighting conditions; see "Display-List Design Philosophy" on page 121.

Creating Light Sources

Light sources have a number of properties, such as color, position, and direction. The following sections explain how to control these properties and what the resulting light looks like. The command used to specify all properties of lights is **glLight*()**; it takes three arguments: to identify the light whose property is being specified, the property, and the desired value for that property.

void **glLight**{if}[v](GLenum *light*, GLenum *pname*, TYPE *param*);

Creates the light specified by *light*, which can be GL_LIGHT0, GL_LIGHT1, ... , or GL_LIGHT7. The characteristic of the light being set is defined by *pname*, which specifies a named parameter (see Table 6-1). The *param* argument indicates the values to which the *pname* characteristic is set; it's a pointer to a group of values if the vector version is used, or the value itself if the nonvector version is used. The nonvector version can be used to set only single-valued light characteristics.

Parameter Name	Default Value	Meaning
GL_AMBIENT	(0.0, 0.0, 0.0, 1.0)	ambient RGBA intensity of light
GL_DIFFUSE	(1.0, 1.0, 1.0, 1.0)	diffuse RGBA intensity of light
GL_SPECULAR	(1.0, 1.0, 1.0, 1.0)	specular RGBA intensity of light
GL_POSITION	(0.0, 0.0, 1.0, 0.0)	(*x, y, z, w*) position of light
GL_SPOT_DIRECTION	(0.0, 0.0, −1.0)	(*x, y, z*) direction of spotlight
GL_SPOT_EXPONENT	0.0	spotlight exponent
GL_SPOT_CUTOFF	180.0	spotlight cutoff angle
GL_CONSTANT_ATTENUATION	1.0	constant attenuation factor
GL_LINEAR_ATTENUATION	0.0	linear attenuation factor
GL_QUADRATIC_ATTENUATION	0.0	quadratic attenuation factor

Table 6-1   Default Values for pname Parameter of glLight*()

Note: The default values listed for GL_DIFFUSE and GL_SPECULAR in Table 6-1 apply only to GL_LIGHT0. For other lights, the default value is (0.0, 0.0, 0.0, 1.0) for both GL_DIFFUSE and GL_SPECULAR.

Here's an example of using **glLight*()**:

```
GLfloat light_ambient[] = { 0.0, 0.0, 0.0, 1.0 };
GLfloat light_diffuse[] = { 1.0, 1.0, 1.0, 1.0 };
GLfloat light_specular[] = { 1.0, 1.0, 1.0, 1.0 };
GLfloat light_position[] = { 1.0, 1.0, 1.0, 0.0 };
```

```
glLightfv(GL_LIGHT0, GL_AMBIENT, light_ambient);
glLightfv(GL_LIGHT0, GL_DIFFUSE, light_diffuse);
glLightfv(GL_LIGHT0, GL_SPECULAR, light_specular);
glLightfv(GL_LIGHT0, GL_POSITION, light_position);
```

As you can see, arrays are defined for the parameter values, and **glLightfv()** is called repeatedly to set the various parameters. In this example, the first three calls to **glLightfv()** are superfluous, since they're being used to specify the default values for the GL_AMBIENT, GL_DIFFUSE, and GL_SPECULAR parameters.

Note: Remember to turn on each light with **glEnable()**; see "Enabling Lighting" on page 179 for more information about how to do this.

All the parameters for **glLight*()** and their possible values are explained in the following sections. These parameters interact with those that define the overall lighting model for a particular scene and an object's material properties. See "Selecting a Lighting Model" on page 177 and "Defining Material Properties" on page 179 for more information about these two topics. "The Mathematics of Lighting" on page 188 explains how all these parameters interact mathematically.

Color

OpenGL allows you to associate three different color-related parameters—GL_AMBIENT, GL_DIFFUSE, and GL_SPECULAR—with any particular light. The GL_AMBIENT parameter refers to the RGBA intensity of the ambient light that a particular light source adds to the scene. As you can see in Table 6-1, by default there is no ambient light since GL_AMBIENT is (0.0, 0.0, 0.0, 1.0). This value was used in Listing 6-1. If this program had specified blue ambient light

```
GLfloat light_ambient[] = { 0.0, 0.0, 1.0, 1.0};
glLightfv(GL_LIGHT0, GL_AMBIENT, light_ambient);
```

the result would have been as shown in the left part of Plate 13a.

The GL_DIFFUSE parameter probably most closely correlates with what you naturally think of as "the color of a light." It defines the RGBA color of the diffuse light that a particular light source adds to a scene. By default, GL_DIFFUSE is (1.0, 1.0, 1.0, 1.0) for GL_LIGHT0, which produces a bright, white light as shown in Plate 13a. The default value for any other light (GL_LIGHT1, ... , GL_LIGHT7) is (0.0, 0.0, 0.0, 0.0).

The GL_SPECULAR parameter affects the color of the specular highlight on an object. Typically, a real-world object such as a glass bottle has a specular highlight that's the color of the light shining on it (which is often white). Therefore, if you want to create a realistic effect, set the GL_SPECULAR parameter to the same value as the GL_DIFFUSE parameter. By default, GL_SPECULAR is (1.0, 1.0, 1.0, 1.0) for GL_LIGHT0 and (0.0, 0.0, 0.0, 0.0) for any other light.

Position and Attenuation

As previously mentioned, you can choose whether to have a light source that's treated as though it's located infinitely far away from the scene or one that's nearer to the scene. The first type is referred to as an *directional* light source; the effect of an infinite location is that the rays of light can be considered parallel by the time they reach an object. An example of a real-world directional light source is the sun. The second type is called a *positional* light source, since its exact position within the scene determines the effect it has on a scene and, specifically, the direction from which the light rays come. A desk lamp is an example of a positional light source. You can see the difference between directional and positional lights in Plate 13b.

The light used in Listing 6-1 is a directional one:

```
GLfloat light_position[] = { 1.0, 1.0, 1.0, 0.0 };
glLightfv(GL_LIGHT0, GL_POSITION, light_position);
```

As shown, you supply a vector of four values (*x*, *y*, *z*, *w*) for the GL_POSITION parameter. If the last value, *w*, is zero, the corresponding light source is a directional one, and the (*x*, *y*, *z*) values describe its direction. This direction is transformed by the modelview matrix just as it would be if it described a normal vector. By default, GL_POSITION is (0, 0, 1, 0), which defines a directional light that points along the negative *z*-axis. (Note that nothing prevents you from creating a directional light with the direction of (0, 0, 0), but such a light won't help you much.)

If the *w* value is nonzero, the light is positional, and the (*x*, *y*, *z*) values specify the location of the light in homogeneous object coordinates (see Appendix G). This location is transformed by the modelview matrix and stored in eye coordinates. See "Controlling a Light's Position and Direction" on page 172 for more information about how to control the transformation of the light's location. Also, by default, a positional light radiates in all directions, but you can restrict it to producing a cone of illumination by defining the light as a spotlight. The next section, "Spotlights" on page 170, explains how to define a light as a spotlight.

Note: Remember that the colors across the face of a smooth-shaded polygon are determined by the colors calculated for the vertices. Because of this, you probably want to avoid using large polygons with local lights—if you locate the light near the middle of the polygon, the vertices might be too far away to receive much light, so the whole polygon will look darker than you intended. To avoid this problem, break up the large polygon into smaller ones.

For real-world lights, the intensity of light decreases as distance from the light increases. Since a directional light is infinitely far away, it doesn't make sense to attenuate its intensity over distance, so attenuation is disabled for a directional light. However, you might want to attenuate the light from a positional light. OpenGL attenuates a light source by multiplying the contribution of that source by an attenuation factor:

$$\text{attenuation factor} = \frac{1}{k_c + k_l d + k_q d^2}$$

where

d = distance between the light's position and the vertex

k_c = GL_CONSTANT_ATTENUATION

k_l = GL_LINEAR_ATTENUATION

k_q = GL_QUADRATIC_ATTENUATION

By default, k_c is 1.0 and both k_l and k_q are zero, but you can give these parameters different values:

```
glLightf(GL_LIGHT0, GL_CONSTANT_ATTENUATION, 2.0);
glLightf(GL_LIGHT0, GL_LINEAR_ATTENUATION, 1.0);
glLightf(GL_LIGHT0, GL_QUADRATIC_ATTENUATION, 0.5);
```

Note that the ambient, diffuse, and specular contributions are all attenuated. Only the emission and global ambient values aren't attenuated.

Spotlights

As previously mentioned, you can have a positional light source act as a spotlight—that is, by restricting the shape of the light it emits to a cone. To create a spotlight, you need to determine the spread of the cone of light you desire. (Remember that since spotlights are positional lights, you also have to locate them where you want them. Again, note that nothing prevents you from creating a directional spotlight, but it probably won't give you the result you want.) To specify the angle between the axis of the cone and a ray along the edge of the cone, use the GL_SPOT_CUTOFF parameter. The angle of the cone at the apex is then twice this value, as shown in Figure 6-2.

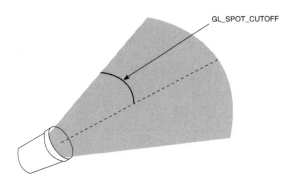

Figure 6-2   The GL_SPOT_CUTOFF Parameter

Note that no light is emitted beyond the edges of the cone. By default, the spotlight feature is disabled because the GL_SPOT_CUTOFF parameter is 180.0. This value means that light is emitted in all directions (the angle at the cone's apex is 360 degrees, so it isn't a cone at all). The value for GL_SPOT_CUTOFF is restricted to being within the range [0.0,90.0] (unless it has the special value 180.0). The following line sets the cutoff parameter to 45 degrees:

```
glLightf(GL_LIGHT0, GL_SPOT_CUTOFF, 45.0);
```

You also need to specify a spotlight's direction, which determines the axis of the cone of light:

```
GLfloat spot_direction[] = { -1.0, -1.0, 0.0 };
glLightfv(GL_LIGHT0, GL_SPOT_DIRECTION, spot_direction);
```

The direction is specified in homogeneous object coordinates. By default, the direction is (0.0, 0.0, −1.0), so if you don't explicitly set the value of GL_SPOT_DIRECTION, the light points down the negative z-axis. Also, keep in mind that a spotlight's direction is transformed by the modelview matrix just as though it were a normal vector, and the result is stored in eye coordinates. (See "Controlling a Light's Position and Direction" on page 172 for more information about such transformations.)

In addition to the spotlight's cutoff angle and direction, you can control the intensity distribution of the light within the cone, in two ways. First, you can set the attenuation factor described earlier, which is multiplied by the light's intensity. You can also set the GL_SPOT_EXPONENT parameter, which is by default zero, to control how concentrated the light is. The light's intensity is highest in the center of the cone. It's attenuated toward the edges of the cone by the cosine of the angle between the direction of the light and the direction from the light to the vertex being lighted, raised to the power of the spot exponent. Thus, higher spot exponents result in a more focused light source. See "The Mathematics of Lighting" on page 188 for more details on the equations used to calculate light intensity.

Multiple Lights

As mentioned, you can have at least eight lights in your scene (possibly more, depending on your OpenGL implementation). Since OpenGL needs to perform calculations to determine how much light each vertex receives from each light source, increasing the number of lights adversely affects performance. The constants used to refer to the eight lights are GL_LIGHT0, GL_LIGHT1, GL_LIGHT2, GL_LIGHT3, and so on. In the preceding discussions, parameters related to GL_LIGHT0 were set. If you want an additional light, you need to specify its parameters; also, remember that the default values are different for these other lights than they are for GL_LIGHT0, as explained in Table 6-1. The following lines of code define a white attenuated spotlight:

```
GLfloat light1_ambient[] = { 0.2, 0.2, 0.2, 1.0 };
GLfloat light1_diffuse[] = { 1.0, 1.0, 1.0, 1.0 };
GLfloat light1_specular[] = { 1.0, 1.0, 1.0, 1.0 };
GLfloat light1_position[] = { -2.0, 2.0, 1.0, 1.0 };
GLfloat spot_direction[] = { -1.0, -1.0, 0.0 };

glLightfv(GL_LIGHT1, GL_AMBIENT, light1_ambient);
glLightfv(GL_LIGHT1, GL_DIFFUSE, light1_diffuse);
glLightfv(GL_LIGHT1, GL_SPECULAR, light1_specular);
glLightfv(GL_LIGHT1, GL_POSITION, light1_position);
```

```
glLightf(GL_LIGHT1, GL_CONSTANT_ATTENUATION, 1.5);
glLightf(GL_LIGHT1, GL_LINEAR_ATTENUATION, 0.5);
glLightf(GL_LIGHT1, GL_QUADRATIC_ATTENUATION, 0.2);

glLightf(GL_LIGHT1, GL_SPOT_CUTOFF, 45.0);
glLightfv(GL_LIGHT0, GL_SPOT_DIRECTION, spot_direction);
glLightf(GL_LIGHT1, GL_SPOT_EXPONENT, 2.0);

glEnable(GL_LIGHT1);
```

If these lines were added to Listing 6-1, the sphere would be lit with two lights, one directional and one spotlight.

Try This

Modify Listing 6-1:

- Change the light to be a positional colored light rather than a directional white one.

- Add an additional colored spotlight. Hint: Use some of the code shown in the preceding section.

- Measure how these two changes affect performance.

Controlling a Light's Position and Direction

OpenGL treats the position and direction of a light source just as it treats the position of a geometric primitive. In other words, a light source is subject to the same matrix transformations as a primitive. More specifically, when **glLight*()** is called to specify the position or the direction of a light source, the position or direction is transformed by the current modelview matrix and stored in eye coordinates. This means you can manipulate a light source's position or direction by changing the contents of the modelview matrix stack. (The projection matrix has no effect on a light's position or direction.) This section explains how to achieve three different effects by changing the point in the program at which the light position is set, relative to modeling or viewing transformations:

- A light position that remains fixed

- A light that moves around a stationary object

- A light that moves along with the viewpoint

In the simplest example, as in Listing 6-1, the light position remains fixed. To achieve this effect, you need to set the light position after whatever viewing and/or modeling transformation you use. Here's what the relevant code from the **myinit()** and **myReshape()** routines might look like:

```
glViewport(0, 0, w, h);
glMatrixMode (GL_PROJECTION);
glLoadIdentity();
if (w <= h)
    glOrtho (-1.5, 1.5, -1.5*h/w, 1.5*h/w, -10.0, 10.0);
else
    glOrtho (-1.5*w/h, 1.5*w/h, -1.5, 1.5, -10.0, 10.0);
glMatrixMode (GL_MODELVIEW);
glLoadIdentity();

/* later in myInit() */
GLfloat light_position[] = { 1.0, 1.0, 1.0, 1.0 };
glLightfv(GL_LIGHT0, GL_POSITION, position);
```

As you can see, the viewport and projection matrices are established first. Then, the identity matrix is loaded as the modelview matrix, after which the light position is set. Since the identity matrix is used, the originally specified light position (1.0, 1.0, 1.0) isn't changed by being multiplied by the modelview matrix. Then, since neither the light position nor the modelview matrix is modified after this point, the light remains pointing at (1.0, 1.0, 1.0).

Now suppose you want to rotate or translate the light position so that the light moves relative to a stationary object. One way to do this is to set the light position after the modeling transformation, which is itself changed specifically to modify the light position. You can begin with the same series of calls in an **init()** routine early in the program. Then, probably within an event loop, you need to perform the desired modeling transformation (on the modelview stack) and reset the light position. Here's what such code might look like:

```
void display(GLint spin)
{
    GLfloat light_position[] = { 0.0, 0.0, 1.5, 1.0 };
    glClear(GL_COLOR_BUFFER_BIT | GL_DEPTH_BUFFER_BIT);

    glPushMatrix();
        glTranslatef(0.0, 0.0, -5.0);
        glPushMatrix();
            glRotated((GLdouble) spin, 1.0, 0.0, 0.0);
            glLightfv(GL_LIGHT0, GL_POSITION, light_position);
        glPopMatrix();
```

```
          auxSolidTorus();
    glPopMatrix();
    glFlush();
}
```

This **display()** command causes the scene to be redrawn with the light rotated *spin* degrees around a stationary torus. Note the two pairs of **glPushMatrix()** and **glPopMatrix()** calls, which are used to isolate the viewing and modeling transformations, all of which occur on the modelview stack. Since in this example the viewpoint remains constant, the current matrix is pushed down the stack and then the desired viewing transformation is loaded with **glTranslatef()**. The matrix stack is pushed again before the modeling transformation **glRotated()** is specified. Then the light position is set in the new, rotated coordinate system so that the light itself appears to be rotated from its previous position. (Remember that the light position is stored in eye coordinates, which are obtained after transformation by the modelview matrix.) After the rotated matrix is popped off the stack, the torus is drawn.

To create a light that moves along with the viewpoint, you need to set the light position before the viewing transformation. Then, the viewing transformation affects both the light and the viewpoint in the same way. For this example, let's use a slightly different set of calls in the **myinit()** routine:

```
GLfloat light_position() = { 0.0, 0.0, 1.0, 1.0 };

glViewport(0, 0, w-1, h-1);
glMatrixMode(GL_PROJECTION);
glLoadIdentity();
gluPerspective(40.0, (GLfloat) w/(GLfloat) h, 1.0, 100.0);
glMatrixMode(GL_MODELVIEW);

glLightfv(GL_LIGHT0, GL_POSITION, light_position);
```

Then, the **display()** routine that's called from the event loop to redraw the scene might look like this:

```
void display(GLint spin)
{
    glClear(GL_COLOR_BUFFER_MASK | GL_DEPTH_BUFFER_MASK);
    glPushMatrix();
        glTranslatef (0.0, 0.0, -5.0);
        glRotatef ((GLfloat) spin, 1.0, 0.0, 0.0);
        auxSolidTorus();
    glPopMatrix();
```

```
    glFlush();
}
```

When the lighted torus is redrawn, both the light position and the viewpoint are moved *spin* degrees. Even though you haven't respecified the light position, the light moves because the eye coordinate system has changed.

Try This

Try This

Modify Listing 6-2:

- Make the light translate past the object instead of rotating around it. Hint: Use **glTranslated()** rather than the first **glRotated()** in **display()**, and choose an appropriate value to use instead of *spin*.

- Change the attenuation so that the light decreases in intensity as it's moved away from the object. Hint: Add calls to **glLight*()** to set the desired attenuation parameters.

Listing 6-2   Moving a Light with Modeling Transformations: movelight.c

```
#include <GL/gl.h>
#include <GL/glu.h>
#include "aux.h"

static int spin = 0;

void movelight (AUX_EVENTREC *event)
{
    spin = (spin + 30) % 360;
}

void myinit (void)
{
    glEnable(GL_LIGHTING);
    glEnable(GL_LIGHT0);

    glDepthFunc(GL_LEQUAL);
    glEnable(GL_DEPTH_TEST);
}

void display(void)
{
    GLfloat position[] = { 0.0, 0.0, 1.5, 1.0 };
```

```
    glClear (GL_COLOR_BUFFER_BIT | GL_DEPTH_BUFFER_BIT);
    glPushMatrix ();
        glTranslatef (0.0, 0.0, -5.0);

        glPushMatrix ();
            glRotated ((GLdouble) spin, 1.0, 0.0, 0.0);
            glRotated (0.0, 1.0, 0.0, 0.0);
            glLightfv (GL_LIGHT0, GL_POSITION, position);

            glTranslated (0.0, 0.0, 1.5);
            glDisable (GL_LIGHTING);
            glColor3f (0.0, 1.0, 1.0);
            auxWireCube (0.1);
            glEnable (GL_LIGHTING);
        glPopMatrix ();

        auxSolidTorus (0.275, 0.85);
    glPopMatrix ();
    glFlush ();
}

void myReshape(GLsizei w, GLsizei h)
{
    glViewport(0, 0, w, h);
    glMatrixMode(GL_PROJECTION);
    glLoadIdentity();
    gluPerspective(40.0, (GLfloat) w/(GLfloat) h, 1.0, 20.0);
    glMatrixMode(GL_MODELVIEW);
}


int main(int argc, char** argv)
{
    auxInitDisplayMode (AUX_SINGLE | AUX_RGBA | AUX_DEPTH);
    auxInitPosition (0, 0, 500, 500);
    auxInitWindow (argv[0]);
    myinit();
    auxMouseFunc (AUX_LEFTBUTTON, AUX_MOUSEDOWN, movelight);
    auxReshapeFunc (myReshape);
    auxMainLoop(display);
}
```

Selecting a Lighting Model

OpenGL's notion of a lighting model has three components:

- The global ambient light intensity

- Whether the viewpoint position is local to the scene or whether it should be considered to be an infinite distance away

- Whether lighting calculations should be performed differently for both the front and back faces of objects

This section explains how to specify a lighting model. It also discusses how to enable lighting—that is, how to tell OpenGL that you want lighting calculations performed.

Global Ambient Light

As discussed earlier, each light source can contribute ambient light to a scene. In addition, there can be other ambient light that's not from any particular source. To specify the RGBA intensity of such global ambient light, use the GL_LIGHT_MODEL_AMBIENT parameter as follows:

```
GLfloat lmodel_ambient[] = { 0.2, 0.2, 0.2, 1.0 };
glLightModelfv(GL_LIGHT_MODEL_AMBIENT, lmodel_ambient);
```

In this example, the values used for *lmodel_ambient* are the default values for GL_LIGHT_MODEL_AMBIENT. Since these numbers yield a small amount of white ambient light, even if you don't add a specific light source to your scene, you can still see the objects in the scene. Plate 14a shows the effect of different amounts of global ambient light.

Local or Infinite Viewpoint

The location of the viewpoint affects the calculations for highlights produced by specular reflectance. More specifically, the intensity of the highlight at a particular vertex depends on the normal at that vertex, the direction from the vertex to the light source, and the direction from the vertex to the viewpoint. Keep in mind that the viewpoint isn't actually being moved by calls to lighting commands (you need to change the projection transformation, as described in "Projection Transformations" on page 90); instead, different assumptions are made for the lighting calculations as if the viewpoint were moved.

With an infinite viewpoint, the direction between it and any vertex in the scene remains constant. A local viewpoint tends to yield more realistic results, but since the direction has to be calculated for each vertex, overall performance is decreased with a local viewpoint. By default, an infinite viewpoint is assumed. Here's how to change to a local viewpoint:

```
glLightModeli(GL_LIGHT_MODEL_LOCAL_VIEWER, GL_TRUE);
```

This call places the viewpoint at (0, 0, 0) in eye coordinates. To switch back to an infinite viewpoint, pass in GL_FALSE as the argument.

Two-sided Lighting

Lighting calculations are performed for all polygons, whether they're front-facing or back-facing. Since you usually set up lighting conditions with the front-facing polygons in mind, however, the back-facing ones typically aren't correctly illuminated. In Listing 6-1 where the object is a sphere, only the front faces are ever seen, since they're the ones on the outside of the sphere. So, in this case, it doesn't matter what the back-facing polygons look like. If the sphere was going to be cut away so that its inside surface would be visible, however, you might want to have the inside surface be fully lit according to the lighting conditions you've defined; you might also want to supply a different material description for the back faces. When you turn on two-sided lighting, as follows

```
glLightModeli(LIGHT_MODEL_TWO_SIDE, GL_TRUE);
```

OpenGL reverses the surface normals for back-facing polygons; typically, this means that the surface normals of visible back- and front-facing polygons face the viewer, rather than pointing away. As a result, all polygons are illumnated correctly.

To turn two-sided lighting off, pass in GL_FALSE as the argument in the preceding call. See "Defining Material Properties" on page 179 for information about how to supply material properties for both faces. You can also control which faces OpenGL considers to be front-facing with the command **glFrontFace()**. See "Reversing and Culling Polygon Faces" on page 46 for more information about this command.

Enabling Lighting

With OpenGL, you need to explicitly enable (or disable) lighting. If lighting isn't enabled, the current color is simply mapped onto the current vertex, and no calculations concerning normals, light sources, the lighting model, and material properties are performed. Here's how to enable lighting:

```
glEnable(GL_LIGHTING);
```

To disable lighting, call **glDisable()** with GL_LIGHTING as the argument.

You also need to explicitly enable each light source that you define, after you've specified the parameters for that source. Listing 6-1 uses only one light, GL_LIGHT0:

```
glEnable(GL_LIGHT0);
```

Defining Material Properties

You've seen how to create light sources with certain characteristics and how to define the desired lighting model. This section describes how to define the material properties of the objects in the scene: the ambient, diffuse, and specular colors, the shininess, and the color of any emitted light. The equations used in the lighting and material-property calculations are described in "The Mathematics of Lighting" on page 188. Most of the material properties are conceptually similar to ones you've already used to create light sources. The mechanism for setting them is similar, except that the command used is called **glMaterial*()**.

void **glMaterial**{if}[v](GLenum *face*, GLenum *pname*, *TYPE param*);

Specifies a current material property for use in lighting calculations. The *face* parameter can be GL_FRONT, GL_BACK, or GL_FRONT_AND_BACK to indicate which face of the object the material should be applied to. The particular material property being set is identified by *pname* and the desired values for that property are given by *param*, which is either a pointer to a group of values (if the vector version is used) or the actual value (if the nonvector version is used). The nonvector version works only for setting GL_SHININESS. The possible values for *pname* are shown in Table 6-2. Note that GL_AMBIENT_AND_DIFFUSE allows you to set both the ambient and diffuse material colors simultaneously to the same RGBA value.

Parameter Name	Default Value	Meaning
GL_AMBIENT	(0.2, 0.2, 0.2, 1.0)	ambient color of material
GL_DIFFUSE	(0.8, 0.8, 0.8, 1.0)	diffuse color of material
GL_AMBIENT_AND_DIFFUSE		ambient and diffuse color of material
GL_SPECULAR	(0.0, 0.0, 0.0, 1.0)	specular color of material
GL_SHININESS	0.0	specular exponent
GL_EMISSION	(0.0, 0.0, 0.0, 1.0)	emissive color of material
GL_COLOR_INDEXES	(0,1,1)	ambient, diffuse, and specular color indices

Table 6-2 Default Values for pname Parameter of glMaterial*()

As discussed in "Selecting a Lighting Model" on page 177, you can choose to have lighting calculations performed differently for the front- and back-facing polygons of objects. If the back faces might indeed be seen, you can supply different material properties for the front and the back surfaces by using the *face* parameter of **glMaterial*()**. See Plate 14b for an example of an object drawn with different inside and outside material properties.

To give you an idea of the possible effects you can achieve by manipulating material properties, see Plate 16. This figure shows the same object drawn with several different sets of material properties. The same light source and lighting model are used for the entire figure. The sections that follow discuss the specific properties used to draw each of these spheres.

Note that most of the material properties set with **glMaterial*()** are (R, G, B, A) colors. Regardless of what alpha values are supplied for other parameters, the alpha value at any particular vertex is the diffuse-material alpha value (that is, the alpha value given to GL_DIFFUSE with the **glMaterial*()** command, as described in the next section. (See "Blending" on page 196 for a complete discussion of alpha values.) Also, none of the RGBA material properties apply in color-index mode; see "Lighting in Color-Index Mode" on page 192 for more information about what parameters are relevant in color-index mode.

Diffuse and Ambient Reflection

The GL_DIFFUSE and GL_AMBIENT parameters set with **glMaterial*()** affect the color of the diffuse and ambient light reflected by an object. Diffuse reflectance plays the most important role in determining what you perceive the color of an object to be. It's affected by the color of the incident diffuse light and the angle of the incident light relative to the normal direction. (It's most intense where the incident light falls perpendicular to the surface.) The position of the viewpoint doesn't affect diffuse reflectance at all.

Ambient reflectance affects the overall color of the object. Because diffuse reflectance is brightest where an object is directly illuminated, ambient reflectance is most noticeable where an object receives no direct illumination. An object's total ambient reflectance is affected by the global ambient light and ambient light from individual light sources. Like diffuse reflectance, ambient reflectance isn't affected by the position of the viewpoint.

For real-world objects, diffuse and ambient reflectance are normally the same color. For this reason, OpenGL provides you with a convenient way of assigning the same value to both simultaneously with **glMaterial*()**:

```
GLfloat mat_amb_diff[] = { 0.1, 0.5, 0.8, 1.0 };
glMaterialfv(GL_FRONT_AND_BACK, GL_AMBIENT_AND_DIFFUSE,
             mat_amb_diff);
```

In this example, the RGBA color (0.1, 0.5, 0.8, 1.0)—a deep blue color— represents the current ambient and diffuse reflectance for both the front- and back-facing polygons.

In Plate 16, the first row of spheres has no ambient reflectance (0.0, 0.0, 0.0, 0.0), and the second row has a significant amount of it (0.7, 0.7, 0.7, 1.0).

Specular Reflection

Specular reflection from an object produces highlights. Unlike ambient and diffuse reflection, the amount of specular reflection seen by a viewer does depend on the location of the viewpoint—it's brightest along the direct angle of reflection. To see this, imagine looking at a metallic ball outdoors in the sunlight. As you move your head, the highlight created by the sunlight moves with you to some extent. However, if you move your head too much, you lose the highlight entirely.

OpenGL allows you to set the RGBA color of a specular highlight (with GL_SPECULAR) and to control the size and brightness of the highlight (with GL_SHININESS). You can assign a number in the range of [0.0, 128.0] to GL_SHININESS—the higher the value, the smaller and brighter (more focused) the highlight. See "The Mathematics of Lighting" on page 188 for the details of how specular highlights are calculated.

In Plate 16, the spheres in the first column have no specular reflection. In the second column, GL_SPECULAR and GL_SHININESS are assigned values as follows:

```
GLfloat mat_specular[] = { 1.0, 1.0, 1.0, 1.0 };
GLfloat low_shininess[] = { 5.0 };
glMaterialfv(GL_FRONT, GL_SPECULAR, mat_specular);
glMaterialfv(GL_FRONT, GL_SHININESS, low_shininess);
```

In the third column, the GL_SHININESS parameter is increased to 100.0.

Emission

By specifying an RGBA color for GL_EMISSION, you can make an object appear to be giving off light of that color. Since most real-world objects (except lights) don't emit light, you'll probably use this feature mostly to simulate lamps and other light sources in a scene. In Plate 16, the spheres in the fourth column have a greenish value for GL_EMISSION:

```
GLfloat mat_emission[] = {0.3, 0.2, 0.2, 0.0};
glMaterialfv(GL_FRONT, GL_EMISSION, mat_emission);
```

Notice that the spheres appear to be slightly glowing; however, they're not actually acting as light sources. You would need to create a light source and position it at the same location as the sphere to create that effect.

Changing Material Properties

Listing 6-1 uses the same material properties for all vertices of the only object in the scene (the sphere). In other situations, you might want to assign different material properties for different vertices on the same object. More likely, you have more than one object in the scene, and each object has different material properties. For example, the code that produced Plate 16 has to draw eight different objects (all spheres), each with different material properties. Listing 6-3 shows some of the code in the **display()** routine.

Listing 6-3   Using Different Material Properties: material.c

```
GLfloat no_mat[] = { 0.0, 0.0, 0.0, 1.0 };
GLfloat mat_ambient[] = { 0.7, 0.7, 0.7, 1.0 };
GLfloat mat_ambient_color[] = { 0.8, 0.8, 0.2, 1.0 };
GLfloat mat_diffuse[] = { 0.1, 0.5, 0.8, 1.0 };
GLfloat mat_specular[] = { 1.0, 1.0, 1.0, 1.0 };
GLfloat no_shininess[] = { 0.0 };
GLfloat low_shininess[] = { 5.0 };
GLfloat high_shininess[] = { 100.0 };
GLfloat mat_emission[] = {0.3, 0.2, 0.2, 0.0};

glClear(GL_COLOR_BUFFER_BIT | GL_DEPTH_BUFFER_BIT);

/* draw sphere in first row, first column
 * diffuse reflection only; no ambient or specular
 */
glPushMatrix();
    glTranslatef (-3.75, 3.0, 0.0);
    glMaterialfv(GL_FRONT, GL_AMBIENT, no_mat);
    glMaterialfv(GL_FRONT, GL_DIFFUSE, mat_diffuse);
    glMaterialfv(GL_FRONT, GL_SPECULAR, no_mat);
    glMaterialfv(GL_FRONT, GL_SHININESS, no_shininess);
    glMaterialfv(GL_FRONT, GL_EMISSION, no_mat);
    auxSolidSphere();
glPopMatrix();

/* draw sphere in first row, second column
 * diffuse and specular reflection; low shininess; no ambient
 */
glPushMatrix();
    glTranslatef (-1.25, 3.0, 0.0);
    glMaterialfv(GL_FRONT, GL_AMBIENT, no_mat);
    glMaterialfv(GL_FRONT, GL_DIFFUSE, mat_diffuse);
    glMaterialfv(GL_FRONT, GL_SPECULAR, mat_specular);
    glMaterialfv(GL_FRONT, GL_SHININESS, low_shininess);
```

```
        glMaterialfv(GL_FRONT, GL_EMISSION, no_mat);
        auxSolidSphere();
    glPopMatrix();

    /* draw sphere in first row, third column
     * diffuse and specular reflection; high shininess; no ambient
     */
    glPushMatrix();
        glTranslatef (1.25, 3.0, 0.0);
        glMaterialfv(GL_FRONT, GL_AMBIENT, no_mat);
        glMaterialfv(GL_FRONT, GL_DIFFUSE, mat_diffuse);
        glMaterialfv(GL_FRONT, GL_SPECULAR, mat_specular);
        glMaterialfv(GL_FRONT, GL_SHININESS, high_shininess);
        glMaterialfv(GL_FRONT, GL_EMISSION, no_mat);
        auxSolidSphere();
    glPopMatrix();

    /* draw sphere in first row, fourth column
     * diffuse refl.; emission; no ambient or specular reflection
     */
    glPushMatrix();
        glTranslatef (3.75, 3.0, 0.0);
        glMaterialfv(GL_FRONT, GL_AMBIENT, no_mat);
        glMaterialfv(GL_FRONT, GL_DIFFUSE, mat_diffuse);
        glMaterialfv(GL_FRONT, GL_SPECULAR, no_mat);
        glMaterialfv(GL_FRONT, GL_SHININESS, no_shininess);
        glMaterialfv(GL_FRONT, GL_EMISSION, mat_emission);
        auxSolidSphere();
    glPopMatrix();
```

As you can see, **glMaterialfv()** is called repeatedly to set the desired material property for each sphere. Note that it's called only to change a property that needs to be changed. The second and third spheres use the same ambient and diffuse properties as the first sphere, for example, so these properties aren't reset. Since **glMaterial*()** has a performance cost associated with its use, it's best to minimize material-property changes.

Another technique for minimizing performance costs associated with changing material properties is to use **glColorMaterial()**.

---

void **glColorMaterial**(GLenum *face*, GLenum *mode*);

Causes the material property (or properties) specified by *mode* of the specified material face (or faces) specified by *face* to track the value of the current color at all times. A change to the current color (using **glColor***()) immediately updates the specified material properties. The *face* parameter can be GL_FRONT, GL_BACK, or GL_FRONT_AND_BACK (the default). The *mode* parameter can be GL_AMBIENT, GL_DIFFUSE, GL_AMBIENT_AND_DIFFUSE (the default), GL_SPECULAR, or GL_EMISSION.

Note that **glColorMaterial**() specifies two independent values: the first specifies which face or faces are updated, and the second specifies which material property or properties of those faces are updated. OpenGL does *not* maintain separate *mode* variables for each face.

After calling **glColorMaterial**(), you need to call **glEnable**() with GL_COLOR_MATERIAL as the parameter. Then, you can change the current color using **glColor***() (or other material properties, using **glMaterial***()) as needed as you draw:

```
glColorMaterial(GL_FRONT, GL_DIFFUSE);
glEnable(GL_COLOR_MATERIAL);
glColor3f(0.2, 0.5, 0.8);
/* draw some objects here */
glColor3f(0.9, 0.0, 0.2);
/* draw other objects here */
glDisable(GL_COLOR_MATERIAL);
```

You should use **glColorMaterial**() whenever you need to change a single material parameter for most vertices in your scene. If you need to change more than one material parameter, as was the case for Plate 16, use **glMaterial***(). When you don't need the capabilities of **glColorMaterial**() anymore, be sure to disable it, so that you don't get undesired material properties and so that you don't incur the performance cost associated with it. The performance value in using **glColorMaterial**() varies, depending on your OpenGL implementation. Some implementations may be able to optimize the vertex routines so that they can quickly update material properties based on the current color.

Listing 6-4 shows an interactive program that uses **glColorMaterial**() to change material parameters. Pressing each of the three mouse buttons changes the color of the diffuse reflection.

Listing 6-4   Using glColorMaterial(): colormat.c

```
#include <GL/gl.h>
#include <GL/glu.h>
#include "aux.h"

GLfloat diffuseMaterial[4] = { 0.5, 0.5, 0.5, 1.0 };

void myinit(void)
{
    GLfloat mat_specular[] = { 1.0, 1.0, 1.0, 1.0 };
    GLfloat light_position[] = { 1.0, 1.0, 1.0, 0.0 };

    glMaterialfv(GL_FRONT, GL_DIFFUSE, diffuseMaterial);
    glMaterialfv(GL_FRONT, GL_SPECULAR, mat_specular);
    glMaterialf(GL_FRONT, GL_SHININESS, 25.0);
    glLightfv(GL_LIGHT0, GL_POSITION, light_position);

    glEnable(GL_LIGHTING);
    glEnable(GL_LIGHT0);
    glDepthFunc(GL_LEQUAL);
    glEnable(GL_DEPTH_TEST);

    glColorMaterial(GL_FRONT, GL_DIFFUSE);
    glEnable(GL_COLOR_MATERIAL);
}

void changeRedDiffuse (AUX_EVENTREC *event)
{
    diffuseMaterial[0] += 0.1;
    if (diffuseMaterial[0] > 1.0)
        diffuseMaterial[0] = 0.0;
    glColor4fv(diffuseMaterial);
}

void changeGreenDiffuse (AUX_EVENTREC *event)
{
    diffuseMaterial[1] += 0.1;
    if (diffuseMaterial[1] > 1.0)
        diffuseMaterial[1] = 0.0;
    glColor4fv(diffuseMaterial);
}
```

```
void changeBlueDiffuse (AUX_EVENTREC *event)
{
    diffuseMaterial[2] += 0.1;
    if (diffuseMaterial[2] > 1.0)
        diffuseMaterial[2] = 0.0;
    glColor4fv(diffuseMaterial);
}

void display(void)
{
    glClear(GL_COLOR_BUFFER_BIT | GL_DEPTH_BUFFER_BIT);
    auxSolidSphere(1.0);
    glFlush();
}

void myReshape(GLsizei w, GLsizei h)
{
    glViewport(0, 0, w, h);
    glMatrixMode(GL_PROJECTION);
    glLoadIdentity();
    if (w <= h)
        glOrtho (-1.5, 1.5, -1.5*(GLfloat)h/(GLfloat)w,
            1.5*(GLfloat)h/(GLfloat)w, -10.0, 10.0);
    else
        glOrtho (-1.5*(GLfloat)w/(GLfloat)h,
            1.5*(GLfloat)w/(GLfloat)h, -1.5, 1.5, -10.0, 10.0);
    glMatrixMode(GL_MODELVIEW);
    glLoadIdentity();
}

int main(int argc, char** argv)
{
    auxInitDisplayMode (AUX_SINGLE | AUX_RGBA | AUX_DEPTH);
    auxInitPosition (0, 0, 500, 500);
    auxInitWindow (argv[0]);
    myinit();
    auxMouseFunc(AUX_LEFTBUTTON, AUX_MOUSEDOWN,
        changeRedDiffuse);
    auxMouseFunc(AUX_MIDDLEBUTTON, AUX_MOUSEDOWN,
        changeGreenDiffuse);
    auxMouseFunc(AUX_RIGHTBUTTON, AUX_MOUSEDOWN,
        changeBlueDiffuse);
    auxReshapeFunc(myReshape);
    auxMainLoop(display);
}
```

Try This

Modify Listing 6-3:

- Change the global ambient light in the scene. Hint: Alter the value of the GL_LIGHT_MODEL_AMBIENT parameter.

- Change the diffuse, ambient, and specular reflection parameters, the shininess exponent, and the emission color. Hint: Use the **glMaterial*()** command, but avoid making excessive calls.

- Use two-sided materials and add an arbitrary clipping plane (see "Additional Clipping Planes" on page 106) so you can see the inside and outside of a row or column of spheres. Hint: Turn on two-sided lighting with GL_LIGHT_MODEL_TWO_SIDE, set the desired material properties, and add a clipping plane.

- Remove all the **glMaterialfv()** calls, and use the more efficient **glColorMaterial()** calls to achieve the same lighting.

The Mathematics of Lighting

This section presents the equations used by OpenGL to perform lighting calculations to determine colors when in RGBA mode. (You can find the corresponding calculations for color-index mode in "The Mathematics of Color-Index Mode Lighting" on page 194.) You don't need to read this section if you're willing to experiment to obtain the lighting conditions you want. Even after reading this section, you'll probably have to experiment, but you'll have a better idea of how the values of parameters affect a vertex's color. Remember that if lighting is not enabled, the color of a vertex is simply the current color; if it is enabled, the lighting computations described here are carried out in eye coordinates.

In the following equations, mathematical operations are performed separately on the R, G, and B components. Thus, for example, when three terms are shown as added together, the R values, the G values, and the B values for each term are separately added to form the final RGB color $(R_1+R_2+R_3, G_1+G_2+G_3, B_1+B_2+B_3)$. When three terms are multiplied, the calculation is $(R_1R_2R_3, G_1G_2G_3, B_1B_2B_3)$. (Remember that the final A or alpha component at a vertex is equal to the material's diffuse alpha value at that vertex.)

The color produced by lighting a vertex is computed as follows:

vertex color = the material emission at that vertex +

the global ambient light scaled by the material's ambient property at that vertex +

the ambient, diffuse, and specular contributions from all the light sources, properly attenuated

After lighting calculations are performed, the color values are clamped (in RGBA mode) to the range [0,1].

Note that OpenGL's lighting calculations don't take into account the possibility of one object blocking light from another, so shadows aren't automatically created. (See "Shadows" on page 401 for a technique to create shadows.) Also keep in mind that with OpenGL, illuminated objects don't radiate light onto other objects.

Material Emission

The material emission term is the simplest. It's the RGB value assigned to the GL_EMISSION parameter.

Scaled Global Ambient Light

The second term is computed by multiplying the global ambient light (as defined by the GL_LIGHT_MODEL_AMBIENT parameter) by the material's ambient property (GL_AMBIENT's values as assigned with **glMaterial*()**):

$$ambient_{light\ model} * ambient_{material}$$

Each of the R, G, and B values for these two parameters are multiplied separately to compute the final RGB value for this term: (R_1R_2, G_1G_2, B_1B_2).

Contributions from Light Sources

Each light source may contribute to a vertex's color, and these contributions are added together. The equation for computing each light source's contribution is as follows:

contribution = attenuation factor * spotlight effect *

(ambient term + diffuse term + specular term)

Attenuation Factor

The *attenuation factor* was described in "Position and Attenuation" on page 168:

$$\text{attenuation factor} = \frac{1}{k_c + k_l d + k_q d^2}$$

where

d = distance between the light's position and the vertex

k_c = GL_CONSTANT_ATTENUATION

k_l = GL_LINEAR_ATTENUATION

k_q = GL_QUADRATIC_ATTENUATION

If the light is a directional one, the attenuation factor is 1.

Spotlight Effect

The *spotlight effect* evaluates to one of three possible values, depending on whether the light is actually a spotlight and whether the vertex lies inside or outside the cone of illumination produced by the spotlight:

- 1 if the light isn't a spotlight (GL_SPOT_CUTOFF is 180.0).

- 0 if the light is a spotlight but the vertex lies outside the cone of illumination produced by the spotlight.

- $(\max\{\mathbf{v} \cdot \mathbf{d}, 0\})^{\text{GL\_SPOT\_EXPONENT}}$ where:

  $\mathbf{v} = (v_x, v_y, v_z)$ is the unit vector that points from the spotlight (GL_POSITION) to the vertex.

  $\mathbf{d} = (d_x, d_y, d_z)$ is the spotlight's direction (GL_SPOT_DIRECTION), assuming the light is a spotlight and the vertex lies inside the cone of illumination produced by the spotlight.

  The dot product of the two vectors $\mathbf{v}$ and $\mathbf{d}$ varies as the cosine of the angle between them; hence, objects directly in line get maximum illumination, and objects off the axis have their illumination drop as the cosine of the angle.

To determine whether a particular vertex lies within the cone of illumination, OpenGL evaluates (max { $\mathbf{v} \cdot \mathbf{d}$, 0 }) where $\mathbf{v}$ and $\mathbf{d}$ are as defined above. If this value is less than the cosine of the spotlight's cutoff angle (GL_SPOT_CUTOFF), then the vertex lies outside the cone; otherwise, it's inside the cone.

Ambient Term

The ambient term is simply the ambient color of the light scaled by the ambient material property:

$ambient_{light}$ *$ambient_{material}$

Diffuse Term

The diffuse term needs to take into account whether light falls directly on the vertex, the diffuse color of the light, and the diffuse material property:

(max { $\mathbf{l} \cdot \mathbf{n}$, 0 }) * $diffuse_{light}$ * $diffuse_{material}$ where:

$\mathbf{l} = (l_x, l_y, l_z)$ is the unit vector that points from the vertex to the light position (GL_POSITION).

$\mathbf{n} = (n_x, n_y, n_z)$ is the unit normal vector at the vertex.

Specular Term

The specular term also depends on whether light falls directly on the vertex. If $\mathbf{l} \cdot \mathbf{n}$ is less than or equal to zero, there is no specular component at the vertex. (If it's less than zero, the light is on the wrong side of the surface.) If there's a specular component, it depends on the following:

- The unit normal vector at the vertex (n_x, n_y, n_z).

- The sum of the two unit vectors that point between (1) the vertex and the light position and (2) the vertex and the viewpoint (assuming that GL_LIGHT_MODEL_LOCAL_VIEWER is true; if it's not true, the vector (0, 0, 1) is used as the second vector in the sum). This vector sum is normalized (by dividing each component by the magnitude of the vector) to yield $\mathbf{s} = (s_x, s_y, s_z)$.

- The specular exponent (GL_SHININESS).

- The specular color of the light (GL_SPECULAR$_{light}$).

- The specular property of the material (GL_SPECULAR$_{material}$).

Using these definitions, here's how OpenGL calculates the specular term:

$(\max \{ \mathbf{s} \cdot \mathbf{n} , 0 \})^{\text{shininess}} *$ specular$_{\text{light}}$ * specular$_{\text{material}}$

However, if $\mathbf{l} \cdot \mathbf{n} = 0$, the specular term is 0.

Putting It All Together

Using the definitions of terms described in the preceding paragraphs, the following represents the entire lighting calculation in RGBA mode.

vertex color = emission$_{\text{material}}$ +

ambient$_{\text{light model}}$ * ambient$_{\text{material}}$ +

$$\sum_{i=0}^{n-1} \left(\frac{1}{k_c + k_1 d + k_q d^2} \right)_i \text{ (spotlight effect)}_i$$

[ambient$_{\text{light}}$ *ambient$_{\text{material}}$ +

$(\max \{ \mathbf{l} \cdot \mathbf{n} , 0 \}) *$ diffuse$_{\text{light}}$ * diffuse$_{\text{material}}$ +

$(\max \{ \mathbf{s} \cdot \mathbf{n} , 0 \})^{\text{shininess}} *$ specular$_{\text{light}}$ * specular$_{\text{material}}$]$_i$

Lighting in Color-Index Mode

In color-index mode, the parameters comprising RGBA values either have no effect or have a special interpretation. Since it's much harder to achieve certain effects in color-index mode, you should use RGBA whenever possible. In fact, the only light-source, lighting-model, or material parameters in an RGBA form that are used in color index mode are the light-source parameters GL_DIFFUSE and GL_SPECULAR and the material parameter GL_SHININESS. These parameters (d_l and s_l, respectively) are used to compute color-index diffuse and specular light intensities (d_{ci} and s_{ci}) as follows:

$d_{ci} = 0.30 \text{ R}(d_l) + 0.59 \text{ G}(d_l) + 0.11 \text{ B}(d_l)$

$s_{ci} = 0.3 \text{ R}(s_l) + 0.59 \text{ G}(s_l) + 0.11 \text{ B}(s_l)$

where R(x), G(x), and B(x) refer to the red, green, and blue components, respectively, of color x. The weighting values 0.30, 0.59, and 0.11 reflect the "perceptual" weights that red, green, and blue have for your eye—your eye is most sensitive to green and least sensitive to blue.

To specify material colors in color-index mode, use **glMaterial*()** with the special parameter GL_COLOR_INDEXES, as follows:

```
GLfloat mat_colormap[] = { 16.0, 47.0, 79.0 };
glMaterialfv(GL_FRONT, GL_COLOR_INDEXES, mat_colormap);
```

The three numbers supplied for GL_COLOR_INDEXES specify the color indices for the ambient, diffuse, and specular material colors, respectively. In other words, OpenGL regards the color associated with the first index (16.0 in this example) as the pure ambient color, with the second index (47.0) as the pure diffuse color, and with the third index (79.0) as the pure specular color. (By default, the ambient color index is 0.0, and the diffuse and specular color indices are both 1.0. Note that **glColorMaterial()** has no effect on color-index lighting.)

As it draws a scene, OpenGL uses colors associated with indices in between these numbers to shade objects in the scene. Therefore, you must build a color ramp between the indicated indices (in this example, between indices 16 and 47, and then between 47 and and 79). Often, the color ramp is built smoothly, but you might want to use other formulations to achieve different effects. Here's an example of a smooth color ramp that starts with a black ambient color and goes through a magenta diffuse color to a white specular color:

```
for (i = 0; i < 32; i++) {
    auxSetOneColor (16 + i, 1.0 * (i/32.0), 0.0, 1.0 * (i/32.0));
    auxSetOneColor (48 + i, 1.0, 1.0 * (i/32.0), 1.0);
}
```

The auxiliary library command **auxSetOneColor()** takes four arguments. It associates the color index indicated by the first argument to the RGB triplet specified by the last three arguments. When $i = 0$, the color index 16 is assigned the RGB value (0.0, 0.0, 0.0), or black. The color ramp builds smoothly up to the diffuse material color at index 47 (when $i = 31$), which is assigned the pure magenta RGB value (1.0, 0.0, 1.0). The second loop builds the ramp between the magenta diffuse color and the white (1.0, 1.0, 1.0) specular color (index 79). Plate 15 shows the result of using this color ramp with a single lighted sphere.

The Mathematics of Color-Index Mode Lighting

As you might expect, since the allowable parameters are different for color-index mode than for RGBA mode, the calculations are different as well. Since there's no material emission and no ambient light, the only terms of interest from the RGBA equations are the diffuse and specular contributions from the light sources and the shininess. Even these need to be modified, however, as explained below.

Begin with the diffuse and specular terms from the RGBA equations. In the diffuse term, instead of $\text{diffuse}_{\text{light}} * \text{diffuse}_{\text{material}}$, substitute d_{ci} as defined in the previous section for color-index mode. Similarly, in the specular term, instead of $\text{specular}_{\text{light}} * \text{specular}_{\text{material}}$, use s_{ci} as defined in the previous section. (Calculate the attenuation, spotlight effect, and all other components of these terms as before.) Call these modified diffuse and specular terms d and s, respectively. Now let $s' = \min\{\, s, 1\,\}$, and then compute

$$c = a_m + d(1-s')(d_m - a_m) + s'(s_m - a_m)$$

where a_m, d_m, and s_m are the ambient, diffuse, and specular material indexes specified using GL_COLOR_INDEXES. The final color index is

$$c' = \min\{\, c, s_m\,\}$$

After lighting calculations are performed, the color-index values are converted to fixed-point (with an unspecified number of bits to the right of the binary point). Then the integer portion is masked (bitwise ANDed) with $2^n - 1$, where n is the number of bits in a color in the color-index buffer.

Chapter 7

Blending, Antialiasing, and Fog

Chapter Objectives

After reading this chapter, you'll be able to do the following:

- Blend colors to achieve such effects as making objects appear translucent

- Smooth jagged edges of lines and polygons with antialiasing

- Create scenes with realistic atmospheric effects

The preceding chapters have given you the basic information you need to create a computer-graphics scene; you've learned how to do the following:

- Draw geometric shapes

- Transform them so that they can be viewed from whatever perspective you wish

- Use display lists to maximize your program's efficiency

- Specify how the geometric shapes in your scene should be colored and shaded

- Add lights and indicate how they should affect the shapes in your scene

Now you're ready to get a little fancier. This chapter discusses three techniques that can add extra detail and polish to your scene. None of these techniques is hard to use—in fact, it's probably harder to explain them than to use them. Each of these techniques is described in its own major section:

- **"Blending"** tells you how to specify a blending function that combines color values from a source and a destination. The final effect is that parts of your scene appear translucent.

- **"Antialiasing"** explains this relatively subtle technique that alters colors so that the edges of points, lines, and polygons appear smooth rather than angular and jagged.

- **"Fog"** describes how to create the illusion of depth by computing the color values of an object based on distance from the viewpoint. Thus, objects that are far away appear to fade into the background, just as they do in real life.

Blending

You've already seen alpha values (alpha is the A in RGBA), but they've always been 1.0, and they haven't been discussed. Alpha values are specified with **glColor*()**, when using **glClearColor()** to specify a clearing color, and when specifying certain lighting parameters such as a material property or light-source intensity. As you learned in Chapter 5, the pixels on a monitor screen emit red, green, and blue light, which is controlled by the red, green, and blue color values. So how does an alpha value affect what gets drawn in a window on the screen? When blending is enabled, the alpha value is used to combine the color value of the fragment being processed with that of the pixel already stored in the framebuffer. Blending occurs after your scene has been rasterized and converted to fragments, but just before the final pixels are drawn in the framebuffer. Alpha values can also be used in the alpha test to accept or reject a fragment based on its alpha value. See Chapter 10 for more information about this process.

Without blending, each new fragment overwrites any existing color values in the framebuffer, as though the fragment is opaque. With blending, you can control how much of the existing color value should be combined with the new fragment's value. Thus, you can use alpha blending to create a translucent fragment, one that lets some of the previously stored color value "show through." Color blending lies at the heart of techniques such as transparency, digital compositing, and painting.

Note: Alpha values aren't specified in color-index mode. Thus, blending operations aren't performed in color-index mode

The most natural way for you to think of blending operations is to view the RGB components of a fragment as representing its color, and the alpha component as representing opacity. Thus, transparent or translucent surfaces have lower opacity than opaque ones. For example, if you're viewing an object through green glass, the color you see is partly green from the glass and partly the color of the object. The percentage varies depending on the transmission properties of the glass: If the glass transmits 80 percent of the light that strikes it (that is, has an opacity of 20 percent), the color you see is a combination of 20 percent glass color and 80 percent of the color of the object behind it. You can easily imagine situations with multiple translucent surfaces. If you look at an automobile, for instance, its interior has one piece of glass between it and your viewpoint; some objects behind the automobile are visible through two pieces of glass.

The Source and Destination Factors

During blending, color values of the incoming fragment (the *source*) are combined with the color values of the corresponding currently stored pixel (the *destination*) in a two-stage process. First, you specify how to compute source and destination factors. These factors are RGBA quadruplets that are multiplied by each component of the R, G, B, and A values in the source and destination, respectively. Then, the corresponding components in the two sets of RGBA quadruplets are added. To show this mathematically, let the source and destination blending factors be (S_r, S_g, S_b, S_a) and

(D_r, D_g, D_b, D_a), respectively, and the RGBA values of the source and destination be indicated with a subscript of s or d. Then, the final, blended RGBA values are given by

$$(R_sS_r+R_dD_r, G_sS_g+G_dD_g, B_sS_b+B_dD_b, A_sS_a+A_dD_a)$$

Each component of this quadruplet is eventually clamped to [0,1].

Now let's look at how the source and destination blending factors are generated. You use **glBlendFunc()** to supply two constants: one that specifies how the source factor should be computed, and one that indicates how the destination factor should be computed. Also, to have blending take effect, you need to enable it:

```
glEnable(GL_BLEND);
```

Use **glDisable()** with GL_BLEND to disable blending. Also, note that using the constants GL_ONE (source) and GL_ZERO (destination) gives the same results as when blending is disabled; these values are the default.

---

void **glBlendFunc**(GLenum *sfactor*, GLenum *dfactor*)

Controls how color values in the fragment being processed (the source) are combined with those already stored in the framebuffer (the destination). The argument *sfactor* indicates how to compute a source blending factor; *dfactor* indicates how to compute a destination blending factor. The possible values for these arguments are explained in Table 7-1. The blend factors are assumed to lie in the range [0,1]; after the color values in the source and destination are combined, they're clamped to the range [0,1].

Note: In Table 7-1, the RGBA values of the source and destination are indicated with the subscripts s and d, respectively. Also, division of an RGBA quadruplet by a scalar means dividing each component by that value. Similarly, subtraction of quadruplets means subtracting them componentwise. The Relevant Factor column indicates whether the corresponding constant can be used to specify the source or destination blend factor.

Constant	Relevant Factor	Computed Blend Factor
GL_ZERO	source or destination	$(0, 0, 0, 0)$
GL_ONE	source or destination	$(1, 1, 1, 1)$
GL_DST_COLOR	source	(R_d, G_d, B_d, A_d)
GL_SRC_COLOR	destination	(R_s, G_s, B_s, A_s)
GL_ONE_MINUS_DST_COLOR	source	$(1, 1, 1, 1)-(R_d, G_d, B_d, A_d)$
GL_ONE_MINUS_SRC_COLOR	destination	$(1, 1, 1, 1)-(R_s, G_s, B_s, A_s)$
GL_SRC_ALPHA	source or destination	(A_s, A_s, A_s, A_s)
GL_ONE_MINUS_SRC_ALPHA	source or destination	$(1, 1, 1, 1)-(A_s, A_s, A_s, A_s)$
GL_DST_ALPHA	source or destination	(A_d, A_d, A_d, A_d)
GL_ONE_MINUS_DST_ALPHA	source or destination	$(1, 1, 1, 1)-(A_d, A_d, A_d, A_d)$
GL_SRC_ALPHA_SATURATE	source	$(f, f, f, 1); f=\min(A_s, 1-A_d)$

Table 7-1 Source and Destination Blending Factors

Sample Uses of Blending

Not all of the combinations of source and destination factors make sense. The majority of applications use a small number of combinations. The following paragraphs describe typical uses for particular combinations of the source and destination factors. Some of these examples use only the incoming alpha value, so they work even when alpha values aren't stored in the framebuffer. Also, note that often there's more than one way to achieve some of these effects.

1. One way to draw a picture composed half of one image and half of another, equally blended, is to set the source factor to GL_ONE, draw the first image, then set the source and destination factors to GL_SRC_ALPHA, and draw the second image with alpha equal to 0.5. If

the picture is supposed to be blended with 0.75 of the first image and 0.25 of the second, draw the first image as before, and draw the second with an alpha of 0.25, but with GL_SRC_ALPHA (source) and GL_ONE_MINUS_SRC_ALPHA (destination). This pair of factors probably represents the most commonly used blending operation.

2. To blend three different images equally, set the destination factor to GL_ONE and the source factor to GL_SRC_ALPHA. Draw each of the images with an alpha equal to 0.3333333. With this technique, each image is only one-third of its original brightness, which is noticeable where the images don't overlap.

3. Suppose you're writing a paint program, and you want to have a brush that gradually adds color so that each brush stroke blends in a little more color with whatever is currently in the image (say 10 percent color with 90 percent image on each pass). To do this, draw the image of the brush with alpha of 10 percent and use GL_SRC_ALPHA (source) and GL_ONE_MINUS_SRC_ALPHA (destination). (Note that you can vary the alphas across the brush to make the brush add more of its color in the middle and less on the edges, for an antialiased brush shape. See "Antialiasing" on page 207.) Similarly, erasers can be implemented by setting the eraser color to the background color.

4. The blending functions that use the source or destination colors— GL_DST_COLOR or GL_ONE_MINUS_DST_COLOR for the source factor and GL_SRC_COLOR or GL_ONE_MINUS_SRC_COLOR for the destination factor—effectively allow you to modulate each color component individually. This operation is equivalent to applying a simple filter—for example, multiplying the red component by 80 percent, the green component by 40 percent, and the blue component by 72 percent would simulate viewing the scene through a photographic filter that blocks 20 percent of red light, 60 percent of green, and 28 percent of blue.

5. Suppose you want to draw a picture composed of three translucent surfaces, some obscuring others and all over a solid background. Assume the farthest surface transmits 80 percent of the color behind it, the next transmits 40 percent, and the closest transmits 90 percent. To compose this picture, draw the background first with the default source and destination factors, and then change the blending factors to GL_SRC_ALPHA (source) and GL_ONE_MINUS_SRC_ALPHA (destination). Next, draw the farthest surface with an alpha of 0.2, then the middle surface with an alpha of 0.6, and finally the closest surface with an alpha of 0.1.

6. If your system has alpha planes, you can render objects one at a time (including their alpha values), read them back, and then perform interesting matting or compositing operations with the fully rendered objects. See "Compositing 3D Rendered Images" by Tom Duff, SIGGRAPH 1985 Proceedings, p. 41-44, for examples of this technique. Note that objects used for picture composition can come from any source—they can be rendered using OpenGL commands, rendered using techniques such as ray-tracing or radiosity that are implemented in another graphics library, or obtained by scanning in existing images.

7. You can create the effect of a nonrectangular raster image by assigning different alpha values to individual fragments in the image. Assign an alpha of 0 to each "invisible" fragment, and an alpha of 1.0 to each opaque fragment. For example, you can draw a polygon in the shape of a tree and apply a texture map of foliage; the viewer can see through parts of the rectangular texture that aren't part of the tree if you've assigned them alpha values of 0. This method, sometimes called *billboarding*, is much faster than creating the tree out of three-dimensional polygons. An example of this technique is shown in Figure 7-1: The tree is a single rectangular polygon that can be rotated about the center of the trunk, as shown by the outlines, so that it's always facing the viewer. See "Modulating and Blending" on page 274 for more information about blending textures.

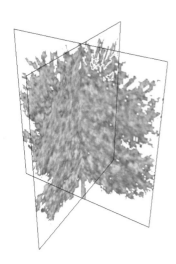

Figure 7-1   Creating a Nonrectangular Raster Image

A Blending Example

Listing 7-1 draws four overlapping colored rectangles—each with an alpha of 0.75—so that the lower left and upper right quadrants of the window are covered twice. In these two quadrants, the colors are blended in different orders using source and destination blending factors of GL_SRC_ALPHA and GL_ONE_MINUS_SRC_ALPHA: In the lower left quadrant, cyan is blended with the original yellow; in the upper right quadrant, yellow is blended with the original cyan. The other quadrants are drawn with unblended colors.

Listing 7-1   A Blending Example: alpha.c

```
#include <GL/gl.h>
#include <GL/glu.h>
#include "aux.h"

void myinit(void)
{
    glEnable(GL_BLEND);
    glBlendFunc(GL_SRC_ALPHA, GL_ONE_MINUS_SRC_ALPHA);
    glShadeModel(GL_FLAT);
    glClearColor(0.0, 0.0, 0.0, 0.0);
}

void display(void)
{
    glClear(GL_COLOR_BUFFER_BIT);

    glColor4f(1.0, 1.0, 0.0, 0.75);
    glRectf(0.0, 0.0, 0.5, 1.0);

    glColor4f(0.0, 1.0, 1.0, 0.75);
    glRectf(0.0, 0.0, 1.0, 0.5);

/* draw colored polygons in reverse order in upper right */
    glColor4f (0.0, 1.0, 1.0, 0.75);
    glRectf (0.5, 0.5, 1.0, 1.0);

    glColor4f (1.0, 1.0, 0.0, 0.75);
    glRectf (0.5, 0.5, 1.0, 1.0);

    glFlush();
}
```

```
void myReshape(GLsizei w, GLsizei h)
{
    glViewport(0, 0, w, h);
    glMatrixMode(GL_PROJECTION);
    glLoadIdentity();
    if (w <= h)
        gluOrtho2D (0.0, 1.0, 0.0, 1.0*(GLfloat)h/(GLfloat)w);
    else
        gluOrtho2D (0.0, 1.0*(GLfloat)w/(GLfloat)h, 0.0, 1.0);
    glMatrixMode(GL_MODELVIEW);
}


int main(int argc, char** argv)
{
    auxInitDisplayMode (AUX_SINGLE | AUX_RGBA);
    auxInitPosition (0, 0, 500, 500);
    auxInitWindow (argv[0]);
    myinit();
    auxReshapeFunc (myReshape);
    auxMainLoop(display);
}
```

As you probably expected, the order in which the rectangles are drawn affects the resulting colors. In the lower left quadrant, the cyan rectangle becomes the source fragment that's blended with the yellow rectangle, which is already in the framebuffer and thus is the destination. In the upper right quadrant, the yellow rectangle is the source and the cyan one the destination. Because the alpha values are all 0.75, the actual blending factors become 0.75 for the source and 1.0 − 0.75 = 0.25 for the destination. In other words, the source rectangle is somewhat translucent, but it has more effect on the final color than the destination rectangle. As a result, the lower left quadrant is light cyan, and the upper left one is light yellow. If you do the arithmetic, you'll find that the lower left RGB color is (0.25, 1.0, 0.75) and the upper right color is (0.75, 1.0, 0.25).

Three-Dimensional Blending with the Depth Buffer

As you saw in the previous example, the order in which polygons are drawn greatly affects the blended result. When drawing three-dimensional translucent objects, you can get different appearances depending on whether you draw the polygons from back to front or from front to back. You also need to consider the effect of the depth buffer when determining the correct order. The depth buffer (sometimes called the z-buffer) is usually used for hidden-surface elimination. (See Chapter 10 for a detailed discussion of the depth buffer.) It keeps track of the distance between the viewpoint and the portion of the object occupying a given pixel in a window on the screen; when another candidate color arrives for that pixel, it's drawn only if its object is closer to the viewpoint, in which case its depth value is stored in the depth buffer. With this method, obscured (or hidden) portions of surfaces aren't necessarily drawn and therefore aren't used for blending.

Typically, you want to render both opaque and translucent objects in the same scene, and you want to use the depth buffer to perform hidden-surface removal for objects that lie behind the opaque objects. If an opaque object hides either a translucent object or another opaque object, you want the depth buffer to eliminate the more distant object. If the translucent object is closer, however, you want to blend it with the opaque object. You can generally figure out the correct order to draw the polygons if everything in the scene is stationary, but the problem can easily become too hard if either the viewpoint or the object is moving.

The solution is to enable depth-buffering but make the depth buffer read-only while drawing the translucent objects. First you draw all the opaque objects, with the depth buffer in normal operation. Then, you preserve these depth values by making the depth buffer read-only. When the translucent objects are drawn, their depth values are still compared to the values established by the opaque objects, so they aren't drawn if they're behind the opaque ones. If they're closer to the viewpoint, however, they don't eliminate the opaque objects, since the depth-buffer values can't change. Instead, they're blended with the opaque objects. To control whether the depth buffer is writable, use **glDepthMask()**; if you pass GL_FALSE as the argument, the buffer becomes read-only, whereas GL_TRUE restores the normal, writable operation.

Listing 7-2 demonstrates how to use this method to draw opaque and translucent three-dimensional objects. In the program, pressing the left mouse button calls **toggleviewpoint()**, which changes the viewpoint position, and thus the ordering of an opaque torus and a translucent cylinder. Keep in mind that this solution is exact only when no pixel in the framebuffer is drawn more than once by a transparent object. If transparent objects overlap, resulting in multiple blended renderings to individual pixels, this solution is only a useful approximation to the correct (sorted) result.

Listing 7-2   Three-Dimensional Blending: alpha3D.c

```c
#include <GL/gl.h>
#include <GL/glu.h>
#include "aux.h"

void myinit(void)
{
    GLfloat mat_ambient[] = { 0.0, 0.0, 0.0, 0.15 };
    GLfloat mat_specular[] = { 1.0, 1.0, 1.0, 0.15 };
    GLfloat mat_shininess[] = { 15.0 };

    glMaterialfv(GL_FRONT, GL_AMBIENT, mat_ambient);
    glMaterialfv(GL_FRONT, GL_SPECULAR, mat_specular);
    glMaterialfv(GL_FRONT, GL_SHININESS, mat_shininess);

    glEnable(GL_LIGHTING);
    glEnable(GL_LIGHT0);
    glDepthFunc(GL_LEQUAL);
    glEnable(GL_DEPTH_TEST);
}

GLboolean eyePosition = GL_FALSE;

void toggleEye(AUX_EVENTREC *event)
{
    if (eyePosition)
        eyePosition = GL_FALSE;
    else
        eyePosition = GL_TRUE;
}

void display(void)
{
    GLfloat position[] = { 0.0, 0.0, 1.0, 1.0 };
    GLfloat mat_torus[] = { 0.75, 0.75, 0.0, 1.0 };
    GLfloat mat_cylinder[] = { 0.0, 0.75, 0.75, 0.15 };

    glClear(GL_COLOR_BUFFER_BIT | GL_DEPTH_BUFFER_BIT);
    glLightfv(GL_LIGHT0, GL_POSITION, position);
    glPushMatrix();
        if (eyePosition)
            gluLookAt(0.0, 0.0, 9.0, 0.0, 0.0, 0.0, 0.0,
                      1.0, 0.0);
        else
            gluLookAt(0.0, 0.0, -9.0, 0.0, 0.0, 0.0, 0.0,
                      1.0, 0.0);
```

```
        glPushMatrix();
            glTranslatef(0.0, 0.0, 1.0);
            glMaterialfv(GL_FRONT, GL_DIFFUSE, mat_torus);
            auxSolidTorus(0.275, 0.85);
        glPopMatrix();

        glEnable(GL_BLEND);
        glDepthMask(GL_FALSE);
        glBlendFunc(GL_SRC_ALPHA, GL_ONE);
        glMaterialfv(GL_FRONT, GL_DIFFUSE, mat_cylinder);
        glTranslatef(0.0, 0.0, -1.0);
        auxSolidCylinder(1.0, 2.0);
        glDepthMask(GL_TRUE);
        glDisable(GL_BLEND);
    glPopMatrix();

    glFlush();
}

void myReshape(GLsizei w, GLsizei h)
{
    glViewport(0, 0, w, h);
    glMatrixMode(GL_PROJECTION);
    glLoadIdentity();
    gluPerspective(30.0, (GLfloat) w/(GLfloat) h, 1.0, 20.0);
    glMatrixMode(GL_MODELVIEW);
    glLoadIdentity();
}


int main(int argc, char** argv)
{
    auxInitDisplayMode(AUX_SINGLE | AUX_RGBA | AUX_DEPTH);
    auxInitPosition(0, 0, 500, 500);
    auxInitWindow(argv[0]);
    auxMouseFunc(AUX_LEFTBUTTON, AUX_MOUSEDOWN, toggleEye);
    myinit();
    auxReshapeFunc(myReshape);
    auxMainLoop(display);
}
```

Antialiasing

You might have noticed in some of your OpenGL pictures that lines, especially nearly horizontal or nearly vertical ones, appear jagged. These jaggies appear because the ideal line is approximated by a series of pixels that must lie on the pixel grid. The jaggedness is called *aliasing*, and this section describes *antialiasing* techniques to reduce it. Figure 7-2 shows two intersecting lines, both aliased and antialiased. The pictures have been magnified to show the effect

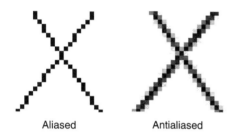

Aliased   Antialiased

Figure 7-2   Aliased and Antialiased Lines

Figure 7-3 shows how a diagonal line one pixel wide covers more of some pixel squares than others. In fact, when performing antialiasing, OpenGL calculates a *coverage* value for each fragment based on the fraction of the pixel square on the screen that it would cover. The figure shows these coverage values for the line. In RGBA mode, OpenGL multiplies the fragment's alpha value by its coverage. You can then use the resulting alpha value to blend the fragment with the corresponding pixel already in the framebuffer. In color-index mode, OpenGL sets the least significant 4 bits of the color index based on the fragment's coverage (0000 for no coverage and 1111 for complete coverage). It's up to you to load your color map and apply it appropriately to take advantage of this coverage information.

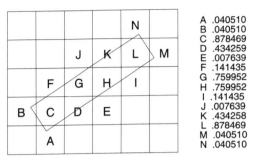

Figure 7-3   Determining Coverage Values

The details of calculating coverage values are complex, difficult to specify in general, and in fact may vary slightly depending on your particular implementation of OpenGL. You can use the **glHint()** command to exercise some control over the trade-off between image quality and speed, but not all implementations will take the hint.

---

void **glHint**(GLenum *target*, GLenum *hint*);

Controls certain aspects of OpenGL behavior. The *target* parameter indicates which behavior is to be controlled; its possible values are shown in Table 7-2. The *hint* parameter can be GL_FASTEST to indicate that the most efficient option should be chosen, GL_NICEST to indicate the highest-quality option, or GL_DONT_CARE to indicate no preference. The interpretation of hints is implementation-dependent; an implementation can ignore them entirely.

For more information about the relevant topics, see "Antialiasing" on page 207 for the details on sampling and "Fog" on page 216 for details on fog. The GL_PERSPECTIVE_CORRECTION_HINT parameter refers to how color values and texture coordinates are interpolated across a primitive: either linearly in screen space (a relatively simple calculation) or in a perspective-correct manner (which requires more computation). Often, systems perform linear color interpolation because the results, while not technically correct, are visually acceptable; textures, however, in most cases require perspective-correct interpolation to be visually acceptable. Thus, an implementation can choose to use this parameter to control the method used for interpolation. Perspective projection is discussed in Chapter 3, color is discussed in Chapter 5, and texture mapping is discussed in Chapter 9.

Parameter	Meaning
GL_POINT_SMOOTH_HINT, GL_LINE_SMOOTH_HINT, GL_POLYGON_SMOOTH_HINT	Specify the desired sampling quality of points, lines, or polygons during antialiasing operations
GL_FOG_HINT	Specifies whether fog calculations are done per pixel (GL_NICEST) or per vertex (GL_FASTEST)
GL_PERSPECTIVE_CORRECTION_HINT	Specifies the desired quality of color and texture-coordinate interpolation

Table 7-2   Values for Use with glHint() and Their Meaning

Antialiasing Points or Lines

To antialias points or lines, you need to turn on antialiasing with
glEnable(), passing in GL_POINT_SMOOTH or GL_LINE_SMOOTH, as
appropriate. You might also want to provide a quality hint with **glHint()**.
(Remember that you can set the size of a point or the width of a line. You
can also stipple a line. See Chapter 2.) Next, follow the procedures
described in one of the following sections, depending on whether you're in
RGBA or color-index mode.

In RGBA Mode

In RGBA mode, you need to enable blending. The blending factors
you most likely want to use are GL_SRC_ALPHA (source) and
GL_ONE_MINUS_SRC_ALPHA (destination). Alternatively, you can
use GL_ONE for the destination factor to make lines a little brighter
where they intersect. Now you're ready to draw whatever points or lines
you want antialiased. The antialiased effect is most noticeable if you use a
fairly high alpha value. Remember that since you're performing blending,
you might need to consider the rendering order as described in "Three-
Dimensional Blending with the Depth Buffer" on page 203; in most cases,
however, the ordering can be ignored without significant adverse effects.
Listing 7-3 initializes the necessary modes for antialiasing and then draws a
wireframe icosahedron. Note that the depth buffer isn't enabled in this
example.

Listing 7-3   An Antialiased Wireframe Icosahedron: anti.c

```c
#include <GL/gl.h>
#include <GL/glu.h>
#include "aux.h"

void myinit(void)
{
    GLfloat values[2];
    glGetFloatv(GL_LINE_WIDTH_GRANULARITY, values);
    printf("GL_LINE_WIDTH_GRANULARITY value is %3.1f\n",
                values[0]);

    glGetFloatv(GL_LINE_WIDTH_RANGE, values);
    printf("GL_LINE_WIDTH_RANGE values are %3.1f %3.1f\n",
                values[0], values[1]);

    glEnable(GL_LINE_SMOOTH);
    glEnable(GL_BLEND);
    glBlendFunc(GL_SRC_ALPHA, GL_ONE_MINUS_SRC_ALPHA);
    glHint(GL_LINE_SMOOTH_HINT, GL_DONT_CARE);
    glLineWidth(1.5);

    glShadeModel(GL_FLAT);
    glClearColor(0.0, 0.0, 0.0, 0.0);
    glDepthFunc(GL_LEQUAL);
    glEnable(GL_DEPTH_TEST);
}

void display(void)
{
    glClear(GL_COLOR_BUFFER_BIT | GL_DEPTH_BUFFER_BIT);
    glColor4f(1.0, 1.0, 1.0, 1.0);
    auxWireIcosahedron(1.0);
    glFlush();
}

void myReshape(GLsizei w, GLsizei h)
{
    glViewport(0, 0, w, h);
    glMatrixMode(GL_PROJECTION);
    glLoadIdentity();
    gluPerspective(45.0, (GLfloat) w/(GLfloat) h, 3.0, 5.0);

    glMatrixMode(GL_MODELVIEW);
    glLoadIdentity();
    glTranslatef(0.0, 0.0, -4.0);
}
```

```
int main(int argc, char** argv)
{
    auxInitDisplayMode(AUX_SINGLE | AUX_RGBA | AUX_DEPTH);
    auxInitPosition(0, 0, 400, 400);
    auxInitWindow(argv[0]);
    myinit();
    auxReshapeFunc(myReshape);
    auxMainLoop(display);
}
```

In Color-Index Mode

The tricky part about antialiasing in color-index mode is loading and using
the color map. Since the last 4 bits of the color index indicate the coverage
value, you need to load sixteen contiguous indices with a color ramp from
the background color to the object's color. (The ramp has to start with an
index value that's a multiple of 16.) Then, you clear the color buffer to the
first of the sixteen colors in the ramp and draw your points or lines using
colors in the ramp. Listing 7-4 demonstrates how to construct the color
ramp to draw an antialiased wireframe icosahedron in color-index mode.
In this example, the color ramp starts at index 32 and contains shades of
gray.

Listing 7-4   Antialiasing in Color-Index Mode: antiindex.c

```
#include <GL/gl.h>
#include <GL/glu.h>
#include "aux.h"

#define RAMPSIZE 16
#define RAMPSTART 32

void myinit(void)
{
    int i;

    for (i = 0; i < RAMPSIZE; i++) {
        GLfloat shade;
        shade = (GLfloat) i/(GLfloat) RAMPSIZE;
        auxSetOneColor(RAMPSTART+(GLint)i, shade, shade, shade);
    }

    glEnable (GL_LINE_SMOOTH);
    glHint (GL_LINE_SMOOTH_HINT, GL_DONT_CARE);
    glLineWidth (1.5);
    glClearIndex ((GLfloat) RAMPSTART);
```

```
        glShadeModel(GL_FLAT);
        glDepthFunc(GL_LEQUAL);
        glEnable(GL_DEPTH_TEST);
}

void display(void)
{
        glClear(GL_COLOR_BUFFER_BIT | GL_DEPTH_BUFFER_BIT);
        glIndexi(RAMPSTART);
        auxWireIcosahedron(1.0);
        glFlush();
}

void myReshape(GLsizei w, GLsizei h)
{
        glViewport(0, 0, w, h);
        glMatrixMode(GL_PROJECTION);
        glLoadIdentity();
        gluPerspective (45.0, (GLfloat) w/(GLfloat) h, 3.0, 5.0);

        glMatrixMode(GL_MODELVIEW);
        glLoadIdentity ();
        glTranslatef (0.0, 0.0, -4.0);
}


int main(int argc, char** argv)
{
        auxInitDisplayMode (AUX_SINGLE | AUX_INDEX | AUX_DEPTH);
        auxInitPosition (0, 0, 400, 400);
        auxInitWindow (argv[0]);
        myinit();
        auxReshapeFunc (myReshape);
        auxMainLoop(display);
}
```

Since the color ramp goes from the background color to the object's color, the antialiased object looks correct only when it's drawn on top of the background. If the antialiased object is drawn on top of another object, places where the objects intersect will have the wrong colors, unless you've constructed your color ramps taking this into consideration. To get the best result, use the depth buffer to ensure that the pixel colors correspond to the "nearest" objects. In RGBA mode, however, the colors of both objects are blended, so the results look more natural. Thus, you typically don't use the depth buffer when rendering a scene consisting of antialiased points and lines.

The trick described in "Three-Dimensional Blending with the Depth Buffer" on page 203 can also be used to mix antialiased points and lines with aliased, depth-buffered polygons. To do this, draw the polygons first, then make the depth buffer read-only and draw the points and lines. The points and lines will intersect nicely with each other but will be obscured by nearer polygons.

■ Advanced

Try This

■ Try This

- Take a previous program, such as the robot arm or solar system program described in "Examples of Composing Several Transformations" on page 109, and draw wireframe objects with antialiasing. Try it with either RGBA or color-index mode. Also try different line widths or point sizes to see their effects.

Antialiasing Polygons

Antialiasing the edges of filled polygons is similar to antialiasing points and lines. When different polygons have overlapping edges, you need to blend the color values appropriately. You can either use the method described in this section, or you can use the accumulation buffer to perform antialiasing for your entire scene. Using the accumulation buffer, which is described in Chapter 10, is easier from your point of view, but it's much more computation-intensive and therefore slower. However, as you'll see, the method described here is rather cumbersome

Note: If you draw your polygons as points at the vertices or as outlines— that is, by passing GL_POINT or GL_LINE to **glPolygonMode()**— point or line antialiasing is applied, if enabled as described earlier. The rest of this section addresses polygon antialiasing when you're using GL_FILL as the polygon mode.

In theory, you can antialias polygons in either RGBA or color-index mode. However, object intersections affect polygon antialiasing more than they affect point or line antialiasing, so rendering order and blending accuracy become more critical. In fact, they're so critical that if you're antialiasing more than one polygon, you need to order the polygons from front to back and then use **glBlendFunc()** with GL_SRC_ALPHA_SATURATE for the source factor and GL_ONE for the destination factor. Thus, antialiasing polygons in color-index mode normally isn't practical.

To antialias polygons in RGBA mode, you use the alpha value to represent coverage values of polygon edges. You need to enable polygon antialiasing by passing GL_POLYGON_SMOOTH to **glEnable()**. This causes pixels on the edges of the polygon to be assigned fractional alpha values based on their coverage, as though they were lines being antialiased. Also, if you desire, you can supply a value for GL_POLYGON_SMOOTH_HINT.

Now you need to blend overlapping edges appropriately. First, turn off the depth buffer so that you have control over how overlapping pixels are drawn. Then set the blending factors to GL_SRC_ALPHA_SATURATE (source) and GL_ONE (destination). With this specialized blending function, the final color is the sum of the destination color and the scaled source color; the scale factor is the smaller of either the incoming source alpha value or one minus the destination alpha value. This means that for a pixel with a large alpha value, successive incoming pixels have little effect on the final color because one minus the destination alpha is almost zero. With this method, a pixel on the edge of a polygon might be blended eventually with the colors from another polygon that's drawn later. Finally, you need to sort all the polygons in your scene so that they're ordered from front to back before drawing them.

Listing 7-5 shows how to antialias filled polygons; clicking the left mouse button toggles the antialiasing on and off. Note that backward-facing polygons are culled and that the alpha values in the color buffer are cleared to zero before any drawing. (Your color buffer must store alpha values for this technique to work correctly.)

Listing 7-5   Antialiasing Filled Polygons: antipoly.c

```
#include <GL/gl.h>
#include <GL/glu.h>
#include "aux.h"

GLboolean polySmooth;

void myinit(void)
{
    GLfloat mat_ambient[] = { 0.0, 0.0, 0.0, 1.00 };
    GLfloat mat_specular[] = { 1.0, 1.0, 1.0, 1.00 };
    GLfloat mat_shininess[] = { 15.0 };

    glMaterialfv(GL_FRONT, GL_AMBIENT, mat_ambient);
    glMaterialfv(GL_FRONT, GL_SPECULAR, mat_specular);
    glMaterialfv(GL_FRONT, GL_SHININESS, mat_shininess);

    glEnable (GL_LIGHTING);
    glEnable (GL_LIGHT0);
    glEnable (GL_BLEND);
```

```
    glCullFace (GL_BACK);
    glEnable (GL_CULL_FACE);
    glEnable (GL_POLYGON_SMOOTH);
    polySmooth = GL_TRUE;

    glClearColor (0.0, 0.0, 0.0, 0.0);
}

void toggleSmooth (AUX_EVENTREC *event)
{
    if (polySmooth) {
        polySmooth = GL_FALSE;
        glDisable (GL_BLEND);
        glDisable (GL_POLYGON_SMOOTH);
        glEnable (GL_DEPTH_TEST);
    }
    else {
        polySmooth = GL_TRUE;
        glEnable (GL_BLEND);
        glEnable (GL_POLYGON_SMOOTH);
        glDisable (GL_DEPTH_TEST);
    }
}

void display(void)
{
    GLfloat position[] = { 0.0, 0.0, 1.0, 0.0 };
    GLfloat mat_cube1[] = { 0.75, 0.75, 0.0, 1.0 };
    GLfloat mat_cube2[] = { 0.0, 0.75, 0.75, 1.0 };

    if (polySmooth)
        glClear (GL_COLOR_BUFFER_BIT);
    else
        glClear (GL_COLOR_BUFFER_BIT | GL_DEPTH_BUFFER_BIT);

    glPushMatrix ();
        glTranslatef (0.0, 0.0, -8.0);
        glLightfv (GL_LIGHT0, GL_POSITION, position);

        glBlendFunc (GL_SRC_ALPHA_SATURATE, GL_ONE);

        glPushMatrix ();
            glRotatef (30.0, 1.0, 0.0, 0.0);
            glRotatef (60.0, 0.0, 1.0, 0.0);
            glMaterialfv(GL_FRONT, GL_DIFFUSE, mat_cube1);
            auxSolidCube (1.0, 1.0, 1.0);
        glPopMatrix ();
```

```
            glTranslatef (0.0, 0.0, -2.0);
            glMaterialfv(GL_FRONT, GL_DIFFUSE, mat_cube2);
            glRotatef (30.0, 0.0, 1.0, 0.0);
            glRotatef (60.0, 1.0, 0.0, 0.0);
            auxSolidCube (1.0);

        glPopMatrix ();

        glFlush ();
    }

    void myReshape(GLsizei w, GLsizei h)
    {
        glViewport(0, 0, w, h);
        glMatrixMode(GL_PROJECTION);
        glLoadIdentity();
        gluPerspective(30.0, (GLfloat) w/(GLfloat) h, 1.0, 20.0);
        glMatrixMode(GL_MODELVIEW);
    }


    int main(int argc, char** argv)
    {
        auxInitDisplayMode (AUX_SINGLE | AUX_RGBA | AUX_DEPTH);
        auxInitPosition (0, 0, 200, 200);
        auxInitWindow (argv[0]);
        auxMouseFunc (AUX_LEFTBUTTON, AUX_MOUSEDOWN, toggleSmooth);
        myinit();
        auxReshapeFunc (myReshape);
        auxMainLoop(display);
    }
```

Fog

Computer images sometimes seem unrealistically sharp and well-defined. Antialiasing makes an object appear more realistic by smoothing its edges. Additionally, you can make an entire image appear more natural by adding fog, which makes objects fade into the distance. *Fog* is a general term that describes similar forms of atmospheric effects; it can be used to simulate haze, mist, smoke, or pollution. Fog is essential in visual-simulation applications, where limited visibility needs to be approximated. It's often incorporated into flight-simulator displays.

When fog is enabled, objects that are farther from the viewpoint begin to fade into the fog color. You can control the density of the fog, which determines the rate at which objects fade as the distance increases, as well as the fog's color. Fog is available in both RGBA and color-index modes, although the calculations are slightly different in the two modes. Since fog is applied after matrix transformations, lighting, and texturing are performed, it affects transformed, lit, and textured objects. Note that with large simulation programs, fog can improve performance, since you can choose not to draw objects that are too fogged to be visible.

Using Fog

Using fog is easy. You enable it by passing GL_FOG to **glEnable()**, and you choose the color and the equation that controls the density with **glFog*()**. If you want, you can supply a value for GL_FOG_HINT with **glHint()**, as described on page 209. Listing 7-6 draws five red teapots, each at a different distance from the viewpoint. Pressing the left mouse button selects among the three different fog equations, which are described in the next section.

Listing 7-6   Five Fogged Teapots in RGBA Mode: fog.c

```
#include <GL/gl.h>
#include <GL/glu.h>
#include <math.h>
#include "aux.h"

GLint fogMode;

void cycleFog (AUX_EVENTREC *event)
{
    if (fogMode == GL_EXP) {
        fogMode = GL_EXP2;
        printf ("Fog mode is GL_EXP2\n");
    }
    else if (fogMode == GL_EXP2) {
        fogMode = GL_LINEAR;
        printf ("Fog mode is GL_LINEAR\n");
        glFogf (GL_FOG_START, 1.0);
        glFogf (GL_FOG_END, 5.0);
    }
    else if (fogMode == GL_LINEAR) {
        fogMode = GL_EXP;
        printf ("Fog mode is GL_EXP\n");
    }
```

```
        glFogi (GL_FOG_MODE, fogMode);
}

void myinit(void)
{
    GLfloat position[] = { 0.0, 3.0, 3.0, 0.0 };
    GLfloat local_view[] = { 0.0 };

    glEnable(GL_DEPTH_TEST);
    glDepthFunc(GL_LEQUAL);
    glLightfv(GL_LIGHT0, GL_POSITION, position);
    glLightModelfv(GL_LIGHT_MODEL_LOCAL_VIEWER, local_view);

    glFrontFace (GL_CW);
    glEnable(GL_LIGHTING);
    glEnable(GL_LIGHT0);
    glEnable(GL_AUTO_NORMAL);
    glEnable(GL_NORMALIZE);
    glEnable(GL_FOG);
    {
        GLfloat density;
        GLfloat fogColor[4] = {0.5, 0.5, 0.5, 1.0};

        fogMode = GL_EXP;
        glFogi (GL_FOG_MODE, fogMode);
        glFogfv (GL_FOG_COLOR, fogColor);
        glFogf (GL_FOG_DENSITY, 0.35);
        glHint (GL_FOG_HINT, GL_DONT_CARE);
        glClearColor(0.5, 0.5, 0.5, 1.0);
    }
}
void renderRedTeapot (GLfloat x, GLfloat y, GLfloat z)
{
    float mat[3];

    glPushMatrix();
    glTranslatef (x, y, z);
    mat[0] = 0.1745; mat[1] = 0.01175; mat[2] = 0.01175;
    glMaterialfv (GL_FRONT, GL_AMBIENT, mat);
    mat[0] = 0.61424; mat[1] = 0.04136; mat[2] = 0.04136;
    glMaterialfv (GL_FRONT, GL_DIFFUSE, mat);
    mat[0] = 0.727811; mat[1] = 0.626959; mat[2] = 0.626959;
    glMaterialfv (GL_FRONT, GL_SPECULAR, mat);
    glMaterialf (GL_FRONT, GL_SHININESS, 0.6*128.0);
    auxSolidTeapot(1.0);
    glPopMatrix();
}
```

```
void display(void)
{
    glClear(GL_COLOR_BUFFER_BIT | GL_DEPTH_BUFFER_BIT);
    renderRedTeapot (-4.0, -0.5, -1.0);
    renderRedTeapot (-2.0, -0.5, -2.0);
    renderRedTeapot (0.0, -0.5, -3.0);
    renderRedTeapot (2.0, -0.5, -4.0);
    renderRedTeapot (4.0, -0.5, -5.0);
    glFlush();
}

void myReshape(GLsizei w, GLsizei h)
{
    glViewport(0, 0, w, h);
    glMatrixMode(GL_PROJECTION);
    glLoadIdentity();
    if (w <= (h*3))
        glOrtho (-6.0, 6.0, -2.0*((GLfloat) h*3)/(GLfloat) w,
            2.0*((GLfloat) h*3)/(GLfloat) w, 0.0, 10.0);
    else
        glOrtho (-6.0*(GLfloat) w/((GLfloat) h*3),
            6.0*(GLfloat) w/((GLfloat) h*3), -2.0, 2.0, 0.0, 10.0);
    glMatrixMode(GL_MODELVIEW);
    glLoadIdentity ();
}


int main(int argc, char** argv)
{
    auxInitDisplayMode (AUX_SINGLE | AUX_RGBA | AUX_DEPTH);
    auxInitPosition (0, 0, 450, 150);
    auxInitWindow (argv[0]);
    auxMouseFunc (AUX_LEFTBUTTON, AUX_MOUSEDOWN, cycleFog);
    myinit();
    auxReshapeFunc (myReshape);
    auxMainLoop(display);
}
```

Fog Equations

Fog blends a fog color with an incoming fragment's color using a fog blending factor. This factor, f, is computed with one of these three equations and then clamped to the range [0,1].

$$f = e^{-(density \cdot z)} \qquad \text{(GL\_EXP)}$$

$$f = e^{-(density \cdot z)^2} \qquad \text{(GL\_EXP2)}$$

$$f = \frac{end - z}{end - start} \qquad \text{(GL\_LINEAR)}$$

where z is the eye-coordinate distance between the viewpoint and the fragment center. The values for *density*, *start*, and *end* are all specified with **glFog*()**. The f factor is used differently, depending on whether you're in RGBA mode or color-index mode, as explained in the next subsections.

void **glFog{if}{v}**(GLenum *pname*, *TYPE param*);

Sets the parameters and function for calculating fog. If *pname* is GL_FOG_MODE, then *param* is either GL_EXP (the default), GL_EXP2, or GL_LINEAR to select one of the three fog factors. If *pname* is GL_FOG_DENSITY, GL_FOG_START, or GL_FOG_END, then *param* is (or points to, with the vector version of the command) a value for *density*, *start*, or *end* in the equations. (The default values are 1, 0, and 1, respectively.) In RGBA mode, *pname* can be GL_FOG_COLOR, in which case *param* points to four values that specify the fog's RGBA color values. The corresponding value for *pname* in color-index mode is GL_FOG_INDEX, for which *param* is a single value specifying the fog's color index.

Figure 7-4 plots the fog-density equations for various values of the parameters. You can use linear fog to achieve a depth-cuing effect, as shown in Plate 2.

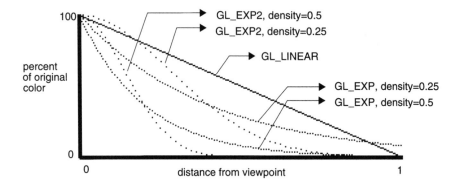

Figure 7-4 Fog-Density Equations

Fog in RGBA Mode

In RGBA mode, the fog factor f is used as follows to calculate the final fogged color:

$$C = f\,C_i + (1-f)\,C_f$$

where C_i represents the incoming fragment's RGBA values and C_f the fog-color values assigned with GL_FOG_COLOR.

Fog in Color-Index Mode

In color-index mode, the final fogged color index is computed as follows:

$$I = I_i + (1-f)\,I_f$$

where I_i is the incoming fragment's color index and I_f is the fog's color index as specified with GL_FOG_INDEX.

To use fog in color-index mode, you have to load appropriate values in a color ramp. The first color in the ramp is the color of the object without fog, and the last color in the ramp is the color of the completely fogged object. You probably want to use **glClearIndex()** to initialize the background color index so that it corresponds to the last color in the ramp; this way, totally fogged objects blend into the background. Similarly, before objects are drawn, you should call **glIndex*()** and pass in the index of the first color in the ramp (the unfogged color). Finally, to apply fog to different colored objects in the scene, you need to create several color ramps, and call **glIndex*()** before each object is drawn to set the current color index to the start of each color ramp. Listing 7-7 illustrates how to initialize appropriate conditions and then apply fog in color-index mode.

Listing 7-7   Using Fog in Color-Index Mode: fogindex.c

```
#include <GL/gl.h>
#include <GL/glu.h>
#include "aux.h"

#define NUMCOLORS 32
#define RAMPSTART 16

void myinit(void)
{
    int i;

    glEnable(GL_DEPTH_TEST);
    glDepthFunc(GL_LEQUAL);
    for (i = 0; i < NUMCOLORS; i++) {
        GLfloat shade;
        shade = (GLfloat) (NUMCOLORS-i)/(GLfloat) NUMCOLORS;
        auxSetOneColor (16 + i, shade, shade, shade);
    }
    glEnable(GL_FOG);

    glFogi (GL_FOG_MODE, GL_LINEAR);
    glFogi (GL_FOG_INDEX, NUMCOLORS);
    glFogf (GL_FOG_START, 0.0);
    glFogf (GL_FOG_END, 4.0);
    glHint (GL_FOG_HINT, GL_NICEST);
    glClearIndex((GLfloat) (NUMCOLORS+RAMPSTART-1));
}

void display(void)
{
    glClear(GL_COLOR_BUFFER_BIT | GL_DEPTH_BUFFER_BIT);
    glPushMatrix ();
        glTranslatef (-1.0, -1.0, -1.0);
        glRotatef (-90.0, 1.0, 0.0, 0.0);
        glIndexi (RAMPSTART);
        auxSolidCone(1.0, 2.0);
    glPopMatrix ();

    glPushMatrix ();
        glTranslatef (0.0, -1.0, -2.25);
        glRotatef (-90.0, 1.0, 0.0, 0.0);
        glIndexi (RAMPSTART);
```

```
            auxSolidCone(1.0, 2.0);
    glPopMatrix ();

    glPushMatrix ();
        glTranslatef (1.0, -1.0, -3.5);
        glRotatef (-90.0, 1.0, 0.0, 0.0);
        glIndexi (RAMPSTART);
        auxSolidCone(1.0, 2.0);
    glPopMatrix ();
    glFlush();
}

void myReshape(GLsizei w, GLsizei h)
{
    glViewport(0, 0, w, h);
    glMatrixMode(GL_PROJECTION);
    glLoadIdentity();
    if (w <= h)
        glOrtho (-2.0, 2.0, -2.0*(GLfloat)h/(GLfloat)w,
            2.0*(GLfloat)h/(GLfloat)w, 0.0, 10.0);
    else
        glOrtho (-2.0*(GLfloat)w/(GLfloat)h,
            2.0*(GLfloat)w/(GLfloat)h, -2.0, 2.0, 0.0, 10.0);
    glMatrixMode(GL_MODELVIEW);
    glLoadIdentity ();
}


int main(int argc, char** argv)
{
    auxInitDisplayMode (AUX_SINGLE | AUX_INDEX | AUX_DEPTH);
    auxInitPosition (0, 0, 200, 200);
    auxInitWindow (argv[0]);
    myinit();
    auxReshapeFunc (myReshape);
    auxMainLoop(display);
}
```

Chapter 8

Drawing Pixels, Bitmaps, Fonts, and Images

Chapter Objectives

After reading this chapter, you'll be able to do the following:

- Position and draw bitmapped data

- Read pixel data (bitmaps and images) from the framebuffer into processor memory and from memory into the framebuffer

- Copy pixel data from one buffer to another, or to another location in the same buffer

- Magnify or reduce an image as it's written to the framebuffer

- Control pixel-data formatting and perform other transformations as the data is moved to and from the framebuffer

So far, most of the discussion in this guide has concerned the rendering of geometric data—points, lines, and polygons. Two other important classes of data that can be rendered by OpenGL are the following:

- Bitmaps, typically used for characters in fonts

- Image data, which might have been scanned in or calculated

Both bitmaps and image data take the form of rectangular arrays of pixels. One difference between them is that a bitmap consists of a single bit of information about each pixel, and image data typically includes several pieces of data per pixel (the complete red, green, blue, and alpha color components, for example). Also, bitmaps are like masks in that they're used to overlay another image, but image data simply overwrites or is blended with whatever data might have existed previously.

This chapter describes how to read pixel data (bitmaps and images) from the framebuffer into processor memory (and vice versa), and how to copy pixel data from one buffer to another, or within a single buffer to another position. This chapter contains the following major sections:

- **"Bitmaps and Fonts"** describes the commands for positioning and drawing bitmapped data. Such data may describe a font.

- **"Images"** presents the basic information about reading and copying pixel data. It also explains how to magnify or reduce an image as it's written to the framebuffer.

- **"Storing, Transforming, and Mapping Pixels"** covers all the details of how pixel data is stored in memory and how to transform it as it's moved into or out of memory.

In most cases, the necessary pixel operations are simple, so the first two sections might be all you need to read for your application. However, pixel manipulation can be complex—there are many ways to store pixel data in memory, and you can apply any of several transformations to pixels as they're moved to and from the framebuffer. These details are the subject of the third section of this chapter; most likely, you'll want to read this section only when you actually need to make use of the information.

Bitmaps and Fonts

A bitmap is a rectangular array of 0s and 1s that serves as a drawing mask for a corresponding rectangular portion of the window. Suppose you're drawing a bitmap and that the current color is red. Everywhere there's a 1 in the bitmap, the corresponding pixel is replaced by a red pixel (or combined with the red pixel, depending on which per-fragment operations are in effect; see "Testing and Operating on Fragments" on page 299). If there's a 0 in the bitmap, the contents of the pixel are unaffected. The most common use for bitmaps is for drawing characters on the screen.

OpenGL provides only the lowest level of support for drawing strings of characters and manipulating fonts. The commands **glRasterPos*()** and **glBitmap()** position and draw a single bitmap on the screen. In addition, through the display-list mechanism, you can use a sequence of character codes to index into a corresponding series of bitmaps representing those characters. See Chapter 4 for more information about display lists. You'll have to write your own routines to provide any other support you need for manipulating bitmaps, fonts, and strings of characters.

As an example, consider Listing 8-1, which draws the character F three times on the screen. Figure 8-1 shows the F as a bitmap and its corresponding bitmap data.

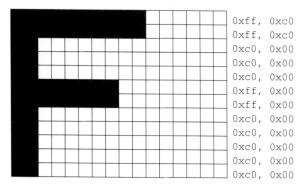

Figure 8-1   A Bitmapped F and Its Data

Listing 8-1   Drawing a Bitmapped Character: drawf.c

```c
#include <GL/gl.h>
#include <GL/glu.h>
#include "aux.h"

GLubyte rasters[24] = {
    0xc0, 0x00, 0xc0, 0x00, 0xc0, 0x00, 0xc0, 0x00,
    0xc0, 0x00, 0xff, 0x00, 0xff, 0x00, 0xc0, 0x00,
    0xc0, 0x00, 0xc0, 0x00, 0xff, 0xc0, 0xff, 0xc0};

void myinit(void)
{
    glPixelStorei(GL_UNPACK_ALIGNMENT, 1);
    glClearColor(0.0, 0.0, 0.0, 0.0);
}

void display(void)
{
    glClear(GL_COLOR_BUFFER_BIT);
    glColor3f(1.0, 1.0, 1.0);
    glRasterPos2i (20.5, 20.5);
    glBitmap(10, 12, 0.0, 0.0, 12.0, 0.0, rasters);
    glBitmap(10, 12, 0.0, 0.0, 12.0, 0.0, rasters);
    glBitmap(10, 12, 0.0, 0.0, 12.0, 0.0, rasters);
    glFlush();
}

void myReshape(GLsizei w, GLsizei h)
{
    glViewport(0, 0, w, h);
    glMatrixMode(GL_PROJECTION);
    glLoadIdentity();
    glOrtho(0, w, 0, h, -1.0, 1.0);
    glMatrixMode(GL_MODELVIEW);
}


int main(int argc, char** argv)
{
    auxInitDisplayMode(AUX_SINGLE | AUX_RGBA);
    auxInitPosition(0, 0, 500, 500);
    auxInitWindow(argv[0]);
    myinit();
    auxReshapeFunc(myReshape);
    auxMainLoop(display);
}
```

In Figure 8-1, note that the visible part of the F character is at most 10 bits wide. Bitmap data is always stored in chunks that are multiples of 8 bits, but the width of the actual bitmap doesn't have to be a multiple of 8. The bits making up a bitmap are drawn starting from the lower left corner: First, the bottom row is drawn, then the next row above it, and so on. As you can tell from the code, the bitmap is stored in memory in this order—the array of rasters begins with 0xc0, 0x00, 0xc0, 0x00 for the bottom two rows of the F and continues to 0xff, 0xc0, 0xff, 0xc0 for the top two rows.

The commands of interest in this example are **glRasterPos2i()** and **glBitmap()**; they're discussed in detail in the next section. For now, ignore the call to **glPixelStorei()**; it describes how the bitmap data is stored in computer memory. This topic is discussed in "Controlling Pixel-Storage Modes" on page 244.

The Current Raster Position

The current raster position is the origin where the next bitmap (or image) is to be drawn. In the F example, the raster position was set using **glRasterPos*()** to (20, 20), which is where the lower left corner of the F was drawn:

```
glRasterPos2i(20, 20);
```

void **glRasterPos{234}{sifd}{v}**(*TYPE x, TYPE y, TYPE z, TYPE w*);

Sets the current raster position. The *x, y, z,* and *w* arguments specify the coordinates of the raster position. If **glRasterPos2*()** is used, *z* is implicitly set to zero and *w* is implicitly set to one; similarly, with **glRasterPos3*()**, *w* is set to one.

The coordinates of the raster position are transformed to screen coordinates in exactly the same way as coordinates supplied with a **glVertex*()** command (that is, with the modelview and perspective matrices). After transformation, they either define a valid spot in the window on the screen, or they're clipped out because the transformed coordinates lie outside the viewport. If the transformed point is clipped out, the current raster position is invalid.

To obtain the current raster position, you can use the query command **glGetFloatv()** with GL_CURRENT_RASTER_POSITION as the first argument. The second argument should be a pointer to an allocated array that can hold the (x, y, z, w) values as floating-point numbers. Call **glGetBooleanv()** with GL_CURRENT_RASTER_POSITION_VALID as the first argument to determine whether the current raster position is valid.

Drawing the Bitmap

Once you've set the desired raster position, you probably want to use the **glBitmap()** command to draw the data.

---

void **glBitmap**(GLsizei *width*, GLsizei *height*, GLfloat x_{bo}, GLfloat y_{bo}, GLfloat x_{bi}, GLfloat y_{bi}, const GLubyte **bitmap*);

Draws the bitmap specified by *bitmap*, which is a pointer to the bitmap image. The origin of the bitmap is placed at the most recently defined current raster position. If the current raster position is invalid, nothing is drawn, and the raster position remains invalid. The *width* and *height* arguments indicate the width and height, in pixels, of the bitmap. The width need not be a multiple of 8, although the data is stored in unsigned characters of 8 bits each. (In the F example, it wouldn't matter if there were garbage bits in the data beyond the tenth bit; since **glBitmap()** was called with a width of 10, only 10 bits of the row are rendered.) Use x_{bo} and y_{bo} to define the origin of the bitmap (positive values move the origin up and to the right; negative values move it down and to the left); x_{bi} and y_{bi} indicate the x and y increments that are added to the raster position after the bitmap is rasterized (see Figure 8-2).

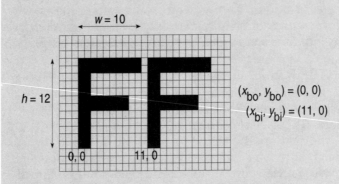

Figure 8-2   A Bitmap and Its Associated Parameters

Allowing the origin of the bitmap to be placed arbitrarily makes it easy for characters to extend below the origin (typically used for characters with descenders, such as g, j, and y), or to extend beyond the left of the origin (used for various swash characters, which have extended flourishes, or for characters in fonts that lean to the left).

After the bitmap is drawn, the current raster position is advanced by x_{bi} and y_{bi} in the x- and y-directions, respectively. For standard Latin fonts, y_{bi} is typically 0.0 and x_{bi} is positive (since successive characters are drawn from left to right). For Hebrew, where characters go from right to left, the x_{bi} values would typically be negative. Fonts that draw successive characters vertically in columns would use zero for x_{bi} and nonzero values for y_{bi}. In Figure 8-2, each time the F is drawn, the current raster position advances by 12 pixels, allowing a 2-pixel space between successive characters.

Since x_{bo}, y_{bo}, x_{bi}, and y_{bi} are floating-point values, characters need not be an integral number of pixels wide. Actual characters are drawn on exact pixel boundaries, but the current raster position is kept in floating point so that each character is drawn as close as possible to where it belongs. For example, if the code in the F example was modified so that x_{bi} is 11.5 instead of 12, and if more characters were drawn, the space between letters would alternate between one and two pixels, giving the best approximation to the requested 1.5-pixel space. Note that bitmaps can't be used for rotatable fonts because the bitmap is always drawn aligned to the x and y framebuffer axes.

Fonts and Display Lists

Display lists are discussed in general terms in Chapter 4. However, a few of the display-list management commands have special relevance for drawing strings of characters. As you read this section, keep in mind that the ideas presented here apply equally well to characters that are drawn using bitmap data as well as those drawn using geometric primitives (points, lines, and polygons). "Executing Multiple Display Lists" on page 132 presents an example of a geometric font.

A font typically consists of a set of characters, where each character has an identifying number (usually the ASCII code), and a drawing method. For a standard ASCII character set, the capital letter A is number 65, B is 66, and so on. The string "DAB" would be represented by the three indices 68, 65, 66. In the simplest approach, display-list number 65 would draw an A, number 66 would draw a B, and so on. Then, to draw the string 68, 65, 66, just execute the corresponding display lists.

You can use the command **glCallLists()** in just this way.

```
void glCallLists(GLsizei n, GLenum type, const GLvoid *lists);
```

The first argument, *n*, indicates the number of characters to be drawn, *type* is usually GL_BYTE, and *lists* is an array of character codes.

Since many applications need to draw character strings in multiple fonts and sizes, this simplest approach isn't convenient. Instead, you'd like to use 65 as A no matter what font is currently active. You could force font 1 to encode A, B, and C as 1065, 1066, 1067, and font 2 as 2065, 2066, 2067, but then any numbers larger than 256 would no longer fit in an 8-bit byte. A better solution is to add an offset to every entry in the string and to choose the display list. In this case, font 1 has A, B, and C represented by 1065, 1066, and 1067, and in font 2, they might be 2065, 2066, and 2067. Then to draw characters in font 1, set the offset to 1000 and draw display lists 65, 66, and 67. To draw that same string in font 2, set the offset to 2000 and draw the same lists.

With this approach, use the command **glListBase()** to set the offset. For the preceding examples, it should be called with 1000 or 2000 as the (only) argument. Now what you need is a contiguous list of unused display-list numbers, which you can obtain from **glGenLists()**.

```
GLuint glGenLists(GLsizei range);
```

This function returns a block of *range* display-list identifiers. The returned lists are all marked as "used" even though they're empty, so that subsequent calls to **glGenLists()** never return the same lists (unless you've explicitly deleted them previously). Thus, if you use 4 as the argument and if **glGenLists()** returns 81, you can use display-list identifiers 81, 82, 83, and 84 for your characters. If **glGenLists()** can't find a block of unused identifiers of the requested length, it returns 0. (Note that the command **glDeleteLists()** makes it easy to delete all the lists associated with a font in a single operation.)

Most American and European fonts have a small number of characters (fewer than 256), so it's easy to represent each character with a different code that can be stored in a single byte. Asian fonts, among others, may require much larger character sets, so a byte-per-character encoding is impossible. OpenGL allows strings to be composed of one-, two-, three-, or four-byte characters through the *type* parameter in **glCallLists()**. This parameter can have any of the following values:

GL_BYTE	GL_UNSIGNED_BYTE
GL_SHORT	GL_UNSIGNED_SHORT
GL_INT	GL_UNSIGNED_INT
GL_FLOAT	GL_2_BYTES
GL_3_BYTES	GL_4_BYTES

See "Executing Multiple Display Lists" on page 132 for more information about these values.

Defining and Using a Complete Font

The sample program in this section defines a complete raster font using the **glBitmap()** command and the display-list mechanism described in the previous section. A complete ASCII font is defined where each character is the same width (although this is by no means necessary). The code is similar to the F example, except that ninety-five different bitmaps are used (one for each of the printable ASCII characters, including the space character), and each is a single command within a display list. Each display-list identifier is equal to the ASCII code for that character, and all have the same offset added to them. Listing 8-2 produces the output shown in Figure 8-3.

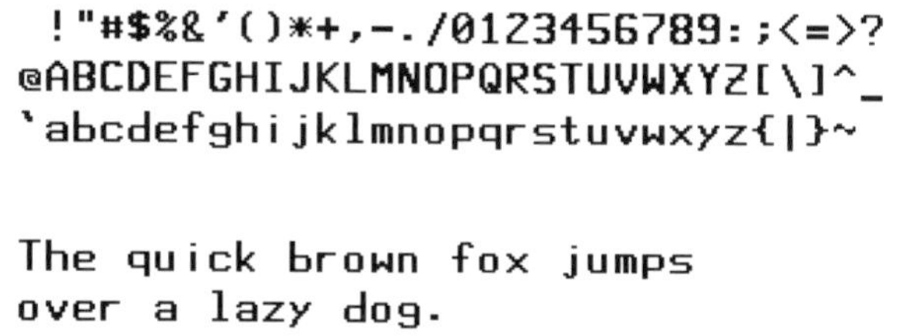

```
 !"#$%&'()*+,-./0123456789:;<=>?
@ABCDEFGHIJKLMNOPQRSTUVWXYZ[\]^_
`abcdefghijklmnopqrstuvwxyz{|}~


The quick brown fox jumps
over a lazy dog.
```

Figure 8-3   A Complete Font Definition

Listing 8-2   Defining a Complete Font: font.c

```c
#include <GL/gl.h>
#include <GL/glu.h>
#include "aux.h"

GLubyte rasters[][13] = {
{0x00, 0x00, 0x00, 0x00, 0x00, 0x00, 0x00, 0x00, 0x00, 0x00, 0x00, 0x00, 0x00},
{0x00, 0x00, 0x18, 0x18, 0x00, 0x00, 0x18, 0x18, 0x18, 0x18, 0x18, 0x18, 0x18},
{0x00, 0x00, 0x00, 0x00, 0x00, 0x00, 0x00, 0x00, 0x00, 0x36, 0x36, 0x36, 0x36},
{0x00, 0x00, 0x00, 0x66, 0x66, 0xff, 0x66, 0x66, 0xff, 0x66, 0x66, 0x00, 0x00},
```

```
{0x00, 0x00, 0x18, 0x7e, 0xff, 0x1b, 0x1f, 0x7e, 0xf8, 0xd8, 0xff, 0x7e, 0x18},
{0x00, 0x00, 0x0e, 0x1b, 0xdb, 0x6e, 0x30, 0x18, 0x0c, 0x76, 0xdb, 0xd8, 0x70},
{0x00, 0x00, 0x7f, 0xc6, 0xcf, 0xd8, 0x70, 0x70, 0xd8, 0xcc, 0xcc, 0x6c, 0x38},
{0x00, 0x00, 0x00, 0x00, 0x00, 0x00, 0x00, 0x00, 0x00, 0x18, 0x1c, 0x0c, 0x0e},
{0x00, 0x00, 0x0c, 0x18, 0x30, 0x30, 0x30, 0x30, 0x30, 0x30, 0x30, 0x18, 0x0c},
{0x00, 0x00, 0x30, 0x18, 0x0c, 0x0c, 0x0c, 0x0c, 0x0c, 0x0c, 0x0c, 0x18, 0x30},
{0x00, 0x00, 0x00, 0x00, 0x99, 0x5a, 0x3c, 0xff, 0x3c, 0x5a, 0x99, 0x00, 0x00},
{0x00, 0x00, 0x00, 0x18, 0x18, 0x18, 0xff, 0xff, 0x18, 0x18, 0x18, 0x00, 0x00},
{0x00, 0x00, 0x30, 0x18, 0x1c, 0x1c, 0x00, 0x00, 0x00, 0x00, 0x00, 0x00, 0x00},
{0x00, 0x00, 0x00, 0x00, 0x00, 0x00, 0xff, 0xff, 0x00, 0x00, 0x00, 0x00, 0x00},
{0x00, 0x00, 0x00, 0x38, 0x38, 0x00, 0x00, 0x00, 0x00, 0x00, 0x00, 0x00, 0x00},
{0x00, 0x60, 0x60, 0x30, 0x30, 0x18, 0x18, 0x0c, 0x0c, 0x06, 0x06, 0x03, 0x03},
{0x00, 0x00, 0x3c, 0x66, 0xc3, 0xe3, 0xf3, 0xdb, 0xcf, 0xc7, 0xc3, 0x66, 0x3c},
{0x00, 0x00, 0x7e, 0x18, 0x18, 0x18, 0x18, 0x18, 0x18, 0x78, 0x38, 0x18},
{0x00, 0x00, 0xff, 0xc0, 0xc0, 0x60, 0x30, 0x18, 0x0c, 0x06, 0x03, 0xe7, 0x7e},
{0x00, 0x00, 0x7e, 0xe7, 0x03, 0x03, 0x07, 0x7e, 0x07, 0x03, 0x03, 0xe7, 0x7e},
{0x00, 0x00, 0x0c, 0x0c, 0x0c, 0x0c, 0x0c, 0xff, 0xcc, 0x6c, 0x3c, 0x1c, 0x0c},
{0x00, 0x00, 0x7e, 0xe7, 0x03, 0x03, 0x07, 0xfe, 0xc0, 0xc0, 0xc0, 0xc0, 0xff},
{0x00, 0x00, 0x7e, 0xe7, 0xc3, 0xc3, 0xc7, 0xfe, 0xc0, 0xc0, 0xc0, 0xe7, 0x7e},
{0x00, 0x00, 0x30, 0x30, 0x30, 0x30, 0x18, 0x0c, 0x06, 0x03, 0x03, 0x03, 0xff},
{0x00, 0x00, 0x7e, 0xe7, 0xc3, 0xc3, 0xe7, 0x7e, 0xe7, 0xc3, 0xc3, 0xe7, 0x7e},
{0x00, 0x00, 0x7e, 0xe7, 0x03, 0x03, 0x03, 0x7f, 0xe7, 0xc3, 0xc3, 0xe7, 0x7e},
{0x00, 0x00, 0x00, 0x38, 0x38, 0x00, 0x00, 0x38, 0x38, 0x00, 0x00, 0x00, 0x00},
{0x00, 0x00, 0x30, 0x18, 0x1c, 0x1c, 0x00, 0x00, 0x1c, 0x1c, 0x00, 0x00, 0x00},
{0x00, 0x00, 0x06, 0x0c, 0x18, 0x30, 0x60, 0xc0, 0x60, 0x30, 0x18, 0x0c, 0x06},
{0x00, 0x00, 0x00, 0x00, 0xff, 0xff, 0x00, 0xff, 0xff, 0x00, 0x00, 0x00, 0x00},
{0x00, 0x00, 0x60, 0x30, 0x18, 0x0c, 0x06, 0x03, 0x06, 0x0c, 0x18, 0x30, 0x60},
{0x00, 0x00, 0x18, 0x00, 0x00, 0x18, 0x18, 0x0c, 0x06, 0x03, 0xc3, 0xc3, 0x7e},
{0x00, 0x00, 0x3f, 0x60, 0xcf, 0xdb, 0xd3, 0xdd, 0xc3, 0x7e, 0x00, 0x00, 0x00},
{0x00, 0x00, 0xc3, 0xc3, 0xc3, 0xc3, 0xff, 0xc3, 0xc3, 0xc3, 0x66, 0x3c, 0x18},
{0x00, 0x00, 0xfe, 0xc7, 0xc3, 0xc3, 0xc7, 0xfe, 0xc7, 0xc3, 0xc3, 0xc7, 0xfe},
{0x00, 0x00, 0x7e, 0xe7, 0xc0, 0xc0, 0xc0, 0xc0, 0xc0, 0xc0, 0xc0, 0xe7, 0x7e},
{0x00, 0x00, 0xfc, 0xce, 0xc7, 0xc3, 0xc3, 0xc3, 0xc3, 0xc3, 0xc7, 0xce, 0xfc},
{0x00, 0x00, 0xff, 0xc0, 0xc0, 0xc0, 0xc0, 0xfc, 0xc0, 0xc0, 0xc0, 0xc0, 0xff},
{0x00, 0x00, 0xc0, 0xc0, 0xc0, 0xc0, 0xc0, 0xc0, 0xfc, 0xc0, 0xc0, 0xc0, 0xff},
{0x00, 0x00, 0x7e, 0xe7, 0xc3, 0xc3, 0xcf, 0xc0, 0xc0, 0xc0, 0xc0, 0xe7, 0x7e},
{0x00, 0x00, 0xc3, 0xc3, 0xc3, 0xc3, 0xc3, 0xff, 0xc3, 0xc3, 0xc3, 0xc3, 0xc3},
{0x00, 0x00, 0x7e, 0x18, 0x18, 0x18, 0x18, 0x18, 0x18, 0x18, 0x18, 0x18, 0x7e},
{0x00, 0x00, 0x7c, 0xee, 0xc6, 0x06, 0x06, 0x06, 0x06, 0x06, 0x06, 0x06, 0x06},
{0x00, 0x00, 0xc3, 0xc6, 0xcc, 0xd8, 0xf0, 0xe0, 0xf0, 0xd8, 0xcc, 0xc6, 0xc3},
{0x00, 0x00, 0xff, 0xc0, 0xc0, 0xc0, 0xc0, 0xc0, 0xc0, 0xc0, 0xc0, 0xc0, 0xc0},
{0x00, 0x00, 0xc3, 0xc3, 0xc3, 0xc3, 0xc3, 0xc3, 0xdb, 0xff, 0xff, 0xe7, 0xc3},
{0x00, 0x00, 0xc7, 0xc7, 0xcf, 0xcf, 0xdf, 0xdb, 0xfb, 0xf3, 0xf3, 0xe3, 0xe3},
{0x00, 0x00, 0x7e, 0xe7, 0xc3, 0xc3, 0xc3, 0xc3, 0xc3, 0xc3, 0xc3, 0xe7, 0x7e},
{0x00, 0x00, 0xc0, 0xc0, 0xc0, 0xc0, 0xc0, 0xfe, 0xc7, 0xc3, 0xc3, 0xc7, 0xfe},
{0x00, 0x00, 0x3f, 0x6e, 0xdf, 0xdb, 0xc3, 0xc3, 0xc3, 0xc3, 0xc3, 0x66, 0x3c},
{0x00, 0x00, 0xc3, 0xc6, 0xcc, 0xd8, 0xf0, 0xfe, 0xc7, 0xc3, 0xc3, 0xc7, 0xfe},
```

```
{0x00, 0x00, 0x7e, 0xe7, 0x03, 0x03, 0x07, 0x7e, 0xe0, 0xc0, 0xc0, 0xe7, 0x7e},
{0x00, 0x00, 0x18, 0x18, 0x18, 0x18, 0x18, 0x18, 0x18, 0x18, 0x18, 0x18, 0xff},
{0x00, 0x00, 0x7e, 0xe7, 0xc3, 0xc3, 0xc3, 0xc3, 0xc3, 0xc3, 0xc3, 0xc3, 0xc3},
{0x00, 0x00, 0x18, 0x3c, 0x3c, 0x66, 0x66, 0xc3, 0xc3, 0xc3, 0xc3, 0xc3, 0xc3},
{0x00, 0x00, 0xc3, 0xe7, 0xff, 0xff, 0xdb, 0xdb, 0xc3, 0xc3, 0xc3, 0xc3, 0xc3},
{0x00, 0x00, 0xc3, 0x66, 0x66, 0x3c, 0x3c, 0x18, 0x3c, 0x3c, 0x66, 0x66, 0xc3},
{0x00, 0x00, 0x18, 0x18, 0x18, 0x18, 0x18, 0x18, 0x3c, 0x3c, 0x66, 0x66, 0xc3},
{0x00, 0x00, 0xff, 0xc0, 0xc0, 0x60, 0x30, 0x7e, 0x0c, 0x06, 0x03, 0x03, 0xff},
{0x00, 0x00, 0x3c, 0x30, 0x30, 0x30, 0x30, 0x30, 0x30, 0x30, 0x30, 0x30, 0x3c},
{0x00, 0x03, 0x03, 0x06, 0x06, 0x0c, 0x0c, 0x18, 0x18, 0x30, 0x30, 0x60, 0x60},
{0x00, 0x00, 0x3c, 0x0c, 0x0c, 0x0c, 0x0c, 0x0c, 0x0c, 0x0c, 0x0c, 0x0c, 0x3c},
{0x00, 0x00, 0x00, 0x00, 0x00, 0x00, 0x00, 0x00, 0x00, 0xc3, 0x66, 0x3c, 0x18},
{0xff, 0xff, 0x00, 0x00, 0x00, 0x00, 0x00, 0x00, 0x00, 0x00, 0x00, 0x00, 0x00},
{0x00, 0x00, 0x00, 0x00, 0x00, 0x00, 0x00, 0x00, 0x00, 0x18, 0x38, 0x30, 0x70},
{0x00, 0x00, 0x7f, 0xc3, 0xc3, 0x7f, 0x03, 0xc3, 0x7e, 0x00, 0x00, 0x00, 0x00},
{0x00, 0x00, 0xfe, 0xc3, 0xc3, 0xc3, 0xc3, 0xfe, 0xc0, 0xc0, 0xc0, 0xc0, 0xc0},
{0x00, 0x00, 0x7e, 0xc3, 0xc0, 0xc0, 0xc0, 0xc3, 0x7e, 0x00, 0x00, 0x00, 0x00},
{0x00, 0x00, 0x7f, 0xc3, 0xc3, 0xc3, 0xc3, 0x7f, 0x03, 0x03, 0x03, 0x03, 0x03},
{0x00, 0x00, 0x7f, 0xc0, 0xc0, 0xfe, 0xc3, 0xc3, 0x7e, 0x00, 0x00, 0x00, 0x00},
{0x00, 0x00, 0x30, 0x30, 0x30, 0x30, 0x30, 0xfc, 0x30, 0x30, 0x30, 0x33, 0x1e},
{0x7e, 0xc3, 0x03, 0x03, 0x7f, 0xc3, 0xc3, 0xc3, 0x7e, 0x00, 0x00, 0x00, 0x00},
{0x00, 0x00, 0xc3, 0xc3, 0xc3, 0xc3, 0xc3, 0xc3, 0xfe, 0xc0, 0xc0, 0xc0, 0xc0},
{0x00, 0x00, 0x18, 0x18, 0x18, 0x18, 0x18, 0x18, 0x18, 0x00, 0x00, 0x18, 0x00},
{0x38, 0x6c, 0x0c, 0x0c, 0x0c, 0x0c, 0x0c, 0x0c, 0x0c, 0x00, 0x00, 0x0c, 0x00},
{0x00, 0x00, 0xc6, 0xcc, 0xf8, 0xf0, 0xd8, 0xcc, 0xc6, 0xc0, 0xc0, 0xc0, 0xc0},
{0x00, 0x00, 0x7e, 0x18, 0x18, 0x18, 0x18, 0x18, 0x18, 0x18, 0x18, 0x18, 0x78},
{0x00, 0x00, 0xdb, 0xdb, 0xdb, 0xdb, 0xdb, 0xdb, 0xfe, 0x00, 0x00, 0x00, 0x00},
{0x00, 0x00, 0xc6, 0xc6, 0xc6, 0xc6, 0xc6, 0xc6, 0xfc, 0x00, 0x00, 0x00, 0x00},
{0x00, 0x00, 0x7c, 0xc6, 0xc6, 0xc6, 0xc6, 0xc6, 0x7c, 0x00, 0x00, 0x00, 0x00},
{0xc0, 0xc0, 0xc0, 0xfe, 0xc3, 0xc3, 0xc3, 0xc3, 0xfe, 0x00, 0x00, 0x00, 0x00},
{0x03, 0x03, 0x03, 0x7f, 0xc3, 0xc3, 0xc3, 0xc3, 0x7f, 0x00, 0x00, 0x00, 0x00},
{0x00, 0x00, 0xc0, 0xc0, 0xc0, 0xc0, 0xc0, 0xe0, 0xfe, 0x00, 0x00, 0x00, 0x00},
{0x00, 0x00, 0xfe, 0x03, 0x03, 0x7e, 0xc0, 0xc0, 0x7f, 0x00, 0x00, 0x00, 0x00},
{0x00, 0x00, 0x1c, 0x36, 0x30, 0x30, 0x30, 0x30, 0xfc, 0x30, 0x30, 0x30, 0x00},
{0x00, 0x00, 0x7e, 0xc6, 0xc6, 0xc6, 0xc6, 0xc6, 0xc6, 0x00, 0x00, 0x00, 0x00},
{0x00, 0x00, 0x18, 0x3c, 0x3c, 0x66, 0x66, 0xc3, 0xc3, 0x00, 0x00, 0x00, 0x00},
{0x00, 0x00, 0xc3, 0xe7, 0xff, 0xdb, 0xc3, 0xc3, 0xc3, 0x00, 0x00, 0x00, 0x00},
{0x00, 0x00, 0xc3, 0x66, 0x3c, 0x18, 0x3c, 0x66, 0xc3, 0x00, 0x00, 0x00, 0x00},
{0xc0, 0x60, 0x60, 0x30, 0x18, 0x3c, 0x66, 0x66, 0xc3, 0x00, 0x00, 0x00, 0x00},
{0x00, 0x00, 0xff, 0x60, 0x30, 0x18, 0x0c, 0x06, 0xff, 0x00, 0x00, 0x00, 0x00},
{0x00, 0x00, 0x0f, 0x18, 0x18, 0x18, 0x38, 0xf0, 0x38, 0x18, 0x18, 0x18, 0x0f},
{0x18, 0x18, 0x18, 0x18, 0x18, 0x18, 0x18, 0x18, 0x18, 0x18, 0x18, 0x18, 0x18},
{0x00, 0x00, 0xf0, 0x18, 0x18, 0x18, 0x1c, 0x0f, 0x1c, 0x18, 0x18, 0x18, 0xf0},
{0x00, 0x00, 0x00, 0x00, 0x00, 0x00, 0x06, 0x8f, 0xf1, 0x60, 0x00, 0x00, 0x00}
};

GLuint fontOffset;
```

```
void makeRasterFont(void)
{
    GLuint i;
    glPixelStorei(GL_UNPACK_ALIGNMENT, 1);
    fontOffset = glGenLists (128);
    for (i = 32; i < 127; i++) {
        glNewList(i+fontOffset, GL_COMPILE);
            glBitmap(8, 13, 0.0, 2.0, 10.0, 0.0, rasters[i-32]);
        glEndList();
    }
}

void myinit(void)
{
    glShadeModel (GL_FLAT);
    makeRasterFont();
}

void printString(char *s)
{
    glPushAttrib (GL_LIST_BIT);
    glListBase(fontOffset);
    glCallLists(strlen(s), GL_UNSIGNED_BYTE, (GLubyte *) s);
    glPopAttrib ();
}

void display(void)
{
    GLfloat white[3] = { 1.0, 1.0, 1.0 };
    int i, j;
    char teststring[33];

    glClear(GL_COLOR_BUFFER_BIT);
    glColor3fv(white);
    for (i = 32; i < 127; i += 32) {
        glRasterPos2i(20, 200 - 18*i/32);
        for (j = 0; j < 32; j++)
            teststring[j] = (char) (i+j);
        teststring[32] = 0;
        printString(teststring);
    }
    glRasterPos2i(20, 100);
    printString("The quick brown fox jumps");
    glRasterPos2i(20, 82);
    printString("over a lazy dog.");
    glFlush ();
}
```

```
void myReshape(GLsizei w, GLsizei h)
{
    glViewport(0, 0, w, h);
    glMatrixMode(GL_PROJECTION);
    glLoadIdentity();
    glOrtho (0.0, w, 0.0, h, -1.0, 1.0);
    glMatrixMode(GL_MODELVIEW);
}


int main(int argc, char** argv)
{
    auxInitDisplayMode (AUX_SINGLE | AUX_RGBA);
    auxInitPosition (0, 0, 500, 500);
    auxInitWindow (argv[0]);
    myinit();
    auxReshapeFunc (myReshape);
    auxMainLoop(display);
}
```

Images

An image is similar to a bitmap, but instead of containing only a single bit for each pixel in a rectangular region of the screen, an image can contain much more information. For example, an image can contain the complete (R, G, B, A) quadruple stored at each pixel. Images can come from several sources, such as:

- A photograph that's digitized with a scanner

- An image that was first generated on the screen by a graphics program using the graphics hardware and then read back, pixel by pixel

- A software program that generated the image in memory pixel by pixel

The images you normally think of as pictures come from the color buffers. However, you can read or write rectangular regions of pixel data from or to the depth buffer or the stencil buffer. See Chapter 10 for an explanation of these other buffers.

In addition to simply being displayed on the screen, images can be used for texture maps, in which case they're essentially pasted onto polygons that are rendered on the screen in the normal way. See Chapter 9 for more information about this technique.

Reading, Writing, and Copying Pixel Data

OpenGL provides three basic commands that manipulate image data:

- **glReadPixels()**—Reads a rectangular array of pixels from the framebuffer and stores the data in processor memory.

- **glDrawPixels()**—Writes a rectangular array of pixels into the framebuffer from data kept in processor memory.

- **glCopyPixels()**—Copies a rectangular array of pixels from one part of the framebuffer to another. This command behaves something like a call to **glReadPixels()** followed by a call to **glDrawPixels()**, but the data is never written into processor memory.

The basic ideas behind these commands are simple, but complexity arises because there are many kinds of framebuffer data, many ways to store pixel information in computer memory, and various data conversions that can be performed during the reading, writing, and copying operations. All these possibilities translate to many different modes of operation. If all your program does is copy images on the screen, or read them into memory temporarily so that they can be copied out later, you can ignore most of these modes. However, if you want your program to modify the data while it's in memory—for example, if you have an image stored in one format but the window requires a different format—or if you want to save image data to a file for future restoration in another session or on another kind of machine with significantly different graphical capabilities, you have to understand the various modes.

The rest of this section describes the basic commands in detail. "Storing, Transforming, and Mapping Pixels" on page 242 discusses the details of pixel-storage modes, pixel-transfer operations, and pixel-mapping operations.

---

void **glReadPixels**(GLint *x*, GLint *y*, GLsizei *width*, GLsizei *height*,
              GLenum *format*, GLenum *type*, GLvoid **pixels*);

Reads pixel data from the framebuffer rectangle whose lower left corner is at (*x*, *y*) and whose dimensions are *width* and *height*, and stores it in the array pointed to by *pixels*. *format* indicates the kind of pixel data elements that are read (an index value or an R, G, B, or A component value, as listed in Table 8-1), and *type* indicates the data type of each element (see Table 8-2).

Name	Kind of Pixel Data
GL_COLOR_INDEX	A single color index
GL_RGB	A red color component, followed by a green color component, followed by a blue color component
GL_RGBA	A red color component, followed by a green color component, followed by a blue color component, followed by an alpha color component
GL_RED	A single red color component
GL_GREEN	A single green color component
GL_BLUE	A single blue color component
GL_ALPHA	A single alpha color component
GL_LUMINANCE	A single luminance component
GL_LUMINANCE_ALPHA	A luminance component followed by an alpha color component
GL_STENCIL_INDEX	A single stencil index
GL_DEPTH_COMPONENT	A single depth component

Table 8-1   Pixel Formats for Use with glReadPixels() or glDrawPixels()

---

void **glDrawPixels**(GLsizei *width*, GLsizei *height*, GLenum *format*,
    GLenum *type*, const GLvoid **pixels*);

Draws a rectangle of pixel data with dimensions *width* and *height*. The pixel rectangle is drawn with its lower left corner at the current raster position. The *format* and *type* parameters have the same meaning as with **glReadPixels**(). The array pointed to by *pixels* contains the pixel data to be drawn. If the current raster position is invalid, nothing is drawn, and it remains invalid.

Remember that, depending on the format, anywhere from one to four elements are read or written. For example, if the format is GL_RGBA, and you're reading into 32-bit integers (that is, if *type* = GL_INT), then every pixel read requires 16 bytes of storage (4 components × 4 bytes/component).

Name	Data Type
GL_UNSIGNED_BYTE	unsigned 8-bit integer
GL_BYTE	signed 8-bit integer
GL_BITMAP	single bits in unsigned 8-bit integers
GL_UNSIGNED_SHORT	unsigned 16-bit integer
GL_SHORT	signed 16-bit integer
GL_UNSIGNED_INT	unsigned 32-bit integer
GL_INT	32-bit integer
GL_FLOAT	single-precision floating point

Table 8-2   Data Types for glReadPixels() or glDrawPixels()

Each element of the saved image is stored in memory as indicated by Table 8-2. If the element represents a continuous value, such as a red, green, blue, or luminance component, each value is scaled to fit into the number of bits available. For example, the red component is a floating-point value between 0.0 and 1.0. If it needs to be packed into an unsigned byte, only 8 bits of precision are kept, even if more bits are allocated to the red component in the framebuffer. GL_UNSIGNED_SHORT and GL_UNSIGNED_INT give 16 and 32 bits of precision, respectively. The normal (signed) versions of GL_BYTE, GL_SHORT, and GL_INT have 7, 15, and 31 bits of precision, since the negative values are typically not used.

If the element is an index (a color index or a stencil index, for example), and the type is not GL_FLOAT, the value is simply masked against the available bits in the type. The signed versions—GL_BYTE, GL_SHORT, and GL_INT—have masks with one fewer bit. For example, if a color index is to be stored in a signed 8-bit integer, it's first masked against 0xff, a mask containing seven 1s. If the type is GL_FLOAT, the index is simply converted into a single-precision floating-point number (for example, the index 17 is converted to the float 17.0).

> void **glCopyPixels**(GLint *x*, GLint *y*, GLsizei *width*, GLsizei *height*,
> GLenum *type*);
>
> Copies pixel data from the framebuffer rectangle whose lower left corner
> is at (*x*, *y*) and whose dimensions are *width* and *height*. The data is copied
> to a new position whose lower left corner is given by the current raster
> position. The *type* parameter is either GL_COLOR, GL_STENCIL, or
> GL_DEPTH. **glCopyPixels**() behaves much like a **glReadPixels**()
> followed by a **glDrawPixels**(), with the following translation for the *type*
> to *format* parameter:
>
> - If *type* is GL_DEPTH or GL_STENCIL, then
>   GL_DEPTH_COMPONENT or GL_STENCIL_INDEX is used,
>   respectively.
>
> - If GL_COLOR is specified, GL_RGBA or GL_COLOR_INDEX is used,
>   depending on whether the system is in RGBA or color-index mode.

glCopyPixels() applies all the pixel transformations, transfer functions,
and so on during what would be the **glReadPixels**() activity. The resulting
data is written as it would be by **glDrawPixels**(), but the transformations
aren't applied a second time. Note that there's no need for a *format* or *data*
parameter for **glCopyPixels**(), since the data is never copied into processor
memory. For all three functions, the exact conversions of the data going to
or from the framebuffer depend on the modes in effect at the time. See the
next section for details.

Magnifying or Reducing an Image

Normally, each pixel in an image is written to a single pixel on the screen.
However, you can arbitrarily magnify or reduce an image by using
glPixelZoom().

> void **glPixelZoom**(GLfloat *zoom_x*, GLfloat *zoom_y*);
>
> Sets the magnification or reduction factors for pixel-write operations, in
> the *x*- and *y*-dimensions. By default, *zoom_x* and *zoom_y* are 1.0. If they're
> both 2.0, each image pixel is drawn to 4 screen pixels. Note that fractional
> magnification or reduction factors are allowed, as are negative factors.

During rasterization, each image pixel is treated as a $zoom_x \times zoom_y$ quadrilateral, and fragments are generated for all the pixels whose centers lie within the quadrilateral. More specifically, let (x_{rp}, y_{rp}) be the current raster position. If a particular group of elements (index or components) is the nth in a row and belongs to the mth column, consider the region in window coordinates bounded by the rectangle with corners at

$(x_{rp} + zoom_x n, y_{rp} + zoom_y m)$ and $(x_{rp} + zoom_x(n+1), y_{rp} + zoom_y(m+1))$

Any fragments whose centers lie inside this rectangle (or on its bottom or left boundaries) are produced in correspondence with this particular group of elements.

Storing, Transforming, and Mapping Pixels

This section discusses the details of the pixel-storage and -transfer modes, including how to set up an arbitrary mapping to convert pixel data as it's transferred. Remember that you need to use these modes only if you need to convert pixel data from one format to another.

Overview of the Pixel Modes

An image stored in memory has between one and four chunks of data, called *elements*, for each pixel in a rectangular portion of the screen. The data might consist of just the color index or the luminance (luminance is the possibly weighted sum of the red, green, and blue values), or it might consist of the red, green, blue, and alpha components for each pixel. The possible arrangements of pixel data, or *formats*, determine the number of elements stored for each pixel and their order.

Some elements (such as a color index or a stencil index) are integers, and others (such as the red, green, blue, and alpha components, or the depth component) are floating-point values, typically ranging between 0.0 and 1.0. Floating-point components are usually stored in your bitplanes in fixed-point with lower resolution than a full floating-point number would require (typically 8 bits are used for color components, for example). The exact number of bits used to represent the components depends on the particular hardware being used. Thus, it's often wasteful to store each component as a full 32-bit floating-point number, especially since images can easily contain a million pixels.

Elements can be stored in memory as various data types, ranging from 8-bit bytes to 32-bit integers or floating-point numbers. OpenGL explicitly defines the conversion of each component in each format to each of the possible data types. Keep in mind that you can lose data if you try to store a high-resolution component in a type represented by a small number of bits.

Image data is typically stored in processor memory in rectangular two- or three-dimensional arrays. Often, you want to display or store a subimage that corresponds to a subrectangle of the array. In addition, you might need to take into account that different machines have different byte-ordering conventions. Finally, some machines have hardware that is far more efficient at moving data to and from the framebuffer if the data is aligned on two-byte, four-byte, or eight-byte boundaries in processor memory. For such machines, you probably want to control the byte alignment. All the issues raised in this paragraph are controlled as pixel-storage modes; you specify these modes using the command **glPixelStore*()**, which you've seen used in a couple of example programs.

As image data is transferred from memory into the framebuffer, or from the framebuffer into memory, OpenGL can perform several operations on it. For example, the ranges of components can be altered—normally, the red component is between 0.0 and 1.0, but you might prefer to keep it in some other range, or perhaps the data you're using from a different graphics system stores the red component in a different range. You can even create maps to perform arbitrary conversion of color indices or color components during pixel transfer. Conversions such as these performed during the transfer of pixels to and from the framebuffer are called pixel-transfer modes. Not too surprisingly, they're controlled with the **glPixelTransfer*()** and **glPixelMap*()** commands.

Other modes that can be controlled include the framebuffer from which pixels are read, and any magnification that's to be performed on pixels as they are written to the framebuffer.

Finally, be aware that although the color, depth, and stencil buffers have many similarities, they don't behave identically, and a few of the modes have special cases for special buffers. All the mode details are covered in the sections that follow, including all the special cases.

Controlling Pixel-Storage Modes

All the possible pixel-storage modes are controlled with the **glPixelStore*()** command. Typically, several successive calls are made with this command to set several parameter values.

---

void **glPixelStore**{if}(GLenum *pname*, *TYPE param*);

Sets the pixel-storage modes, which affect the operation of **glDrawPixels*()**, **glReadPixels*()**, **glBitmap()**, **glPolygonStipple()**, **glTexImage1D()**, **glTexImage2D()**, and **glGetTexImage()**. The possible parameter names for *pname* are shown in Table 8-3, along with their data type, initial value, and valid range of values. The GL_UNPACK* parameters control how data is unpacked from memory by **glDrawPixels*()**, **glBitmap()**, **glPolygonStipple()**, **glTexImage1D()**, and **glTexImage2D()**. The GL_PACK* parameters control how data is packed into memory by **glReadPixels*()** and **glGetTexImage()**.

Parameter Name	Type	Initial Value	Valid Range
GL_UNPACK_SWAP_BYTES, GL_PACK_SWAP_BYTES	GLboolean	FALSE	TRUE/FALSE
GL_UNPACK_LSB_FIRST, GL_PACK_LSB_FIRST	GLboolean	FALSE	TRUE/FALSE
GL_UNPACK_ROW_LENGTH, GL_PACK_ROW_LENGTH	GLint	0	any nonnegative integer
GL_UNPACK_SKIP_ROWS, GL_PACK_SKIP_ROWS	GLint	0	any nonnegative integer
GL_UNPACK_SKIP_PIXELS, GL_PACK_SKIP_PIXELS	GLint	0	any nonnegative integer
GL_UNPACK_ALIGNMENT, GL_PACK_ALIGNMENT	GLint	4	1, 2, 4, 8

Table 8-3   Parameters for Use with glPixelStore()

Since the corresponding parameters for packing and unpacking have the same meanings, they're discussed together in the rest of this section and referred to without the GL_PACK or GL_UNPACK prefix. For example, *SWAP_BYTES refers to GL_PACK_SWAP_BYTES and GL_UNPACK_SWAP_BYTES.

If the *SWAP_BYTES parameter is FALSE (the default), the ordering of the bytes in memory is whatever is native for the OpenGL client; otherwise, the bytes are reversed. The byte reversal applies to any size element.

Note: As long as your OpenGL application doesn't share images with other machines, you can ignore the issue of byte ordering. If your application must render an OpenGL image that was created on a different machine, and the "endianness" of the two machines differs, byte ordering can be swapped using *SWAP_BYTES.

The *LSB_FIRST parameter applies when drawing or reading 1-bit images or bitmaps, for which a single bit of data is saved or restored for each pixel. If *LSB_FIRST is FALSE (the default), the bits are taken from the bytes starting with the most significant bit; otherwise, they're taken in the opposite order. For example, if *LSB_FIRST is FALSE, and the byte in question is 0x31, the bits, in order, are {0, 0, 1, 1, 0, 0, 0, 1}. If *LSB_FIRST is TRUE, the order is {1, 0, 0, 0, 1, 1, 0, 0}.

Sometimes you want to draw or read only a subrectangle of the entire rectangle of image data that's stored in memory. If the rectangle in memory is larger than the subrectangle that's being drawn or read, you need to specify the actual length of the larger rectangle with *ROW_LENGTH. If *ROW_LENGTH is zero (which it is by default), the row length is understood to be the same as the width that's specified with **glReadPixels*()**, **glDrawPixels*()**, or **glCopyPixels()**. You also need to specify the number of rows and pixels to skip before starting to copy the data for the subrectangle. These numbers are set using the parameters *SKIP_ROWS and *SKIP_PIXELS, as shown in Figure 8-4. By default, both parameters are 0, so you start at the lower left corner.

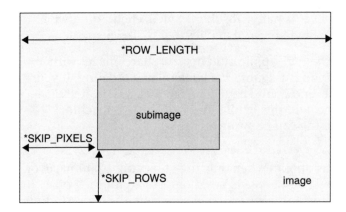

Figure 8-4   The *SKIP_ROWS, *SKIP_PIXELS, and *ROW_LENGTH Parameters

Often, a particular machine's hardware is optimized for moving pixel data to and from memory if the data is saved in memory with a particular byte alignment. For example, in a machine with 32-bit words, hardware can often retrieve data much faster if it's initially aligned on a 32-bit boundary, which typically has an address that is a multiple of 4. Likewise, 64-bit architectures might work better when the data is aligned to eight-byte boundaries. On some machines, however, byte alignment makes no difference.

As an example, suppose your machine works better with pixel data aligned to a four-byte boundary. Images are most efficiently saved by forcing the data for each row of the image to begin on a four-byte boundary. If the image is 5 pixels wide, and each pixel consists of one byte each of red, green, and blue information, a row requires 5×3 = 15 bytes of data. Maximum display efficiency can be achieved if the first row, and each successive row, begins on a four-byte boundary, so there is one byte of waste in the memory storage for each row. If your data is stored like this, set the *ALIGNMENT parameter appropriately (to 4, in this case).

If *ALIGNMENT is set to 1, the next available byte is used. If it's 2, at the end of each row, a byte is skipped if necessary, so that the first byte of the next row has an address that's a multiple of 2. In the case of bitmaps (or one-bit images) where a single bit is saved for each pixel, the same byte alignment works, although you have to count individual bits. For example, if you're saving a single bit per pixel, the row length is 75, and the alignment is 4, each row requires 75/8, or 9 3/8 bytes. Since 12 is the smallest multiple of 4 that is bigger than 9 3/8, twelve bytes of memory are used for each row.

Pixel-Transfer Operations

You can perform various operations on pixels as they're transferred from and to the framebuffer. The continuous components, including the red, green, blue, alpha, and depth components, can have an affine transformation applied. In addition, after transformation, these components—as well as the color-index and stencil values—can be transformed by an arbitrary table lookup.

Some of the pixel-transfer function characteristics are set with **glPixelTransfer*()**. The other characteristics are specified with **glPixelMap*()**, which is described in the next section.

---

void **glPixelTransfer**{if}(GLenum *pname*, *TYPE param*);

Sets pixel-transfer modes that affect the operation of **glDrawPixels*()**, **glReadPixels*()**, **glCopyPixels()**, **glTexImage1D()**, **glTexImage2D()**, and **glGetTexImage()**. The parameter *pname* must be one of those listed in the first column of Table 8-4, and its value, *param*, must be in the valid range shown.

Parameter Name	Type	Initial Value	Valid Range
GL_MAP_COLOR	GLboolean	FALSE	TRUE/FALSE
GL_MAP_STENCIL	GLboolean	FALSE	TRUE/FALSE
GL_INDEX_SHIFT	GLint	0	$(-\infty, \infty)$
GL_INDEX_OFFSET	GLint	0	$(-\infty, \infty)$
GL_RED_SCALE	GLfloat	1.0	$(-\infty, \infty)$
GL_GREEN_SCALE	GLfloat	1.0	$(-\infty, \infty)$
GL_BLUE_SCALE	GLfloat	1.0	$(-\infty, \infty)$
GL_ALPHA_SCALE	GLfloat	1.0	$(-\infty, \infty)$
GL_DEPTH_SCALE	GLfloat	1.0	$(-\infty, \infty)$
GL_RED_BIAS	GLfloat	0	$(-\infty, \infty)$
GL_GREEN_BIAS	GLfloat	0	$(-\infty, \infty)$
GL_BLUE_BIAS	GLfloat	0	$(-\infty, \infty)$
GL_ALPHA_BIAS	GLfloat	0	$(-\infty, \infty)$
GL_DEPTH_BIAS	GLfloat	0	$(-\infty, \infty)$

Table 8-4   Parameters for Use with glPixelTransfer*()

If the GL_MAP_COLOR or GL_MAP_STENCIL parameter is TRUE, then mapping is enabled. See the next section to learn how the mapping is done and how to change the contents of the maps. All the other parameters directly affect the pixel component values.

The pixel conversions performed when going from framebuffer to memory (reading) are similar but not identical to the conversions performed when going in the opposite direction (drawing), as explained in the following sections.

The Pixel Rectangle-Drawing Process in Detail

Figure 8-5 and the following paragraphs describe the operation of drawing pixels into the framebuffer.

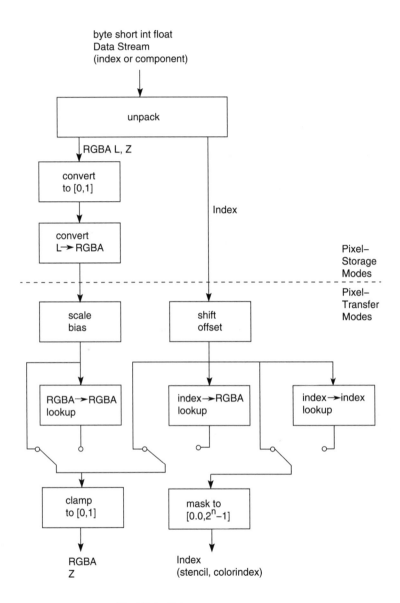

Figure 8-5 Drawing Pixels with glDrawPixels*()

1. If the pixels aren't indices (color or stencil), the first step is to convert the components to floating-point format if necessary. See Table 5-1 on page 151 for the details of the conversion.

2. If the format is GL_LUMINANCE or GL_LUMINANCE_ALPHA, the luminance element is converted into R, G, and B, by using the luminance value for each of the R, G, and B components. In GL_LUMINANCE_ALPHA format, the alpha value becomes the A value. If A is missing, it's set to 1.0.

3. Each component (R, G, B, A, or depth) is multiplied by the appropriate scale, and the appropriate bias is added. For example, the R component is multiplied by the value corresponding to GL_RED_SCALE, and added to the value corresponding to GL_RED_BIAS.

4. If GL_MAP_COLOR is true, each of the R, G, B, and A components is clamped to the range [0.0,1.0], multiplied by an integer one less than the table size, truncated, and looked up in the table. See "Pixel Mapping" on page 252 for more details.

5. Next, the R, G, B, and A components are clamped to [0.0,1.0] if they weren't already, and they're converted to fixed-point with as many bits to the left of the binary point as there are in the corresponding framebuffer component.

6. If you're working with index values (stencil or color indices), then the values are first converted to fixed-point (if they were initially floating-point numbers) with some unspecified bits to the right of the binary point. Indices that were initially fixed-point remain so, and any bits to the right of the binary point are set to zero.

7. The resulting index value is then shifted right or left by the absolute value of GL_INDEX_SHIFT bits; the value is shifted left if GL_INDEX_SHIFT > 0 and right otherwise. Finally, GL_INDEX_OFFSET is added to the index.

8. The next step with indices depends on whether you're using RGBA mode or index mode. In RGBA mode, a color index is converted to RGBA using the color components specified by GL_PIXEL_MAP_I_TO_R, GL_PIXEL_MAP_I_TO_G, GL_PIXEL_MAP_I_TO_B, and GL_PIXEL_MAP_I_TO_A (see the next section for details). Otherwise, if GL_MAP_COLOR is TRUE, a color index is looked up through the table GL_PIXEL_MAP_I_TO_I. (If GL_MAP_COLOR is FALSE, the index is unchanged.) If the image is made up of stencil indices rather than color indices, and if GL_MAP_STENCIL is TRUE, the index is looked up in the table corresponding to GL_PIXEL_MAP_S_TO_S. If GL_MAP_STENCIL is FALSE, the stencil index is unchanged.

The Pixel Rectangle-Reading Process in Detail

During the pixel reading process, many of the same conversions are done, as shown in Figure 8-6 and as described in the following paragraphs.

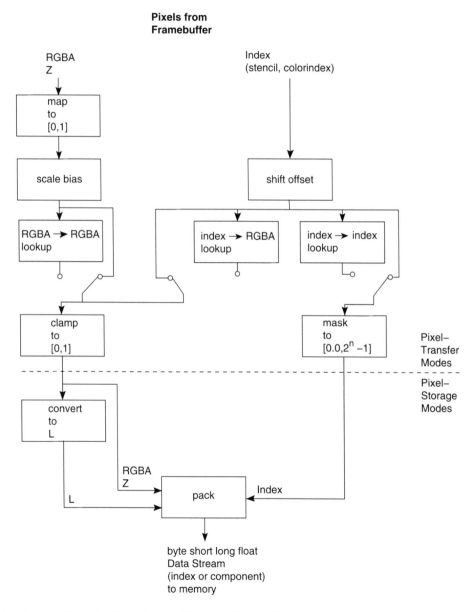

Figure 8-6   Reading Pixels with glReadPixels*()

If the pixels to be read aren't indices (color or stencil), the components are mapped to [0.0,1.0]—that is, in exactly the opposite way that they are when written. Next, the scales and biases are applied to each component. If GL_MAP_COLOR is TRUE, they're mapped and again clamped to [0.0,1.0]. If luminance is desired instead of RGB, the R, G, and B components are added (L = R + G + B). Finally, the results are packed into memory according to the GL_PACK* modes set with **glPixelStore*()**.

If the pixels are indices (color or stencil), they're shifted and offset, and mapped if GL_MAP_COLOR is TRUE. If the storage format is either GL_COLOR_INDEX or GL_STENCIL_INDEX, the pixel indices are masked to the number of bits of the storage type (1, 8, 16, or 32) and packed into memory as described previously. If the storage format is one of the component kind (such as luminance or RGB), the pixels are always mapped by the index-to-RGBA maps. Then, they're treated as though they had been RGBA pixels in the first place (including perhaps being converted to luminance).

The scaling, bias, shift, and offset values are the same as those used when drawing pixels, so if you're doing both reading and drawing of pixels, be sure to reset these components to the appropriate values before doing a read or a draw. Similarly, the various maps (see the next section) must also be properly reset if you intend to use maps for both reading and drawing.

Note: It might seem that luminance is handled incorrectly in both the reading and drawing operations. For example, luminance is not usually equally dependent on the R, G, and B components as it seems above. If you wanted your luminance to be calculated such that the R component contributed 30 percent, the G 59 percent, and the B 11 percent, you could set GL_RED_SCALE to .30, GL_RED_BIAS to 0.0, and so on. Then the computed L is then .30R + .59G + .11B.

Pixel Mapping

As mentioned in the previous section, all the color components, color indices, and stencil indices can be modified by means of a table lookup before being placed in screen memory. The command for controlling this mapping is **glPixelMap*()**.

void **glPixelMap**[ui us f}**v**(GLenum *map*, GLint *mapsize*,
                         const *TYPE *values*);

Loads the pixel map indicated by *map* with *mapsize* entries, whose values
are pointed to by *values*. Table 8-5 lists the map names and values; the
default sizes are all 1 and the default values are all 0. Each map's size must
be a power of 2.

Map Name	Address	Value
GL_PIXEL_MAP_I_TO_I	color index	color index
GL_PIXEL_MAP_S_TO_S	stencil index	stencil index
GL_PIXEL_MAP_I_TO_R	color index	R
GL_PIXEL_MAP_I_TO_G	color index	G
GL_PIXEL_MAP_I_TO_B	color index	B
GL_PIXEL_MAP_I_TO_A	color index	A
GL_PIXEL_MAP_R_TO_R	R	R
GL_PIXEL_MAP_G_TO_G	G	G
GL_PIXEL_MAP_B_TO_B	B	B
GL_PIXEL_MAP_A_TO_A	A	A

Table 8-5   Valid Parameter Names and Values for Use with glPixelMap*()

The maximum size of the maps is machine-dependent. You can find the
sizes of the pixel maps supported on your machine with the **glGet*()**
command: Use the query argument GL_MAX_PIXEL_MAP_TABLE to
obtain the maximum size for all the pixel map tables, and use
GL_PIXEL_MAP_*_TO_*_SIZE to obtain the current size of the specified
map. The six maps whose address is a color index must always be sized to
an integral power of 2. The four RGBA maps can be any size from 1
through GL_MAX_PIXEL_MAP_TABLE.

To illustrate how a table works, let's look at a simple example. Suppose that
you want to create a 256-entry table that maps color indices to color
indices using GL_PIXEL_MAP_I_TO_I. You create a table with an entry for
each of the values between 0 and 255, and initialize the table with
glPixelMap*(). Let's say that you're using the table for thresholding, for

example, and you want to map all indices 100 and below to 0, and all indices 101 and above to 255. In this case, your table consists of 101 0s and 155 255s. The pixel map is enabled using the routine **glPixelTransfer*()** to set the parameter GL_MAP_COLOR to TRUE. Once the pixel map is loaded and enabled, incoming color indices below 101 come out as 0, and incoming pixels between 101 and 255 are mapped to 255. If the incoming pixel is larger than 255, it's first masked by 255, throwing out all the bits beyond the eighth, and the resulting masked value is looked up in the table. If the incoming index is a floating-point value (say 88.14585), it's rounded to the nearest integer value (giving 88), and that number is looked up in the table (giving 0).

Chapter 9

Texture Mapping

Chapter Objectives

After reading this chapter, you'll be able to do the following:

- Understand what texture mapping can add to your scene

- Specify a texture map and how its coordinates relate to those of the objects in your scene

- Control how a texture image is filtered as it's applied to a fragment

- Specify how the color values in the image combine with those of the fragment to which it's being applied

- Use automatic texture coordinate generation to produce effects like contour maps and environment maps

So far in this guide, every geometric primitive has been drawn as either a solid color or smoothly shaded between the colors at its vertices—that is, they've been drawn without texture mapping. If you want to draw a large brick wall without texture mapping, for example, each brick must be drawn as a separate polygon. Without texturing, a large flat wall—which is really a single rectangle—might require thousands of individual bricks, and even then the bricks would appear too smooth and regular to be realistic.

Texture mapping allows you to glue an image of a brick wall (obtained, perhaps, by scanning in a photograph of a real wall) to a polygon, and to draw the entire wall as a single polygon. Texture mapping ensures that all the right things happen as the polygon is transformed and rendered: When the wall is viewed in perspective, for example, the bricks decrease in size along with the wall as the wall gets farther from the viewpoint. Other uses for texture mapping include vegetation to be textured on large polygons representing the ground for a flight simulator; wallpaper patterns; and textures that make polygons appear to be made of natural substances such as marble, wood, or cloth. The possibilities are endless. Although it's most natural to think of applying textures to polygons, textures can be applied to all primitives—points, lines, polygons, bitmaps, and images. Plates 6, 8, 18-21, 24-27, and 29-31 all demonstrate the use of textures.

Because there are so many possibilities, texture mapping is a fairly large, complex subject, and you must make several programming choices when using it. For instance, you can map textures to surfaces made of a set of polygons or to curved surfaces, and you can repeat a texture in one or both directions to cover the surface. A texture can even be one-dimensional. In addition, you can automatically map a texture onto an object in such a way that the texture indicates contours or other properties of the item being viewed. Shiny objects can be textured so that they appear as if they were in the center of a room or other environment, reflecting the surroundings off their surfaces. Finally, a texture can be applied to a surface in different ways. It can be painted on directly (like a decal placed on a surface), it can be used to modulate the color the surface would have been painted otherwise, or it can be used to blend a texture color with the surface color. If this is your first exposure to texture mapping, you might find that the discussion in this chapter moves fairly quickly. As an additional reference, you might look at the chapter on texture mapping in *Fundamentals of Three-Dimensional Computer Graphics* by Alan Watt (Reading, Mass.: Addison-Wesley, 1990).

Textures are simply rectangular arrays of data—for example, color data, luminance data, or color and alpha data. The individual values in a texture array are often called *texels*. What makes texture mapping tricky is that a rectangular texture can be mapped to nonrectangular regions, and this must be done in a reasonable way.

Figure 9-1 illustrates the texture-mapping process. The left side of the figure represents the entire texture, and the black outline represents a quadrilateral shape whose corners are mapped to those spots on the texture. When the quadrilateral is displayed on the screen, it might be distorted by applying various transformations—rotations, translations, scaling, and projections. The right side of the figure shows how the texture-mapped quadrilateral might appear on your screen after these transformations. (Note that this quadrilateral is concave and might not be rendered correctly by OpenGL.)

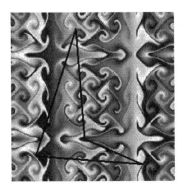 

Figure 9-1   The Texture-Mapping Process

Notice how the texture is distorted to match the distortion of the quadrilateral. In this case, it's stretched in the x direction and compressed in the y direction; there's a bit of rotation and shearing going on as well. Depending on the texture size, the quadrilateral's distortion, and the size of the screen image, some of the texels might be mapped to more than one fragment, and some fragments might be covered by multiple texels. Since the texture is made up of discrete texels (in this case, 256×256 of them), filtering operations must be performed to map texels to fragments. For example, if many texels correspond to a fragment, they're averaged down to fit; if texel boundaries fall across fragment boundaries, a weighted average of the applicable texels is performed. Because of these calculations, texturing is computationally expensive, which is why many specialized graphics systems include hardware support for texture mapping.

This chapter covers the OpenGL's texture-mapping facility in the following major sections:

- **"An Overview and an Example"** gives a brief, broad look at the steps required to perform texture mapping. It also presents a relatively simple example of texture mapping.

- **"Specifying the Texture"** explains how to specify a two- or one-dimensional texture. It also discusses how to use a texture's borders, how to supply a series of related textures of different sizes, and how to control the filtering methods used to determine how an applied texture is mapped to screen coordinates.

- **"Modulating and Blending"** discusses the methods used for painting a texture onto a surface. You can choose to have the texture color values replace those that would be used if texturing wasn't in effect, or you can have the final color be a combination of the two.

- **"Assigning Texture Coordinates"** describes how to compute and assign appropriate texture coordinates to the vertices of an object. It also explains how to control the behavior of coordinates that lie outside the default range—that is, how to repeat or clamp textures across a surface.

- **"Automatic Texture-Coordinate Generation"** shows you how to have OpenGL automatically generate texture coordinates for you, in order to achieve such effects as contour and environment maps.

- **"Advanced Features"** explains how to manipulate the texture matrix stack and how to use the q texture coordinate.

Remember that you might be able to use display lists to store defined textures for maximum performance efficiency. See "Display-List Design Philosophy" on page 121.

An Overview and an Example

This section gives an overview of the steps necessary to perform texture mapping. It also presents a relatively simple texture-mapping program— *relatively* because, remember, texture mapping is a fairly involved process.

Steps in Texture Mapping

To use texture mapping, you perform these steps:

1. Specify the texture.
2. Indicate how the texture is to be applied to each pixel.
3. Enable texture mapping.
4. Draw the scene, supplying both texture and geometric coordinates.

Keep in mind that texture mapping works only in RGB mode; the results in color-index mode are undefined.

Specify the Texture

In the simplest case, the texture is a single image. A texture is usually thought of as being two-dimensional, like most images, but it can also be one-dimensional. The data describing a texture can consist of one, two, three, or four elements per texel, representing anything from a modulation constant to an (R, G, B, A) quadruple.

Using an advanced technique, called *mipmapping*, you can specify a single texture at many different resolutions; this allows you to avoid mapping a full-resolution image of a brick wall on a wall that's so far away from the viewer that it appears on the screen as a single pixel, for example. Also, the specification of the map can include boundary values to use when the object's texture coordinates get outside the valid range. Boundary values allow you to paste together multiple texture maps smoothly, thereby increasing the effective size of the largest available texture.

Indicate How the Texture Is to Be Applied to Each Pixel

You can choose any of three possible functions for computing the final RGBA value from the fragment color and the texture-image data. One possibility is to simply use the texture color as the final color; this is the *decal* mode, in which the texture is painted on top of the fragment, just as a decal would be applied. Another method is to use the texture to *modulate*, or scale, the fragment's color; this technique is useful for combining the effects of lighting with texturing. Finally, a constant color can be *blended* with that of the fragment, based on the texture value.

Enable Texture Mapping

You need to enable texturing before drawing your scene. Texturing is enabled or disabled using **glEnable()** or **glDisable()** with the symbolic constant GL_TEXTURE_1D or GL_TEXTURE_2D for one- or two-dimensional texturing, respectively. (If both are enabled, *2D is preferred.)

Draw the Scene, Supplying Both Texture and Geometric Coordinates

You need to indicate how the texture should be aligned relative to the fragments to which it's to be applied before it's "glued on." That is, you need to specify both texture coordinates and geometric coordinates as you specify the objects in your scene. For a two-dimensional texture map, for example, the texture coordinates range from 0.0 to 1.0 in both directions, but the coordinates of the items being textured can be anything. For the brick-wall example, if the wall is square and meant to represent one copy of the texture, the code would probably assign texture coordinates (0, 0), (1, 0), (1, 1), and (0, 1) to the four corners of the wall. If the wall is large, you might want to paint several copies of the texture map on it. If you do so, the texture map must be designed so that the bricks on the left edge blend nicely with the bricks on the right edge, and similarly for the bricks on the top and those on the bottom.

You must also indicate how texture coordinates outside the range [0.0,1.0] should be treated. Do the textures *wrap* to cover the object, or are they clamped to a boundary value?

A Sample Program

One of the problems with showing sample programs to illustrate texture mapping is that interesting textures are large. Typically, textures are read from an image file, since specifying a texture programmatically could take hundreds of lines of code. In Listing 9-1, the texture—which consists of alternating white and black squares, like a checkerboard—is generated by the program. The program applies this texture to two squares, which are then rendered in perspective, one of them facing the viewer squarely and the other tilting back at 45 degrees, as shown in Figure 9-2. In object coordinates, both squares are the same size.

Figure 9-2   Texture-Mapped Squares

Listing 9-1   A Texture-Mapped Checkerboard: checker.c

```
#include <GL/gl.h>
#include <GL/glu.h>
#include "aux.h"

#define     checkImageWidth 64
#define     checkImageHeight 64
GLubyte checkImage[checkImageWidth][checkImageHeight][3];

void makeCheckImage(void)
{
    int i, j, r, c;

    for (i = 0; i < checkImageWidth; i++) {
        for (j = 0; j < checkImageHeight; j++) {
            c = ((((i&0x8)==0)^((j&0x8))==0))*255;
            checkImage[i][j][0] = (GLubyte) c;
            checkImage[i][j][1] = (GLubyte) c;
            checkImage[i][j][2] = (GLubyte) c;
        }
    }
}

void myinit(void)
{
    glClearColor (0.0, 0.0, 0.0, 0.0);
    glEnable(GL_DEPTH_TEST);
    glDepthFunc(GL_LEQUAL);
```

```
    makeCheckImage();
    glPixelStorei(GL_UNPACK_ALIGNMENT, 1);
    glTexImage2D(GL_TEXTURE_2D, 0, 3, checkImageWidth,
        checkImageHeight, 0, GL_RGB, GL_UNSIGNED_BYTE,
        &checkImage[0][0][0]);
    glTexParameterf(GL_TEXTURE_2D, GL_TEXTURE_WRAP_S, GL_CLAMP);
    glTexParameterf(GL_TEXTURE_2D, GL_TEXTURE_WRAP_T, GL_CLAMP);
    glTexParameterf(GL_TEXTURE_2D, GL_TEXTURE_MAG_FILTER,
        GL_NEAREST);
    glTexParameterf(GL_TEXTURE_2D, GL_TEXTURE_MIN_FILTER,
        GL_NEAREST);
    glTexEnvf(GL_TEXTURE_ENV, GL_TEXTURE_ENV_MODE, GL_DECAL);
    glEnable(GL_TEXTURE_2D);
    glShadeModel(GL_FLAT);
}

void display(void)
{
    glClear(GL_COLOR_BUFFER_BIT | GL_DEPTH_BUFFER_BIT);
    glBegin(GL_QUADS);
    glTexCoord2f(0.0, 0.0); glVertex3f(-2.0, -1.0, 0.0);
    glTexCoord2f(0.0, 1.0); glVertex3f(-2.0, 1.0, 0.0);
    glTexCoord2f(1.0, 1.0); glVertex3f(0.0, 1.0, 0.0);
    glTexCoord2f(1.0, 0.0); glVertex3f(0.0, -1.0, 0.0);

    glTexCoord2f(0.0, 0.0); glVertex3f(1.0, -1.0, 0.0);
    glTexCoord2f(0.0, 1.0); glVertex3f(1.0, 1.0, 0.0);
    glTexCoord2f(1.0, 1.0); glVertex3f(2.41421, 1.0, -1.41421);
    glTexCoord2f(1.0, 0.0); glVertex3f(2.41421, -1.0, -1.41421);
    glEnd();
    glFlush();
}

void myReshape(GLsizei w, GLsizei h)
{
    glViewport(0, 0, w, h);
    glMatrixMode(GL_PROJECTION);
    glLoadIdentity();
    gluPerspective(60.0, 1.0*(GLfloat)w/(GLfloat)h, 1.0, 30.0);
    glMatrixMode(GL_MODELVIEW);
    glLoadIdentity();
    glTranslatef(0.0, 0.0, -3.6);
}
```

```
int main(int argc, char** argv)
{
    auxInitDisplayMode (AUX_SINGLE | AUX_RGBA | AUX_DEPTH);
    auxInitPosition (0, 0, 500, 500);
    auxInitWindow (argv[0]);
    myinit();
    auxReshapeFunc (myReshape);
    auxMainLoop(display);
}
```

The checkerboard texture is generated in the routine **makeCheckImage()**, and all the texture-mapping initialization occurs in the routine **myinit()**. The single, full-resolution texture map is specified by **glTexImage2D()**, whose parameters indicate the size of the image, type of the image, location of the image, and other properties of it. See the next section for more information about this command.

The next four calls to **glTexParameter*()** specify how the texture is to be wrapped (see "Repeating and Clamping Textures" on page 280) and how the colors are to be filtered if there isn't an exact match between pixels in the texture and pixels on the screen (see "Controlling Filtering" on page 271). Next, **glTexEnv*()** sets the drawing mode to GL_DECAL so that the textured polygons are drawn using the colors from the texture map (rather than taking into account what color the polygons would have been drawn without the texture). Finally, **glEnable()** turns on texturing.

The routine **display()** draws the two polygons. Note that texture coordinates are specified along with vertex coordinates. The **glTexCoord*()** command behaves similarly to the **glNormal()** command: It sets the current texture coordinates; any subsequent vertex command has those texture coordinates associated with it until **glTexCoord*()** is called again.

Note: The checkerboard image on the tilted polygon might look wrong when you compile and run it on your machine—for example, it might look like two triangles with different projections of the checkerboard image on them. If so, try setting the parameter GL_PERSPECTIVE_CORRECTION_HINT to GL_NICEST and running the example again. To do this, use **glHint()**, as described on page 208.

Specifying the Texture

The command **glTexImage2D**() defines a two-dimensional texture. It takes several arguments, which are described briefly here and in more detail in the subsections that follow. The related command for one-dimensional textures, **glTexImage1D**(), is described in "One-Dimensional Textures" on page 274.

---

void **glTexImage2D**(GLenum *target*, GLint *level*, GLint *components*,
  GLsizei *width*, GLsizei *height*, GLint *border*,
  GLenum *format*, GLenum *type*, const GLvoid **pixels*);

Defines a two-dimensional texture. The *target* parameter is intended for future use by OpenGL; for this release, it must be set to the constant GL_TEXTURE_2D. You use the *level* parameter if you're supplying multiple resolutions of the texture map; with only one resolution, *level* should be 0. (See "Multiple Levels of Detail" on page 266 for more information about using multiple resolutions.)

The next parameter, *components*, is an integer from 1 to 4 indicating which of the R, G, B, and A components are selected for use in modulating or blending. A value of 1 selects the R component, 2 selects the R and A components, 3 selects R, G, and B, and 4 selects R, B, G, and A. See "Modulating and Blending" on page 274 for a discussion of how these selected components are used.

The *width* and *height* parameters give the dimensions of the texture image; *border* indicates the width of the border, which is usually zero. (See "Using a Texture's Borders" on page 265.) Both *width* and *height* must have the form 2^m+2b, where *m* is an integer (which can have a different value for *width* than for *height*) and *b* is the value of *border*. The maximum size of a texture map depends on the implementation of OpenGL, but it must be at least 64×64 (or 66×66 with borders). If *width* or *height* is set to zero, texture mapping is effectively disabled.

The *format* and *type* parameters describe the format and data type of the texture image data. They have the same meaning as they do for **glDrawPixels**(), which is described in "Storing, Transforming, and Mapping Pixels" on page 242. In fact, texture data is in the same format as the data used by **glDrawPixels**(), so the settings of such modes as GL_ALIGNMENT apply. (In the checkered-squares example, the call

```
glPixelStorei(GL_ALIGNMENT, 1);
```

is made because the data in the example isn't padded at the end of each texel row.) The *format* parameter can be GL_COLOR_INDEX, GL_RGB, GL_RGBA, GL_RED, GL_GREEN, GL_BLUE, GL_ALPHA, GL_LUMINANCE, or GL_LUMINANCE_ALPHA—that is, the same formats available for **glDrawPixels()** with the exceptions of GL_STENCIL_INDEX and GL_DEPTH_COMPONENT. Similarly, the *type* parameter can be GL_BYTE, GL_UNSIGNED_BYTE, GL_SHORT, GL_UNSIGNED_SHORT, GL_INT, GL_UNSIGNED_INT, GL_FLOAT, or GL_BITMAP.

Finally, *pixels* contains the texture-image data. This data describes the texture image itself as well as its border.

The next sections give more detail about using the *border* and *level* parameters. The *level* parameter, which specifies textures of different resolutions, naturally raises the topic of filtering textures as they're applied; filtering is the subject of "Controlling Filtering" on page 271. Finally, one-dimensional textures are discussed in "One-Dimensional Textures" on page 274.

Using a Texture's Borders

Advanced

If you need to apply a larger texture map than your implementation of OpenGL allows, you can, with a little care, effectively make larger textures by tiling with several different textures. For example, if you need a texture twice as large as the maximum allowed size mapped to a square, draw the square as four subsquares, and load a different texture before drawing each piece.

Since only a single texture map is available at one time, this approach might lead to problems at the edges of the textures, especially if some form of linear filtering is enabled. The texture value to be used for pixels at the edges must be averaged with something off the edge, which, ideally, should come from the adjacent texture map. If you define a border for each texture whose texel values are equal to the values of the texels on the edge of the adjacent texture map, then when linear averaging takes place, the correct behavior results.

To do this correctly, notice that each map can have eight neighbors—one adjacent to each edge, and one touching each corner. The values of the texels in the corner of the border need to correspond with the texels in the texture maps that touch the corners. If your texture is an edge or corner of the whole tiling, you need to decide what values would be reasonable to put in the borders. The easiest reasonable thing to do is to copy the value of the adjacent texel in the texture map. Remember that the border values need to be supplied at the same time as the texture-image data, so you need to figure this out ahead of time.

A texture's border color is also used if the texture is applied in such a way that it only partially covers a primitive. See "Repeating and Clamping Textures" on page 280 for more information about this situation.

Advanced

Multiple Levels of Detail

Textured objects can be viewed, like any other objects in a scene, at different distances from the viewpoint. In a dynamic scene, for example, as a textured object moves farther from the viewpoint, the texture map must decrease in size along with the size of the projected image. To accomplish this, OpenGL has to filter the texture map down to an appropriate size for mapping onto the object, without introducing visually disturbing artifacts. To avoid such artifacts, you can specify a series of prefiltered texture maps of decreasing resolutions, called *mipmaps*, as shown in Figure 9-3. Then, OpenGL automatically determines which texture map to use based on the size (in pixels) of the object being mapped. With this approach, the level of detail in the texture map is appropriate for the image that's drawn on the screen—as the image of the object gets smaller, the size of the texture map decreases. Mipmapping requires some extra computation, but, when it's not used, textures that are mapped onto smaller objects might shimmer and flash as the objects move.

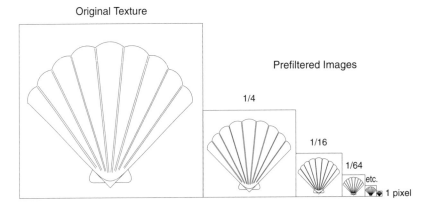

Figure 9-3   Mipmaps

This technique is called *mipmapping*. (*Mip* stands for the Latin *multim im parvo*, meaning "many things in a small place." Mipmapping uses some clever methods to pack the image data into memory. See "Pyramidal Parametrics " by Lance Williams, SIGGRAPH 1983 Proceedings.)

To use mipmapping, you provide all sizes of your texture in powers of 2 between the largest size and a 1×1 map. For example, if your highest-resolution map is 64×16, you must also provide maps of size 32×8, 16×4, 8×2, 4×1, 2×1, and 1×1. The smaller maps are typically filtered and averaged-down versions of the largest map in which each texel in a smaller texture is an average of the corresponding four texels in the larger texture. OpenGL doesn't require any particular method for calculating the smaller maps, however, so the differently sized textures could be totally unrelated.

To specify these textures, call **glTexImage2D()** once for each resolution of the texture map, with different values for the *level*, *width*, *height*, and *image* parameters. Starting with zero, *level* identifies which texture in the series is specified; with the previous example, the largest texture of size 64×16 would be declared with *level* = 0, the 32×8 texture with *level* = 1, and so on. In addition, for the mipmapped textures to take effect, you need to choose one of the appropriate filtering methods described in the next section.

Listing 9-2 illustrates the use of a series of six texture maps decreasing in size from 32×32 to 1×1. This program draws a rectangle that extends from the foreground far back in the distance, eventually disappearing at a point, as shown in Plate 20. Note that sixty-four copies of the texture map are required to tile the rectangle, eight in each direction. To illustrate how one texture map succeeds another, each map has a different color.

Listing 9-2   A Mipmapping Example: mipmap.c

```
#include <GL/gl.h>
#include <GL/glu.h>
#include "aux.h"

GLubyte mipmapImage32[32][32][3];
GLubyte mipmapImage16[16][16][3];
GLubyte mipmapImage8[8][8][3];
GLubyte mipmapImage4[4][4][3];
GLubyte mipmapImage2[2][2][3];
GLubyte mipmapImage1[1][1][3];

void loadImages(void)
{
    int i, j;
```

```
        for (i = 0; i < 32; i++) {
            for (j = 0; j < 32; j++) {
                mipmapImage32[i][j][0] = 255;
                mipmapImage32[i][j][1] = 255;
                mipmapImage32[i][j][2] = 0;
            }
        }
        for (i = 0; i < 16; i++) {
            for (j = 0; j < 16; j++) {
                mipmapImage16[i][j][0] = 255;
                mipmapImage16[i][j][1] = 0;
                mipmapImage16[i][j][2] = 255;
            }
        }
        for (i = 0; i < 8; i++) {
            for (j = 0; j < 8; j++) {
                mipmapImage8[i][j][0] = 255;
                mipmapImage8[i][j][1] = 0;
                mipmapImage8[i][j][2] = 0;
            }
        }
        for (i = 0; i < 4; i++) {
            for (j = 0; j < 4; j++) {
                mipmapImage4[i][j][0] = 0;
                mipmapImage4[i][j][1] = 255;
                mipmapImage4[i][j][2] = 0;
            }
        }
        for (i = 0; i < 2; i++) {
            for (j = 0; j < 2; j++) {
                mipmapImage2[i][j][0] = 0;
                mipmapImage2[i][j][1] = 0;
                mipmapImage2[i][j][2] = 255;
            }
        }
    mipmapImage1[0][0][0] = 255;
    mipmapImage1[0][0][1] = 255;
    mipmapImage1[0][0][2] = 255;
}

void myinit(void)
{
    glEnable(GL_DEPTH_TEST);
    glDepthFunc(GL_LEQUAL);
    glShadeModel(GL_FLAT);
```

```
    glTranslatef(0.0, 0.0, -3.6);
    loadImages();
    glPixelStorei(GL_UNPACK_ALIGNMENT, 1);
    glTexImage2D(GL_TEXTURE_2D, 0, 3, 32, 32, 0,
        GL_RGB, GL_UNSIGNED_BYTE, &mipmapImage32[0][0][0]);
    glTexImage2D(GL_TEXTURE_2D, 1, 3, 16, 16, 0,
        GL_RGB, GL_UNSIGNED_BYTE, &mipmapImage16[0][0][0]);
    glTexImage2D(GL_TEXTURE_2D, 2, 3, 8, 8, 0,
        GL_RGB, GL_UNSIGNED_BYTE, &mipmapImage8[0][0][0]);
    glTexImage2D(GL_TEXTURE_2D, 3, 3, 4, 4, 0,
        GL_RGB, GL_UNSIGNED_BYTE, &mipmapImage4[0][0][0]);
    glTexImage2D(GL_TEXTURE_2D, 4, 3, 2, 2, 0,
        GL_RGB, GL_UNSIGNED_BYTE, &mipmapImage2[0][0][0]);
    glTexImage2D(GL_TEXTURE_2D, 5, 3, 1, 1, 0,
        GL_RGB, GL_UNSIGNED_BYTE, &mipmapImage1[0][0][0]);
    glTexParameterf(GL_TEXTURE_2D, GL_TEXTURE_WRAP_S,
        GL_REPEAT);
    glTexParameterf(GL_TEXTURE_2D, GL_TEXTURE_WRAP_T,
        GL_REPEAT);
    glTexParameterf(GL_TEXTURE_2D, GL_TEXTURE_MAG_FILTER,
        GL_NEAREST);
    glTexParameterf(GL_TEXTURE_2D, GL_TEXTURE_MIN_FILTER,
        GL_NEAREST_MIPMAP_NEAREST);
    glTexEnvf(GL_TEXTURE_ENV, GL_TEXTURE_ENV_MODE, GL_DECAL);
    glEnable(GL_TEXTURE_2D);
}

void display(void)
{
    glClear(GL_COLOR_BUFFER_BIT | GL_DEPTH_BUFFER_BIT);
    glBegin(GL_QUADS);
    glTexCoord2f(0.0, 0.0); glVertex3f(-2.0, -1.0, 0.0);
    glTexCoord2f(0.0, 8.0); glVertex3f(-2.0, 1.0, 0.0);
    glTexCoord2f(8.0, 8.0); glVertex3f(2000.0, 1.0, -6000.0);
    glTexCoord2f(8.0, 0.0); glVertex3f(2000.0, -1.0, -6000.0);
    glEnd();
    glFlush();
}

void myReshape(GLsizei w, GLsizei h)
{
    glViewport(0, 0, w, h);
    glMatrixMode(GL_PROJECTION);
    glLoadIdentity();
    gluPerspective(60.0, 1.0*(GLfloat)w/(GLfloat)h, 1.0,
        30000.0);
```

```
        glMatrixMode(GL_MODELVIEW);
        glLoadIdentity();
    }

    int main(int argc, char** argv)
    {
        auxInitDisplayMode (AUX_SINGLE | AUX_RGBA | AUX_DEPTH);
        auxInitPosition (0, 0, 500, 500);
        auxInitWindow (argv[0]);
        myinit();
        auxReshapeFunc (myReshape);
        auxMainLoop(display);
    }
```

Listing 9-2 illustrates mipmapping by making each mipmap a different color so that it's obvious when one map is replaced by another. In a real situation, you define mipmaps so that the transition is as smooth as possible. Thus, the maps of lower resolution are usually filtered versions of an original, high-resolution map. The construction of a series of such mipmaps is a software process, and thus isn't part of OpenGL, which is simply a rendering library. Since mipmap construction is such an important operation, however, the OpenGL Utility Library contains three routines that aid in the manipulation of images to be used as texture maps.

Assuming that you have constructed the level 0, or highest-resolution map, the routines **gluBuild1DMipmaps()** and **gluBuild2DMipmaps()** construct and define the pyramid of mipmaps down to a resolution of 1×1 (or 1, for one-dimensional texture maps). Both these routines require that the original image already be suitable for a texture map, namely that its dimensions must be powers of 2. Most scanned images don't satisfy this property, so you have to scale the incoming image to some appropriate size. The GLU provides the routine **gluScaleImage()** to perform such scaling.

int **gluBuild1DMipmaps**(GLenum *target*, GLint *components*,
                    GLint *width*, GLenum *format*, GLenum *type*,
                    void **data*);

int **gluBuild2DMipmaps**(GLenum *target*, GLint *components*,
                    GLint *width*, GLint *height*, GLenum *format*,
                    GLenum *type*, void **data*);

Construct a series of mipmaps. The parameters for *target*, *components*, *width*, *height*, *format*, *type*, and *data* are exactly the same as those for **glTexImage1D()** and **glTexImage2D()**. A value of 0 is returned if all the mipmaps are constructed successfully; otherwise, a GLU error code is returned.

int **gluScaleImage**(GLenum *format*, GLint *widthin*, GLint *heightin*,
                 GLenum *typein*, const void **datain*,
                 GLint *widthout*, GLint *heightout*, GLenum *typeout*,
                 void **dataout*);

Scales an image using the appropriate pixel-storage modes to unpack the data from *datain*. The *format*, *typein*, and *typeout* parameters can refer to any of the formats or data types supported by **glDrawPixels()**. The image is scaled using linear interpolation and box filtering (from the size indicated by *widthin* and *heightin* to *widthout* and *heightout*), and the resulting image is written to *dataout*. A value of 0 is returned on success, and a GLU error code is returned on failure.

Controlling Filtering

Texture maps are square or rectangular, but after being mapped to a polygon or surface and transformed into screen coordinates, the individual texels of a texture rarely correspond to individual pixels of the final screen image. Depending on the transformations used and the texture mapping applied, a single pixel on the screen can correspond to anything from a tiny portion of a texel (magnification) to a large collection of texels (minification), as shown in Figure 9-4. In either case, it's unclear exactly which texel values should be used and how they should be averaged or interpolated. Consequently, OpenGL allows you to specify any of several filtering options to determine these calculations. The options provide different trade-offs between speed and image quality. Also, you can specify the filtering methods for magnification and minification independently.

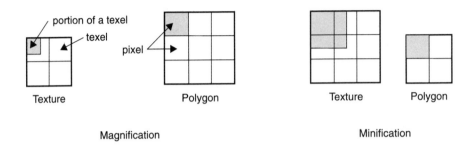

Figure 9-4 Texture Magnification and Minification

In some cases, it isn't obvious whether magnification or minification is called for. If the mipmap needs to be stretched (or shrunk) in both the x and y directions, then magnification (or minification) is needed. If the mipmap needs to be stretched in one direction and shrunk in the other, however, OpenGL makes a choice between magnification and minification that in most cases gives the best result possible. It's best to try to avoid these situations by using texture coordinates that map without such distortion; see "Computing Appropriate Texture Coordinates" on page 278.

The following lines are examples of how to use **glTexParameter*()** to specify the magnification and minification filtering methods:

```
glTexParameteri(GL_TEXTURE_2D, GL_TEXTURE_MAG_FILTER,
                GL_NEAREST);
glTexParameteri(GL_TEXTURE_2D, GL_TEXTURE_MIN_FILTER,
                GL_NEAREST);
```

The first argument to **glTexParameter*()** is either GL_TEXTURE_2D or GL_TEXTURE_1D, depending on whether you're working with two- or one-dimensional textures. For the purposes of this discussion, the second argument is either GL_TEXTURE_MAG_FILTER or GL_TEXTURE_MIN_FILTER to indicate whether you're specifying the filtering method for magnification or minification. The third argument specifies the filtering method; Table 9-1 lists the possible values.

Parameter	Values
GL_TEXTURE_MAG_FILTER	GL_NEAREST or GL_LINEAR
GL_TEXTURE_MIN_FILTER	GL_NEAREST, GL_LINEAR, GL_NEAREST_MIPMAP_NEAREST, GL_NEAREST_MIPMAP_LINEAR, GL_LINEAR_MIPMAP_NEAREST, or GL_LINEAR_MIPMAP_LINEAR

Table 9-1   Filtering Methods for Magnification and Minification

If you choose GL_NEAREST, the texel with coordinates nearest the center of the pixel is used for both magnification and minification. This can result in aliasing artifacts (sometimes severe). If you choose GL_LINEAR, a weighted linear average of the 2×2 array of texels that lies nearest to the center of the pixel is used, again for both magnification and minification. When the texture coordinates are near the edge of the texture map, the nearest 2×2 array of texels might include some that are outside the texture map. In these cases, the texel values used depend on whether GL_REPEAT or GL_CLAMP is in effect and whether you've assigned a border for the texture, as described in "Using a Texture's Borders" on page 265. GL_NEAREST requires less computation than GL_LINEAR and therefore might execute more quickly, but GL_LINEAR provides smoother results.

With magnification, even if you've supplied mipmaps, the largest texture map (*level* = 0) is always used. With minification, you can choose a filtering method that uses the most appropriate one or two mipmaps, as described in the next paragraph. (If GL_NEAREST or GL_LINEAR is specified with minification, the largest texture map is used.)

As shown in Table 9-1, four additional filtering choices are available when minifying with mipmaps. Within an individual mipmap, you can choose the nearest texel value with GL_NEAREST_MIPMAP_NEAREST, or you can interpolate linearly by specifying GL_LINEAR_MIPMAP_NEAREST. Using the nearest texels is faster but yields less desirable results. The particular mipmap chosen is a function of the amount of minification required, and there's a cutoff point from the use of one particular mipmap to the next. To avoid a sudden transition, use GL_NEAREST_MIPMAP_LINEAR or GL_LINEAR_MIPMAP_LINEAR to linearly interpolate texel values from the two nearest best choices of mipmaps. GL_NEAREST_MIPMAP_LINEAR selects the nearest texel in each of the two maps and then interpolates linearly between these two values. GL_LINEAR_MIPMAP_LINEAR uses linear interpolation to compute the value in each of two maps and then interpolates lineraly between these two values. As you might expect, GL_LINEAR_MIPMAP_LINEAR generally produces the smoothest results, but it requires the most computation and therefore might be the slowest.

One-Dimensional Textures

Sometimes a one-dimensional texture is sufficient—for example, if you're drawing textured bands where all the variation is in one direction. A one-dimensional texture behaves like a two-dimensional one with *height* = 1, and without borders along the top and bottom. To specify a one-dimensional texture, use **glTexImage1D()**.

---

void **glTexImage1D**(GLenum *target*, GLint *level*, GLint *components*,
  GLsizei *width*, GLint *border*, GLenum *format*,
  GLenum *type*, const GLvoid **pixels*);

Defines a one-dimensional texture. All the parameters have the same meanings as for **glTexImage2D()**, except that the image is now a one-dimensional array of texels. As before, the value of *width* must be a power of 2 (2^m, or 2^m+2 if there's a border). You can supply mipmaps, and the same filtering options are available as well.

For a sample program that uses a one-dimensional texture map, see Listing 9-3 on page 284.

Modulating and Blending

In all the examples so far in this chapter, the values in the texture map have been used directly as colors to be painted on the surface being rendered. You can also use the values in the texture map to modulate the color that the surface would be painted without texturing, or to blend the color in the texture map with the nontextured color of the surface. You choose one of these three texturing functions by supplying the appropriate arguments to **glTexEnv*()**.

> void **glTexEnv{if}{v}**(GLenum *target*, GLenum *pname*,
> TYPE *param*);
>
> Sets the current texturing function. *target* must be GL_TEXTURE_ENV. If *pname* is GL_TEXTURE_ENV_MODE, *param* can be GL_DECAL, GL_MODULATE, or GL_BLEND, to specify how texture values are to be combined with the color values of the fragment being processed. In decal mode and with a three-component texture, the texture's colors replace the fragment's colors. With either of the other modes or with a four-component texture, the final color is a combination of the texture's and the fragment's values. If *pname* is GL_TEXTURE_ENV_COLOR, *param* is an array of four floating-point values representing R, G, B, and A components. These values are used only if the GL_BLEND texture function has been specified as well.

The texturing function operates on selected components of the texture and the color values that would be used with no texturing. Recall that when you specify your texture map with **glTexImage*d**(), the third argument is the number of R, G, B, A components to be selected for each texel. A single selected component is interpreted as a luminance value (L); if there are two, the first is luminance, and the second is an alpha value (A). Three components form an RGB color triple (C), and four components provide an RGB triple and a value for alpha. Note that this selection is performed after the pixel-transfer function has been applied. Therefore, it makes sense, for example, to specify a texture with a GL_COLOR_INDEX image because the indices are converted to RGBA values by table lookup before they're used to form the texture image. These components are used by the texturing functions as shown in Table 9-2.

Components	Decal Mode	Modulate Mode	Blend Mode
1	undefined	$C = L_t C_f,$ $A = A_f$	$C = (1-L_t)C_f + L_t C_c,$ $A = A_f$
2	undefined	$C = L_t C_f,$ $A = A_t A_f$	$C = (1-L_t)C_f + L_t C_c,$ $A = A_t A_f$
3	$C = C_t,$ $A = A_f$	$C = C_t C_f,$ $A = A_f$	undefined
4	$C = (1-A_t)C_f + A_t C_t,$ $A = A_f$	$C = C_t C_f,$ $A = A_t A_f$	undefined

Table 9-2 Decal, Modulate, and Blend Functions

Note: In the table, a subscript of t indicates a texture value, f indicates a fragment value, c indicates the values assigned with GL_TEXTURE_ENV_COLOR, and no subscript indicates the final, computed value. Also in the table, multiplication of a color triple by a scalar means multiplying each of the R, G, and B components by the scalar; multiplying (or adding) two color triples means multiplying (or adding) each component of the second by the corresponding component of the first.

Decal mode makes sense only if the number of components is three or four (remember that texture mapping doesn't work in color-index mode). With three selected components, the color that would have been painted in the absence of any texture mapping (the fragment's color) is replaced by the texture color, and its alpha is unchanged. With four components, the fragment's color is blended with the texture color in a ratio determined by the texture alpha, and the fragment's alpha is unchanged. You use decal mode in situations where you want to apply an opaque texture to an object—if you were drawing a soup can with an opaque label, for example.

For modulation, the fragment's color is modulated by the contents of the texture map. For one or two components, the color values are multiplied by the same value, so the texture map modulates between the fragment's color (if the luminance is 1) to black (if it's 0). With three or four components, each of the incoming color components is multiplied by a corresponding (possibly different) value in the texture. If there's an alpha value (which there is for two or four components), it's multiplied by the fragment's alpha. You need to use modulation to create a texture that responds to lighting conditions; most of the texture-mapping examples in the color plates use modulation for this reason.

Blending mode makes sense only for one- or two-component textures. The luminance is used somewhat like an alpha value to blend the fragment's color with the color specified by GL_TEXTURE_ENV_COLOR. With two components, the fragment's alpha is also multiplied by the alpha in the texture. See "Sample Uses of Blending" on page 199 for the billboarding example, which uses a blended texture.

Assigning Texture Coordinates

As you draw your texture-mapped scene, you must provide both object coordinates and texture coordinates for each vertex. After transformation, the object coordinates determine where on the screen that particular vertex is rendered. The texture coordinates determine which texel in the texture map is assigned to that vertex. In exactly the same way that colors are interpolated between two vertices of shaded polygons and lines, texture coordinates are linearly interpolated between vertices. (Remember that textures are rectangular arrays of data.)

Texture coordinates can comprise one, two, three, or four coordinates. They're usually referred to as the $s, t, r,$ and q coordinates to distinguish them from object coordinates ($x, y, z,$ and w) and from evaluator coordinates (u and v; see Chapter 11). For one-dimensional textures, you use the s coordinate; for two-dimensional textures, you use s and t. Currently, the r coordinate is ignored (although it might have meaning in the future). The q coordinate, like w, is typically given the value 1 and can be used to create homogeneous coordinates; it's described as an advanced feature in "The q Coordinate" on page 290. The command to specify texture coordinates, **glTexCoord*()**, is similar to **glVertex*()**, **glColor*()**, and **glNormal*()**—it comes in similar variations and is used the same way between **glBegin()** and **glEnd()** pairs. Usually, texture-coordinate values range between 0 and 1; values can be assigned outside this range, however, with the results described in "Repeating and Clamping Textures" on page 280.

---

void **glTexCoord**{1234}{sifd}{v}(*TYPE coords*);

Sets the current texture coordinates (s, t, r, q). Subsequent calls to **glVertex*()** result in those vertices being assigned the current texture coordinates. With **glTexCoord1*()**, the s coordinate is set to the specified value, t and r are set to 0, and q is set to 1. Using **glTexCoord2*()** allows you to specify s and t; r and q are set to 0 and 1, respectively. With **glTexCoord3*()**, q is set to 1 and the other coordinates are set as specified. You can specify all coordinates with **glTexCoord4*()**. Use the appropriate suffix (s, i, f, or d) and the corresponding value for *TYPE* (GLshort, GLint, GLfloat, or GLdouble) to specify the coordinates' data type. You can supply the coordinates individually, or you can use the vector version of the command to supply them in a single array. Texture coordinates are multiplied by the 4×4 texture matrix before any texture mapping occurs, as described in "The Texture Matrix Stack" on page 289. Note that integer texture coodinates are interpreted directly rather than being mapped to the range [−1,1] as normal coordinates are.

The next section discusses how to calculate appropriate texture coordinates. Instead of explicitly assigning them yourself, you can choose to have texture coordinates calculated automatically by OpenGL as a function of the vertex coordinates. This technique is described in "Automatic Texture-Coordinate Generation" on page 283.

Computing Appropriate Texture Coordinates

Two-dimensional textures are square or rectangular images that are typically mapped to the polygons that make up a polygonal model. In the simplest case, you're mapping a rectangular texture onto a model that's also rectangular—for example, your texture is a scanned image of a brick wall, and your rectangle is to represent a brick wall of a building. Suppose the brick wall is square, and the texture is square, and you want to map the whole texture to the whole wall. The texture coordinates of the texture square are (0, 0), (1, 0), (1, 1), and (0, 1) in counterclockwise order. When you're drawing the wall, just give those four coordinate sets as the texture coordinates as you specify the wall's vertices in counterclockwise order.

Now suppose that the wall is two-thirds as high as it is wide, that the texture is again square. To avoid distorting the texture, you need to map the wall to a portion of the texture map so that the aspect ratio of the texture is preserved. Suppose that you decide to use the lower two-thirds of the texture map to texture the wall. In this case, use texture coordinates of (0,0), (1,0), (1,2/3), and (0,2/3) for the texture coordinates as the wall vertices are traversed in a counterclockwise order.

As a slightly more complicated example, suppose you'd like to display a tin can with a label wrapped around it on the screen. To obtain the texture, you purchase a can, remove the label, and scan it in. Suppose the label is 4 units tall and 12 units around, which yields an aspect ratio of 3 to 1. Since textures must have aspect ratios of 2^n to 1, you can either simply not use the top third of the texture, or you can cut and paste the texture until it has the necessary aspect ratio. Let's say you decide to not use the top third. Now suppose the tin can is a cylinder approximated by thirty polygons of length 4 units (the height of the can) and width 12/30 (1/30 of the circumference of the can). You can use the following texture coordinates for each of the thirty approximating rectangles:

1: (0, 0), (1/30, 0), (1/30, 2/3), (0, 2/3)

2: (1/30, 0), (2/30, 0), (2/30, 2/3), (1/30, 2/3)

3: (2/30, 0), (3/30, 0), (3/30, 2/3), (2/30, 2/3)

. . .

30: (29/30, 0), (1, 0), (1, 2/3), (29/30, 2/3)

Only a few curved surfaces such as cones and cylinders can be mapped to a flat surface without geodesic distortion. Any other shape requires some distortion. In general, the higher the curvature of the surface, the more distortion of the texture is required.

If you don't care about texture distortion, it's often quite easy to find a reasonable mapping. For example, consider a sphere whose surface coordinates are given by ($\cos \theta \cos \phi$, $\cos \theta \sin \phi$, $\sin \theta$), where $0 \leq \theta \leq 2\pi$, and $0 \leq \phi \leq \pi$. The θ-ϕ rectangle can be mapped directly to a rectangular texture map, but the closer you get to the poles, the more distorted the texture is. The entire top edge of the texture map is mapped to the north pole, and the entire bottom edge to the south pole. For other surfaces, such as that of a torus (doughnut) with a large hole, the natural surface coordinates map to the texture coordinates in a way that produces only a little distortion, so it might be suitable for many applications. Figure 9-5 shows two tori, one with a small hole (and therefore a lot of distortion near the center) and one with a large hole (and only a little distortion).

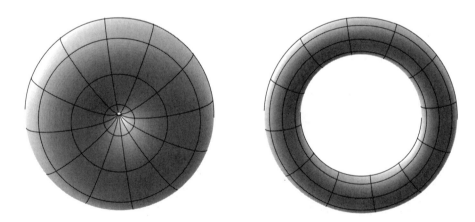

Figure 9-5   Texture-Map Distortion

If you're texturing spline surfaces generated with evaluators (see Chapter 11), the u and v parameters for the surface can sometimes be used as texture coordinates. In general, however, there's a large artistic component to successfully mapping textures to polygonal approximations of curved surfaces.

Repeating and Clamping Textures

You can assign texture coordinates outside the range [0,1] and have them either clamp or repeat in the texture map. With repeating textures, if you have a large plane with texture coordinates running from 0.0 to 10.0 in both directions, for example, you'll get 100 copies of the texture tiled together on the screen. During repeating, the integer part of texture coordinates is ignored, and copies of the texture map tile the surface. For most applications where the texture is to be repeated, the texels at the top of the texture should match those at the bottom, and similarly for the left and right edges.

The other possibility is to clamp the texture coordinates: Any values greater than 1.0 are set to 1.0, and any values less than 0.0 are set to 0.0. Clamping is useful for applications where you want a single copy of the texture to appear on a large surface. If the surface-texture coordinates range from 0.0 to 10.0 in both directions, one copy of the texture appears in the lower corner of the surface. The rest of the surface is painted with the texture's border colors as needed. If you've chosen GL_LINEAR as the filtering method (see "Controlling Filtering" on page 271), an equally weighted combination of the border color and the texture color is used, as follows:

- When repeating, the 2×2 array wraps to the opposite edge of the texture. Thus, texels on the right edge are averaged with those on the left, and top and bottom texels are also averaged.

- If there is a border, then the texel from the border is used. Otherwise, GL_TEXTURE_BORDER_COLOR is used.

Note that you can avoid having the rest of the surface affected by the texture. To do this, use blending with alpha values of 0 to eliminate the drawing. (See "Blending" on page 196.)

If you haven't specified a border with **glTexImage*d**(), the color value of GL_TEXTURE_BORDER_COLOR is used to paint the rest of the surface. By default, this value is (0, 0, 0, 0); use **glTexParameter***() to change this value, as described near the end of this section.

In Listing 9-1, if the texture coordinates for the squares are mapped from 0.0 to 3.0 as follows, the result is as shown in Figure 9-6.

```
glBegin(GL_POLYGON);
  glTexCoord2f(0.0, 0.0); glVertex3f(-2.0, -1.0, 0.0);
  glTexCoord2f(0.0, 3.0); glVertex3f(-2.0, 1.0, 0.0);
```

```
  glTexCoord2f(3.0, 3.0); glVertex3f(0.0, 1.0, 0.0);
  glTexCoord2f(3.0, 0.0); glVertex3f(0.0, -1.0, 0.0);
glEnd();

glBegin(GL_POLYGON);
  glTexCoord2f(0.0, 0.0); glVertex3f(1.0, -1.0, 0.0);
  glTexCoord2f(0.0, 3.0); glVertex3f(1.0, 1.0, 0.0);
  glTexCoord2f(3.0, 3.0); glVertex3f(2.41421, 1.0, -1.41421);
  glTexCoord2f(3.0, 0.0); glVertex3f(2.41421, -1.0, -1.41421);
glEnd();
```

Figure 9-6   Repeating a Texture

In this case, the texture is repeated in both the *s* and *t* directions, since the following calls are made to **glTexParameter*()**:

```
glTexParameterfv(GL_TEXTURE_2D, GL_TEXTURE_S_WRAP, GL_REPEAT);
glTexParameterfv(GL_TEXTURE_2D, GL_TEXTURE_T_WRAP, GL_REPEAT);
```

If GL_CLAMP is used instead of GL_REPEAT, you see the picture shown in Figure 9-7.

Figure 9-7   Clamping a Texture

Notice that the border colors are continued outside the range of the texture map. You can also clamp in one direction and repeat in the other, as shown in Figure 9-8.

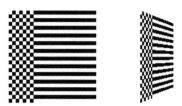

Figure 9-8   Repeating and Clamping a Texture

You've now seen all the possible arguments for **glTexParameter***(), which is summarized here.

void **glTexParameter**{if}{v}(GLenum *target*, GLenum *pname*,
                              TYPE param);

Sets various parameters that control how a texture is treated as it's
applied to a fragment. The *target* parameter is either GL_TEXTURE_2D or
GL_TEXTURE_1D to indicate a two- or one-dimensional texture. The
possible values for *pname* and *param* are shown in Table 9-3. You can use
the vector version of the command to supply an array of values for
GL_TEXTURE_BORDER_COLOR, or you can supply them individually
using the nonvector version. If these values are supplied as integers,
they're converted to floating-point according to Table 5-1 on
page 151; they're also clamped to the range [0,1].

Parameter	Values
GL_TEXTURE_WRAP_S	GL_CLAMP, GL_REPEAT
GL_TEXTURE_WRAP_T	GL_CLAMP, GL_REPEAT
GL_TEXTURE_MAG_FILTER	GL_NEAREST, GL_LINEAR
GL_TEXTURE_MIN_FILTER	GL_NEAREST, GL_LINEAR, GL_NEAREST_MIPMAP_NEAREST, GL_NEAREST_MIPMAP_LINEAR, GL_LINEAR_MIPMAP_NEAREST, GL_LINEAR_MIPMAP_LINEAR
GL_TEXTURE_BORDER_COLOR	any four values in [0, 1]

Table 9-3   Arguments for glTexParameter*()

Automatic Texture-Coordinate Generation

You can use texture mapping to make contours on your models or to
simulate the reflections from an arbitrary environment on a shiny model.
To achieve these effects, let OpenGL automatically generate the texture
coordinates for you, rather than explicitly assigning them with
glTexCoord*(). Actually, the mechanism for automatic texture-coordinate
generation is useful for many different applications such as showing
contours and environment mapping. To generate texture coordinates
automatically, use the command **glTexGen()**.

void **glTexGen**{ifd}{v}(GLenum *coord*, GLenum *pname*, *TYPE param*);

Specifies the functions for automatically generating texture coordinates. The first parameter, *coord*, must be GL_S, GL_T, GL_R, or GL_Q to indicate whether texture coordinate *s, t, r,* or *q* is to be generated. The *pname* parameter is GL_TEXTURE_GEN_MODE, GL_OBJECT_PLANE, or GL_EYE_PLANE. If it's GL_TEXTURE_GEN_MODE, *param* is an integer (or, in the vector version of the command, points to an integer) that's either GL_OBJECT_LINEAR, GL_EYE_LINEAR, or GL_SPHERE_MAP. These symbolic constants determine which function is used to generate the texture coordinate. With either of the other possible values for *pname*, *param* is either a pointer to an array of values (in the vector version) or a single value specifying parameters for the texture-generation function.

Creating Contours

When GL_TEXTURE_GEN_MODE and GL_OBJECT_LINEAR are specified, the generation function is a linear combination of the object coordinates of the vertex (x_0, y_0, z_0, w_0):

generated coordinate = $p_1 x_0 + p_2 y_0 + p_3 z_0 + p_4 w_0$

The $p_1, ..., p_4$ values are supplied as the *param* argument to **glTexGen*()** with *pname* set to GL_OBJECT_PLANE. With $p_1, ..., p_4$ correctly normalized, this function gives the distance from the vertex to a plane. For example, if $p_1 = p_3 = p_4 = 0$ and $p_2 = 1$, the function gives the distance between the vertex and the plane $y = 0$. The distance is positive on one side of the plane, negative on the other, and zero if the vertex lies on the plane.

In Listing 9-3, equally spaced contour lines are drawn on a teapot; the lines indicate the distance from the plane $y = 0$. Since only one property is being shown (the distance from the plane), a one-dimensional texture map suffices. The texture map is a constant green color, except that at equally spaced intervals it includes a red mark. Since the teapot is sitting on the *x-y* plane, the contours are all perpendicular to its base. Plate 18a shows the picture drawn by the program.

Listing 9-3   Automatic Texture-Coordinate Generation: texgen.c

```
#include <GL/gl.h>
#include <GL/glu.h>
#include "aux.h"
```

```
#define    stripeImageWidth 32
GLubyte    stripeImage[3*stripeImageWidth];

void loadStripeImage(void)
{
    int j;

    for (j = 0; j < stripeImageWidth; j++) {
        stripeImage[3*j] = (j<=4) ? 255 : 0;
        stripeImage[3*j+1] = (j>4) ? 255 : 0;
        stripeImage[3*j+2] = 0;
    }
}

GLfloat sgenparams[] = {1.0, 0.0, 0.0, 0.0};

void myinit(void)
{
    glClearColor (0.0, 0.0, 0.0, 0.0);

    loadStripeImage();
    glPixelStorei(GL_UNPACK_ALIGNMENT, 1);
    glTexEnvf(GL_TEXTURE_ENV, GL_TEXTURE_ENV_MODE, GL_MODULATE);
    glTexParameterf(GL_TEXTURE_1D, GL_TEXTURE_WRAP_S,
        GL_REPEAT);
    glTexParameterf(GL_TEXTURE_1D, GL_TEXTURE_MAG_FILTER,
        GL_LINEAR);
    glTexParameterf(GL_TEXTURE_1D, GL_TEXTURE_MIN_FILTER,
        GL_LINEAR);
    glTexImage1D(GL_TEXTURE_1D, 0, 3, stripeImageWidth, 0,
        GL_RGB, GL_UNSIGNED_BYTE, stripeImage);
    glTexGeni(GL_S, GL_TEXTURE_GEN_MODE, GL_OBJECT_LINEAR);
    glTexGenfv(GL_S, GL_OBJECT_PLANE, sgenparams);
    glEnable(GL_DEPTH_TEST);
    glDepthFunc(GL_LEQUAL);
    glEnable(GL_TEXTURE_GEN_S);
    glEnable(GL_TEXTURE_1D);
    glEnable(GL_CULL_FACE);
    glEnable(GL_LIGHTING);
    glEnable(GL_LIGHT0);
    glEnable(GL_AUTO_NORMAL);
    glEnable(GL_NORMALIZE);
    glFrontFace(GL_CW);
    glCullFace(GL_BACK);
    glMaterialf (GL_FRONT, GL_SHININESS, 64.0);
}
```

Automatic Texture-Coordinate Generation   **285**

```
void display(void)
{
    glClear(GL_COLOR_BUFFER_BIT | GL_DEPTH_BUFFER_BIT);
    glPushMatrix ();
        glRotatef(45.0, 0.0, 0.0, 1.0);
        auxSolidTeapot(2.0);
    glPopMatrix ();
    glFlush();
}

void myReshape(GLsizei w, GLsizei h)
{
    glViewport(0, 0, w, h);
    glMatrixMode(GL_PROJECTION);
    glLoadIdentity();
    if (w <= h) glOrtho (-3.5, 3.5, -3.5*(GLfloat)h/(GLfloat)w,
            3.5*(GLfloat)h/(GLfloat)w, -3.5, 3.5);
    else glOrtho (-3.5*(GLfloat)w/(GLfloat)h,
            3.5*(GLfloat)w/(GLfloat)h, -3.5, 3.5, -3.5, 3.5);
    glMatrixMode(GL_MODELVIEW);
    glLoadIdentity();
}

int main(int argc, char** argv)
{
    auxInitDisplayMode (AUX_SINGLE | AUX_RGBA | AUX_DEPTH);
    auxInitPosition (0, 0, 200, 200);
    auxInitWindow (argv[0]);
    myinit();
    auxReshapeFunc (myReshape);
    auxMainLoop(display);
}
```

As shown, you have to enable texture-coordinate generation for the *s* coordinate by passing GL_TEXTURE_GEN_S to **glEnable**(); if you were generating other coordinates, you'd have to enable them with GL_TEXTURE_GEN_T, GL_TEXTURE_GEN_R, or GL_TEXTURE_GEN_Q. (Use **glDisable**() with the appropriate constant to disable coordinate generation.) Also note the use of GL_REPEAT to cause the contour lines to be repeated across the teapot.

If you change the line that defines the parameter array *sgenparams* to

```
GLfloat sgenparams[] = {1, 1, 1, 0};
```

the contour stripes are parallel to the plane $x + y + z = 0$, slicing across the teapot at an angle, as shown in Plate 18b.

The GL_OBJECT_LINEAR function calculates the texture coordinates in the model's coordinate system. In Listing 9-3, where the contour lines are perpendicular to the base of the teapot, they would remain so, no matter how the teapot was rotated or viewed. Sometimes you'd like the contour lines to be calculated relative to the eye's coordinate system. In other words, you want to multiply the vector $(p_1\ p_2\ p_3\ p_4)$ by the inverse of the modelview matrix before calculating the distance to the plane. If you specify GL_TEXTURE_GEN_MODE with GL_EYE_LINEAR, this is exactly what happens. The texture coordinate is generated with the following function:

$$\text{generated coordinate} = p_1'\, x_e + p_2'\, y_e + p_3'\, z_e + p_4'\, w_e$$

where $(p_1'\ p_2'\ p_3'\ p_4') = (p_1\ p_2\ p_3\ p_4)\mathbf{M}^{-1}$

In this case, $(x_e,\ y_e,\ z_e,\ w_e)$ are the eye coordinates of the vertex, and p_1, ..., p_4 are supplied as the *param* argument to **glTexGen*()** with *pname* set to GL_EYE_PLANE. The primed values are calculated only once, at the time they're specified, so this operation isn't as computationally expensive as it looks. To see the effect of this function, in the example above, change *sgenparams* back to {1, 0, 0, 0}, and change GL_OBJECT_LINEAR to GL_EYE_LINEAR. The result is red stripes parallel to the *y-z* plane from the eye's point of view, as shown in Plate 18c.

In all these examples, a single texture coordinate is used to generate contours. The *s* and *t* texture coordinates can be generated independently, however, to indicate the distances to two different planes. With a properly constructed two-dimensional texture map, the resulting two sets of contours can be viewed simultaneously. For an added level of complexity, you can calculate the *s* coordinate using GL_OBJECT_LINEAR and the *t* coordinate using GL_EYE_LINEAR.

Environment Mapping

The goal of environment mapping is to render an object as if it were perfectly reflective, so that the colors on its surface are those reflected to the eye from its surroundings. In other words, if you look at a perfectly polished, perfectly reflective silver object in a room, you see the walls, floor, and other objects in the room reflected off the object. The objects whose reflections you see depend on the position of your eye and on the position and surface angles of the silver object. To perform environment mapping, all you have to do is create an appropriate texture map and then have OpenGL generate the texture coordinates for you.

Environment mapping is an approximation based on the assumption that the items in the environment are far away compared to the surfaces of the shiny object—that is, it's a small object in a large room. With this assumption, to find the color of a point on the surface, take the ray from the eye to the surface, and reflect the ray off the surface. The direction of the reflected ray completely determines the color to be painted there. Encoding a color for each direction on a flat texture map is equivalent to putting a polished perfect sphere in the middle of the environment and taking a picture of it with a camera that has a lens with a very long focal length placed far away. Mathematically, the lens has an infinite focal length and the camera is infinitely far away. The encoding therefore covers a circular region of the texture map, tangent to the top, bottom, left, and right edges of the map. The texture values outside the circle make no difference, as they are never accessed in environment mapping.

To make a perfectly correct environment texture map, you need to obtain a large silvered sphere, take a photograph of it in some environment with a camera located an infinite distance away and with a lens that has an infinite focal length, and scan in the photograph. To approximate this result, you can use a scanned-in photograph of an environment taken with an extremely wide-angle (or fish-eye) lens. Plate 21 shows a photograph taken with a such a lens and the results when that image is used as an environment map.

Once you've created a texture designed for environment mapping, you need to invoke OpenGL's environment-mapping algorithm. This algorithm finds the point on the surface of the sphere with the same tangent surface as the point on the object being rendered, and it paints the object's point with the color visible on the sphere at the corresponding point. Programmatically, all you need to do is change these lines from Listing 9-3:

```
glTexGenfv(GL_S, GL_OBJECT_LINEAR, sgenparams);
glEnable(GL_TEXTURE_GEN_S);
```

to:

```
glTexGenfv(GL_S, GL_SPHERE_MAP, 0);
glTexGenfv(GL_T, GL_SPHERE_MAP, 0);
glEnable(GL_TEXTURE_GEN_S);
glEnable(GL_TEXTURE_GEN_T);
```

The GL_SPHERE_MAP constant is what invokes the environment mapping. As shown, you need to specify it for both the *s* and *t* directions. You don't have to specify any parameters for the texture-coordinate generation function, however.

Advanced Features

▨ Advanced

This section describes how to manipulate the texture matrix stack and how to use the *q* coordinate. Both techniques are considered advanced, since you don't need them for many applications of texture mapping.

The Texture Matrix Stack

Just as your model coordinates are transformed by a matrix before being rendered, texture coordinates are multiplied by a 4×4 matrix before any texture mapping occurs. By default, the texture matrix is the identity, so the texture coordinates you explicitly assign or those that are automatically generated remain unchanged. By modifying the texture matrix while redrawing an object, however, you can make the texture slide over the surface, rotate around it, stretch and shrink, or any combination of the three. In fact, since the texture matrix is a completely general 4×4 matrix, effects such as perspective can be achieved.

When the four texture coordinates (s, t, r, q) are multiplied by the texture matrix, the resulting vector $(s'\ t'\ r'\ q')$ is interpreted as homogeneous texture coordinates. In other words, the texture map is indexed by s'/q' and t'/q'. (Remember that r'/q' is currently ignored, but it might be used in the future.) The texture matrix is actually the top matrix on a stack whose depth must be at least two. All the standard matrix-manipulation commands such as **glPushMatrix()**, **glPopMatrix()**, **glMultMatrix()**, and **glRotate()** can be applied to the texture matrix. To modify the current texture matrix, you need to set the matrix mode to GL_TEXTURE, as follows:

```
glMatrixMode(GL_TEXTURE); /* enter texture matrix mode */
glRotate(...);
/* ... other matrix manipulations ... */
glMatrixMode(GL_MODELVIEW); /* back to modelview mode */
```

The q Coordinate

The mathematics of the q coordinate in a general four-dimensional texture coordinate is as described in the previous section. You can make use of q in cases where more than one projection or perspective transformation is needed.

For example, suppose you want to model a spotlight that has some nonuniform pattern—brighter in the center, perhaps, or noncircular, because of flaps or lenses that modify the shape of the beam. You can emulate shining such a light on a flat surface by making a texture map that corresponds to the shape and intensity of a light, and then projecting it on the surface in question using projection transformations. Projecting the cone of light onto surfaces in the scene requires a perspective transformation ($q \neq 1$), since the lights might shine on surfaces that aren't perpendicular to them. A second perspective transformation occurs because the viewer sees the scene from a different (but perspective) point of view. See Plate 27 for an example, and see "Fast Shadows and Lighting Effects Using Texture Mapping" by Mark Segal, Carl Korobkin, Rolf van Widenfelt, Jim Foran, and Paul Haeberli, SIGGRAPH 1992 Proceedings, (*Computer Graphics*, 26:2, July 1992, p. 249-252) for more details.

Another example might arise if the texture map to be applied comes from a photograph that itself was taken in perspective. In the same way as for spotlights, the final view depends on the combination of two perspective transformations.

Chapter 10

The Framebuffer

Chapter Objectives

After reading this chapter, you'll be able to do the following:

- Understand what buffers make up the framebuffer and how they're used

- Clear selected buffers and enable them for writing

- Control the parameters of the scissoring, alpha, stencil, and depth-buffer tests that are applied to pixels

- Perform dithering and logical operations

- Use the accumulation buffer for such purposes as scene antialiasing

An important goal of almost every graphics program is to draw pictures on the screen. The screen is composed of a rectangular array of pixels, each capable of displaying a tiny square of color at that point in the image. To draw these pixels, you need to know what color they are, which is the information that's stored in the color buffer. Whenever data is stored uniformly for each pixel, such storage for all the pixels is called a *buffer*. Different buffers might contain different amounts of data per pixel, but within a given buffer, each pixel is assigned the same amount of data. A buffer that stores a single bit of information about pixels is called a *bitplane*.

As shown in Figure 10-1, the lower left pixel in an OpenGL window is pixel (0, 0), corresponding to the window coordinates of the lower left corner of the 1×1 region occupied by this pixel. In general, pixel (x, y) fills the region bounded by x on the left, x+1 on the right, y on the bottom, and y+1 on the top.

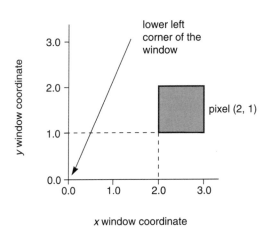

Figure 10-1   The Region Occupied by a Pixel

As an example of a buffer, let's look more closely at the color buffer, which holds the color information that's to be displayed on the screen. Assume that the screen is 1280 pixels wide and 1024 pixels high and that it's a full *24-bit color* screen—in other words, there are 2^{24} (or 16,777,216) different colors that can be displayed. Since 24 bits translates to three bytes (8 bits/byte), the color buffer in this example has to store at least three bytes of data for each of the 1024*1280 (= 1,310,720) pixels on the screen. A particular hardware system might have more or fewer pixels on the physical screen as well as more or less color data per pixel. Any particular color buffer, however, has the same amount of data saved for each pixel on the screen.

The color buffer is only one of several buffers that hold information about a pixel. In "Hidden-Surface Removal Survival Kit" on page 27, for example, you learned that the depth buffer holds depth information for each pixel. The color buffer itself can consist of several subbuffers. The *framebuffer* on a system comprises all of these buffers. With the exception of the color buffer(s), you don't view these other buffers directly; instead, you use them to perform such tasks as hidden-surface elimination, antialiasing of an entire scene, stenciling, drawing smooth motion, and other operations.

This chapter describes all the buffers that can exist in an OpenGL implementation and how they're used. It also discusses the series of tests and pixel operations that are performed before any data is written to the viewable color buffer. Finally, it explains how to use the accumulation buffer, which is used to accumulate images that are drawn into the color buffer. This chapter has the following major sections:

- "Buffers and Their Uses" describes the possible buffers, what they're for, and how to clear them and enable them for writing.

- "Testing and Operating on Fragments" explains the scissoring, alpha, stencil, and depth-buffer tests that occur after a pixel's position and color have been calculated but before this information is drawn on the screen. Several operations—blending, dithering, and logical operations—can also be performed before a fragment updates the screen.

- "The Accumulation Buffer" describes how to perform several advanced techniques using the accumulation buffer. These techniques include antialiasing an entire scene, using motion blur, and simulating photographic depth of field.

Buffers and Their Uses

An OpenGL system can manipulate the following buffers:

- Color buffers: front-left, front-right, back-left, back-right, and any number of auxiliary color buffers

- Depth buffer

- Stencil buffer

- Accumulation buffer

Your particular OpenGL implementation determines which buffers are available and how many bits per pixel each holds. Additionally, you can have multiple visuals, or window types, that have different buffers available. At a minimum, you're guaranteed to have one color buffer for use in RGBA mode with associated stencil, depth, and accumulation buffers that have color components of nonzero size, and one color buffer for use in color-index mode with associated depth and stencil buffers. Table 10-1 lists the parameters to use with **glGetIntegerv()** to query your OpenGL system about per-pixel buffer storage for a particular visual. If you're using the X Window System, you'll probably want to use **glXGetConfig()** to query your visuals; see Appendix D and the *OpenGL Reference Manual* for more information about this routine.

Parameter	Meaning
GL_RED_BITS, GL_GREEN_BITS, GL_BLUE_BITS, GL_ALPHA_BITS	Number of bits per R, G, B, or A component in the color buffers
GL_DEPTH_BITS	Number of bits per pixel in the depth buffer
GL_STENCIL_BITS	Number of bits per pixel in the stencil buffer
GL_ACCUM_RED_BITS, GL_ACCUM_GREEN_BITS, GL_ACCUM_BLUE_BITS, GL_ACCUM_ALPHA_BITS	Number of bits per R, G, B, or A component in the accumulation buffer

Table 10-1 Query Parameters for Per-Pixel Buffer Storage

Color Buffers

The color buffers are usually the ones you draw to. They contain either color-index or RGB color data and may also contain alpha values. An OpenGL implementation that supports stereoscopic viewing has left and right color buffers for the left and right stereo images. If stereo isn't supported, only the left buffers are used. Similarly, double-buffered systems have front and back buffers, and a single-buffered system has the front buffers only. Every OpenGL implementation must provide a front-left color buffer.

Up to four optional, nondisplayable auxiliary color buffers can also be supported. OpenGL doesn't specify any particular uses for these buffers, so you can define and use them however you please. For example, you might use them for saving an image that you use repeatedly; rather than redrawing the image, you can just copy it into the usual color buffers. See the description of **glCopyPixels()** in "Reading, Writing, and Copying Pixel Data" on page 238 for more information about how to do this.

You can use GL_STEREO or GL_DOUBLE_BUFFER with **glGetBooleanv()** to find out if your system supports stereo (that is, has left and right buffers) or double-buffering (has front and back buffers). To find out how many auxiliary buffers are present, use **glGetIntegerv()** with GL_AUX_BUFFERS.

Depth Buffer

The depth buffer stores a depth value for each pixel. As described in "Hidden-Surface Removal Survival Kit" on page 27, depth is usually measured in terms of distance to the eye, so pixels with larger depth-buffer values are overwritten by pixels with smaller values. This is just a useful convention, however, and the depth buffer's behavior can be modified as described in "Depth Test" on page 307. The depth buffer is sometimes called the *z buffer* (the z comes from the fact that x and y values measure horizontal and vertical displacement on the screen, and the z value measures distance perpendicular to the screen).

Stencil Buffer

One use for the stencil buffer is to restrict drawing to certain portions of the screen, just as a cardboard stencil can be used with a can of spray paint to make fairly precise painted images. For example, if you want to draw an image as it would appear through an odd-shaped windshield, you can store an image of the windshield's shape in the stencil buffer, and then draw the entire scene. The stencil buffer prevents anything that wouldn't be visible through the windshield from being drawn. Thus, if your application is a driving simulation, you can draw all the instruments and other items inside the automobile once, and as the car moves, only the outside scene need be updated.

Accumulation Buffer

The accumulation buffer holds RGBA color data just like the color buffers do in RGBA mode. (The results of using the accumulation buffer in color-index mode are undefined.) It's typically used for accumulating a series of images into a final, composite image. With this method, you can perform operations like scene antialiasing by supersampling an image and then averaging the samples to produce the values that are finally painted into the pixels of the color buffers. You don't draw directly into the accumulation buffer; accumulation operations are always performed in rectangular blocks, usually transfers of data to or from a color buffer.

Clearing Buffers

In graphics programs, clearing the screen (or any of the buffers) is typically one of the most expensive operations you can perform—on a 1280 by 1024 monitor, it requires touching well over a million pixels. For simple graphics applications, the clear operation can take more time than the rest of the drawing. If you need to clear not only the color buffer but also the depth and stencil buffers, say, the clear operation can be three times as expensive.

To address this problem, some machines have hardware that can clear more than one buffer at once. The OpenGL clearing commands are structured to take advantage of architectures like this. First, you specify the values to be written into each buffer to be cleared. Then you issue a single command to perform the clear operation, passing in a list of all the buffers to be cleared. If the hardware is capable of simultaneous clears, they all occur at once; otherwise, each buffer is cleared sequentially.

The following commands set the clearing values for each buffer.

---

void **glClearColor**(GLclampf *red*, GLclampf *green*, GLclampf *blue*,
          GLclampf *alpha*);
void **glClearIndex**(GLfloat *index*);
void **glClearDepth**(GLclampd *depth*);
void **glClearStencil**(GLint *s*);
void **glClearAccum**(GLfloat *red*, GLfloat *green*, GLfloat *blue*,
          GLfloat *alpha*);

Specifies the current clearing values for the color buffer (in RGBA mode), the color buffer (in color-index mode), the depth buffer, the stencil buffer, and the accumulation buffer. The GLclampf and GLclampd types (clamped GLfloat and clamped GLdouble) are clamped to be between 0.0 and 1.0. The default depth-clearing value is 1.0; all the other default clearing values are 0. The values set with the clear commands remain in effect until they're changed by another call to the same command.

After you've selected your clearing values and you're ready to clear the buffers, use **glClear**().

---

void **glClear**(GLbitfield *mask*);

Clears the specifed buffers. The value of *mask* is the bitwise logical OR of some combination of GL_COLOR_BUFFER_BIT, GL_DEPTH_BUFFER_BIT, GL_STENCIL_BUFFER_BIT, and GL_ACCUM_BUFFER_BIT, to identify which buffers are to be cleared. GL_COLOR_BUFFER_BIT clears either the RGBA color or the color-index buffer, depending on the mode of the system at the time. When you clear the color or color-index buffer, all the color buffers that are enabled for writing (see the next section) are cleared.

Selecting Color Buffers for Writing

The results of a drawing operation can go into any of the color buffers: front, back, front-left, back-left, front-right, back-right, or any of the auxiliary buffers. You can choose an individual buffer to be the drawing target, or you can also set the target to be a combination of these buffers. In a double-buffered application, for example, you might want to draw a common background into both the back and front buffers; from then on, you want to draw only in the back buffer (and swap the buffers when you're finished drawing). In some cases, however, you might want to treat part of a particular double-buffered window as though it were single-buffered by drawing to both front and back buffers. You use the **glDrawBuffer**() command to select the buffers to be written.

---

void **glDrawBuffer**(GLenum *mode*);

Selects the buffers enabled for writing or clearing. The value of *mode* can be one of the following:

GL_FRONT	GL_FRONT_RIGHT	GL_AUX*i*
GL_BACK	GL_FRONT_LEFT	GL_FRONT_AND_BACK
GL_RIGHT	GL_BACK_RIGHT	GL_NONE
GL_LEFT	GL_BACK_LEFT	

Arguments that omit RIGHT or LEFT refer to both the left and right buffers; similarly, arguments that omit FRONT or BACK refer to both. The *i* in GL_AUX*i* is a digit identifying a particular auxiliary buffer.

Note: You can enable drawing to nonexistent buffers as long as you enable drawing to at least one buffer that does exist. If none of the specified buffers exist, an error results.

Masking Buffers

Before OpenGL writes data into the enabled color, depth, or stencil buffers, a masking operation is applied to the data, as specified with one of the following commands. A bitwise logical AND is performed with each mask and the corresponding data to be written.

---

void **glIndexMask**(GLuint *mask*);
void **glColorMask**(GLboolean *red*, GLboolean *green*, GLboolean *blue*,
                           GLboolean *alpha*);
void **glDepthMask**(GLboolean *flag*);
void **glStencilMask**(GLuint *mask*);

Sets the masks used to control writing into the indicated buffers. The mask set by **glIndexMask**() applies only in color-index mode. If a 1 appears in *mask*, the corresponding bit in the color-index buffer is written; where a 0 appears, the bit isn't written. Similarly, **glColorMask**() affects drawing in RGBA mode only. The *red*, *green*, *blue*, and *alpha* values control whether the corresponding component is written. (GL_TRUE means it is written.) If *flag* is GL_TRUE for **glDepthMask**(), the depth buffer is enabled for writing; otherwise, it's disabled. The mask for **glStencilMask**() is used for stencil data in the same way as the mask is used for color-index data in **glIndexMask**(). The default values of all the GLboolean masks are GL_TRUE, and the default values for the two GLuint masks are all 1s.

You can do plenty of tricks with color masking in color-index mode. For example, you can use each bit in the index as a different layer, and set up interactions between arbitrary layers with appropriate settings of the color map. You can create overlays and underlays, and do so-called color-map animations. See Chapter 13 for examples of using color masking. Masking in RGBA mode is useful less often, but you can use it for loading separate image files into the red, green, and blue bitplanes, for example.

You've seen one use for disabling the depth buffer in "Three-Dimensional Blending with the Depth Buffer" on page 203. Disabling the depth buffer for writing can also be useful if a common background is desired for a series of frames, and you want to add some features that may be obscured by parts of the background. For example, suppose your background is a forest, and you would like to draw repeated frames with the same trees, but with objects moving among them. After the trees are drawn with their depths recorded in the depth buffer, then the image of the trees is saved, and the new items are drawn with the depth buffer disabled for writing. As long as the new items don't overlap each other, the picture is correct. To draw the next frame, restore the image of the trees and continue. You don't need to restore the values in the depth buffer. This trick is most useful if the background is extremely complex—so complex that it's much faster just to recopy the image into the color buffer than to recompute it from the geometry.

Masking the stencil buffer can allow you to use a multiple-bit stencil buffer to hold multiple stencils (one per bit). You might use this technique to perform capping as explained in "Stencil Test" on page 302 or to implement the Game of Life as described in "Life in the Stencil Buffer" on page 407.

Note: The mask specified by **glStencilMask()** controls which stencil bitplanes are written. This mask isn't related to the mask that's specified as the third parameter of **glStencilFunc()**, which specifies which bitplanes are considered by the stencil function.

Testing and Operating on Fragments

When you draw geometry, text, or images on the screen, OpenGL performs several calculations to rotate, translate, scale, determine the lighting, project the object(s) into perspective, figure out which pixels in the window are affected, and determine what colors those pixels should be drawn. Many of the earlier chapters in this book give some information about how to control these operations. After OpenGL determines that an individual fragment should be generated and what its color should be, several processing stages remain that control how and whether the fragment is drawn as a pixel into the framebuffer. For example, if it's outside the window or if it's farther from the viewpoint than the pixel that's already in the framebuffer, it isn't drawn. In another stage, the fragment's color is blended with the color of the pixel already in the framebuffer.

This section describes both the complete set of tests that a fragment must pass before it goes into the framebuffer and the possible final operations that can be performed on the fragment as it's written. The tests and operations occur in the following order; if a fragment is eliminated in an early test, none of the later tests or operations take place.

1. Scissor test
2. Alpha test
3. Stencil test
4. Depth test
5. Blending
6. Dithering
7. Logical operation

Each of these tests and operations is described in detail in the following sections.

Scissor Test

You can define a rectangular portion of your window and restrict drawing to take place within it by using the **glScissor()** command. If a fragment lies inside the rectangle, it passes the scissor test.

---

void **glScissor**(GLint *x*, GLint *y*, GLsizei *width*, GLsizei *height*);

Sets the location and size of the scissor rectangle. The parameters define the lower left corner (*x*, *y*), and the width and height of the rectangle. Pixels that lie inside the rectangle pass the scissor test. Scissoring is enabled and disabled by passing GL_SCISSOR to **glEnable()** and **glDisable()**. By default, the rectangle matches the size of the window and scissoring is disabled.

The scissor test is just a version of a stencil test using a rectangular region of the screen. It's fairly easy to create a blindingly fast hardware implementation of scissoring, while a given system might be much slower at stenciling—perhaps because the stenciling is performed in software.

Advanced

As an advanced use of scissoring, you might use it to perform nonlinear projection. First, divide the window into a regular grid of subregions, specifying viewport and scissor parameters that limit rendering to one region at a time. Then project the entire scene to each region using a different projection matrix.

You can use GL_SCISSOR_TEST with **glIsEnabled()** and GL_SCISSOR_BOX with **glGetIntegerv()** to determine whether scissoring is enabled and to obtain the values that define the scissor rectangle.

Alpha Test

In RGBA mode, the alpha test allows you to accept or reject a fragment based on its alpha value. If enabled, the test compares the incoming alpha value with a reference value. The fragment is accepted or rejected depending on the result of the comparison. Both the reference value and the comparison function are set with **glAlphaFunc()**. To determine whether the alpha test is enabled and to obtain the reference value and the comparison function, use GL_ALPHA_TEST with **glIsEnabled()** and GL_ALPHA_TEST_FUNC or GL_ALPHA_TEST_REF with **glGetIntegerv()**.

---

void **glAlphaFunc**(GLenum *func*, GLclampf *ref*);

Sets the reference value and comparison function for the alpha test. The reference value *ref* is clamped to be between 0 and 1. The possible values for *func* and their meaning are listed in Table 10-2.

Parameter	Meaning
GL_NEVER	Never accept the fragment
GL_ALWAYS	Always accept the fragment
GL_LESS	Accept fragment if fragment alpha < reference alpha
GL_LEQUAL	Accept fragment if fragment alpha ≤ reference alpha
GL_EQUAL	Accept fragment if fragment alpha = reference alpha
GL_GEQUAL	Accept fragment if fragment alpha ≥ reference alpha
GL_GREATER	Accept fragment if fragment alpha > reference alpha
GL_NOTEQUAL	Accept fragment if fragment alpha ≠ reference alpha

Table 10-2 Parameter Values for Use with glAlphaFunc()

The alpha test is enabled and disabled by passing GL_ALPHA_TEST to **glEnable()** and **glDisable()**. By default, the reference value is zero, the comparison function is GL_ALWAYS, and the alpha test is disabled.

One application for the alpha test is to implement a transparency algorithm. Render your entire scene twice, the first time accepting only fragments with alpha values of one, and the second time accepting fragments with alpha values that aren't equal to one. Turn the depth buffer on during both passes, but disable depth buffer writing during the second pass.

Another use might be to make decals with texture maps where you can see through certain parts of the decals. Set the alphas in the decals to 0.0 where you want to see through, set them to 1.0 otherwise, set the reference value to 0.5 (or anything between 0.0 and 1.0), and set the comparison function to GL_GREATER. The decal has see-through parts, and the values in the depth buffer aren't affected. This technique, called billboarding, is described in "Sample Uses of Blending" on page 199.

Stencil Test

The stencil test takes place only if there is a stencil buffer. (If there is no stencil buffer, the stencil test always passes.) Stenciling applies a test that compares a reference value with the value stored at a pixel in the stencil buffer. Depending on the result of the test, the value in the stencil buffer is modified. You can choose the particular comparison function used, the reference value, and the modification performed with the **glStencilFunc()** and **glStencilOp()** commands.

---

void **glStencilFunc**(GLenum *func*, GLint *ref*, GLuint *mask*);

Sets the comparison function (*func*), reference value (*ref*), and a mask (*mask*) for use with the stencil test. The reference value is compared to the value in the stencil buffer using the comparison function, but the comparison applies only to those bits where the corresponding bits of the mask are 1. The function can be GL_NEVER, GL_ALWAYS, GL_LESS, GL_LEQUAL, GL_EQUAL, GL_GEQUAL, GL_GREATER, or GL_NOTEQUAL. If it's GL_LESS, for example, then the fragment passes if *ref* is less than the value in the stencil buffer. If the stencil buffer contains *s* bitplanes, the low-order *s* bits of *mask* are bitwise ANDed with the value in the stencil buffer and with the reference value before the comparison is performed. The masked values are all interpreted as nonnegative values. The stencil test is enabled and disabled by passing GL_STENCIL_TEST to **glEnable()** and **glDisable()**. By default, *func* is GL_ALWAYS, *ref* is 0, *mask* is all 1s, and stenciling is disabled.

---

void **glStencilOp**(GLenum *fail*, GLenum *zfail*, GLenum *zpass*);

Specifies how the data in the stencil buffer is modified when a fragment passes or fails the stencil test. The three functions *fail*, *zfail*, and *zpass* can be GL_KEEP, GL_ZERO, GL_REPLACE, GL_INCR, GL_DECR, or GL_INVERT. They correspond to keeping the current value, replacing it with zero, replacing it with the reference value, incrementing it, decrementing it, and bitwise-inverting it. The result of the increment and decrement functions is clamped to lie between 0 and the maximum unsigned integer value (2^s-1 if the stencil buffer holds *s* bits). The *fail* function is applied if the fragment fails the stencil test; if it passes, then *zfail* is applied if the depth test fails and *zpass* if the depth test passes, or if no depth test is performed. (See "Depth Test" on page 307.) By default, all three stencil operations are GL_KEEP.

Stencil Queries

You can obtain the values for all six stencil-related parameters by using the query function **glGetIntegerv()** and one of the values shown in Table 10-3. You can also determine whether the stencil test is enabled by passing GL_STENCIL_TEST to **glIsEnabled()**.

Query Value	Meaning
GL_STENCIL_FUNC	Stencil function
GL_STENCIL_REF	Stencil reference value
GL_STENCIL_VALUE_MASK	Stencil mask
GL_STENCIL_FAIL	Stencil fail action
GL_STENCIL_PASS_DEPTH_FAIL	Stencil pass and depth buffer fail action
GL_STENCIL_PASS_DEPTH_PASS	Stencil pass and depth buffer pass action

Table 10-3 Query Values for the Stencil Test

Stencil Examples

Probably the most typical use of the stencil test is to mask out an irregularly shaped region of the screen to prevent drawing from occurring within it (as in the windshield example in "Buffers and Their Uses" on page 293). To do this, fill the stencil mask with 0, and then draw the desired shape in the stencil buffer with 1. You can't draw directly into the stencil buffer, but you can achieve the same result by drawing into the color buffer and choosing a suitable value for the *zpass* function (such as GL_REPLACE). Whenever drawing occurs, a value is also written into the stencil buffer (in this case, the reference value). To prevent the stencil-buffer drawing from affecting the contents of the color buffer, set the color mask to zero (or GL_FALSE). You might also want to disable writing into the depth buffer.

After you've defined the stencil area, set the reference value to 1, and the comparison function such that the fragment passes if the reference value is equal to the stencil-plane value. During drawing, don't modify the contents of the stencil planes.

Listing 10-1 demonstrates how to use the stencil test in this way. Two tori are drawn, with a diamond-shaped cutout in the center of the scene. Within the diamond-shaped stencil mask, a sphere is drawn. In this example, drawing into the stencil buffer takes place only when the window is redrawn, so the color buffer is cleared after the stencil mask has been created.

Listing 10-1   Using the Stencil Test: stencil.c

```
#include <GL/gl.h>
#include <GL/glu.h>
#include "aux.h"

#define YELLOWMAT    1
#define BLUEMAT 2

void myinit (void)
{
    GLfloat yellow_diffuse[] = { 0.7, 0.7, 0.0, 1.0 };
    GLfloat yellow_specular[] = { 1.0, 1.0, 1.0, 1.0 };

    GLfloat blue_diffuse[] = { 0.1, 0.1, 0.7, 1.0 };
    GLfloat blue_specular[] = { 0.1, 1.0, 1.0, 1.0 };

    GLfloat position_one[] = { 1.0, 1.0, 1.0, 0.0 };
```

```
    glNewList(YELLOWMAT, GL_COMPILE);
        glMaterialfv(GL_FRONT, GL_DIFFUSE, yellow_diffuse);
        glMaterialfv(GL_FRONT, GL_SPECULAR, yellow_specular);
        glMaterialf(GL_FRONT, GL_SHININESS, 64.0);
    glEndList();

    glNewList(BLUEMAT, GL_COMPILE);
        glMaterialfv(GL_FRONT, GL_DIFFUSE, blue_diffuse);
        glMaterialfv(GL_FRONT, GL_SPECULAR, blue_specular);
        glMaterialf(GL_FRONT, GL_SHININESS, 45.0);
    glEndList();

    glLightfv(GL_LIGHT0, GL_POSITION, position_one);

    glEnable(GL_LIGHT0);
    glEnable(GL_LIGHTING);
    glDepthFunc(GL_LEQUAL);
    glEnable(GL_DEPTH_TEST);

    glClearStencil(0x0);
    glEnable(GL_STENCIL_TEST);
}

void display(void)
{
    glClear(GL_COLOR_BUFFER_BIT | GL_DEPTH_BUFFER_BIT);

/* draw blue sphere where the stencil is 1 */
    glStencilFunc (GL_EQUAL, 0x1, 0x1);
    glCallList (BLUEMAT);
    auxSolidSphere (0.5);

/* draw the tori where the stencil is not 1 */
    glStencilFunc (GL_NOTEQUAL, 0x1, 0x1);
    glStencilOp (GL_KEEP, GL_KEEP, GL_KEEP);
    glPushMatrix();
        glRotatef (45.0, 0.0, 0.0, 1.0);
        glRotatef (45.0, 0.0, 1.0, 0.0);
        glCallList (YELLOWMAT);
        auxSolidTorus (0.275, 0.85);
        glPushMatrix();
            glRotatef (90.0, 1.0, 0.0, 0.0);
            auxSolidTorus (0.275, 0.85);
        glPopMatrix();
    glPopMatrix();
}
```

```
void myReshape(GLsizei w, GLsizei h)
{
    glViewport(0, 0, w, h);

    glClear(GL_STENCIL_BUFFER_BIT);
/* create a diamond-shaped stencil area */
    glMatrixMode(GL_PROJECTION);
    glLoadIdentity();
    glOrtho(-3.0, 3.0, -3.0, 3.0, -1.0, 1.0);
    glMatrixMode(GL_MODELVIEW);
    glLoadIdentity();

    glStencilFunc (GL_ALWAYS, 0x1, 0x1);
    glStencilOp (GL_REPLACE, GL_REPLACE, GL_REPLACE);
    glBegin(GL_QUADS);
        glVertex3f (-1.0, 0.0, 0.0);
        glVertex3f (0.0, 1.0, 0.0);
        glVertex3f (1.0, 0.0, 0.0);
        glVertex3f (0.0, -1.0, 0.0);
    glEnd();

    glMatrixMode(GL_PROJECTION);
    glLoadIdentity();
    gluPerspective(45.0, (GLfloat) w/(GLfloat) h, 3.0, 7.0);
    glMatrixMode(GL_MODELVIEW);
    glLoadIdentity();
    glTranslatef(0.0, 0.0, -5.0);
}


int main(int argc, char** argv)
{
    auxInitDisplayMode (AUX_SINGLE | AUX_RGBA
    | AUX_DEPTH | AUX_STENCIL);
    auxInitPosition (0, 0, 400, 400);
    auxInitWindow (argv[0]);
    myinit ();
    auxReshapeFunc (myReshape);
    auxMainLoop(display);
}
```

The following examples illustrate other uses of the stencil test. See Chapter 13 for additional ideas.

- Capping—Suppose you're drawing a closed convex object (or several of them, as long as they don't intersect or enclose each other) made up of several polygons, and you have a clipping plane that may or may not slice off a piece of it. Suppose that if the plane does intersect the object, you want to cap the object with some constant-colored surface, rather than seeing the inside of it. To do this, clear the stencil buffer to 0, and begin drawing with stenciling enabled and the stencil comparison function set to always accept fragments. Invert the value in the stencil planes each time a fragment is accepted. After all the objects are drawn, regions of the screen where no capping is required have 0 in the stencil planes, and regions requiring capping are nonzero. Reset the stencil function so that it draws only where the stencil value is nonzero, and draw a large polygon of the capping color across the entire screen.

- Overlapping translucent polygons—Suppose you have a translucent surface that's made up of polygons that overlap slightly. If you simply use alpha blending, portions of the underlying objects are covered by more than one transparent surface, which doesn't look right. Use the stencil planes to make sure that each fragment is covered by at most one portion of the transparent surface. Do this by clearing the stencil planes to zero, drawing only when the stencil plane is zero, and incrementing the value in the stencil plane when you draw.

- Stippling—Suppose you want to draw an image with a stipple pattern (see "Displaying Points, Lines, and Polygons" on page 39 for more information about stippling). You can do this by writing the stipple pattern into the stencil buffer, and then drawing conditionally on the contents of the stencil buffer. After the original stipple pattern is drawn, the stencil buffer aren't altered while drawing the image, so the object gets stippled by the pattern in the stencil planes.

Depth Test

For each pixel on the screen, the depth buffer keeps track of the distance between the viewpoint and the object occupying that pixel. Then, if the specified depth test passes, the incoming depth value replaces the one already in the depth buffer.

The depth buffer is usually used for hidden-surface elimination. If a new candidate color for that pixel appears, it's drawn only if the corresponding object is closer than the previous object. In this way, only objects that aren't obscured by other items remain after the entire scene has been rendered. During initialization, the depth buffer is typically filled with a value that's as far from the viewpoint as possible, so any object is nearer than that. If this is how you want to use the depth buffer, you simply have to enable it by passing GL_DEPTH_TEST to **glEnable()** and remember to clear the depth buffer before you redraw each frame (see "Clearing Buffers" on page 296). You can also choose a different comparison function for the depth test with **glDepthFunc()**.

---

void **glDepthFunc**(GLenum *func*);

Sets the comparison function for the depth test. The value for *func* must be GL_NEVER, GL_ALWAYS, GL_LESS, GL_LEQUAL, GL_EQUAL, GL_GEQUAL, GL_GREATER, or GL_NOTEQUAL. An incoming fragment passes the depth test if its *z* value has the specified relation to the value already stored in the depth buffer. The default is GL_LESS, which means that an incoming fragment passes the test if its *z* value is less than that already stored in the depth buffer. In this case, the *z* value represents the distance from the object to the viewpoint, and smaller values mean the corresponding objects are closer to the viewpoint.

Blending, Dithering, and Logical Operations

Once an incoming fragment has passed all the tests described in the previous section, it can be combined with the current contents of the color buffer in one of several ways. The simplest way, which is also the default, is to overwrite the existing values. Alternatively, if you're using RGBA mode and you want the fragment to be translucent or antialiased, you might average its value with the value already in the buffer (blending). On systems with a small number of available colors, you might want to dither color values to increase the number of colors available at the cost of a loss in resolution. Finally, in color-index mode, you can use arbitrary bitwise logical operations to combine the incoming fragment and the pixel that's already written.

Blending

Blending combines the incoming fragment's R, G, B, and alpha values with those of the pixel already stored at the location. Different blending operations can be applied, and the blending that occurs depends on the values of the incoming alpha value and the alpha value (if any) stored at the pixel. Blending is discussed extensively in "Blending" on page 196.

Dithering

On systems with a small number of color bitplanes, you can improve the color resolution at the expense of spatial resolution by dithering the color in the image. Dithering is like halftoning in newspapers. Although a newspaper has only two colors—black and white—it can show photographs by representing the shades of gray with combinations of black and white dots. Comparing a newspaper image of a photo (having no shades of gray) with the original photo (with grayscale) makes the loss of spatial resolution obvious. Since even the lowest-quality color displays typically have at least a few different values of red, green, and blue available (not just two as in a newspaper), there's less loss in spatial resolution in exchange for a better range of colors.

The dithering operation that takes place is hardware-dependent; all OpenGL allows you to do is to turn it on and off. In fact, on some machines, enabling dithering might do nothing at all, which makes sense if the machine already has high color resolution. To enable and disable dithering, pass GL_DITHER to **glEnable()** and **glDisable()**. Dithering is enabled by default.

Dithering applies in both RGBA and color-index mode: The colors or color indices alternate in some hardware-dependent way between the two nearest possibilities. For example, in color-index mode, if dithering is enabled and the color index to be painted is 4.4, then six-tenths of the pixels are painted with index 4 and four-tenths of the pixels with index 5. In RGBA mode, dithering is performed separately for each component (including alpha). To use dithering in color-index mode, you generally need to arrange the colors in the color map appropriately in ramps, or bizarre images might result.

In RGBA mode, dithering is the final step before the resulting values are written into the color buffers; in color-index mode, you can perform one of the logical operations described in the next section.

Logical Operations

In color-index mode, the color indices can be interpreted as integers or as bit patterns. For shading and dithering, the integer interpretation is usually best, but for images composed as combinations of drawings on different layers—for instance, if you're using writemasks to limit drawing to different sets of bitplanes—a bit-pattern interpretation makes more sense. Logical operations, such as OR or XOR, are applied to the incoming fragment values and/or those currently in the color buffer.

Such fragment operations are especially useful on bit-blt-type machines, on which the primary graphics operation is copying a rectangle of data from one place in the window to another, from the window to processor memory, or from memory to the window. Typically, the copy doesn't write the data directly into memory but instead allows you to perform an arbitrary logical operation on the incoming data and the data already present; then it replaces the existing data with the results of the operation. Since this process can be implemented fairly cheaply in hardware, many such machines are available. As an example of using a logical operation, XOR can be used to draw on an image in an undoable way; simply XOR the same drawing again, and the original image is restored.

You choose among the sixteen logical operations with **glLogicOp()**, and you enable and disable logical operations by passing GL_LOGIC_OP to **glEnable()** and **glDisable()**.

---

void **glLogicOp**(GLenum *opcode*);

In color-index mode, selects the logical operation to be performed, given an incoming (source) fragment and the pixel currently stored in the color buffer (destination). Table 10-4 shows the possible values for *opcode* and their meaning (*s* represents source and *d* destination). The default value is GL_COPY.

Paramter	Operation	Parameter	Operation
GL_CLEAR	0	GL_AND	$s \wedge d$
GL_COPY	s	GL_OR	$s \vee d$
GL_NOOP	d	GL_NAND	$\neg(s \wedge d)$
GL_SET	1	GL_NOR	$\neg(s \vee d)$
GL_COPY_INVERTED	$\neg s$	GL_XOR	$sXORd$
GL_INVERT	$\neg d$	GL_EQUIV	$\neg(sXORd)$
GL_AND_REVERSE	$s \wedge \neg d$	GL_AND_INVERTED	$\neg s \wedge d$
GL_OR_REVERSE	$s \vee \neg d$	GL_OR_INVERTED	$\neg s \vee d$

Table 10-4 The Sixteen Logical Operations

The Accumulation Buffer

Advanced

The accumulation buffer can be used for such things as scene antialiasing, motion blur, simulating photographic depth of field, and calculating the soft shadows that result from multiple light sources. Other techniques are possible, especially in combination with some of the other buffers. (For more information on the uses for the accumulation buffer, see *The Accumulation Buffer: Hardware Support for High-Quality Rendering* by Paul Haeberli and Kurt Akeley (SIGGRAPH 1990 Proceedings, p. 309-318).

OpenGL graphics operations don't write directly into the accumulation buffer. Typically, a series of images is generated in one of the standard color buffers, and these are accumulated, one at a time, into the accumulation buffer. When the accumulation is finished, the result is copied back into a color buffer for viewing. To reduce rounding errors, the accumulation buffer may have higher precision (more bits per color) than the standard color buffers. Rendering a scene several times obviously takes longer than rendering it once, but the result is higher quality. You can decide what trade-off between quality and rendering time is appropriate for your application.

You can use the accumulation buffer the same way a photographer can use film for multiple exposures. A photographer typically creates a multiple exposure by taking several pictures of the same scene without advancing the film. If anything in the scene moves, that object appears blurred. Not surprisingly, a computer can do more with an image than a photographer can do with a camera. For example, a computer has exquisite control over the viewpoint, but a photographer can't shake a camera a predictable and controlled amount.

See "Clearing Buffers" on page 296 for information about how to clear the accumulation buffer; use **glAccum()** to control it.

---

void **glAccum**(GLenum *op*, GLfloat *value*);

Controls the accumulation buffer. The *op* parameter selects the operation, and *value* is a number to be used in that operation. The possible operations are GL_ACCUM, GL_LOAD, GL_RETURN, GL_ADD, and GL_MULT:

- GL_ACCUM reads each pixel from the buffer currently selected for reading with **glReadBuffer()** (see Chapter 8), multiplies the R, G, B, and alpha values by *value*, and adds the result to the accumulation buffer.

- GL_LOAD does the same thing, except that the values replace those in the accumulation buffer rather than being added to them.

- GL_RETURN takes values from the accumulation buffer, multiplies them by *value*, and places the result in the color buffer(s) enabled for writing.

- GL_ADD and GL_MULT simply add or multiply the value of each pixel in the accumulation buffer by *value*, and then return it to the accumulation buffer. For GL_MULT, *value* is clamped to be in the range [–1.0,1.0]. For GL_ADD, no clamping occurs.

Scene Antialiasing

To perform scene antialiasing, first clear the accumulation buffer and enable the front buffer for reading and writing. Then loop several times (say, *n*) through code that draws the image in a slightly different position, accumulating the data with

```
glAccum(GL_ACCUM, 1.0/n);
```

and finally calling

```
glAccum(GL_RETURN, 1.0);
```

Note that this method is a bit faster if, on the first pass through the loop, GL_LOAD is used and clearing the accumulation buffer is omitted. See the section on "Logical Operations" on page 323 later in this chapter for possible jittering values. With this code, the image is drawn *n* times before the final image is drawn. If you want to avoid showing the user the intermediate images, draw into a color buffer that's not displayed, accumulate from that, and use the GL_RETURN call to draw into a displayed buffer (or into a back buffer that you subsequently swap to the front).

You could instead present a user interface that shows the viewed image improving as each additional piece is accumulated and that allows the user to halt the process when the image is good enough. To accomplish this, in the loop that draws successive images, call **glAccum()** with GL_RETURN after each accumulation, using 16.0/1.0, 16.0/2.0, 16.0/3.0, ... as the second argument. With this technique, after one pass, 1/16 of the final image is shown, after two passes, 2/16 is shown, and so on. After the GL_RETURN, the code should check to see if the user wants to interrupt the process. This interface is slightly slower, since the resultant image must be copied in after each pass.

To decide what *n* should be, you need to trade off speed (the more times you draw the scene, the longer it takes to obtain the final image) and quality (the more times you draw the scene, the smoother it gets, until you make maximum use of the accumulation buffer's resolution). Plates 22 and 23 show improvements made using scene antialiasing.

Listing 10-2 defines two routines for jittering that you might find useful: **accPerspective()** and **accFrustum()**. The routine **accPerspective()** is used in place of **gluPerspective()**, and the first four parameters of both routines are the same. To jitter the viewing frustum for scene antialiasing, pass the *x* and *y* jitter values (of less than one pixel) to the fifth and sixth parameters of **accPerspective()**. Also, pass 0.0 for the seventh and eighth parameters to **accPerspective()** and a nonzero value for the ninth parameter (to prevent division by zero inside **accPerspective()**). These last three parameters are used for depth-of-field effects, which are described later in this chapter.

Listing 10-2   Useful Routines for Jittering the Viewing Volume: accpersp.c

```
void accFrustum(GLdouble left, GLdouble right, GLdouble bottom,
    GLdouble top, GLdouble near, GLdouble far, GLdouble pixdx,
    GLdouble pixdy, GLdouble eyedx, GLdouble eyedy,
    GLdouble focus)
{
    GLdouble xwsize, ywsize;
    GLdouble dx, dy;
    GLint viewport[4];

    glGetIntegerv (GL_VIEWPORT, viewport);
```

```
        xwsize = right - left;
        ywsize = top - bottom;
        dx = -(pixdx*xwsize/(GLdouble) viewport[2] +
                eyedx*near/focus);
        dy = -(pixdy*ywsize/(GLdouble) viewport[3] +
                eyedy*near/focus);

        glMatrixMode(GL_PROJECTION);
        glLoadIdentity();
        glFrustum (left + dx, right + dx, bottom + dy, top + dy,
            near, far);
        glMatrixMode(GL_MODELVIEW);
        glLoadIdentity();
        glTranslatef (-eyedx, -eyedy, 0.0);
}

void accPerspective(GLdouble fovy, GLdouble aspect,
    GLdouble near, GLdouble far, GLdouble pixdx, GLdouble pixdy,
    GLdouble eyedx, GLdouble eyedy, GLdouble focus)
{
    GLdouble fov2,left,right,bottom,top;
    fov2 = ((fovy*PI_) / 180.0) / 2.0;

    top = near / (fcos(fov2) / fsin(fov2));
    bottom = -top;
    right = top * aspect;
    left = -right;

    accFrustum (left, right, bottom, top, near, far,
        pixdx, pixdy, eyedx, eyedy, focus);
}
```

Listing 10-3 uses these two routines to perform scene antialiasing.

Listing 10-3 Scene Antialiasing: accpersp.c

```
#include <GL/gl.h>
#include <GL/glu.h>
#include <math.h>
#include "aux.h"
#include "jitter.h"

void myinit(void)
{
    GLfloat mat_ambient[] = { 1.0, 1.0, 1.0, 1.0 };
    GLfloat mat_specular[] = { 1.0, 1.0, 1.0, 1.0 };
    GLfloat light_position[] = { 0.0, 0.0, 10.0, 1.0 };
    GLfloat lm_ambient[] = { 0.2, 0.2, 0.2, 1.0 };
```

```
    glMaterialfv(GL_FRONT, GL_AMBIENT, mat_ambient);
    glMaterialfv(GL_FRONT, GL_SPECULAR, mat_specular);
    glMaterialf(GL_FRONT, GL_SHININESS, 50.0);
    glLightfv(GL_LIGHT0, GL_POSITION, light_position);
    glLightModelfv(GL_LIGHT_MODEL_AMBIENT, lm_ambient);

    glEnable(GL_LIGHTING);
    glEnable(GL_LIGHT0);
    glDepthFunc(GL_LEQUAL);
    glEnable(GL_DEPTH_TEST);
    glShadeModel (GL_FLAT);

    glClearColor(0.0, 0.0, 0.0, 0.0);
    glClearAccum(0.0, 0.0, 0.0, 0.0);
}

void displayObjects(void)
{
    GLfloat torus_diffuse[] = { 0.7, 0.7, 0.0, 1.0 };
    GLfloat cube_diffuse[] = { 0.0, 0.7, 0.7, 1.0 };
    GLfloat sphere_diffuse[] = { 0.7, 0.0, 0.7, 1.0 };
    GLfloat octa_diffuse[] = { 0.7, 0.4, 0.4, 1.0 };

    glPushMatrix ();
        glTranslatef (0.0, 0.0, -5.0);
        glRotatef (30.0, 1.0, 0.0, 0.0);

        glPushMatrix ();
            glTranslatef (-0.80, 0.35, 0.0);
            glRotatef (100.0, 1.0, 0.0, 0.0);
            glMaterialfv(GL_FRONT, GL_DIFFUSE, torus_diffuse);
            auxSolidTorus (0.275, 0.85);
        glPopMatrix ();

        glPushMatrix ();
            glTranslatef (-0.75, -0.50, 0.0);
            glRotatef (45.0, 0.0, 0.0, 1.0);
            glRotatef (45.0, 1.0, 0.0, 0.0);
            glMaterialfv(GL_FRONT, GL_DIFFUSE, cube_diffuse);
            auxSolidCube (1.5);
        glPopMatrix ();

        glPushMatrix ();
            glTranslatef (0.75, 0.60, 0.0);
            glRotatef (30.0, 1.0, 0.0, 0.0);
            glMaterialfv(GL_FRONT, GL_DIFFUSE, sphere_diffuse);
```

```
                auxSolidSphere (1.0);
            glPopMatrix ();

            glPushMatrix ();
                glTranslatef (0.70, -0.90, 0.25);
                glMaterialfv(GL_FRONT, GL_DIFFUSE, octa_diffuse);
                auxSolidOctahedron (1.0);
            glPopMatrix ();

        glPopMatrix ();
}

#define ACSIZE   8

void display(void)
{
    GLint viewport[4];
    int jitter;

    glGetIntegerv (GL_VIEWPORT, viewport);

    glClear(GL_ACCUM_BUFFER_BIT);
    for (jitter = 0; jitter < ACSIZE; jitter++) {
        glClear(GL_COLOR_BUFFER_BIT | GL_DEPTH_BUFFER_BIT);
        accPerspective (50.0,
            (GLdouble) viewport[2]/(GLdouble) viewport[3],
            1.0, 15.0, j8[jitter].x, j8[jitter].y,
            0.0, 0.0, 1.0);
        displayObjects ();
        glAccum(GL_ACCUM, 1.0/ACSIZE);
    }
    glAccum (GL_RETURN, 1.0);
    glFlush();
}

void myReshape(GLsizei w, GLsizei h)
{
    glViewport(0, 0, w, h);
}


int main(int argc, char** argv)
{
    auxInitDisplayMode (AUX_SINGLE | AUX_RGBA
            | AUX_ACCUM | AUX_DEPTH);
    auxInitPosition (0, 0, 250, 250);
    auxInitWindow (argv[0]);
```

```
    myinit();
    auxReshapeFunc (myReshape);
    auxMainLoop(display);
}
```

You don't have to use a perspective projection to perform scene antialiasing. You can antialias a scene with orthographic projection simply by using **glTranslate*()** to jitter the scene. Keep in mind that **glTranslate*()** operates in world coordinates, but you want the apparent motion of the scene to be less than one pixel, measured in screen coordinates. Thus, you must reverse the world-coordinate mapping by calculating the jittering translation values, using its width or height in world coordinates divided by its viewport size. Then, multiply that world-coordinate value by the amount of jitter to determine how much the scene should be moved in world coordinates to get a predictable jitter of less than one pixel. Listing 10-4 shows how the **display()** and **myReshape()** routines might look with a world-coordinate width and height of 4.5.

Listing 10-4 Jittering with an Orthographic Projection: accanti.c

```
#define ACSIZE   8

void display(void)
{
    GLint viewport[4];
    int jitter;

    glGetIntegerv (GL_VIEWPORT, viewport);

    glClear(GL_ACCUM_BUFFER_BIT);
    for (jitter = 0; jitter < ACSIZE; jitter++) {
        glClear(GL_COLOR_BUFFER_BIT | GL_DEPTH_BUFFER_BIT);
/* Note that 4.5 is the distance in world space between
 * left and right and bottom and top. The following formula
 * converts fractional pixel movement to world coordinates.
 */
        glPushMatrix ();
            glTranslatef (j8[jitter].x*4.5/viewport[2],
                j8[jitter].y*4.5/viewport[3], 0.0);
            displayObjects ();
        glPopMatrix ();
        glAccum(GL_ACCUM, 1.0/ACSIZE);
    }
    glAccum (GL_RETURN, 1.0);
    glFlush();
}
```

```
void myReshape(GLsizei w, GLsizei h)
{
    glViewport(0, 0, w, h);
    glMatrixMode(GL_PROJECTION);
    glLoadIdentity();
    if (w <= h)
        glOrtho (-2.25, 2.25, -2.25*h/w, 2.25*h/w, -10.0, 10.0);
    else
        glOrtho (-2.25*w/h, 2.25*w/h, -2.25, 2.25, -10.0, 10.0);
    glMatrixMode(GL_MODELVIEW);
}
```

Motion Blur

Similar methods can be used to simulate motion blur, as shown in Plate 7 and Figure 10-2. Suppose your scene has some stationary and some moving objects in it, and you want to make a motion-blurred image extending over a small interval of time. Set up the accumulation buffer in the same way, but instead of spatially jittering the images, jitter them temporally. The entire scene can be made successively dimmer by calling

```
glAccum (GL_MULT, decayFactor);
```

as the scene is drawn into the accumulation buffer, where *decayFactor* is a number between 0.0 and 1.0. Smaller numbers for *decayFactor* cause the object to appear to be moving faster. You can transfer the completed scene with the object's current position and "vapor trail" of previous positions from the accumulation buffer to the standard color buffer with

```
glAccum (GL_RETURN, 1.0);
```

The image looks correct even if the items move at different speeds, or if some of them are accelerated. As before, the more jitter points you use, the better the final image, at least up to the point where you begin to lose resolution due to finite precision in the accumulation buffer. You can combine motion blur with antialiasing by jittering in both the spatial and temporal domains, but you pay for higher quality with longer rendering times.

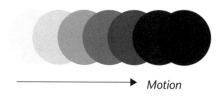

Motion

Figure 10-2   A Motion-Blurred Object

Depth of Field

A photograph made with a camera is in perfect focus only for items lying on a single plane a certain distance from the film. The farther an item is from this plane, the more out of focus it is. The depth of field for a camera is a region about the plane of perfect focus where items are out of focus by a small enough amount.

Under normal conditions, everything you draw with OpenGL is in focus (unless your monitor's bad, in which case everything is out of focus). The accumulation buffer can be used to approximate what you would see in a photograph where items are more and more blurred as their distance from a plane of perfect focus increases. It isn't an exact simulation of the effects produced in a camera, but the result looks similar to what a camera would produce.

To achieve this result, draw the scene repeatedly using calls with different argument values to **glFrustum**(). Choose the arguments so that the position of the viewpoint varies slightly around its true position and so that each frustum shares a common rectangle that lies in the plane of perfect focus, as shown in Figure 10-3. The results of all the renderings should be averaged in the usual way using the accumulation buffer.

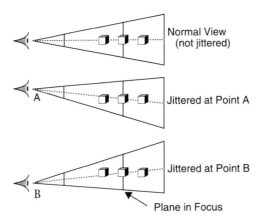

Figure 10-3 A Jittered Viewing Volume for Depth-of-Field Effects

Plate 10 shows an image of five teapots drawn using the depth-of-field effect. The gold teapot (second from the left) is in focus, and the other teapots get progressively blurrier, depending upon their distance from the focal plane (gold teapot). The code to draw this image is shown in Listing 10-5 (which assumes **accPerspective()** and **accFrustum()** are defined as described in Listing 10-2). The scene is drawn eight times, each with a slightly jittered viewing volume, by calling **accPerspective()**. As you recall, with scene antialiasing, the fifth and sixth parameters jitter the viewing volumes in the x and y directions. For the depth-of-field effect, however, you want to jitter the volume while holding it stationary at the focal plane. The focal plane is the depth value defined by the ninth (last) parameter to **accPerspective()**, which is $z = 0$ in this example. The amount of blur is determined by multiplying the x and y jitter values (seventh and eighth parameters of **accPerspective()**) by a constant. Determining the constant is not a science; experiment with values until the depth of field is as pronounced as you want. (Note that in Listing 10-5, the fifth and sixth parameters to **accPerspective()** are set to 0.0, so scene antialiasing is turned off.)

Listing 10-5 Creating a Depth-of-Field Effect: dof.c

```
#include <GL/gl.h>
#include <GL/glu.h>
#include <math.h>
#include "aux.h"
#include "jitter.h"
```

```
void myinit(void)
{
    GLfloat ambient[] = { 0.0, 0.0, 0.0, 1.0 };
    GLfloat diffuse[] = { 1.0, 1.0, 1.0, 1.0 };
    GLfloat specular[] = { 1.0, 1.0, 1.0, 1.0 };
    GLfloat position[] = { 0.0, 3.0, 3.0, 0.0 };

    GLfloat lmodel_ambient[] = { 0.2, 0.2, 0.2, 1.0 };
    GLfloat local_view[] = { 0.0 };

    glEnable(GL_DEPTH_TEST);
    glDepthFunc(GL_LEQUAL);

    glLightfv(GL_LIGHT0, GL_AMBIENT, ambient);
    glLightfv(GL_LIGHT0, GL_DIFFUSE, diffuse);
    glLightfv(GL_LIGHT0, GL_POSITION, position);

    glLightModelfv(GL_LIGHT_MODEL_AMBIENT, lmodel_ambient);
    glLightModelfv(GL_LIGHT_MODEL_LOCAL_VIEWER, local_view);

    glFrontFace (GL_CW);
    glEnable(GL_LIGHTING);
    glEnable(GL_LIGHT0);
    glEnable(GL_AUTO_NORMAL);
    glEnable(GL_NORMALIZE);

    glMatrixMode (GL_MODELVIEW);
    glLoadIdentity ();

    glClearColor(0.0, 0.0, 0.0, 0.0);
    glClearAccum(0.0, 0.0, 0.0, 0.0);
}

void renderTeapot (GLfloat x, GLfloat y, GLfloat z,
    GLfloat ambr, GLfloat ambg, GLfloat ambb,
    GLfloat difr, GLfloat difg, GLfloat difb,
    GLfloat specr, GLfloat specg, GLfloat specb, GLfloat shine)
{
    float mat[3];

    glPushMatrix();
    glTranslatef (x, y, z);
    mat[0] = ambr; mat[1] = ambg; mat[2] = ambb;
    glMaterialfv (GL_FRONT, GL_AMBIENT, mat);
    mat[0] = difr; mat[1] = difg; mat[2] = difb;
    glMaterialfv (GL_FRONT, GL_DIFFUSE, mat);
```

```
        mat[0] = specr; mat[1] = specg; mat[2] = specb;
        glMaterialfv (GL_FRONT, GL_SPECULAR, mat);
        glMaterialf (GL_FRONT, GL_SHININESS, shine*128.0);
        auxSolidTeapot(0.5);
        glPopMatrix();
    }

    void display(void)
    {
        int jitter;
        GLint viewport[4];

        glGetIntegerv (GL_VIEWPORT, viewport);
        glClear(GL_ACCUM_BUFFER_BIT);

        for (jitter = 0; jitter < 8; jitter++) {
            glClear(GL_COLOR_BUFFER_BIT | GL_DEPTH_BUFFER_BIT);
            accPerspective (45.0,
                (GLdouble) viewport[2]/(GLdouble) viewport[3],
                1.0, 15.0, 0.0, 0.0,
                0.33*j8[jitter].x, 0.33*j8[jitter].y, 5.0);
            renderTeapot (-1.1, -0.5, -4.5, 0.1745, 0.01175,
                          0.01175, 0.61424, 0.04136, 0.04136,
                          0.727811, 0.626959, 0.626959, 0.6);
            renderTeapot (-0.5, -0.5, -5.0, 0.24725, 0.1995, 0.0745,
                          0.75164, 0.60648, 0.22648, 0.628281,
                          0.555802, 0.366065, 0.4);
            renderTeapot (0.2, -0.5, -5.5, 0.19225, 0.19225,
                          0.19225, 0.50754, 0.50754, 0.50754,
                          0.508273, 0.508273, 0.508273, 0.4);
            renderTeapot (1.0, -0.5, -6.0, 0.0215, 0.1745, 0.0215,
                          0.07568, 0.61424, 0.07568, 0.633,
                          0.727811, 0.633, 0.6);
            renderTeapot (1.8, -0.5, -6.5, 0.0, 0.1, 0.06, 0.0,
                          0.50980392, 0.50980392, 0.50196078,
                          0.50196078, 0.50196078, .25);
            glAccum (GL_ACCUM, 0.125);
        }

        glAccum (GL_RETURN, 1.0);
        glFlush();
    }

    void myReshape(GLsizei w, GLsizei h)
    {
        glViewport(0, 0, w, h);
    }
```

```
int main(int argc, char** argv)
{
    auxInitDisplayMode (AUX_SINGLE | AUX_RGBA
            | AUX_ACCUM | AUX_DEPTH);
    auxInitPosition (0, 0, 400, 400);
    auxInitWindow (argv[0]);
    myinit();
    auxReshapeFunc (myReshape);
    auxMainLoop(display);
}
```

Soft Shadows

To accumulate soft shadows due to multiple light sources, render the shadows with one light turned on at a time, and accumulate them together. This can be combined with spatial jittering to antialias the scene at the same time. See "Shadows" on page 401 for more information about drawing shadows.

Jittering

If you need to take nine or sixteen samples to antialias an image, you might think that the best choice of points is an equally spaced grid across the pixel. Surprisingly, this is not necessarily true. In fact, sometimes it's a good idea to take points that lie in adjacent pixels. You might want a uniform distribution or a normalized distribution, clustering toward the center of the pixel. The SIGGRAPH paper cited on page 311 discusses these issues. In addition, Table 10-5 shows a few sets of reasonable jittering values to be used for some selected sample counts. Most of the examples in the table are uniformly distributed in the pixel, and all lie within the pixel.

Count	Values
2	{0.25, 0.75}, {0.75, 0.25}
3	{0.5033922635, 0.8317967229}, {0.7806016275, 0.2504380877}, {0.2261828938, 0.4131553612}
4	{0.375, 0.25}, {0.125, 0.75}, {0.875, 0.25}, {0.625, 0.75}
5	{0.5, 0.5}, {0.3, 0.1}, {0.7, 0.9}, {0.9, 0.3}, {0.1, 0.7}
6	{0.4646464646, 0.4646464646}, {0.1313131313, 0.7979797979}, {0.5353535353, 0.8686868686}, {0.8686868686, 0.5353535353}, {0.7979797979, 0.1313131313}, {0.2020202020, 0.2020202020}
8	{0.5625, 0.4375}, {0.0625, 0.9375}, {0.3125, 0.6875}, {0.6875, 0.8125}, {0.8125, 0.1875}, {0.9375, 0.5625}, {0.4375, 0.0625}, {0.1875, 0.3125}
9	{0.5, 0.5}, {0.1666666666, 0.9444444444}, {0.5, 0.1666666666}, {0.5, 0.8333333333}, {0.1666666666, 0.2777777777}, {0.8333333333, 0.3888888888}, {0.1666666666, 0.6111111111}, {0.8333333333, 0.7222222222}, {0.8333333333, 0.0555555555}
12	{0.4166666666, 0.625}, {0.9166666666, 0.875}, {0.25, 0.375}, {0.4166666666, 0.125}, {0.75, 0.125}, {0.0833333333, 0.125}, {0.75, 0.625}, {0.25, 0.875}, {0.5833333333, 0.375}, {0.9166666666, 0.375}, {0.0833333333, 0.625}, { 0.583333333, 0.875}
16	{0.375, 0.4375}, {0.625, 0.0625}, {0.875, 0.1875}, {0.125, 0.0625}, {0.375, 0.6875}, {0.875, 0.4375}, {0.625, 0.5625}, {0.375, 0.9375}, {0.625, 0.3125}, {0.125, 0.5625}, {0.125, 0.8125}, {0.375, 0.1875}, {0.875, 0.9375}, {0.875, 0.6875}, {0.125, 0.3125}, {0.625, 0.8125}

Table 10-5 Sample Jittering Values

Evaluators and NURBS

Chapter Objectives

After reading this chapter, you'll be able to do the following:

- Use OpenGL's evaluator commands to draw basic curves and surfaces

- Use the GLU's higher-level NURBS facility to draw more complex curves and surfaces

Note that this chapter presumes a number of prerequisites; they're listed in "Prerequisites" on page 327.

At the lowest level, graphics hardware draws points, line segments, and polygons, which are usually triangles and quadrilaterals. Smooth curves and surfaces are drawn by approximating them with large numbers of small line segments or polygons. However, many useful curves and surfaces can be described mathematically by a small number of parameters such as a few *control points*. Saving the sixteen control points for a surface requires much less storage than saving 1000 triangles together with the normal vector information at each vertex. In addition, the 1000 triangles only approximate the true surface, but the control points can accurately describe the real surface.

Evaluators provide a way to specify points on a curve or surface (or part of one) using only the control points. The curve or surface can then be rendered at any precision. In addition, normal vectors can be calculated for surfaces automatically. You can use the points generated by an evaluator in many ways—to draw dots where the surface would be, to draw a wireframe version of the surface, or to draw a fully lighted and shaded version.

You can use evaluators to describe any polynomial or rational polynomial splines or surfaces of any degree. These include almost all splines and spline surfaces in use today, including B-splines, NURBS (Non-Uniform Rational B-Spline) surfaces, Bézier curves and surfaces, and Hermite splines. Since evaluators provide only a low-level description of the points on a curve or surface, however, they're typically used underneath utility libraries that provide a higher-level interface to the programmer. The GLU's NURBS facility is such a higher-level interface—the NURBS routines encapsulate lots of complicated code, but the final rendering is done with evaluators.

This chapter contains the following major sections:

- **"Prerequisites"** discusses what knowledge is assumed for this chapter. It also gives several references where you can obtain this information.

- **"Evaluators"** explains how evaluators work and how to control them using the appropriate OpenGL commands.

- **"The GLU NURBS Interface"** describes the GLU routines for creating NURBS surfaces.

Prerequisites

Evaluators make splines and surfaces that are based on a Bézier (or Bernstein) basis. The defining formulas for the functions in this basis are given in this chapter, but the discussion doesn't include derivations or even lists of all their interesting mathematical properties. If you want to use evaluators to draw curves and surfaces using other bases, you must know how to convert your basis to a Bézier basis. In addition, when you render a Bézier surface or part of it using evaluators, you need to determine the granularity of your subdivision. Your decision needs to take into account the trade-off between high-quality (highly subdivided) images and high speed. Determining an appropriate subdivision strategy can be quite complicated, and it's not discussed here.

Similarly, a complete discussion of NURBS is beyond the scope of this book. The GLU NURBS interface is documented here, however, and programming examples are provided for readers who already understand the subject. In what follows, we assume that you know about NURBS control points, knot sequences, and trimming curves.

If you lack some of these prerequisites, the following references will help.

- Burns, Derrick. *Dynamic Trimmed Surface Rendering.* Ph.D. dissertation, Stanford University, 1993.

- de Boor, Carl. *A Practical Guide to Splines.* New York: Springer-Verlag, 1985.

- Farin, Gerald. *Curves and Surfaces for Computer-Aided Geometric Design.* San Diego, Calif: Academic Press, 1990.

- Mortenson, Michael. *Geometric Modeling.* New York: John Wiley & Sons, 1985.

- Newman, William and Sproull, Robert. *Principles of Interactive Computer Graphics.* New York: McGraw-Hill, 1979.

Note: Some of the terms used in this chapter might have slightly different meanings in other books on spline curves and surfaces, since there isn't total agreement among the practitioners of this art. Generally, the OpenGL meanings are a bit more restrictive. For example, OpenGL evaluators always use Bézier bases; in other contexts, evaluators might refer to the same concept, but with an arbitrary basis.

Evaluators

A Bézier curve is a vector-valued function of one variable

$$C(u) = [X(u) \quad Y(u) \quad Z(u)]$$

where u varies in some domain (say [0,1]). A Bézier surface patch is a vector-valued function of two variables

$$S(u,v) = [X(u,v) \quad Y(u,v) \quad Z(u,v)]$$

where u and v can both vary in some domain. The range isn't necessarily three-dimensional as shown here. You might want two-dimensional output for curves on a plane or texture coordinates, or you might want four-dimensional output to specify RGBA information. Even one-dimensional output may make sense for gray levels, for example.

For each u (or u and v, in the case of a surface), the formula for C() (or S()) calculates a point on the curve (or surface). To use an evaluator, first define the function C() or S(), enable it, and then use the **glEvalCoord1()** or **glEvalCoord2()** command instead of **glVertex()**. This way, the curve or surface vertices can be used like any other vertices—to form points or lines, for example. In addition, other commands automatically generate series of vertices that produce a regular mesh uniformly spaced in u (or in u and v). One- and two-dimensional evaluators are similar, but the description is somewhat simpler in one dimension, so that case is discussed first.

One-Dimensional Evaluators

This section presents an example of using one-dimensional evaluators to draw a curve. It then describes the commands and equations that control evaluators.

One-Dimensional Example: A Simple Bézier Curve

The program shown in Listing 11-1 draws a cubic Bézier curve using four control points, as shown in Figure 11-1.

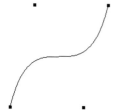

Figure 11-1 A Bézier Curve

Listing 11-1 Drawing a Bézier Curve Using Four Control Points: bezcurve.c

```
#include <GL/gl.h>
#include <GL/glu.h>
#include "aux.h"

GLfloat ctrlpoints[4][3] = {
    { -4.0, -4.0, 0.0}, { -2.0, 4.0, 0.0},
    {2.0, -4.0, 0.0}, {4.0, 4.0, 0.0}};

void myinit(void)
{
    glClearColor(0.0, 0.0, 0.0, 1.0);
    glMap1f(GL_MAP1_VERTEX_3, 0.0, 1.0, 3, 4,&ctrlpoints[0][0]);
    glEnable(GL_MAP1_VERTEX_3);
    glShadeModel(GL_FLAT);
}

void display(void)
{
    int i;

    glClear(GL_COLOR_BUFFER_BIT | GL_DEPTH_BUFFER_BIT);
    glColor3f(1.0, 1.0, 1.0);
    glBegin(GL_LINE_STRIP);
        for (i = 0; i <= 30; i++)
            glEvalCoord1f((GLfloat) i/30.0);
    glEnd();
    /* The following code displays the control points as dots. */
    glPointSize(5.0);
    glColor3f(1.0, 1.0, 0.0);
    glBegin(GL_POINTS);
        for (i = 0; i < 4; i++)
            glVertex3fv(&ctrlpoints[i][0]);
    glEnd();
```

```
        glFlush();
}

void myReshape(GLsizei w, GLsizei h)
{
    glViewport(0, 0, w, h);
    glMatrixMode(GL_PROJECTION);
    glLoadIdentity();
    if (w <= h)
        glOrtho(-5.0, 5.0, -5.0*(GLfloat)h/(GLfloat)w,
            5.0*(GLfloat)h/(GLfloat)w, -5.0, 5.0);
    else
        glOrtho(-5.0*(GLfloat)w/(GLfloat)h,
            5.0*(GLfloat)w/(GLfloat)h, -5.0, 5.0, -5.0, 5.0);
    glMatrixMode(GL_MODELVIEW);
    glLoadIdentity();
}

int main(int argc, char** argv)
{
    auxInitDisplayMode (AUX_SINGLE | AUX_RGBA);
    auxInitPosition (0, 0, 500, 500);
    auxInitWindow (argv[0]);
    myinit();
    auxReshapeFunc (myReshape);
    auxMainLoop(display);
}
```

A cubic Bézier curve is described by four control points, which appear in this example in the *ctrlpoints[][]* array. This array is one of the arguments to **glMap1f()**. All the arguments for this command are as follows:

GL_MAP1_VERTEX_3	Three-dimensional vertices are produced
0	Low value of parameter *u*
1	High value of parameter *u*
3	The number of floating-point values to advance in the data between one control point and the next
4	The order of the spline, which is the degree+1; in this case, the degree is 3 (since the curve is a cubic)
&ctrlpoints[0][0]	Pointer to the first control point's data

Note that the second and third arguments control the parameterization of the curve—as the variable u ranges from 0 to 1, the curve goes from one end to the other. The call to **glEnable()** enables the one-dimensional evaluator for two-dimensional vertices.

The curve is drawn in the routine **display()** between the **glBegin()** and **glEnd()** calls. Since the evaluator is enabled, the command **glEvalCoord1f()** is just like issuing a **glVertex()** command with coordinates that are the coordinates of a vertex on the curve corresponding to the input parameter u.

Defining and Evaluating a One-Dimensional Evaluator

The Bernstein polynomial of degree n (or order $n+1$) is given by

$$B_i^n(u) = \binom{n}{i} u^i (1-u)^{n-i}$$

If P_i represents a set of control points (one-, two-, three-, or even four-dimensional), then the equation

$$C(u) = \sum_{i=0}^{n} B_i^n(u) P_i$$

represents a Bézier curve as u varies from 0 to 1. To represent the same curve but allowing u to vary between u_1 and u_2 instead of 0 and 1, evaluate

$$C\left(\frac{u - u_1}{u_2 - u_1}\right)$$

The command **glMap1()** defines a one-dimensional evaluator that uses these equations.

---

void **glMap1**{fd}(GLenum *target, TYPE u1, TYPE u2*, GLint *stride*,
GLint *order, const TYPE *points*);

Defines a one-dimensional evaluator. The *target* parameter specifies what the control points represent, as shown in Table 11-1, and therefore how many values need to be supplied in *points*. The points can represent vertices, RGBA color data, normal vectors, or texture coordinates. Forexample, with GL_MAP1_COLOR_4, the evaluator generates color data along a curve in four-dimensional (RGBA) color space. You also use the parameter values listed in Table 11-1 to enable each defined evaluator before you invoke it. Pass the appropriate value to **glEnable()** or **glDisable()** to enable or disable the evaluator.

The second two parameters for **glMap1*()**, *u1* and *u2*, indicate the range for the variable *u*. The variable *stride* is the number of single- or double-precision values (as appropriate) in each block of storage. Thus, it's an offset value between the beginning of one control point and the beginning of the next.

The *order* is the degree plus one, and it should agree with the number of control points. The *points* parameter points to the first coordinate of the first control point. Using the example data structure for **glMap1*()**, use the following for *points*:

```
(GLfloat *)(&ctlpoints[0].x)
```

Parameter	Meaning
GL_MAP1_VERTEX_3	*x, y, z* vertex coordinates
GL_MAP1_VERTEX_4	*x, y, z, w* vertex coordinates
GL_MAP1_INDEX	color index
GL_MAP1_COLOR_4	R, G, B, A
GL_MAP1_NORMAL	normal coordinates
GL_MAP1_TEXTURE_COORD_1	*s* texture coordinates
GL_MAP1_TEXTURE_COORD_2	*s, t* texture coordinates
GL_MAP1_TEXTURE_COORD_3	*s, t, r* texture coordinates
GL_MAP1_TEXTURE_COORD_4	*s, t, r, q* texture coordinates

Table 11-1 Types of Control Points for Use with glMap1*()

More than one evaluator can be evaluated at a time. If you have both a GL_MAP1_VERTEX_3 and a GL_MAP1_COLOR_4 evaluator defined and enabled, for example, then calls to **glEvalCoord1()** generate both a position and a color. Only one of the vertex evaluators can be enabled at a time, although you might have defined both of them. Similarly, only one of the texture evaluators can be active. Other than that, however, evaluators can be used to generate any combination of vertex, normal, color, and texture-coordinate data. If more than one evaluator of the same type is defined and enabled, the one of highest dimension is used.

Use **glEvalCoord1*()** to evaluate a defined and enabled one-dimensional map.

---

void **glEvalCoord1**{fd}{v}(*TYPE u*);

Causes evaluation of the enabled one-dimensional maps. The argument *u* is the value (or a pointer to the value, in the vector version of the command) that's the domain coordinate.

Defining Evenly Spaced Coordinate Values in One Dimension

You can use **glEvalCoord1()** with any values for *u*, but by far the most common use is with evenly spaced values, as shown previously in Listing 11-1. To obtain evenly spaced values, define a one-dimensional grid using **glMapGrid1*()** and then apply it using **glEvalMesh1()**.

---

void **glMapGrid1**{fd}(GLint *n, TYPE u1, TYPE u2*);

Defines a grid that goes from *u1* to *u2* in *n* steps, which are evenly spaced.

> void **glEvalMesh1**(GLenum *mode*, GLint *p1*, GLint *p2*);
>
> Applies the currently defined map grid to all enabled evaluators. The *mode* can be either GL_POINT or GL_LINE, depending on whether you want to draw points or a connected line along the curve. The call has exactly the same effect as issuing a **glEvalCoord1()** for each of the steps between and including *p1* and *p2*, where $0 <= p1, p2 <= n$. Programatically, it's equivalent to the following:
>
> ```
> glBegin(GL_POINTS);     /* OR glBegin(GL_LINE_STRIP); */
> for (i = p1; i <= p2; i++)
>     glEvalCoord1(u1 + i*(u2-u1)/n);
> glEnd();
> ```
>
> except that if $i = 0$ or $i = n$, then **glEvalCoord()** is called with exactly *u1* or *u2* as its parameter.

Two-Dimensional Evaluators

In two dimensions, everything is similar to the one-dimensional case, except that all the commands must take two parameters, *u* and *v*, into account. Points, colors, normals, or texture coordinates must be supplied over a surface instead of a curve. Mathematically, the definition of a Bézier surface patch is given by

$$S(u, v) = \sum_{i=0}^{n} \sum_{j=0}^{m} B_i^n(u) B_j^m(v) P_{ij}$$

where P_{ij} are a set of $m*n$ control points, and the B_i are the same Bernstein polynomials for one dimension. As before, the P_{ij} can represent vertices, normals, colors, or texture coordinates.

The procedure to use two-dimensional evaluators is similar to the procedure for one dimension:

1. Define the evaluator(s) with **glMap2*()**.

2. Enable them by passing the appropriate value to **glEnable()**.

3. Invoke them either by calling **glEvalCoord2()** between a **glBegin()** and **glEnd()** pair, or by specifying and then applying a mesh with **glMapGrid2()** and **glEvalMesh2()**.

Defining and Evaluating a Two-Dimensional Evaluator

Use **glMap2*()** and **glEvalCoord2*()** to define and then invoke a two-dimensional evaluator.

---

void **glMap2**{fd}(GLenum *target*, TYPE *u1*, TYPE *u2*, GLint *ustride*,
  GLint *uorder*, TYPE *v1*, TYPE *v2*, GLint *vstride*,
  GLint *vorder*, TYPE *points*);

The *target* parameter can have any of the values in Table 11-1 (see page 332), except that the string MAP1 is replaced with MAP2. As before, these values are also used with **glEnable()** to enable the corresponding evaluator. Minimum and maximum values for both *u* and *v* are provided as *u1*, *u2*, *v1*, and *v2*. The parameters *ustride* and *vstride* indicate the number of single- or double-precision values (as appropriate) between independent settings for these values allows users to select a subrectangle of control points out of a much larger array. For example, if the data appears in the form

```
GLfloat ctlpoints[100][100][3];
```

and you want to use the 4×4 subset beginning at ctlpoints[20][30], choose *ustride* to be 100*3, and *vstride* to be 3. The starting point, *points*, should be set to &ctlpoints[20][30][0]. Finally, the order parameters, *uorder* and *vorder*, can be different, allowing patches that are cubic in one direction and quadratic in the other, for example.

---

void **glEvalCoord2**{fd}{v}(TYPE *u*, TYPE *v*);

Causes evaluation of the enabled two-dimensional maps. The arguments *u* and *v* are the values (or a pointer to the value, in the vector version of the command) for the domain coordinates. If either of the vertex evaluators is enabled (GL_MAP2_VERTEX_3 or GL_MAP2_VERTEX_4), then the normal to the surface is computed analytically. This normal is associated with the generated vertex if automatic normal generation has been enabled by passing GL_AUTO_NORMAL to **glEnable()**. If it's disabled, the corresponding enabled normal map is used to produce a normal. If no such map exists, the current normal is used.

Two-Dimensional Example: A Bézier Surface

Listing 11-2 draws a wireframe Bézier surface using evaluators, as shown in Figure 11-2. In this example, the surface is drawn with nine curved lines in each direction. Each curve is drawn as 30 segments. To get the whole program, add the **myReshape()** and **main()** routines from Listing 11-1.

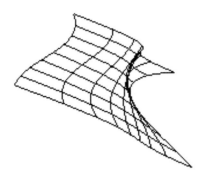

Figure 11-2   A Bézier Surface

Listing 11-2   Drawing a Bézier Surface: bezsurf.c

```
#include <GL/gl.h>
#include <GL/glu.h>
#include "aux.h"

GLfloat ctrlpoints[4][4][3] = {
    {{-1.5, -1.5, 4.0}, {-0.5, -1.5, 2.0},
        {0.5, -1.5, -1.0}, {1.5, -1.5, 2.0}},
    {{-1.5, -0.5, 1.0}, {-0.5, -0.5, 3.0},
        {0.5, -0.5, 0.0}, {1.5, -0.5, -1.0}},
    {{-1.5, 0.5, 4.0}, {-0.5, 0.5, 0.0},
        {0.5, 0.5, 3.0}, {1.5, 0.5, 4.0}},
    {{-1.5, 1.5, -2.0}, {-0.5, 1.5, -2.0},
        {0.5, 1.5, 0.0}, {1.5, 1.5, -1.0}}
};

void display(void)
{
    int i, j;

    glClear(GL_COLOR_BUFFER_BIT | GL_DEPTH_BUFFER_BIT);
    glColor3f(1.0, 1.0, 1.0);
```

```
    glPushMatrix ();
    glRotatef(85.0, 1.0, 1.0, 1.0);
    for (j = 0; j <= 8; j++) {
        glBegin(GL_LINE_STRIP);
            for (i = 0; i <= 30; i++)
                glEvalCoord2f((GLfloat)i/30.0, (GLfloat)j/8.0);
        glEnd();
        glBegin(GL_LINE_STRIP);
            for (i = 0; i <= 30; i++)
                glEvalCoord2f((GLfloat)j/8.0, (GLfloat)i/30.0);
        glEnd();
    }
    glPopMatrix ();
    glFlush();
}

void myinit(void)
{
    glClearColor (0.0, 0.0, 0.0, 1.0);
    glMap2f(GL_MAP2_VERTEX_3, 0, 1, 3, 4,
        0, 1, 12, 4, &ctrlpoints[0][0][0]);
    glEnable(GL_MAP2_VERTEX_3);
    glEnable(GL_DEPTH_TEST);
    glShadeModel(GL_FLAT);
}
```

Defining Evenly Spaced Coordinate Values in Two Dimensions

In two dimensions, the **glMapGrid2*()** and **glEvalMesh2()** commands are similar to the one-dimensional versions, except that both *u* and *v* information must be included.

---

void **glMapGrid2**{fd}(GLint *nu*, *TYPE u1*, *TYPE u2*, GLint *nv*, *TYPE v1*,
            TYPE v2);
void **glEvalMesh2**(GLenum *mode*, GLint *p1*, GLint *p2*, GLint *q2*,
            GLint *q2*);

Defines a two-dimensional map grid that goes from *u1* to *u2* in *nu* evenly spaced steps and from *v1* to *v2* in *nv* steps (**glMapGrid2*()**), and then applies this grid to all enabled evaluators (**glEvalMesh2()**). The only significant difference from the one-dimensional versions of these two commands is that in **glEvalMesh2()**, the *mode* parameter can be GL_FILL as well as GL_POINT or GL_LINE. GL_FILL generates filled polygons using the quad-mesh primitive. Stated precisely, **glEvalMesh2()** is nearly equivalent to one of the following three code fragments. (It's nearly equivalent because when *i* is equal to *nu* or *j* to *nv*, the parameter is exactly equal to *u2* or *v2*, not to *u1+nu*(u2–u1)/nu*, which might be slightly different due to round-off error.)

```
glBegin(GL_POINTS);                      /* mode == GL_POINT */
for (i = nu1; i <= nu2; i++)
    for (j = nv1; j <= nv2; j++)
        glEvalCoord2(u1 + i*(u2-u1)/nu, v1+j*(v2-v1)/nv);
glEnd();
```

or

```
for (i = nu1; i <= nu2; i++) {       /* mode == GL_LINE */
    glBegin(GL_LINES);
        for (j = nv1; j <= nv2; j++)
            glEvalCoord2(u1 + i*(u2-u1)/nu, v1+j*(v2-v1)/nv);
    glEnd();
}
for (j = nv1; j <= nv2; j++) {
    glBegin(GL_LINES);
    for (i = nu1; i <= nu2; i++)
        glEvalCoord2(u1 + i*(u2-u1)/nu, v1+j*(v2-v1)/nv);
    glEnd();
}
```

or

```
for (i = nu1; i < nu2; i++) {       /* mode == GL_FILL */
    glBegin(GL_QUAD_STRIP);
    for (j = nv1; j <= nv2; j++) {
        glEvalCoord2(u1 + i*(u2-u1)/nu, v1+j*(v2-v1)/nv);
        glEvalCoord2(u1 + (i+1)*(u2-u1)/nu, v1+j*(v2-v1)/nv);
    glEnd();
}
```

Listing 11-3 shows the differences necessary to draw the same Bézier surface as Listing 11-2, but using **glMapGrid2()** and **glEvalMesh2()** to subdivide the square domain into a uniform 8×8 grid. This program also adds lighting and shading, as shown in Figure 11-3.

Figure 11-3 A Lit, Shaded Bézier Surface Drawn Using a Mesh

Listing 11-3 Drawing a Lit, Shaded Bézier Surface Using a Mesh: bezmesh.c

```
void initlights(void)
{
    GLfloat ambient[] = { 0.2, 0.2, 0.2, 1.0 };
    GLfloat position[] = { 0.0, 0.0, 2.0, 1.0 };
    GLfloat mat_diffuse[] = { 0.6, 0.6, 0.6, 1.0 };
    GLfloat mat_specular[] = { 1.0, 1.0, 1.0, 1.0 };
    GLfloat mat_shininess[] = { 50.0 };

    glEnable(GL_LIGHTING);
    glEnable(GL_LIGHT0);

    glLightfv(GL_LIGHT0, GL_AMBIENT, ambient);
    glLightfv(GL_LIGHT0, GL_POSITION, position);
    glMaterialfv(GL_FRONT_AND_BACK, GL_DIFFUSE, mat_diffuse);
    glMaterialfv(GL_FRONT_AND_BACK, GL_SPECULAR, mat_specular);
    glMaterialfv(GL_FRONT_AND_BACK,GL_SHININESS, mat_shininess);
}

void display(void)
{
    glClear(GL_COLOR_BUFFER_BIT | GL_DEPTH_BUFFER_BIT);
    glPushMatrix();
        glRotatef(85.0, 1.0, 1.0, 1.0);
        glEvalMesh2(GL_FILL, 0, 8, 0, 8);
    glPopMatrix();
    glFlush();
}
```

```
void myinit(void)
{
    glClearColor (0.0, 0.0, 0.0, 1.0);
    glEnable(GL_DEPTH_TEST);
    glMap2f(GL_MAP2_VERTEX_3, 0, 1, 3, 4,
        0, 1, 12, 4, &ctrlpoints[0][0][0]);
    glEnable(GL_MAP2_VERTEX_3);
    glEnable(GL_AUTO_NORMAL);
    glMapGrid2f(8, 0.0, 1.0, 8, 0.0, 1.0);
    initlights();
}
```

Example: Using Evaluators for Textures

Listing 11-4 enables two evaluators at the same time: The first generates three-dimensional points on the same Bézier surface as Listing 11-3, and the second generates texture coordinates. In this case, the texture coordinates are the same as the *u* and *v* coordinates of the surface, but a special flat Bézier patch must be created to do this.

The flat patch is defined over a square with corners at (0, 0), (0, 1), (1, 0), and (1, 1); it generates (0, 0) at corner (0, 0), (0, 1) at corner (0, 1), and so on. Since it's of order 2 (linear degree plus one), evaluating this texture at the point (*u*, *v*) generates texture coordinates (*s*, *t*). It's enabled at the same time as the vertex evaluator, so both take effect when the surface is drawn. See Plate 19. If you want the texture to repeat three times in each direction, change every 1.0 in the array *texpts[][][]* to 3.0. Since the texture wraps in this example, the surface is rendered with nine copies of the texture map.

Listing 11-4 Using Evaluators for Textures: texturesurf.c

```
#include <GL/gl.h>
#include <GL/glu.h>
#include "aux.h"
#include <math.h>

GLfloat ctrlpoints[4][4][3] = {
    {{ -1.5, -1.5, 4.0}, { -0.5, -1.5, 2.0},
        {0.5, -1.5, -1.0}, {1.5, -1.5, 2.0}},
    {{ -1.5, -0.5, 1.0}, { -0.5, -0.5, 3.0},
        {0.5, -0.5, 0.0}, {1.5, -0.5, -1.0}},
    {{ -1.5, 0.5, 4.0}, { -0.5, 0.5, 0.0},
        {0.5, 0.5, 3.0}, {1.5, 0.5, 4.0}},
    {{ -1.5, 1.5, -2.0}, { -0.5, 1.5, -2.0},
        {0.5, 1.5, 0.0}, {1.5, 1.5, -1.0}}
};
```

```
GLfloat texpts[2][2][2] = {{{0.0, 0.0}, {0.0, 1.0}},
        {{1.0, 0.0}, {1.0, 1.0}}};

void display(void)
{
    glClear(GL_COLOR_BUFFER_BIT | GL_DEPTH_BUFFER_BIT);
    glColor3f(1.0, 1.0, 1.0);
    glEvalMesh2(GL_FILL, 0, 20, 0, 20);
    glFlush();
}

#define    imageWidth 64
#define    imageHeight 64
GLubyte    image[3*imageWidth*imageHeight];

void loadImage(void)
{
    int i, j;
    float ti, tj;

    for (i = 0; i < imageWidth; i++) {
        ti = 2.0*3.14159265*i/imageWidth;
        for (j = 0; j < imageHeight; j++) {
            tj = 2.0*3.14159265*j/imageHeight;
            image[3*(imageHeight*i+j)] =
                (GLubyte) 127*(1.0+sin(ti));
            image[3*(imageHeight*i+j)+1] =
                (GLubyte) 127*(1.0+cos(2*tj));
            image[3*(imageHeight*i+j)+2] =
                (GLubyte) 127*(1.0+cos(ti+tj));
        }
    }
}

void myinit(void)
{
    glMap2f(GL_MAP2_VERTEX_3, 0, 1, 3, 4,
        0, 1, 12, 4, &ctrlpoints[0][0][0]);
    glMap2f(GL_MAP2_TEXTURE_COORD_2, 0, 1, 2, 2,
        0, 1, 4, 2, &texpts[0][0][0]);
    glEnable(GL_MAP2_TEXTURE_COORD_2);
    glEnable(GL_MAP2_VERTEX_3);
    glMapGrid2f(20, 0.0, 1.0, 20, 0.0, 1.0);
    loadImage();
    glTexEnvf(GL_TEXTURE_ENV, GL_TEXTURE_ENV_MODE, GL_DECAL);
    glTexParameterf(GL_TEXTURE_2D, GL_TEXTURE_WRAP_S,
                    GL_REPEAT);
```

```
        glTexParameterf(GL_TEXTURE_2D, GL_TEXTURE_WRAP_T,
                        GL_REPEAT);
        glTexParameterf(GL_TEXTURE_2D, GL_TEXTURE_MAG_FILTER,
                        GL_NEAREST);
        glTexParameterf(GL_TEXTURE_2D, GL_TEXTURE_MIN_FILTER,
                        GL_NEAREST);
        glTexImage2D(GL_TEXTURE_2D, 0, 3, imageWidth, imageHeight,
                     0, GL_RGB, GL_UNSIGNED_BYTE, image);
        glEnable(GL_TEXTURE_2D);
        glEnable(GL_DEPTH_TEST);
        glEnable(GL_NORMALIZE);
        glShadeModel (GL_FLAT);
}

void myReshape(GLsizei w, GLsizei h)
{
    glViewport(0, 0, w, h);
    glMatrixMode(GL_PROJECTION);
    glLoadIdentity();
    if (w <= h)
        glOrtho(-4.0, 4.0, -4.0*(GLfloat)h/(GLfloat)w,
                4.0*(GLfloat)h/(GLfloat)w, -4.0, 4.0);
    else
        glOrtho(-4.0*(GLfloat)w/(GLfloat)h,
                4.0*(GLfloat)w/(GLfloat)h, -4.0, 4.0, -4.0, 4.0);

    glMatrixMode(GL_MODELVIEW);
    glLoadIdentity();
    glRotatef(85.0, 1.0, 1.0, 1.0);
}

int main(int argc, char** argv)
{
    auxInitDisplayMode (AUX_SINGLE | AUX_RGBA | AUX_DEPTH);
    auxInitPosition (0, 0, 300, 300);
    auxInitWindow (argv[0]);
    myinit();
    auxReshapeFunc (myReshape);
    auxMainLoop(display);
}
```

The GLU NURBS Interface

Although evaluators are the only OpenGL primitive available to directly draw curves and surfaces, and even though they can be implemented very efficiently in hardware, they're often accessed by applications through higher-level libraries. The GLU provides a NURBS (Non-Uniform Rational B-Spline) interface built on top of the OpenGL evaluator commands.

A Simple NURBS Example

If you understand NURBS, writing OpenGL code to manipulate NURBS curves and surfaces is relatively easy, even with lighting and texture mapping. Follow these steps to draw NURBS curves or untrimmed NURBS surfaces. (Trimmed surfaces are discussed in "Trimming" on page 349.)

1. If you intend to use lighting with a NURBS surface, call **glEnable()** with GL_AUTO_NORMAL to automatically generate surface normals. (Or you can calculate your own.)

2. Use **gluNewNurbsRenderer()** to create a pointer to a NURBS object, which is referred to when creating your NURBS curve or surface.

3. If desired, call **gluNurbsProperty()** to choose rendering values, such as the maximum size of lines or polygons that are used to render your NURBS object.

4. Call **gluNurbsCallback()** if you want to be notified when an error is encountered. (Error checking may slightly degrade performance.)

5. Start your curve or surface by calling **gluBeginCurve()** or **gluBeginSurface()**.

6. Generate and render your curve or surface. Call **gluNurbsCurve()** or **gluNurbsSurface()** at least once with the control points (rational or nonrational), knot sequence, and order of the polynomial basis function for your NURBS object. You might call these functions additional times to specify surface normals and/or texture coordinates.

7. Call **gluEndCurve()** or **gluEndSurface()** to complete the curve or surface.

Listing 11-5 renders a NURBS surface in the shape of a symmetrical hill with control points ranging from −3.0 to 3.0. The basis function is a cubic B-spline, but the knot sequence is nonuniform, with a multiplicity of 4 at each endpoint, causing the basis function to behave like a Bézier curve in each direction. The surface is lighted, with a dark gray diffuse reflection

and white specular highlights. Figure 11-4 shows the surface as a
wireframe and lighted.

Figure 11-4   A NURBS Surface

Listing 11-5   Drawing a NURBS Surface: surface.c

```c
#include <GL/gl.h>
#include <GL/glu.h>
#include "aux.h"

GLfloat ctlpoints[4][4][3];
GLUnurbsObj *theNurb;

void init_surface(void)
{
    int u, v;
    for (u = 0; u < 4; u++) {
        for (v = 0; v < 4; v++) {
            ctlpoints[u][v][0] = 2.0*((GLfloat)u - 1.5);
            ctlpoints[u][v][1] = 2.0*((GLfloat)v - 1.5);

            if ( (u == 1 || u == 2) && (v == 1 || v == 2))
                ctlpoints[u][v][2] = 3.0;
            else
                ctlpoints[u][v][2] = -3.0;
        }
    }
}
```

```
void myinit(void)
{
    GLfloat mat_diffuse[] = { 0.7, 0.7, 0.7, 1.0 };
    GLfloat mat_specular[] = { 1.0, 1.0, 1.0, 1.0 };
    GLfloat mat_shininess[] = { 100.0 };

    glClearColor (0.0, 0.0, 0.0, 1.0);
    glMaterialfv(GL_FRONT, GL_DIFFUSE, mat_diffuse);
    glMaterialfv(GL_FRONT, GL_SPECULAR, mat_specular);
    glMaterialfv(GL_FRONT, GL_SHININESS, mat_shininess);

    glEnable(GL_LIGHTING);
    glEnable(GL_LIGHT0);
    glDepthFunc(GL_LEQUAL);
    glEnable(GL_DEPTH_TEST);
    glEnable(GL_AUTO_NORMAL);
    glEnable(GL_NORMALIZE);

    init_surface();

    theNurb = gluNewNurbsRenderer();
    gluNurbsProperty(theNurb, GLU_SAMPLING_TOLERANCE, 25.0);
    gluNurbsProperty(theNurb, GLU_DISPLAY_MODE, GLU_FILL);
}

void display(void)
{
    GLfloat knots[8] = {0.0, 0.0, 0.0, 0.0, 1.0, 1.0, 1.0, 1.0};

    glClear(GL_COLOR_BUFFER_BIT | GL_DEPTH_BUFFER_BIT);

    glPushMatrix();
        glRotatef(330.0, 1.,0.,0.);
        glScalef (0.5, 0.5, 0.5);

        gluBeginSurface(theNurb);
        gluNurbsSurface(theNurb,
            8, knots,
            8, knots,
            4 * 3,
            3,
            &ctlpoints[0][0][0],
            4, 4,
            GL_MAP2_VERTEX_3);
        gluEndSurface(theNurb);

    glPopMatrix();
```

```
        glFlush();
}

void myReshape(GLsizei w, GLsizei h)
{
    glViewport(0, 0, w, h);
    glMatrixMode(GL_PROJECTION);
    glLoadIdentity();
    gluPerspective (45.0, (GLdouble)w/(GLdouble)h, 3.0, 8.0);

    glMatrixMode(GL_MODELVIEW);
    glLoadIdentity();
    glTranslatef (0.0, 0.0, -5.0);
}


int main(int argc, char** argv)
{
    auxInitDisplayMode (AUX_SINGLE | AUX_RGBA);
    auxInitPosition (0, 0, 500, 500);
    auxInitWindow (argv[0]);
    myinit();
    auxReshapeFunc (myReshape);
    auxMainLoop(display);
}
```

As shown in Listing 11-5, **gluNewNurbsRenderer()** returns a new NURBS object, whose type is a pointer to a GLUnurbsObj structure. The **gluBeginSurface()** and **gluEndSurface()** pair bracket the rendering routine, saving and restoring the evaluator state. These three routines are summarized in Appendix C. The more complex routines, **gluNurbsProperty()** and **gluNurbsSurface()**, are discussed in this section.

void **gluNurbsProperty**(GLUnurbsObj *nobj*, GLenum *property*,
                GLfloat *value*);

Controls attributes of a NURBS object, *nobj*. The *property* argument
specifies the property and can be GLU_SAMPLING_TOLERANCE,
GLU_DISPLAY_MODE, GLU_CULLING, or GLU_AUTO_LOAD_MATRIX.
The *value* argument indicates what the property should be. Since a NURBS
object is rendered as primitives, it's sampled at different values of its
parameter(s) (*u* and *v*) and broken down into small line segments or
polygons for rendering. GLU_SAMPLING_TOLERANCE controls how
often the NURBS object is sampled. The default value of 50.0 makes the
largest sampled line segment or polygon edge 50.0 pixels long.

The default value for GLU_DISPLAY_MODE is GLU_FILL, which causes
the surface to be rendered as polygons. If GLU_OUTLINE_POLYGON is
used for the display-mode property, the outlines of polygons are
rendered. Finally, GLU_OUTLINE_PATCH renders the outlines of
patches and trimming curves (see the next section on trimming).

GLU_CULLING can speed up performance by not performing
tessellation if the NURBS object falls completely outside the viewing
volume; set this property to GL_TRUE to enable culling (the default is
GL_FALSE). The GLU_AUTO_LOAD_MATRIX property determines
whether the projection matrix, modelview matrix, and viewport are
downloaded from the OpenGL server (GL_TRUE, the default), or
whether the application must supply these matrices with
gluLoadSamplingMatrices() (GL_FALSE).

---

void **gluNurbsSurface** (GLUnurbsObj *nobj*, GLint *uknot_count*,
GLfloat **uknot*, GLint *vknot_count*, GLfloat **vknot*,
GLint *u_stride*, GLint *v_stride*, GLfloat **ctlarray*,
GLint *uorder*, GLint *vorder*, GLenum *type*);

Describes the vertices (or surface normals or texture coordinates) of a NURBS surface, *nobj*. Several of the values must be specified for both *u* and *v* parametric directions, such as the knot sequences (*uknot* and *vknot*), knot counts (*uknot_count* and *vknot_count*), and order of the polynomial (*uorder* and *vorder*) for the NURBS surface. Note that the number of control points isn't specified. Instead, it's derived by determining the number of control points along each parameter as the number of knots minus the order. Then, the number of control points for the surface is equal to the number of control points in each parametric direction, multiplied by one another. The *ctlarray* argument points to an array of control points.

The last parameter, *type*, is one of the two-dimensional evaluator types. Commonly, you might use GL_MAP2_VERTEX_3 for nonrational or GL_MAP2_VERTEX_4 for rational control points, respectively. You might also use other types, such as GL_MAP2_TEXTURE_COORD_* or GL_MAP2_NORMAL to calculate and assign texture coordinates or surface normals.

The *u_stride* and *v_stride* arguments represent the number of floating-point values between control points in each parametric direction. The evaluator type, as well as its order, affects the *u_stride* and *v_stride* values. In Listing 11-5, *u_stride* is 12 (4 * 3) because there are three coordinates for each vertex (set by GL_MAP2_VERTEX_3) and four control points in the parametric *v* direction; *v_stride* is 3 because each vertex had three coordinates, and *v* control points are adjacent to one another.

Drawing a NURBS curve is similar to drawing a surface, except that all calculations are done with one parameter, *u*, rather than two. Also, for curves, **gluBeginCurve()** and **gluEndCurve()** are the bracketing routines.

void **gluNurbsCurve** (GLUnurbsObj **nobj*, GLint *uknot_count*,
                 GLfloat **uknot*, GLint *u_stride*, GLfloat **ctlarray*,
                 GLint *uorder*, GLenum *type*);

Defines a NURBS curve for the object *nobj*. The arguments have the same meaning as those for **gluNurbsSurface()**. Note that this routine requires only one knot sequence, and one declaration of the order of the NURBS object. If this curve is defined within a **gluBeginCurve()/gluEndCurve()** pair, then the type can be any of the valid one-dimensional evaluator types (such as GL_MAP1_VERTEX_3 or GL_MAP1_VERTEX_4).

Trimming

To create a trimmed NURBS surface with OpenGL, start as if you were creating an untrimmed surface. After calling **gluBeginSurface()** and **gluNurbsSurface()** but before calling **gluEndSurface()**, start a trim by calling **gluBeginTrim()**. You can create two kinds of trimming curves, a piecewise linear curve with **gluPwlCurve()** or a NURBS curve with **gluNurbsCurve()**. A piecewise linear curve doesn't look like what's conventionally called a curve, because it's a series of straight lines. A NURBS curve for trimming must lie within the unit square of parametric (u, v) space. The type for a NURBS trimming curve is usually GLU_MAP1_TRIM2. Less often, the type is GLU_MAP1_TRIM3, where the curve is described in a two-dimensional homogeneous space (u', v', w') by $(u, v) = (u'/w', v'/w')$.

void **gluPwlCurve** (GLUnurbsObj **nobj*, GLint *count*, GLfloat **array*,
                GLint *stride*, GLenum *type*);

Describes a piecewise linear trimming curve for the NURBS object *nobj*. There are *count* points on the curve, and they're given by *array*. The *type* can be either GLU_MAP1_TRIM_2 (the most common) or GLU_MAP1_TRIM_3 ((u, v, w) homogeneous parameter space). The type affects whether *stride*, the number of floating-point values to the next vertex, is 2 or 3.

You need to consider the orientation of trimming curves—that is, whether they're counterclockwise or clockwise—to make sure you include the desired part of the surface. If you imagine walking along a curve, everything to the left is included and everything to the right is trimmed away. For example, if your trim consists of a single counterclockwise loop, everything inside the loop is included. If the trim consists of two nonintersecting counterclockwise loops with nonintersecting interiors, everything inside either of them is included. If it consists of a counterclockwise loop with two clockwise loops inside it, the trimming region has two holes in it. The outermost trimming curve must be counterclockwise. Often, you run a trimming curve around the entire unit square to include everything within it, which is what you get by default by not specifying any trimming curves.

Trimming curves must be closed and nonintersecting. You can combine trimming curves, so long as the endpoints of the trimming curves meet to form a closed curve. You can nest curves, creating islands that float in space. Be sure to get the curve orientations right. For example, an error results if you specify a trimming region with two counterclockwise curves, one enclosed within another: The region between the curves is to the left of one and to the right of the other, so it must be both included and excluded, which is impossible. Figure 11-5 illustrates a few valid possibilities.

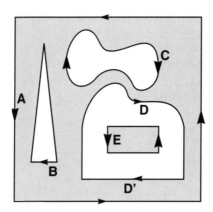

```
gluBeginSurface();
    gluNurbsSurface(...);
    gluBeginTrim();
        gluPwlCurve(...); /* A */
    gluEndTrim();
    gluBeginTrim();
        gluPwlCurve(...); /* B */
    gluEndTrim();
    gluBeginTrim();
        gluNurbsCurve(...);/* C */
    gluEndTrim();
    gluBeginTrim();
        gluNurbsCurve(...);/* D */
        gluPwlCurve(...); /* D' */
    gluEndTrim();
    gluBeginTrim();
        gluPwlCurve(...); /* E */
    gluEndTrim();
gluEndSurface();
```

Figure 11-5 Parametric Trimming Curves

Figure 11-6 shows the same small hill as in Figure 11-4 , this time with a trimming curve that's a combination of a piecewise linear curve and a NURBS curve. The program that creates this figure is similar to that shown in Listing 11-5; the differences are in the routines shown in Listing 11-6.

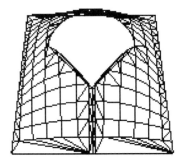 

Figure 11-6   A Trimmed NURBS Surface

Listing 11-6   Trimming a NURBS Surface: trim.c

```
void myinit(void)
{
    GLfloat mat_diffuse[] = { 0.6, 0.6, 0.6, 1.0 };
    GLfloat mat_specular[] = { 0.9, 0.9, 0.9, 1.0 };
    GLfloat mat_shininess[] = { 128.0 };

    glClearColor (0.0, 0.0, 0.0, 1.0);
    glMaterialfv(GL_FRONT, GL_DIFFUSE, mat_diffuse);
    glMaterialfv(GL_FRONT, GL_SPECULAR, mat_specular);
    glMaterialfv(GL_FRONT, GL_SHININESS, mat_shininess);

    glEnable(GL_LIGHTING);
    glEnable(GL_LIGHT0);
    glDepthFunc(GL_LEQUAL);
    glEnable(GL_DEPTH_TEST);
    glEnable(GL_AUTO_NORMAL);
    glEnable(GL_NORMALIZE);

    init_surface();

    theNurb = gluNewNurbsRenderer();
    gluNurbsProperty(theNurb, GLU_SAMPLING_TOLERANCE, 50.0);
    gluNurbsProperty(theNurb, GLU_DISPLAY_MODE, GLU_FILL);
}
```

```
void display(void)
{
    GLfloat knots[8] = {0.0, 0.0, 0.0, 0.0, 1.0, 1.0, 1.0, 1.0};
    GLfloat edgePt[5][2] = /* counter clockwise */
        {{0.0, 0.0}, {1.0, 0.0}, {1.0, 1.0}, {0.0, 1.0},
        {0.0, 0.0}};
    GLfloat curvePt[4][2] = /* clockwise */
        {{0.25, 0.5}, {0.25, 0.75}, {0.75, 0.75}, {0.75, 0.5}};
    GLfloat curveKnots[8] =
        {0.0, 0.0, 0.0, 0.0, 1.0, 1.0, 1.0, 1.0};
    GLfloat pwlPt[4][2] = /* clockwise */
        {{0.75, 0.5}, {0.5, 0.25}, {0.25, 0.5}};

    glClear(GL_COLOR_BUFFER_BIT | GL_DEPTH_BUFFER_BIT);
    glPushMatrix();
        glRotatef(330.0, 1.,0.,0.);
        glScalef (0.5, 0.5, 0.5);

        gluBeginSurface(theNurb);
        gluNurbsSurface(theNurb,
            8, knots,
            8, knots,
            4 * 3,
            3,
            &ctlpoints[0][0][0],
            4, 4,
            GL_MAP2_VERTEX_3);
        gluBeginTrim (theNurb);
            gluPwlCurve(theNurb, 5, &edgePt[0][0], 2,
                    GLU_MAP1_TRIM_2);
        gluEndTrim (theNurb);
        gluBeginTrim (theNurb);
            gluNurbsCurve(theNurb, 8, curveKnots, 2,
                    &curvePt[0][0], 4, GLU_MAP1_TRIM_2);
            gluPwlCurve (theNurb, 3, &pwlPt[0][0], 2,
                    GLU_MAP1_TRIM_2);
        gluEndTrim (theNurb);
        gluEndSurface(theNurb);

    glPopMatrix();
    glFlush();
}
```

In Listing 11-6, **gluBeginTrim()** and **gluEndTrim()** bracket each trimming curve. The first trim, with vertices defined by the array *edgePt[][]*, goes counterclockwise around the entire unit square of parametric space. This ensures that everything is drawn, provided it isn't removed by a clockwise trimming curve inside of it. The second trim is a combination of a NURBS trimming curve and a piecewise linear trimming curve. The NURBS curve ends at the points (0.9, 0.5) and (0.1, 0.5), where it is met by the piecewise linear curve, forming a closed clockwise curve.

Chapter 12

Selection and Feedback

Chapter Objectives

After reading this chapter, you'll be able to do the following:

- Create applications that allow the user to select a region of the screen or pick an object drawn on the screen

- Use OpenGL's feedback mode to obtain the results of rendering calculations

Some graphics applications simply draw static images of two- and three-dimensional objects. Other applications allow the user to identify objects on the screen and then to move, modify, delete, or otherwise manipulate those objects. OpenGL is designed to support exactly such interactive applications. Since objects drawn on the screen typically undergo multiple rotations, translations, and perspective transformations, it can be difficult for you to determine which object a user is selecting in a three-dimensional scene. To help you, OpenGL provides a selection mechanism that automatically tells you which objects are drawn inside a specified region of the window. You can use this mechanism together with a special utility routine to determine which object within the region the user is specifying, or *picking*, with the cursor.

Selection is actually a mode of operation for OpenGL; feedback is another such mode. In feedback mode, you use your graphics hardware and OpenGL to perform the usual rendering calculations. Instead of using the calculated results to draw an image on the screen, however, OpenGL returns (or feeds back) the drawing information to you. If you want to draw three-dimensional objects on a plotter rather than the screen, for example, you would draw the items in feedback mode, collect the drawing instructions, and then convert them to commands the plotter can understand.

In both selection and feedback modes, drawing information is returned to the application rather than being sent to the framebuffer, as it is in rendering mode. Thus, the screen remains frozen—no drawing occurs—while OpenGL is in selection or feedback mode. This chapter explains each of these modes in its own section:

- **"Selection"** discusses how to use selection mode and related routines to allow a user of your application to pick an object drawn on the screen.

- **"Feedback"** describes how to obtain information about what would be drawn on the screen and how that information is formatted.

Selection

Typically, when you're planning to use OpenGL's selection mechanism, you first draw your scene into the framebuffer and then you enter selection mode and redraw the scene. Once you're in selection mode, however, the contents of the framebuffer don't change until you exit selection mode. When you exit, OpenGL returns a list of the primitives that would have intersected the viewing volume (remember that the viewing volume is defined by the current modelview and projection matrices and any clipping planes you've specified, as explained in "Additional Clipping Planes" on page 106). Each primitive that intersects the viewing volume causes a selection *hit*. The list of primitives is actually returned as an array of integer-valued *names* and related data—the *hit records*—that correspond to the current contents of the *name stack*. You construct the name stack by loading names onto it as you issue primitive drawing commands while in selection mode. Thus, when the list of names is returned, you can use it to determine which primitives might have been selected on the screen by the user.

In addition to this selection mechanism, OpenGL provides a utility routine designed to simplify selection in some cases by restricting drawing to a small region of the viewport. Typically, you use this routine to determine which objects are drawn near the cursor, so that you can identify which object the user is picking. You can also delimit a selection region by specifying additional clipping planes; see "Additional Clipping Planes" on page 106 for more information about how to do this. Since picking is a special case of selection, selection is described first in this chapter, and then picking.

The Basic Steps

To use the selection mechanism, you need to perform the following steps.

1. Specify the array to be used for the returned hit records with **glSelectBuffer()**.

2. Enter selection mode by specifying GL_SELECT with **glRenderMode()**.

3. Initialize the name stack using **glInitNames()** and **glPushName()**.

4. Define the viewing volume you want to use for selection. Usually, this is different from the viewing volume you used to draw the scene originally, so you probably want to save and then restore the current transformation state with **glPushMatrix()** and **glPopMatrix()**.

5. Alternately issue primitive drawing commands and commands to manipulate the name stack so that each primitive of interest has an appropriate name assigned.

6. Exit selection mode and process the returned selection data (the hit records).

The following paragraphs describe **glSelectBuffer()** and **glRenderMode()**. In the next section, the commands to manipulate the name stack are described.

---

void **glSelectBuffer**(GLsizei *size*, GLuint **buffer*);

Specifies the array to be used for the returned selection data. The *buffer* argument is a pointer to an array of unsigned integers into which the data is put, and *size* indicates the maximum number of values that can be stored in the array. You need to call **glSelectBuffer()** before entering selection mode.

GLint **glRenderMode**(GLenum *mode*);

Controls whether the application is in rendering, selection, or feedback mode. The *mode* argument can be one of GL_RENDER (the default), GL_SELECT, or GL_FEEDBACK. The application remains in a given mode until **glRenderMode()** is called again with a different argument. Before entering selection mode, **glSelectBuffer()** must be called to specify the selection array. Similarly, before entering feedback mode, **glFeedbackBuffer()** must be called to specify the feedback array. The return value for **glRenderMode()** has meaning if the current render mode (that is, not the *mode* parameter) is either GL_SELECT or GL_FEEDBACK: The return value is the number of selection hits or the number of values placed in the feedback array when either mode is exited; a negative value means that the selection or feedback array has overflowed. You can use GL_RENDER_MODE with **glGetIntegerv()** to obtain the current mode.

Creating the Name Stack

As mentioned in the previous section, the name stack forms the basis for the selection information that's returned to you. To create the name stack, first you initialize it with **glInitNames()**, which simply clears the stack, and then you add integer names to it as you issue corresponding drawing commands. As you might expect, the commands to manipulate the stack allow you to push a name onto it (**glPushName()**), pop a name off of it (**glPopName()**), and replace the name on the top of the stack with a different one (**glLoadName()**). Listing 12-1 shows what your name-stack manipulation code might look like with these commands.

Listing 12-1 Creating a Name Stack

```
glInitNames();
glPushName(-1);

glPushMatrix();    /* save the current transformation state */

    /* create your desired viewing volume here */

    glLoadName(1);
    drawSomeObject();
    glLoadName(2);
    drawAnotherObject();
    glLoadName(3);
    drawYetAnotherObject();
    drawJustOneMoreObject();

glPopMatrix ();    /* restore the previous transformation state*/
```

In this example, the first two objects to be drawn have their own names, and the third and fourth objects share a single name. With this setup, if either or both of the third and fourth objects causes a selection hit, only one hit record is returned to you. You can have multiple objects share the same name if you don't need to differentiate between them when processing the hit records.

---

void **glInitNames**(void);

Clears the name stack so that it's empty.

---

void **glPushName**(GLuint *name*);

Pushes *name* onto the name stack. Pushing a name beyond the capacity of the stack generates the error GL_STACK_OVERFLOW. The name stack's depth can vary among different OpenGL implementations, but it must be able to contain at least sixty-four names. You can use the parameter GL_NAME_STACK_DEPTH with **glGetIntegerv()** to obtain the depth of the name stack.

---

void **glPopName**(void);

Pops one name off the top of the name stack. Popping an empty stack generates the error GL_STACK_UNDERFLOW.

---

void **glLoadName**(GLuint *name*);

Replaces the value on the top of the name stack with *name*. If the stack is empty, which it is right after **glInitNames()** is called, **glLoadName()** generates the error GL_INVALID_OPERATION. To avoid this, if the stack is initially empty, call **glPushName()** at least once to put something on the name stack before calling **glLoadName()**.

Calls to **glPushName()**, **glPopName()**, and **glLoadName()** are ignored if you're not in selection mode. You might find that it simplifies your code to use these calls throughout your drawing code, and then use the same drawing code for both selection and normal rendering modes.

The Hit Record

In selection mode, a primitive that intersects the viewing volume causes a selection hit. Whenever a name-stack manipulation command is executed or **glRenderMode()** is called, OpenGL writes a hit record into the selection array if there's been a hit since the last time the stack was manipulated or **glRenderMode()** was called. With this process, objects that share the same name—for example, an object that's composed of more than one primitive—don't generate multiple hit records. Also, hit records aren't guaranteed to be written into the array until **glRenderMode()** is called.

Note: In addition to primitives, valid coordinates produced by **glRasterPos()** can cause a selection hit. In the case of polygons, no hit occurs if the polygon would have been culled.

Each hit record consists of four items, in order:

- The number of names on the name stack when the hit occurred.

- Both the minimum and maximum window-coordinate z values of all vertices of the primitives that intersected the viewing volume since the last recorded hit. These two values, which lie in the range [0,1], are each multiplied by $2^{32}-1$ and rounded to the nearest unsigned integer.

- The contents of the name stack at the time of the hit, with the bottommost element first.

When you enter selection mode, OpenGL initializes a pointer to the beginning of the selection array. Each time a hit record is written into the array, the pointer is updated accordingly. If writing a hit record would cause the number of values in the array to exceed the *size* argument specified with **glSelectBuffer()**, OpenGL writes as much of the record as fits in the array and sets an overflow flag. When you exit selection mode with **glRenderMode()**, this command returns the number of hit records that were written (including a partial record if there was one), clears the name stack, resets the overflow flag, and resets the stack pointer. If the overflow flag had been set, the return value is –1.

A Selection Example

In Listing 12-2, four triangles (green, red, and two yellow ones) are drawn in selection mode, and the corresponding hit records are processed. The first triangle generates a hit, the second one doesn't, and the third and fourth ones together generate a single hit. Routines are defined to draw a triangle (**drawTriangle()**) and to draw a wireframe box representing the viewing volume (**drawViewVolume()**). The **processHits()** routine prints out the selection array. Finally, **selectObjects()** draws the triangles in selection mode to generate the hit records.

Listing 12-2 A Selection Example: select.c

```
#include <GL/gl.h>
#include <GL/glu.h>
#include "aux.h"

void drawTriangle (GLfloat x1, GLfloat y1, GLfloat x2,
    GLfloat y2, GLfloat x3, GLfloat y3, GLfloat z)
{
    glBegin (GL_TRIANGLES);
    glVertex3f (x1, y1, z);
    glVertex3f (x2, y2, z);
    glVertex3f (x3, y3, z);
    glEnd ();
}
```

```
void drawViewVolume (GLfloat x1, GLfloat x2, GLfloat y1,
    GLfloat y2, GLfloat z1, GLfloat z2)
{
    glColor3f (1.0, 1.0, 1.0);
    glBegin (GL_LINE_LOOP);
        glVertex3f (x1, y1, -z1);
        glVertex3f (x2, y1, -z1);
        glVertex3f (x2, y2, -z1);
        glVertex3f (x1, y2, -z1);
    glEnd ();

    glBegin (GL_LINE_LOOP);
        glVertex3f (x1, y1, -z2);
        glVertex3f (x2, y1, -z2);
        glVertex3f (x2, y2, -z2);
        glVertex3f (x1, y2, -z2);
    glEnd ();

    glBegin (GL_LINES);/*  4 lines*/
        glVertex3f (x1, y1, -z1);
        glVertex3f (x1, y1, -z2);
        glVertex3f (x1, y2, -z1);
        glVertex3f (x1, y2, -z2);
        glVertex3f (x2, y1, -z1);
        glVertex3f (x2, y1, -z2);
        glVertex3f (x2, y2, -z1);
        glVertex3f (x2, y2, -z2);
    glEnd ();
}

void drawScene (void)
{
    glMatrixMode (GL_PROJECTION);
    glLoadIdentity ();
    gluPerspective (40.0, 4.0/3.0, 0.01, 100.0);

    glMatrixMode (GL_MODELVIEW);
    glLoadIdentity ();
    gluLookAt (7.5, 7.5, 12.5, 2.5, 2.5, -5.0, 0.0, 1.0, 0.0);
    glColor3f (0.0, 1.0, 0.0);      /*  green triangle */
    drawTriangle (2.0, 2.0, 3.0, 2.0, 2.5, 3.0, -5.0);
    glColor3f (1.0, 0.0, 0.0);      /*  red triangle */
    drawTriangle (2.0, 7.0, 3.0, 7.0, 2.5, 8.0, -5.0);
    glColor3f (1.0, 1.0, 0.0);      /*  yellow triangles */
    drawTriangle (2.0, 2.0, 3.0, 2.0, 2.5, 3.0, 0.0);
    drawTriangle (2.0, 2.0, 3.0, 2.0, 2.5, 3.0, -10.0);
```

```
    drawViewVolume (0.0, 5.0, 0.0, 5.0, 0.0, 10.0);
}

void processHits (GLint hits, GLuint buffer[])
{
    unsigned int i, j;
    GLuint names, *ptr;

    printf ("hits = %d\n", hits);
    ptr = (GLuint *) buffer;
    for (i = 0; i < hits; i++) {              /* for each hit */
        names = *ptr;
        printf(" number of names for hit = %d\n", names); ptr++;
        printf ("  z1 is %u;", *ptr); ptr++;
        printf (" z2 is %u\n", *ptr); ptr++;
        printf ("   the name is ");
        for (j = 0; j < names; j++) {         /* for each name */
            printf ("%d ", *ptr); ptr++;
        }
        printf ("\n");
    }
}

#define BUFSIZE 512

void selectObjects(void)
{
    GLuint selectBuf[BUFSIZE];
    GLint hits, viewport[4];

    glSelectBuffer (BUFSIZE, selectBuf);
    (void) glRenderMode (GL_SELECT);

    glInitNames();
    glPushName(-1);

    glPushMatrix ();
        glMatrixMode (GL_PROJECTION);
        glLoadIdentity ();
        glOrtho (0.0, 5.0, 0.0, 5.0, 0.0, 10.0);
        glMatrixMode (GL_MODELVIEW);
        glLoadIdentity ();
        glLoadName(1);
        drawTriangle (2.0, 2.0, 3.0, 2.0, 2.5, 3.0, -5.0);
        glLoadName(2);
        drawTriangle (2.0, 7.0, 3.0, 7.0, 2.5, 8.0, -5.0);
```

```
            glLoadName(3);
            drawTriangle (2.0, 2.0, 3.0, 2.0, 2.5, 3.0, 0.0);
            drawTriangle (2.0, 2.0, 3.0, 2.0, 2.5, 3.0, -10.0);
        glPopMatrix ();
        glFlush ();

        hits = glRenderMode (GL_RENDER);
        processHits (hits, selectBuf);
}

void myinit (void)
{
    glDepthFunc(GL_LEQUAL);
    glEnable(GL_DEPTH_TEST);
    glShadeModel(GL_FLAT);
}

void display(void)
{
    glClearColor (0.0, 0.0, 0.0, 0.0);
    glClear(GL_COLOR_BUFFER_BIT | GL_DEPTH_BUFFER_BIT);
    drawScene ();
    selectObjects ();
    glFlush();
}

int main(int argc, char** argv)
{
    auxInitDisplayMode (AUX_SINGLE | AUX_RGBA | AUX_DEPTH);
    auxInitPosition (0, 0, 200, 200);
    auxInitWindow (argv[0]);
    myinit ();
    auxMainLoop(display);
}
```

Picking

As an extension of the process described in the previous section, you can use selection mode to determine if objects are picked. To do this, you use a special picking matrix in conjunction with the projection matrix to restrict drawing to a small region of the viewport, typically near the cursor. Then you allow some form of input, such as clicking a mouse button, to initiate selection mode. With selection mode established and with the special picking matrix used, objects that are drawn near the cursor cause selection hits. Thus, during picking you're typically determining which objects are drawn near the cursor.

Picking is set up almost exactly like regular selection mode is, with the following major differences:

- Picking is usually triggered by an input device. In the following code examples, pressing the left mouse button invokes a function that performs picking.

- You use the utility routine **gluPickMatrix()** to multiply a special projection matrix onto the current matrix. This routine should be called prior to multiplying a projection matrix onto the stack.

Another, completely different way to perform picking is described in "Object Selection Using the Back Buffer" on page 389. This technique uses color values to identify different components of an object.

---

void **gluPickMatrix**(GLdouble *x*, GLdouble *y*, GLdouble *width*,
  GLdouble *height*, GLint *viewport[4]*);

Creates a projection matrix that restricts drawing to a small region of the viewport and multiplies that matrix onto the current matrix stack. The center of the picking region is (x, y) in window coordinates, typically the cursor location. *width* and *height* define the size of the picking region in screen coordinates. (You can think of the width and height as the sensitivity of the picking device.) *viewport[]* indicates the current viewport boundaries, which can be obtained by calling

```
glGetIntegerv(GL_VIEWPORT, GLint *viewport);
```

The net result of the matrix created by **gluPickMatrix()** is to transform the clipping region into the unit cube $-1 \le (x, y, z) \le 1$ (or $-w \le (wx, wy, wz) \le w$). The picking matrix effectively performs an orthogonal transformation that maps a subregion of this unit cube to the unit cube. Since the transformation is arbitrary, you can make picking work for different sorts of regions—for example, for rotated rectangular portions of the window. In certain situations, you might find it easier to specify additional clipping planes to define the picking region.

⊓ Advanced

Listing 12-3 illustrates simple picking. It also demonstrates how to use multiple names to identify different components of a primitive, in this case the row and column of a selected object. A 3×3 grid of squares is drawn, with each square a different color. The board[3][3] array maintains the current amount of blue for each square. When the left mouse button is pressed, the **pickSquares()** routine is called to identify which squares were picked by the mouse. Two names identify each square in the grid—one identifies the row, and the other the column. Also, when the left mouse button is pressed, the color of all squares under the cursor position changes.

Listing 12-3 A Picking Example: picksquare.c

```
#include <GL/gl.h>
#include <GL/glu.h>
#include "aux.h"

int board[3][3];      /*  amount of color for each square */

/* Clear color value for every square on the board */
void myinit(void)
{
    int i, j;
    for (i = 0; i < 3; i++)
        for (j = 0; j < 3; j ++)
            board[i][j] = 0;
    glClearColor (0.0, 0.0, 0.0, 0.0);
}

void drawSquares(GLenum mode)
{
    GLuint i, j;
    for (i = 0; i < 3; i++) {
        if (mode == GL_SELECT)
            glLoadName (i);
        for (j = 0; j < 3; j ++) {
            if (mode == GL_SELECT)
                glPushName (j);
            glColor3f ((GLfloat) i/3.0, (GLfloat) j/3.0,
                (GLfloat) board[i][j]/3.0);
            glRecti (i, j, i+1, j+1);
            if (mode == GL_SELECT)
                glPopName ();
        }
    }
}

void processHits (GLint hits, GLuint buffer[])
{
    unsigned int i, j;
    GLuint ii, jj, names, *ptr;
```

```
    printf ("hits = %d\n", hits);
    ptr = (GLuint *) buffer;
    for (i = 0; i < hits; i++) {      /* for each hit */
        names = *ptr;
        printf (" number of names for this hit = %d\n", names);
            ptr++;
        printf ("   z1 is %u;", *ptr); ptr++;
        printf ("  z2 is %u\n", *ptr); ptr++;
        printf ("   names are ");
        for (j = 0; j < names; j++) {/*  for each name */
            printf ("%d ", *ptr);
            if (j == 0)/*  set row and column  */
                ii = *ptr;
            else if (j == 1)
                jj = *ptr;
            ptr++;
        }
    printf ("\n");
    board[ii][jj] = (board[ii][jj] + 1) % 3;
    }
}

#define BUFSIZE 512

void pickSquares(AUX_EVENTREC *event)
{
    GLuint selectBuf[BUFSIZE];
    GLint hits;
    GLint viewport[4];
    int x, y;

    x = event->data[AUX_MOUSEX];
    y = event->data[AUX_MOUSEY];
    glGetIntegerv (GL_VIEWPORT, viewport);

    glSelectBuffer (BUFSIZE, selectBuf);
    (void) glRenderMode (GL_SELECT);

    glInitNames ();
    glPushName(-1);

    glMatrixMode (GL_PROJECTION);
    glPushMatrix ();
        glLoadIdentity ();
/* create 5x5 pixel picking region near cursor location */
        gluPickMatrix((GLdouble) x,
            (GLdouble) (viewport[3] - y), 5.0, 5.0, viewport);
```

```
        gluOrtho2D (0.0, 3.0, 0.0, 3.0);
        drawSquares (GL_SELECT);
    glPopMatrix ();
    glFlush ();

    hits = glRenderMode (GL_RENDER);
    processHits (hits, selectBuf);
}

void display(void)
{
    glClear(GL_COLOR_BUFFER_BIT);
    drawSquares (GL_RENDER);
    glFlush();
}

void myReshape(GLsizei w, GLsizei h)
{
    glViewport(0, 0, w, h);
    glMatrixMode(GL_PROJECTION);
    glLoadIdentity();
    gluOrtho2D (0.0, 3.0, 0.0, 3.0);
    glMatrixMode(GL_MODELVIEW);
    glLoadIdentity();
}


int main(int argc, char** argv)
{
    auxInitDisplayMode (AUX_SINGLE | AUX_RGBA);
    auxInitPosition (0, 0, 100, 100);
    auxInitWindow (argv[0]);
    myinit ();
    auxMouseFunc (AUX_LEFTBUTTON, AUX_MOUSEDOWN, pickSquares);
    auxReshapeFunc (myReshape);
    auxMainLoop(display);
}
```

Picking with Multiple Names and a Hierarchical Model

Multiple names can also be used to choose parts of a hierarchical object in a scene. For example, if you were rendering an assembly line of automobiles, you might want the user to move the mouse to pick the third bolt on the left front tire of the third car in line. A different name can be used to identify each level of hierarchy: which car, which tire, and finally which bolt. As another example, one name can be used to describe a single molecule among other molecules, and additional names can differentiate individual atoms within that molecule.

Listing 12-4 is a modification of Listing 3-4 on page 104 that draws an automobile with four identical wheels, each of which has five identical bolts. Code has been added to manipulate the name stack with the object hierarchy.

Listing 12-4 Creating Multiple Names

```
draw_wheel_and_bolts()
{
    long i;

    draw_wheel_body();
    for (i = 0; i < 5; i++) {
        glPushMatrix();
            glRotate(72.0*i, 0.0, 0.0, 1.0);
            glTranslatef(3.0, 0.0, 0.0);
            glPushName(i);
                draw_bolt_body();
            glPopName();
        glPopMatrix();
    }
 }

draw_body_and_wheel_and_bolts()
{
    draw_car_body();
    glPushMatrix();
        glTranslate(40, 0, 20);   /* first wheel position*/
        glPushName(1);            /* name of wheel number 1 */
            draw_wheel_and_bolts();
        glPopName();
    glPopMatrix();
    glPushMatrix();
        glTranslate(40, 0, -20); /* second wheel position */
        glPushName(2);            /* name of wheel number 2 */
            draw_wheel_and_bolts();
        glPopName();
    glPopMatrix();

    /* draw last two wheels similarly */
 }
```

Listing 12-5 uses the routines in Listing 12-4 to draw three different cars, numbered 1, 2, and 3.

Listing 12-5 Using Multiple Names

```
draw_three_cars()
{
    glInitNames();
    glPushMatrix();
        translate_to_first_car_position();
        glPushName(1);
            draw_body_and_wheel_and_bolts();
        glPopName();
    glPopMatrix();

    glPushMatrix();
        translate_to_second_car_position();
        glPushName(2);
            draw_body_and_wheel_and_bolts();
        glPopName();
    glPopMatrix();

    glPushMatrix();
        translate_to_third_car_position();
        glPushName(3);
            draw_body_and_wheel_and_bolts();
        glPopName();
    glPopMatrix();
}
```

Assuming that picking is performed, the following are some possible name-stack return values and their interpretations. In these examples, at most one hit record is returned; also, $d1$ and $d2$ are depth values.

empty	The pick was outside all cars
2 $d1$ $d2$ 2 1	Car 2, wheel 1
1 $d1$ $d2$ 3	Car 3 body
3 $d1$ $d2$ 1 1 0	Bolt 0 on wheel 1 on car 1

The last interpretation assumes that the bolt and wheel don't occupy the same picking region. A user might well pick both the wheel and the bolt, yielding two hits. If you receive multiple hits, you have to decide which hit to process, perhaps by using the depth values to determine which picked object is closest to the viewpoint. The use of depth values is explored further in the next section.

Picking and Depth Values

Listing 12-6 demonstrates how to use depth values when picking to determine which object is picked. This program draws three overlapping rectangles in normal rendering mode. When the left mouse button is pressed, the **pickRects()** routine is called. This routine returns the cursor position, enters selection mode, initializes the name stack, and multiplies the picking matrix onto the stack before the orthographic projection matrix. A selection hit occurs for each rectangle the cursor is over when the left mouse button is clicked. Finally, the contents of the selection buffer is examined to identify which named objects were within the picking region near the cursor.

The rectangles in this program are drawn at different depth, or z, values. Since only one name is used to identify all three rectangles, only one hit can be recorded. However, if more than one rectangle is picked, that single hit has different minimum and maximum z values.

Listing 12-6 Picking with Depth Values: pickdepth.c

```
#include <GL/gl.h>
#include <GL/glu.h>
#include "aux.h"

void myinit(void)
{
    glClearColor (0.0, 0.0, 0.0, 0.0);
    glDepthFunc(GL_LEQUAL);
    glEnable(GL_DEPTH_TEST);
    glShadeModel(GL_FLAT);
    glDepthRange (0.0, 1.0);    /* The default z mapping */
}

void drawRects(GLenum mode)
{
    if (mode == GL_SELECT)
        glLoadName (1);
    glBegin (GL_QUADS);
        glColor3f (1.0, 1.0, 0.0);
        glVertex3i (2, 0, 0);
        glVertex3i (2, 6, 0);
        glVertex3i (6, 6, 0);
        glVertex3i (6, 0, 0);
        glColor3f (0.0, 1.0, 1.0);
        glVertex3i (3, 2, -1);
        glVertex3i (3, 8, -1);
        glVertex3i (8, 8, -1);
```

```
            glVertex3i (8, 2, -1);
            glColor3f (1.0, 0.0, 1.0);
            glVertex3i (0, 2, -2);
            glVertex3i (0, 7, -2);
            glVertex3i (5, 7, -2);
            glVertex3i (5, 2, -2);
        glEnd ();
}

void processHits (GLint hits, GLuint buffer[])
{
    unsigned int i, j;
    GLuint names, *ptr;

    printf ("hits = %d\n", hits);
    ptr = (GLuint *) buffer;
    for (i = 0; i < hits; i++) {           /* for each hit */
        names = *ptr;
        printf (" number of names for hit = %d\n", names);
            ptr++;
        printf ("  z1 is %u;", *ptr); ptr++;
        printf ("  z2 is %u\n", *ptr); ptr++;
        printf ("   the name is ");
        for (j = 0; j < names; j++) {    /* for each name */
            printf ("%d ", *ptr); ptr++;
        }
        printf ("\n");
    }
}

#define BUFSIZE 512

void pickRects(AUX_EVENTREC *event)
{
    GLuint selectBuf[BUFSIZE];
    GLint hits;
    GLint viewport[4];
    int x, y;

    x = event->data[AUX_MOUSEX];
    y = event->data[AUX_MOUSEY];
    glGetIntegerv (GL_VIEWPORT, viewport);

    glSelectBuffer (BUFSIZE, selectBuf);
    (void) glRenderMode (GL_SELECT);
```

```
    glInitNames ();
    glPushName (-1);

    glMatrixMode (GL_PROJECTION);
    glPushMatrix ();
        glLoadIdentity ();
/* create 5x5 pixel picking region near cursor location */
        gluPickMatrix ((GLdouble) x,
            (GLdouble) (viewport[3] - y), 5.0, 5.0, viewport);
        glOrtho (0.0, 8.0, 0.0, 8.0, 0.0, 2.0);
        drawRects (GL_SELECT);
    glPopMatrix ();
    glFlush ();

    hits = glRenderMode (GL_RENDER);
    processHits (hits, selectBuf);
}

void display(void)
{
    glClear(GL_COLOR_BUFFER_BIT | GL_DEPTH_BUFFER_BIT);
    drawRects (GL_RENDER);
    glFlush();
}

void myReshape(GLsizei w, GLsizei h)
{
    glViewport(0, 0, w, h);
    glMatrixMode(GL_PROJECTION);
    glLoadIdentity(),
    glOrtho (0.0, 8.0, 0.0, 8.0, 0.0, 2.0);
    glMatrixMode(GL_MODELVIEW);
    glLoadIdentity();
}


int main(int argc, char** argv)
{
    auxInitDisplayMode (AUX_SINGLE | AUX_RGBA | AUX_DEPTH);
    auxInitPosition (0, 0, 100, 100);
    auxInitWindow (argv[0]);
    myinit ();
    auxMouseFunc (AUX_LEFTBUTTON, AUX_MOUSEDOWN, pickRects);
    auxReshapeFunc (myReshape);
    auxMainLoop(display);
}
```

Try This

- Modify Listing 12-6 to add additional calls to **glPushName()** so that multiple names are on the stack when the selection hit occurs. What will the contents of the selection buffer be?

- By default, **glDepthRange()** sets the mapping of the z values to [0.0,1.0]. Try modifying the **glDepthRange()** values and see how it affects the z values that are returned in the selection array.

Hints for Writing a Program That Uses Selection

Most programs that allow a user to interactively edit some geometry provide a mechanism for the user to pick items or groups of items for editing. For two-dimensional drawing programs (for example, text editors, page-layout programs, circuit-design programs), it might be easier to do your own picking calculations instead of using the OpenGL picking mechanism. Often, it's easy to find bounding boxes for two-dimensional objects and to organize them in some hierarchical data structure to speed up searches. For example, OpenGL-style picking in a VLSI layout program that has millions of rectangles can be relatively slow. However, using simple bounding-box information when rectangles are typically aligned with the screen could make picking in such a program extremely fast. The code is probably simpler to write, too.

As another example, since only geometric objects cause hits, you might want to create your own method for picking text. Setting the current raster position is a geometric operation, but it effectively creates only a single pickable point at the current raster position, which is typically at the lower left-hand corner of the text. If your editor needs to manipulate individual characters within a text string, some other picking mechanism must be used. You could draw little rectangles around each character during picking mode, but it's almost certainly easier to handle text as a special case.

If you decide to use OpenGL picking, organize your program and its data structures so that it's easy to draw appropriate lists of objects in either selection or normal drawing mode. This way, when the user picks something, you can use the same data structures for the pick operation that you use to display the items on the screen. Also, consider whether you want to allow the user to select multiple objects. One way to do this is to store a bit for each item indicating whether it's selected, but with this method, you have to traverse your entire list of items to find the selected items. You might find it useful to maintain a list of pointers to selected items to speed up this search. It's probably a good idea to keep the selection bit for each item as well, since when you're drawing the entire picture, you might want to draw selected items differently (for example, in a different color or with a selection box around them). Finally, consider the selection user interface. You might want to allow the user to do the following:

- Select an item

- Sweep-select a group of items (see the next paragraphs for a description of this behavior)

- Add an item to the selection

- Add a sweep selection to the current selections

- Delete an item from a selection

- Choose a single item from a group of overlapping items

A typical solution for a two-dimensional drawing program might work as follows.

1. All selection is done by pointing with the mouse cursor and using the left mouse button. In what follows, *cursor* means the cursor tied to the mouse, and *button* means the left mouse button.

2. Clicking on an item selects it and deselects all other currently selected items. If the cursor is on top of multiple items, the smallest is selected. (In three dimensions, many other strategies work to disambiguate a selection.)

3. Clicking down where there is no item, holding the button down while dragging the cursor, and then releasing the button selects all the items in a screen-aligned rectangle whose corners are determined by the cursor positions when the button went down and where it came up. This is called a *sweep selection*. All items not in the swept-out region are deselected. (You must decide whether an item is selected only if it's completely within the sweep region, or if any part of it falls within the region. The completely within strategy usually works best.)

4. If the Shift key is held down and the user clicks on an item that isn't currently selected, that item is added to the selected list. If the clicked-upon item is selected, it's deleted from the selection list.

5. If a sweep selection is performed with the Shift key pressed, the items swept out are added to the current selection.

6. In an extremely cluttered region, it's often hard to do a sweep selection. When the button goes down, the cursor might lie on top of some item, and normally, that item would be selected. You can make any operation a sweep selection, but a typical user interface interprets a button-down on an item plus a mouse motion as a select-plus-drag operation. To solve this problem, you can have an enforced sweep selection by holding down, say, the Alt key. With this, the following set of operations constitutes a sweep selection: Alt-button down, sweep, button up. Items under the cursor when the button goes down are ignored.

7. If the Shift key is held during this sweep selection, the items enclosed in the sweep region are added to the current selection.

8. Finally, if the user clicks on multiple items, select just one of them. If the cursor isn't moved (or maybe not moved more than a pixel), and the user clicks again in the same place, deselect the item originally selected, and select a different item under the cursor. Use repeated clicks at the same point to cycle through all the possibilities.

Different rules can apply in particular situations. In a text editor, you probably don't have to worry about characters on top of each other, and selections of multiple characters are always contiguous characters in the document. Thus, you need to mark only the first and last selected characters to identify the complete selection. With text, often the best way to handle selection is to identify the positions between characters rather than the characters themselves. This allows you to have an empty selection when the beginning and end of the selection are between the same pair of characters, and to put the cursor before the first character in the document or after the final one with no special-case code.

In three-dimensional editors, you might provide ways to rotate and zoom between selections, so sophisticated schemes for cycling through the possible selections might be unnecessary. On the other hand, selection in three dimensions is difficult because the cursor's position on the screen usually gives no indication of its depth.

Feedback

Feedback is similar to selection in that once you're in either mode, no pixels are produced and the screen is frozen. Instead of drawing occurring, information about primitives that would have been rendered is sent back to the application. The key difference between selection and feedback modes is what information is sent back. In selection mode, assigned names are returned to an array of integer values. In feedback mode, information about transformed primitives is sent back to an array of floating-point values. The values sent back to the feedback array consist of tokens that specify what type of primitive (point, line, polygon, image, or bitmap) has been processed and transformed, followed by vertex, color, or other data for that primitive. The values returned are fully transformed by lighting and viewing operations. Feedback mode is initiated by calling **glRenderMode()** with GL_FEEDBACK as the argument.

Here's how you enter and exit feedback mode:

1. Call **glFeedbackBuffer()** to specify the array to hold the feedback information. The arguments to this command describe what type of data and how much of it gets written into the array.

2. Call **glRenderMode()** with GL_FEEDBACK as the argument to enter feedback mode. (You can ignore the value returned by **glRenderMode()**.) After this point, until you exit feedback mode, primitives aren't rasterized to produce pixels, and the contents of the framebuffer don't change.

3. Draw your primitives. As you issue drawing commands, you can make several calls to **glPassThrough()** to insert markers into the returned feedback data to help you parse it more easily.

4. Exit feedback mode by calling **glRenderMode()**, with GL_RENDER as the argument if you want to return to normal drawing mode. The integer value returned by **glRenderMode()** is the number of values stored in the feedback array.

5. Parse the data in the feedback array.

void **glFeedbackBuffer**(GLsizei *size*, GLenum *type*, GLfloat *buffer);

Establishes a buffer for the feedback data: *buffer* is a pointer to an array where the data is stored. The *size* argument indicates the maximum number of values that can be stored in the array. The *type* argument describes the information fed back for each vertex in the feedback array; its possible values and their meaning are shown in Table 12-1. **glFeedbackBuffer()** must be called before feedback mode is entered. In the table, k is 1 in color-index mode and 4 in RGBA mode.

Type Argument	Coordinates	Color	Texture	Total Values
GL_2D	x, y	-	-	2
GL_3D	x, y, z	-	-	3
GL_3D_COLOR	x, y, z	k	-	$3 + k$
GL_3D_COLOR_TEXTURE	x, y, z	k	4	$7 + k$
GL_4D_COLOR_TEXTURE	x, y, z, w	k	4	$8 + k$

Table 12-1 Values for the Type Argument to glFeedbackBuffer()

The Feedback Array

In feedback mode, each primitive that would be rasterized (or each call to **glDrawPixels()** or **glCopyPixels()**, if the raster position is valid) generates a block of values that's copied into the feedback array. The number of values is determined by the *type* argument to **glFeedbackBuffer()**, as listed in Table 12-1. Use the appropriate value for the type of primitives you're drawing: GL_2D or GL_3D for unlit two- or three-dimensional primitives, GL_3D_COLOR for lit, three-dimensional primitives, and GL_3D_COLOR_TEXTURE or GL_4D_COLOR_TEXTURE for lit, textured, three- or four-dimensional primitives.

Each block of feedback values begins with a code indicating the primitive type, followed by values that describe the primitive's vertices and associated data. Entries are also written for pixel rectangles. In addition, pass-through markers that you've explicitly created can be returned in the array; the next section explains these markers in more detail. Table 12-2 shows the syntax for the feedback array; remember that the data associated with each returned vertex is as described in Table 12-1. Note that a polygon can have *n* vertices returned. Also, the *x, y, z* coordinates returned by feedback are window coordinates; if *w* is returned, it's in clip coordinates. For bitmaps and pixel rectangles, the coordinates returned are those of the current raster position. In the table, note that GL_LINE_RESET_TOKEN is returned only when the line stipple is reset for that line segment.

Primitive Type	Code	Associated Data
Point	GL_POINT_TOKEN	vertex
Line	GL_LINE_TOKEN or GL_LINE_RESET_TOKEN	vertex vertex
Polygon	GL_POLYGON_TOKEN	*n* vertex vertex ... vertex
Bitmap	GL_BITMAP_TOKEN	vertex
Pixel Rectangle	GL_DRAW_PIXEL_TOKEN or GL_COPY_PIXEL_TOKEN	vertex
Pass-through	GL_PASS_THROUGH_TOKEN	a floating-point number

Table 12-2 Feedback Array Syntax

Using Markers in Feedback Mode

Feedback occurs after transformations, lighting, polygon culling, and interpretation of polygons by **glPolygonMode()**. It might also occur after polygons with more than three edges are broken up into triangles (if your particular OpenGL implementation renders polygons by performing this decomposition). Thus, it might be hard for you to recognize the primitives you drew in the feedback data you receive. To help yourself parse the feedback data, call **glPassThrough()** as needed in your sequence of drawing commands to insert a marker. You might use the markers to separate the feedback values returned from different primitives, for example. This command causes GL_PASS_THROUGH_TOKEN to be written into the feedback array, followed by the floating-point value you pass in as an argument.

---

void **glPassThrough**(GLfloat *token*);

Inserts a marker into the stream of values written into the feedback array, if called in feedback mode. The marker consists of the code GL_PASS_THROUGH_TOKEN followed by a single floating-point value, *token*. This command has no effect when called outside of feedback mode. Calling **glPassThrough**() between **glBegin**() and **glEnd**() generates a GL_INVALID_OPERATION error.

A Feedback Example

Listing 12-7 demonstrates the use of feedback mode. This program draws a lit, three-dimensional scene in normal rendering mode. Then, feedback mode is entered, and the scene is redrawn. Since the program draws lit, untextured, three-dimensional objects, the type of feedback data is GL_3D_COLOR. Since RGBA mode is used, each unclipped vertex generates seven values for the feedback buffer: *x, y, z, r, g, b,* and *a.*

In feedback mode, the program draws two lines as part of a line strip and then inserts a pass-through marker. Next, a point is drawn at (–100.0, –100.0, –100.0), which falls outside the orthographic viewing volume and thus doesn't put any values into the feedback array. Finally, another pass-through marker is inserted, and another point is drawn.

Listing 12-7   Using Feedback Mode: feedback.c

```
#include <GL/gl.h>
#include <GL/glu.h>
#include "aux.h"

void myinit(void)
{
    glEnable(GL_LIGHTING);
    glEnable(GL_LIGHT0);
}

void drawGeometry (GLenum mode)
{
    glBegin (GL_LINE_STRIP);
        glNormal3f (0.0, 0.0, 1.0);
        glVertex3f (30.0, 30.0, 0.0);
```

```
        glVertex3f (50.0, 60.0, 0.0);
        glVertex3f (70.0, 40.0, 0.0);
    glEnd ();
    if (mode == GL_FEEDBACK)
        glPassThrough (1.0);

    glBegin (GL_POINTS);
        glVertex3f (-100.0, -100.0, -100.0);
    glEnd ();
    if (mode == GL_FEEDBACK)
        glPassThrough (2.0);

    glBegin (GL_POINTS);
        glNormal3f (0.0, 0.0, 1.0);
        glVertex3f (50.0, 50.0, 0.0);
    glEnd ();
}

void print3DcolorVertex (GLint size, GLint *count,
        GLfloat *buffer)
{
    int i;

    printf ("   ");
    for (i = 0; i < 7; i++) {
        printf ("%4.2f ", buffer[size-(*count)]);
        *count = *count - 1;
    }
    printf ("\n");
}

void printBuffer(GLint size, GLfloat *buffer)
{
    GLint count;
    GLfloat token;

    count = size;
    while (count) {
        token = buffer[size-count]; count--;
        if (token == GL_PASS_THROUGH_TOKEN) {
            printf ("GL_PASS_THROUGH_TOKEN\n");
            printf ("  %4.2f\n", buffer[size-count]);
            count--;
        }
```

```
            else if (token == GL_POINT_TOKEN) {
                printf ("GL_POINT_TOKEN\n");
                print3DcolorVertex (size, &count, buffer);
            }
            else if (token == GL_LINE_TOKEN) {
                printf ("GL_LINE_TOKEN\n");
                print3DcolorVertex (size, &count, buffer);
                print3DcolorVertex (size, &count, buffer);
            }
            else if (token == GL_LINE_RESET_TOKEN) {
                printf ("GL_LINE_RESET_TOKEN\n");
                print3DcolorVertex (size, &count, buffer);
                print3DcolorVertex (size, &count, buffer);
            }
        }
}

void display(void)
{
    GLfloat feedBuffer[1024];
    GLint size;

    glMatrixMode (GL_PROJECTION);
    glLoadIdentity ();
    glOrtho (0.0, 100.0, 0.0, 100.0, 0.0, 1.0);

    glClearColor (0.0, 0.0, 0.0, 0.0);
    glClear(GL_COLOR_BUFFER_BIT);
    drawGeometry (GL_RENDER);

    glFeedbackBuffer (1024, GL_3D_COLOR, feedBuffer);
    (void) glRenderMode (GL_FEEDBACK);
    drawGeometry (GL_FEEDBACK);

    size = glRenderMode (GL_RENDER);
    printBuffer (size, feedBuffer);
}


int main(int argc, char** argv)
{
    auxInitDisplayMode (AUX_SINGLE | AUX_RGBA);
    auxInitPosition (0, 0, 100, 100);
    auxInitWindow (argv[0]);
    myinit ();
    auxMainLoop(display);
}
```

Running this program generates the following output:

```
GL_LINE_RESET_TOKEN
  30.00 30.00 0.00 0.84 0.84 0.84 1.00
  50.00 60.00 0.00 0.84 0.84 0.84 1.00
GL_LINE_TOKEN
  50.00 60.00 0.00 0.84 0.84 0.84 1.00
  70.00 40.00 0.00 0.84 0.84 0.84 1.00
GL_PASS_THROUGH_TOKEN
  1.00
GL_PASS_THROUGH_TOKEN
  2.00
GL_POINT_TOKEN
  50.00 50.00 0.00 0.84 0.84 0.84 1.00
```

Thus, the line strip drawn with these commands results in two primitives:

```
glBegin(GL_LINE_STRIP);
    glNormal3f (0.0, 0.0, 1.0);
    glVertex3f (30.0, 30.0, 0.0);
    glVertex3f (50.0, 60.0, 0.0);
    glVertex3f (70.0, 40.0, 0.0);
glEnd();
```

The first primitive begins with GL_LINE_RESET_TOKEN, which indicates that the primitive is a line segment and that the line stipple is reset. The second primitive begins with GL_LINE_TOKEN, so it's also a line segment, but the line stipple isn't reset and hence continues from where the previous line segment left off. Each of the two vertices for these lines generates seven values for the feedback array. Note that the RGBA values for all four vertices in these two lines are (0.84, 0.84, 0.84, 1.0), which is a very light gray color with the maximum alpha value. These color values are a result of the interaction of the surface normal and lighting parameters.

Since no feedback data is generated between the first and second pass-through markers, you can deduce that any primitives drawn between the first two calls to **glPassThrough()** were clipped out of the viewing volume. Finally, the point at (50.0, 50.0, 0.0) is drawn, and its associated data is copied into the feedback array.

Try This

Try This

- Make changes to Listing 12-7 and see how they affect the feedback values that are returned. For example, change the coordinate values of **glOrtho()**. Change the lighting variables, or eliminate lighting altogether and change the feedback type to GL_3D. Or add more primitives to see what other geometry (such as filled polygons) contributes to the feedback array.

Chapter 13

Now That You Know

Chapter Objectives

This chapter doesn't have objectives in the same way that previous chapters do. It's simply a collection of topics that describe ideas you might find useful for your application.

OpenGL is kind of a bag of low-level tools; now that you know about those tools, you can use them to implement higher-level functions. This chapter presents several examples of such higher-level capabilities.

This chapter discusses a variety of techniques based on OpenGL commands that illustrate some of the not-so-obvious uses to which you can put these commands. The examples are in no particular order and aren't related to each other. The idea is to read the section headings and skip to the examples that you find interesting. For your convenience, the headings are listed and explained briefly here.

Note: Most of the examples in the rest of this guide are complete and can be compiled and run as is. In this chapter, however, there are no complete programs, and you have to do a bit of work on your own to make them run.

- "Cheesy Translucency" (page 387) explains how to use polygon stippling to achieve translucency; this is particularly useful when you don't have blending hardware available.

- "An Easy Fade Effect" (page 388) shows how to use polygon stippling to create the effect of a fade into the background.

- "Object Selection Using the Back Buffer" (page 389) describes how to use the back buffer in a double-buffered system to handle simple object picking.

- "Cheap Image Transformation" (page 390) discusses how to draw a distorted version of a bitmapped image by drawing each pixel as a quadrilateral.

- "Displaying Layers" (page 392) explains how to display multiple different layers of materials and indicate where the materials overlap.

- "Antialiased Characters" (page 393) describes how to draw smoother fonts.

- "Drawing Round Points" (page 396) describes how to draw near-round points.

- "Interpolating Images" (page 396) shows how to smoothly blend from one image to the another.

- "Making Decals" (page 397) explains how to draw two images, where one is a sort of decal that should always appear on top of the other.

- "Drawing Filled, Concave Polygons Using the Stencil Buffer" (page 398) tells you how to draw concave polygons, nonsimple polygons, and polygons with holes by using the stencil buffer.

- "Finding Interference Regions" (page 399) describes how to determine where three-dimensional pieces overlap.

- "Shadows" (page 401) describes how to draw shadows of lit objects.

- **"Hidden-Line Removal"** (page 402) discusses how to draw a wireframe object with hidden lines removed by using the stencil buffer.

- **"Texture-Mapping Applications"** (page 403) describes several clever uses for texture mapping, such as rotating and warping images.

- **"Drawing Depth-Buffered Images"** (page 404) tells you how to combine images in a depth-buffered environment.

- **"Dirichlet Domains"** (page 405) explains how to find the Dirichlet domain of a set of points using the depth buffer.

- **"Life in the Stencil Buffer"** (page 407) explains how to implement the Game of Life using the stencil buffer.

- **"Alternative Uses for glDrawPixels() and glCopyPixels()"** (page 408) describes how to use these two commands for such effects as fake video, airbrushing, and transposed images.

Cheesy Translucency

You can use polygon stippling to simulate a translucent material. This is an especially good solution for systems that don't have blending hardware. Since polygon stipple patterns are 32×32 bits, or 1024 bits, you can go from opaque to transparent in 1023 steps. For example, if you want a surface that lets through 29 percent of the light, simply make up a stipple pattern where 29 percent (roughly 297) of the pixels in the mask are 0 and the rest are 1. Even if your surfaces have the same translucency, don't use the same stipple pattern for each one, as they cover exactly the same bits on the screen. Make up a different pattern for each by randomly selecting the appropriate number of pixels to be 0. See "Displaying Points, Lines, and Polygons" on page 39 for more information about polygon stippling.

If you don't like the effect with random pixels turned on, you can use regular patterns, but they don't work as well when transparent surfaces are stacked. This is often not a problem because most scenes have relatively few translucent regions that overlap. In a picture of an automobile with translucent windows, your line of sight can go through at most two windows, and usually it's only one.

An Easy Fade Effect

Suppose you have an image that you want to fade gradually to some background color. Define a series of polygon stipple patterns, each of which has more bits turned on so that they represent denser and denser patterns. Then use these patterns repeatedly with a polygon large enough to cover the region over which you want to fade. For example, suppose you want to fade to black in sixteen steps. First define sixteen different pattern arrays:

```
GLubyte stips[16][4*32];
```

Then load them in such a way that each has one-sixteenth of the pixels in a 32×32 stipple pattern turned on. After that, the following code does the trick:

```
draw_the_picture();
glColor3f(0.0, 0.0, 0.0);        /* set color to black */
for (i = 0; i < 16; i++) {
    glPolygonStipple(&stips[i][0]);
    draw_a_polygon_large_enough_to_cover_the_whole_region();
}
```

In some OpenGL implementations, you might get better performance by first compiling the stipple patterns into display lists. During your initialization, do something like this:

```
#define STIP_OFFSET 100
for (i = 0; i < 16; i++) {
    glNewList(i+STIP_OFFSET, GL_COMPILE);
    glPolygonStipple(&stips[i][0]);
    glEndList();
}
```

Then, replace this line in the first code fragment

```
glPolygonStipple(&stips[i][0]);
```

with

```
glCallList(i);
```

By compiling the command to set the stipple into a display list, OpenGL might be able to rearrange the data in the stips[ ][ ] array into the hardware-specific form required for maximum stipple-setting speed.

Another application for this technique is if you're drawing a changing picture, and you want to leave some blur behind that gradually fades out to give some indication of past motion. For example, suppose you're simulating a planetary system, and you want to leave trails on the planets to show a recent portion of their path. Again, assuming you want to fade in sixteen steps, set up the stipple patterns as before (using the display-list version, say), and have the main simulation loop look something like this:

```
current_stipple = 0;
while (1) {                          /* loop forever */
    draw_the_next_frame();
    glCallList(current_stipple++);
    if (current_stipple == 16) current_stipple = 0;
    glColor3f(0.0, 0.0, 0.0);        /* set color to black */
    draw_a_polygon_large_enough_to_cover_the_whole_region();
}
```

Each time through the loop, you clear one-sixteenth of the pixels. Any pixel that hasn't had a planet on it for sixteen frames is certain to be cleared to black. Of course, if your system supports blending in hardware, it's easier to blend in a certain amount of background color with each frame.

See "Displaying Points, Lines, and Polygons" on page 39 for polygon stippling details, Chapter 4 for more information about display lists, and "Blending" on page 196 for information about blending.

Object Selection Using the Back Buffer

Although OpenGL's selection mechanism (see "Selection" on page 356) is powerful and flexible, it can be cumbersome to use. Often, the situation is simple: Your application draws a scene composed of a substantial number of objects; the user points to an object with the mouse, and the application needs to find the item under the tip of the cursor.

One way to do this requires your application to be running in double-buffer mode. When the user picks an object, the application redraws the entire scene in the back buffer, but instead of using the normal colors for objects, it encodes some kind of object identifier for each object's color. The application then simply reads back the pixel under the cursor, and the value of that pixel encodes the number of the picked object.

Note that this scheme has an advantage over standard selection in that it picks the object that's in front, if multiple objects appear at the same pixel, one behind the other. Since the image with false colors is drawn in the back buffer, the user never sees it; you can redraw the back buffer (or copy it from the front buffer) before swapping the buffers. In color-index mode, the encoding is simple—send the object identifier as the index. In RGBA mode, encode the bits of the identifier into the R, G, and B components.

Be aware that you can run out of identifiers if there are too many objects in the scene. For example, suppose you're running in color-index mode on a system that has 4-bit buffers for color-index information (sixteen possible different indices) in each of the color buffers, but the scene has thousands of pickable items. To address this issue, the picking can be done in a few passes. For definiteness, assume there are fewer than 4096 items, so all the object identifiers can be encoded in 12 bits. In the first pass, draw the scene using indices composed of the 4 high-order bits, then use the second and third passes to draw the middle 4 bits and the 4 low-order bits. After each pass, read the pixel under the cursor, extract the bits, and pack them together at the end to get the object identifier.

With this method, the picking takes three times as long, but that's often acceptable. Note that after you have the high-order 4 bits, you eliminate fifteen of the sixteen possible objects, so you really only need to draw one-sixteenth of them for the second pass. Similarly, after the second pass, 255 of the 256 possible items have been eliminated. The first pass thus takes about as long as drawing a single frame does, but the second and third passes can be up to 16 and 256 times as fast.

If you're trying to write portable code that works on different systems, break up your object identifiers into chunks that fit on the lowest common denominator of those systems. Also, keep in mind that your system might perform automatic dithering in RGB mode. If this is the case, turn off dithering.

Cheap Image Transformation

Suppose you want to draw a distorted version of a bitmapped image (perhaps simply stretched or rotated, or perhaps drastically modified by some mathematical function). In many cases, you can achieve good results by drawing the image of each pixel as a quadrilateral. Although this scheme doesn't produce images as nice as those you would get by applying a sophisticated filtering algorithm (and it might not be sufficient for sophisticated users), it's a lot quicker.

To make the problem more concrete, assume that the original image is m pixels by n pixels, with coordinates chosen from $[0, m-1] \times [0, n-1]$. Let the distortion functions be $x(m,n)$ and $y(m,n)$. For example, if the distortion is simply a zooming by a factor of 3.2, then $x(m,n) = 3.2*m$ and $y(m,n) = 3.2*n$. The following code draws the distorted image:

```
glShadeModel(GL_FLAT);
glScale(3.2, 3.2, 1.0);
for (j=0; j < n; j++) {
    glBegin(GL_QUAD_STRIP);
    for (i=0; i <= m; i++) {
        glVertex2i(i,j);
        glVertex2i(i, j+1);
        set_color(i,j);
    }
    glEnd();
}
```

This code draws each transformed pixel in a solid color equal to that pixel's color and scales the image size by 3.2. The routine **set_color()** stands for whatever the appropriate OpenGL command is to set the color of the image pixel.

The following is a slightly more complex version that distorts the image using the functions $x(i,j)$ and $y(i,j)$:

```
glShadeModel(GL_FLAT);
for (j=0; j < n; j++) {
    glBegin(GL_QUAD_STRIP);
    for (i=0; i <= m; i++) {
        glVertex2i(x(i,j), y(i,j));
        glVertex2i(x(i,j+1), y(i,j+1));
        set_color(i,j);
    }
    glEnd();
}
```

An even better distorted image can be drawn with the following code:

```
glShadeModel(GL_SMOOTH);
for (j=0; j < (n-1); j++) {
    glBegin(GL_QUAD_STRIP);
    for (i=0; i < m; i++) {
        set_color(i,j);
        glVertex2i(x(i,j), y(i,j));
```

```
        set_color(i,j+1);
        glVertex2i(x(i,j+1), y(i,j+1));
    }
    glEnd();
}
```

This code smoothly interpolates color across each quadrilateral. Note that this version produces one fewer quadrilateral in each dimension than do the flat-shaded versions because the color image is being used to specify colors at the quadrilateral vertices. In addition, you can antialias the polygons with the appropriate blending function (GL_SRC_ALPHA, GL_ONE) to get an even nicer image.

Displaying Layers

In some applications such as semiconductor layout programs, you want to display multiple different layers of materials and indicate where the materials overlap each other.

As a simple example, suppose you have three different substances that can be layered. At any point, eight possible combinations of layers can occur, as shown in Table 13-1.

	Layer 1	Layer 2	Layer 3	Color
0	absent	absent	absent	black
1	present	absent	absent	red
2	absent	present	absent	green
3	present	present	absent	blue
4	absent	absent	present	pink
5	present	absent	present	yellow
6	absent	present	present	white
7	present	present	present	gray

Table 13-1 Eight Combinations of Layers

You want your program to display eight different colors, depending on the layers present. One arbitrary possibility is shown in the last column of the table. To use this method, use color-index mode and load your color map so that entry 0 is black, entry 1 is red, entry 2 is green, and so on. Note that if the numbers from 0 through 7 are written in binary, the 4 bit is turned on whenever layer 3 appears, the 2 bit whenever layer 2 appears, and the 1 bit whenever layer 1 appears.

To clear the window, set the writemask to 7 (all three layers) and set the clearing color to 0. To draw your image, set the color to 7, and then when you want to draw something in layer n, set the writemask to n. In other types of applications, it might be necessary to selectively erase in a layer, in which case you would use the same writemasks as above, but set the color to 0 instead of 7.

See "Masking Buffers" on page 298 for more information about writemasks.

Antialiased Characters

Using the standard technique for drawing characters with **glBitmap()**, drawing each pixel of a character is an all-or-nothing affair—the pixel is either turned on or not. If you're drawing black characters on a white background, for example, the resulting pixels are either black or white, never a shade of gray. Much smoother, higher-quality images can be achieved if intermediate colors are used when rendering characters (grays, in this example).

Assuming that you're drawing black characters on a white background, imagine a highly magnified picture of the pixels on the screen, with a high-resolution character outline superimposed on it, as shown in the left side of Figure 13-1.

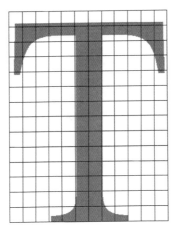

Figure 13-1 Antialiased Characters

Notice that some of the pixels are completely enclosed by the character's outline and should be painted black; some pixels are completely outside the outline and should be painted white; but many pixels should ideally be painted some shade of gray, where the darkness of the gray corresponds to the amount of black in the pixel. If this technique is used, the resulting image on the screen looks better.

If speed and memory usage are of no concern, each character can be drawn as a small image instead of as a bitmap. If you're using RGBA mode, however, this method might require up to 32 bits per pixel of the character to be stored and drawn, instead of the one bit per pixel in a standard character. Alternatively, you could use one 8-bit index per pixel and convert these indices to RGBA by table lookup during transfer. In many cases, a compromise is possible that allows you to draw the character with a few gray levels between black and white (say, two or three), and the resulting font description requires only 2 or 3 bits per pixel of storage.

The numbers in the right side of Figure 13-1 indicate the approximate percentage coverage of each pixel: 0 means approximately empty, 1 means approximately one-third coverage, 2 means two-thirds, and 3 means completely covered. If pixels labeled 0 are painted white, pixels labeled 3 are painted black, and pixels labeled 1 and 2 are painted one-third and two-thirds black, respectively, the resulting character looks quite good. Only 2 bits are required to store the numbers 0, 1, 2, and 3, so for 2 bits per pixel, four levels of gray can be saved.

There are basically two methods to implement antialiased characters, depending on whether you're in RGBA mode.

In RGBA mode, define three different character bitmaps, corresponding to where 1, 2, and 3 appear in Figure 13-1. Set the color to white and clear for the background. Set the color to one-third gray (RGB = (0.666, 0.666, 0.666)) and draw all the pixels with a 1 in them. Then set RGB = (0.333, 0.333, 0.333), draw with the 2 bitmap, and use RGB = (0.0, 0.0, 0.0) for the 3 bitmap. What you're doing is defining three different fonts, and redrawing the string three times, where each pass fills in the bits of the appropriate color densities.

In color-index mode, you can do exactly the same thing, but if you're willing to set up the color map correctly and use writemasks, you can get away with only two bitmaps per character and two passes per string. In the preceding example, set up one bitmap that has a 1 wherever 1 or 3 appears in the character. Set up a second bitmap that has a 1 wherever a 2 or a 3 appears. Load the color map so that 0 gives white, 1 gives light gray, 2 gives dark gray, and 3 gives black. Set the color to 3 (11 in binary) and the writemask to 1, and draw the first bitmap. Then change the writemask to 2, and draw the second. Where 0 appears in Figure 13-1, nothing is drawn in the framebuffer. Where 1, 2, and 3 appear, 1, 2, and 3 appear in the framebuffer.

For this example with only four gray levels, the savings is small—two passes instead of three. If eight gray levels were used instead, the RGBA method would require seven passes, and the color-map masking technique would require only three. With sixteen gray levels, the comparison is fifteen passes to four passes.

See "Masking Buffers" on page 298 for more information about writemasks and "Bitmaps and Fonts" on page 227 for more information about drawing bitmaps.

Try This

| Try This |

- Can you see how to do RGBA rendering using no more images than the optimized color-index case? Hint: How are RGB fragments normally merged into the color buffer when antialiasing is desired?

Drawing Round Points

Draw near-round, aliased points by enabling point antialiasing, turning blending off, and using an alpha function that passes only fragments with alpha greater than 0.5.

See "Antialiasing" on page 207 and "Blending" on page 196 for more information about these topics.

Interpolating Images

Suppose you have a pair of images (where *image* can mean a bitmap image, or a picture generated using geometry in the usual way), and you want to smoothly blend from one to the other. This can be done easily using the alpha component and appropriate blending operations. Let's say you want to accomplish the blending in ten steps, where image A is shown in frame 0 and image B is shown in frame 9. The obvious approach is to draw image A with alpha equal to $(9-i)/9$ and image B with an alpha of $i/9$ in frame i.

The problem with this method is that both images must be drawn in each frame. A faster approach is to draw image A in frame 0. To get frame 1, blend in 1/9 of image B and 8/9 of what's there. For frame 2, blend in 1/8 of image B with 7/8 of what's there. For frame 3, blend in 1/7 of image B with 6/7 of what's there, and so on. For the last step, you're just drawing 1/1 of image B blended with 0/1 of what's left, yielding image B exactly.

To see that this works, if for frame i you have

$$\frac{(9-i)A}{9} + \frac{iB}{9}$$

and you blend in $B/(9-i)$ with $(8-i)/(9-i)$ of what's there, you get

$$\frac{B}{9-i} + \frac{8-i}{9-i}\left[\frac{(9-i)A}{9} + \frac{iB}{9}\right] = \frac{9-(i+1)A}{9} + \frac{(i+1)B}{9}$$

See "Blending" on page 196.

Making Decals

Suppose you're drawing a complex three-dimensional picture using depth-buffering to eliminate the hidden surfaces. Suppose further that one part of your picture is composed of coplanar figures A and B, where B is a sort of decal that should always appear on top of figure A.

Your first approach might be to draw B after you've drawn A, setting the depth-buffering function to replace on greater or equal. Due to the finite precision of the floating-point representations of the vertices, however, round-off error can cause polygon B to be sometimes a bit in front and sometimes a bit behind figure A. Here's one solution to this problem:

1. Disable the depth buffer for writing, and render A.
2. Enable the depth buffer for writing, and render B.
3. Disable the color buffer for writing, and render A again.
4. Enable the color buffer for writing.

Note that during the entire process, the depth-buffer test is enabled. In step 1, A is rendered wherever it should be, but none of the depth-buffer values are changed, so in step 2, wherever B appears over A, B is guaranteed to be drawn. Step 3 simply makes sure that all of the depth values under A are updated correctly, but since RGBA writes are disabled, the color pixels are unaffected. Finally, step 4 returns the system to the default state (writing is enabled both in the depth buffer and in the color buffer).

If a stencil buffer is available, the following simpler technique works:

1. Configure the stencil buffer to write 1 if the depth test passes, and 0 otherwise. Render A.
2. Configure the stencil buffer to make no stencil value change, but to render only where stencil values are 1. Disable the depth-buffer test and its update. Render B.

With this method, it's not necessary to initialize the contents of the stencil buffer at any time, because the stencil value of all pixels of interest (that is, those rendered by A) are set when A is rendered. Be sure to reenable the depth test and disable the stencil test before additional polygons are drawn.

See "Selecting Color Buffers for Writing" on page 297, "Depth Test" on page 307, and "Stencil Test" on page 302.

Drawing Filled, Concave Polygons Using the Stencil Buffer

Consider the concave polygon 1234567 shown in Figure 13-2. Imagine that it's drawn as a series of triangles: 123, 134, 145, 156, 167, all of which are shown in the figure. The heavier line represents the original polygon boundary. Drawing all these triangles divides the buffer into nine regions A, B, C, ..., I, where region I is outside all the triangles.

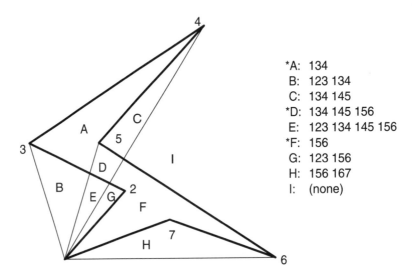

Figure 13-2   A Concave Polygon

In the text of the figure, each of the region names is followed by a list of the triangles that cover it. Regions A, D, and F make up the original polygon; note that these three regions are covered by an odd number of triangles. Every other region is covered by an even number of triangles (possibly zero). Thus, to render the inside of the concave polygon, you just need to render regions that are enclosed by an odd number of triangles. This can be done using the stencil buffer, with a two-pass algorithm.

First, clear the stencil buffer and disable writing into the color buffer. Next, draw each of the triangles in turn, using the GL_INVERT function in the stencil buffer. This flips the value between zero and a nonzero value every time a triangle is drawn that covers a pixel. After all the triangles are drawn, if a pixel is covered an even number of times, the value in the stencil buffers is zero; otherwise, it's nonzero. Finally, draw a large polygon over the whole region (or redraw the triangles), but allow drawing only where the stencil buffer is nonzero.

Note: There's a slight generalization of the preceding technique, where you don't need to start with a polygon vertex. In the 1234567 example, let P be any point on or off the polygon. Draw the triangles: P12, P23, P34, P45, P56, P67, and P71. Regions covered by an odd number of triangles are inside; other regions are outside. This is a generalization in that if P happens to be one of the polygon's edges, one of the triangles is empty.

This technique can be used to fill both nonsimple polygons (polygons whose edges cross each other) and polygons with holes. The following example illustrates how to handle a complicated polygon with two regions, one four-sided and one five-sided. Assume further that there's a triangular and a four-sided hole (it doesn't matter in which regions the holes lie). Let the two regions be abcd and efghi, and the holes jkl and mnop. Let z be any point on the plane. Draw the following triangles:

zab zbc zcd zda zef zfg zgh zhi zie zjk zkl zlj zmn zno zop zpm

Mark regions covered by an odd number of triangles as *in*, and those covered by an even number as *out*.

See "Stencil Test" on page 302 for more information about the stencil buffer.

Finding Interference Regions

If you're designing a mechanical part made from smaller three-dimensional pieces, you often want to display regions where the pieces overlap. In many cases, such regions indicate design errors where parts of a machine interfere with each other. In the case of moving parts, it can be even more valuable, since a search for interfering regions can be done through a complete mechanical cycle of the design. The method for doing this is complicated, and the description here might be too brief. Complete details can be found in the paper *Interactive Inspection of Solids: Cross-sections and Interferences*, by Jarek Rossignac, Abe Megahed, and Bengt-Olaf Schneider (SIGGRAPH 1992 Proceedings).

The method is related to the capping algorithm described in "Stencil Test" on page 302. The idea is to pass an arbitrary clipping plane through the objects that you want to test for interference, and then determine when a portion of the clipping plane is inside more than one object at a time. For a static image, the clipping plane can be moved manually to highlight interfering regions; for a dynamic image, it might be easier to use a grid of clipping planes to search for all possible interferences.

Draw each of the objects you want to check and clip them against the clipping plane. Note which pixels are inside the object at that clipping plane using an odd-even count in the stencil buffer, as explained in the preceding section. (For properly formed objects, a point is inside the object if a ray drawn from that point to the eye intersects an odd number of surfaces of the object.) To find interferences, you need to find pixels in the framebuffer where the clipping plane is in the interior of two or more regions at once; in other words, in the intersection of the interiors of any pair of objects.

If multiple objects need to be tested for mutual intersection, store one bit every time some intersection appears, and another bit wherever the clipping buffer is inside any of the objects (the union of the objects' interiors). For each new object, determine its interior, find the intersection of that with the union of the interiors of the objects so far tested, and keep track of the intersection points. Then add the interior points of the new object to the union of the other objects' interiors.

You can perform the operations described in the preceding paragraph by using different bits in the stencil buffer together with various masking operations. Three bits of stencil buffer are required per pixel—one for the toggling to determine the interior of each object, one for the union of all interiors discovered so far, and one for the regions where interference has occurred so far. For concreteness, assume the 1 bit of the stencil buffer is for toggling interior/exterior, the 2 bit is the running union, and the 4 bit is for interferences so far. For each object that you're going to render, clear the 1 bit (using a stencil mask of 1 and clearing to 0), then toggle the 1 bit by keeping the stencil mask as 1 and using the GL_INVERT stencil operation.

You can find intersections and unions of the bits in the stencil buffers using the stenciling operations. For example, to make bits in buffer 2 be the union of the bits in buffers 1 and 2, mask the stencil to those two bits, and draw something over the entire object with the stencil function set to pass if anything nonzero occurs. This happens if the bits in buffer 1, buffer 2, or both are turned on. If the comparison succeeds, write a 1 in buffer 2. Also, make sure that drawing in the color buffer is disabled. An intersection calculation is similar—set the function to pass only if the value in the two buffers is equal to 3 (bits turned on in both buffers 1 and 2). Write the result into the correct buffer.

See "Additional Clipping Planes" on page 106 and "Stencil Test" on page 302.

Shadows

Every possible projection of three-dimensional space to three-dimensional space can be achieved with a suitable 4×4 invertible matrix and homogeneous coordinates. If the matrix isn't invertible but has rank 3, it projects three-dimensional space onto a two-dimensional plane. Every such possible projection can be achieved with a suitable rank-3 4×4 matrix. To find the shadow of an arbitrary object on an arbitrary plane from an arbitrary light source (possibly at infinity), you need to find a matrix representing that projection, multiply it on the matrix stack, and draw the object in the shadow color. Keep in mind that you need to project onto each plane that you're calling the "ground."

As a simple illustration, assume the light is at the origin, and the equation of the ground plane is $ax+by+c+d=0$. Given a vertex $S=(sx,sy,sz,1)$, the line from the light through S includes all points αS, where α is an arbitrary real number. The point where this line intersects the plane occurs when

$\alpha(a{*}sz+b{*}sy+c{*}sz) + d = 0,$

so

$\alpha = -d/(a{*}sx+b{*}sy+c{*}sz).$

Plugging this back into the line, we get:

$-d(sx,sy,sz)/(a{*}sx+b{*}sy+c{*}sz)$

for the point of intersection.

The matrix that maps S to this point for every S is

$$\begin{bmatrix} -d & 0 & 0 & a \\ 0 & -d & 0 & b \\ 0 & 0 & -d & c \\ 0 & 0 & 0 & 0 \end{bmatrix}$$

This matrix can be used if you first translate the world so that the light is at the origin.

If the light is from an infinite source, all you have is a point S and a direction D = (dx,dy,dz). Points along the line are given by

S + αD

Proceeding as before, the intersection of this line with the plane is given by

a(sx+αdx)+b(sy+αdy)+c(sz+αdz)+d = 0

Solving for α, plugging that back into the equation for a line, and then determining a projection matrix gives

$$
\begin{bmatrix}
b*dy+c*dz & -a*dy & -a*dz & 0 \\
-b*dx & a*dx+c*dz & -b*dz & 0 \\
-c*dx & -c*dy & a*dx+b*dy & 0 \\
-d*dx & -d*dy & -d*dz & a*dx+b*dy*c*dz
\end{bmatrix}
$$

This matrix works given the plane and an arbitrary direction vector. There's no need to translate anything first.

See Chapter 3, "Viewing," and Appendix G.

Hidden-Line Removal

If you want to draw a wireframe object with hidden lines removed, one approach is to draw the outlines using lines, and then fill the interiors of the polygons making up the surface with polygons having the background color. With depth-buffering enabled, this interior fill covers any outlines that would be obscured by faces closer to the eye. This method would work, except that there's no guarantee that the interior of the object falls entirely inside the polygon's outline, and in fact it might overlap it in various places.

There's an easy, two-pass solution using the stencil buffer. For each polygon, clear the stencil buffer, and then draw the outline both in the framebuffer and in the stencil buffer. Then when you fill the interior, enable drawing only where the stencil buffer is still clear. To avoid doing an entire stencil-buffer clear for each polygon, an easy way to clear it is simply to draw 0s into the buffer using the same polygon outline. In this way, you need to clear the entire stencil buffer only once.

For example, the following code represents the inner loop you might use to perform such hidden-line removal. Each polygon is outlined in the foreground color, filled with the background color, and then outlined again in the foreground color. The stencil buffer is used to keep the fill color of each polygon from overwriting its outline. To optimize performance, the stencil and color parameters are changed only twice per loop by using the same values both times the polygon outline is drawn.

```
glEnable(GL_STENCIL_TEST);
glEnable(GL_DEPTH_TEST);
glClear(GL_STENCIL_BUFFER_BIT);
glStencilFunc(GL_ALWAYS, 0, 1);
glStencilOp(GL_INVERT, GL_INVERT, GL_INVERT);
set_color(foreground);
for (i=0; i < max; i++) {
    outline_polygon(i);
    set_color(background);
    glStencilFunc(GL_EQUAL, 0, 1);
    glStencilOp(GL_KEEP, GL_KEEP, GL_KEEP);
    fill_polygon(i);
    set_color(foreground);
    glStencilFunc(GL_ALWAYS, 0, 1);
    glStencilOp(GL_INVERT, GL_INVERT, GL_INVERT);
    outline_polygon(i);
}
```

See "Stencil Test" on page 302.

Texture-Mapping Applications

Texture mapping is quite powerful, and it can be used in some interesting ways. Here are a few advanced applications of texture mapping:

- Antialiased text—Define a texture map for each character at a relatively high resolution, and then map them onto smaller areas using the filtering provided by texturing. This also makes text appear correctly on surfaces that aren't aligned with the screen, but are tilted and have some perspective distortion.

- Antialiased lines—These can be done like antialiased text: Make the line in the texture several pixels wide, and use the texture filtering to antialias the lines.

- Image scaling and rotation—If you put an image into a texture map and use that texture to map onto a polygon, rotating and scaling the polygon effectively rotates and scales the image.

- Image warping—As in the preceding example, store the image as a texture map, but map it to some spline-defined surface (use evaluators). As you warp the surface, the image follows the warping.

- Projecting images—Put the image in a texture map, and project it as a spotlight, creating a slide projector effect. See "The q Coordinate" on page 290 for more information about how to model a spotlight using textures.

See Chapter 3 for information about rotating and scaling, Chapter 9 for more information about creating textures, and Chapter 11 for details on evaluators.

Drawing Depth-Buffered Images

For complex static backgrounds, the rendering time for the geometric description of the background can be greater than the time it takes to draw a pixel image of the rendered background. If there's a fixed background and a relatively simple changing foreground, you may want to draw the background and its associated depth-buffered version as an image rather than render it geometrically. The foreground might also consist of items that are time-consuming to render, but whose framebuffer images and depth buffers are available. You can render these items into a depth-buffered environment using a two-pass algorithm.

For example, if you're drawing a model of a molecule made of spheres, you might have an image of a beautifully rendered sphere and its associated depth-buffer values that were calculated using Phong shading or ray-tracing, or using some other scheme that isn't directly available through OpenGL. To draw a complex model, you might be required to draw hundreds of such spheres, which should be depth-buffered together.

To add a depth-buffered image to the scene, first draw the image's depth-buffer values into the depth buffer using **glDrawPixels()**. Then enable depth-buffering, set the writemask to zero so that no drawing occurs, and enable stenciling such that the stencil buffers get drawn whenever a write to the depth buffer occurs.

Then draw the image into the color buffer, masked by the stencil buffer you've just written so that writing occurs only when there's a 1 in the stencil buffer. During this write, set the stenciling function to zero out the stencil buffer so that it's automatically cleared when it's time to add the next image to the scene. If the objects are to be moved nearer to or farther from the viewer, you need to use an orthographic projection; in these cases, you use GL_DEPTH_BIAS with **glPixelTransfer*()** to move the depth image.

See "Hidden-Surface Removal Survival Kit" on page 27, "Depth Test" on page 307, see "Stencil Test" on page 302, and see Chapter 8 for details on **glDrawPixels()** and **glPixelTransfer*()**.

Dirichlet Domains

Given a set S of points on a plane, the Dirichlet domain or Voronoi polygon of one of the points is the set of all points in the plane closer to that point than to any other point in the set S. These points provide the solution to many problems in computational geometry. Figure 13-3 shows outlines of the Dirichlet domains for a set of points.

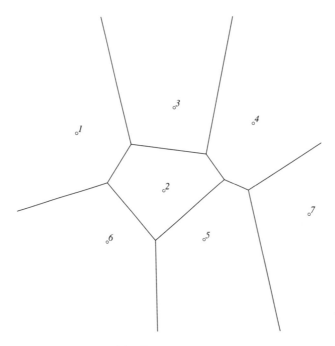

Figure 13-3 Dirichlet Domains

If you draw a depth-buffered cone with its apex at the point in a different color than each of the points in S, the Dirichlet domain for each point is drawn in that color. The easiest way to do this is to precompute a cone's depth in an image, and use the image as the depth-buffer values as described in the preceding section. You don't need an image to draw in the framebuffer as in the case of shaded spheres, however. While you're drawing into the depth buffer, use the stencil buffer to record the pixels where drawing should occur by first clearing it, and then writing nonzero values wherever the depth test succeeds. To draw the Dirichlet region, draw a polygon over the entire window, but enable drawing only where the stencil buffers are nonzero.

You can do this perhaps more easily by rendering cones of uniform color with a simple depth buffer, but a good cone might require thousands of polygons. The technique described in this section can render much higher-quality cones much more quickly.

See "Hidden-Surface Removal Survival Kit" on page 27 and "Depth Test" on page 307.

Life in the Stencil Buffer

The Game of Life, invented by John Conway, is played on a rectangular grid where each grid location is "alive" or "dead." To calculate the next generation from the current one, count the number of live neighbors for each grid location (the eight adjacent grid locations are neighbors). A grid location is alive in generation $n+1$ if it was alive in generation n and has exactly two or three live neighbors, or if it was dead in generation n and has exactly three live neighbors. In all other cases, it is dead in generation $n+1$. This game generates some incredibly interesting patterns given different initial configurations. (See Martin Gardner, "Mathematical Games," *Scientific American*, vol. 223, no. 4, October 1970, p. 120-123.) Figure 13-4 shows six generations from a game.

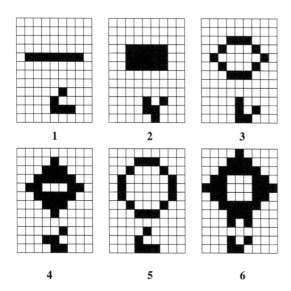

Figure 13-4 Six Generations from the Game of Life

One way to create this game using OpenGL is to use a multipass algorithm. Keep the data in the color buffer, one pixel for each grid point. Assume that black (all zeros) is the background color, and the color of a live pixel is nonzero. Initialize by clearing the depth and stencil buffers to zero, set the depth-buffer writemask to zero, and set the depth comparison function so that it passes on not-equal. To iterate, read the image off the screen, enable drawing into the depth buffer, and set the stencil function so that it increments whenever a depth comparison succeeds but leaves the stencil buffer unchanged otherwise. Disable drawing into the color buffer.

Next, draw the image eight times, offset one pixel in each vertical, horizontal, and diagonal direction. When you're done, the stencil buffer contains a count of the number of live neighbors for each pixel. Enable drawing to the color buffer, set the color to the color for live cells, and set the stencil function to draw only if the value in the stencil buffer is 3 (three live neighbors). In addition, if this drawing occurs, decrement the value in the stencil buffer. Then draw a rectangle covering the image; this paints each cell that has exactly three live neighbors with the "alive" color.

At this point, the stencil buffers contain 0, 1, 2, 4, 5, 6, 7, 8, and the values under the 2s are correct. The values under 0, 1, 4, 5, 6, 7, and 8 must be cleared to the "dead" color. Set the stencil function to draw whenever the value is not 2, and to zero the stencil values in all cases. Then draw a large polygon of the "dead" color across the entire image. You're done.

For a usable demonstration program, you might want to zoom the grid up to a size larger than a single pixel; it's hard to see detailed patterns with a single pixel per grid point.

See "Hidden-Surface Removal Survival Kit" on page 27, "Depth Test" on page 307, and "Stencil Test" on page 302.

Alternative Uses for glDrawPixels() and glCopyPixels()

You might think of **glDrawPixels()** as a way to draw a rectangular region of pixels to the screen. Although this is often what it's used for, some other interesting uses are outlined here.

- Video—Even if your machine doesn't have special video hardware, you can display short movie clips by repeatedly drawing frames with **glDrawPixels()** in the same region of the back buffer and then swapping the buffers. The size of the frames you can display with reasonable performance using this method depends on your hardware's drawing speed, so you might be limited to 100×100 pixel movies (or smaller) if you want smooth fake video.

- Airbrush—In a paint program, your airbrush (or paintbrush) shape can be simulated using alpha values. The color of the paint is represented as the color values. To paint with a circular brush in blue, repeatedly draw a blue square with **glDrawPixels()** where the alpha values are largest in the center and taper to zero at the edges of a circle centered in the square. Draw using a blending function that uses alpha of the incoming color and (1–alpha) of the color already at the pixel. If the alpha values in the brush are all much less than 1, you have to paint over an area repeatedly to get a solid color. If the alpha values are near 1, each brush stroke pretty much obliterates the colors underneath.

- Filtered Zooms—If you zoom a pixel image by a nonintegral amount, OpenGL effectively uses a box filter, which can lead to rather severe aliasing effects. To improve the filtering, jitter the resulting image by amounts less than a pixel and redraw it multiple times, using alpha blending to average the resulting pixels. The result is a filtered zoom.

- Transposing Images—You can swap same-size images in place with **glCopyPixels()** using the XOR operation. With this method, you can avoid having to read the images back into processor memory. If A and B represent the two images, the operation looks like this:

  1. A = A XOR B

  2. B = A XOR B

  3. A = A XOR B

Order of Operations

This guide describes all the operations performed between the time vertices are specified and when fragments are finally written into the framebuffer. The chapters of this guide are arranged in an order that facilitates learning rather than in the exact order in which these operations are actually performed. Sometimes the exact order of operations doesn't matter—for example, surfaces can be converted to polygons and then transformed, or transformed first and then converted to polygons, with identical results— and different implementations of OpenGL might do things differently. This appendix describes a possible order; any implementation is required to give equivalent results. If you want more details than are presented here, see the *OpenGL Reference Manual*.

This appendix has the following major sections:

- "Overview"
- "Geometric Operations"
- "Pixel Operations"
- "Fragment Operations"
- "Odds and Ends"

Overview

This section gives an overview of the order of operations, as shown in Figure A-1. Geometric data (vertices, lines, and polygons) follows the path through the row of boxes that includes evaluators and per-vertex operations, while pixel data (pixels, images, and bitmaps) is treated differently for part of the process. Both types of data undergo the rasterization and per-fragment operations before the final pixel data is written into the framebuffer.

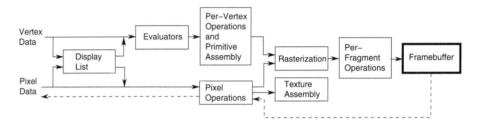

Figure A-1   Order of Operations

All data, whether it describes geometry or pixels, can be saved in a display list or processed immediately. When a display list is executed, the data is sent from the display list just as if it were sent by the application.

All geometric primitives are eventually described by vertices. If evaluators are used, that data is converted to vertices and treated as vertices from then on. Per-vertex calculations are performed on each vertex, followed by rasterization to fragments. For pixel data, pixel operations are performed, and the results are either stored in the texture memory, used for polygon stippling, or rasterized to fragments.

Finally, the fragments are subjected to a series of per-fragment operations, after which the final pixel values are drawn into the framebuffer.

Geometric Operations

Geometric data, whether it comes from a display list, an evaluator, the vertices of a rectangle, or as raw data, consists of a set of vertices and the type of primitive it describes (a vertex, line, or polygon). Vertex data includes not only the (x, y, z, w) coordinates, but also a normal vector, texture coordinates, a color or index, and edge-flag data. All these elements except the vertex's coordinates can be specified in any order, and default values exist as well. As soon as the vertex command **glVertex*()** is issued, the components are padded, if necessary, to four dimensions (using $z = 0$ and $w = 1$), and the current values of all the elements are associated with the vertex. The complete set of vertex data is then processed.

Per-Vertex Operations

In the per-vertex operations stage of processing, each vertex's spatial coordinates are transformed by the modelview matrix, while the normal vector is transformed by that matrix's inverse and renormalized if specified. If automatic texture generation is enabled, new texture coordinates are generated from the transformed vertex coordinates, and they replace the vertex's old texture coordinates. The texture coordinates are then transformed by the current texture matrix and passed on to the primitive assembly step.

Meanwhile, the lighting calculations, if enabled, are performed using the transformed vertex and normal vector coordinates, and the current material, lights, and lighting model. These calculations generate new colors or indices that are clamped or masked to the appropriate range and passed on to the primitive assembly step.

Primitive Assembly

Primitive assembly differs, depending on whether the primitive is a point, a line, or a polygon. If flat shading is enabled, the colors or indices of all the vertices in a line or polygon are set to the same value. If special clipping planes are defined and enabled, they're used to clip primitives of all three types. (The clipping-plane equations are transformed by the inverse of the modelview matrix when they're specified.) Point clipping simply passes or rejects vertices; line or polygon clipping can add additional vertices depending on how the line or polygon is clipped. After this clipping, the spatial coordinates of each vertex are transformed by the projection matrix, and the results are clipped against the standard viewing planes $x = \pm w$, $y = \pm w$, and $z = \pm w$.

If selection is enabled, any primitive not eliminated by clipping generates a selection-hit report, and no further processing is performed. Without selection, perspective division by w occurs and the viewport and depth-range operations are applied. Also, if the primitive is a polygon, it's then subjected to a culling test (if culling is enabled). A polygon might convert to vertices or lines, depending on the polygon mode.

Finally, points, lines, and polygons are rasterized to fragments, taking into account polygon or line stipples, line width, and point size. Rasterization involves determining which squares of an integer grid in window coordinates are occupied by the primitive. Color and depth values are also assigned to each such square.

Pixel Operations

Pixels from host memory are first unpacked into the proper number of components. The OpenGL unpacking facility handles a number of different formats. Next, the data is scaled, biased, and processed using a pixel map. The results are clamped to an appropriate range depending on the data type, and then either written in the texture memory for use in texture mapping or rasterized to fragments.

If pixel data is read from the framebuffer, pixel-transfer operations (scale, bias, mapping, and clamping) are performed. The results are packed into an appropriate format and then returned to processor memory.

The pixel copy operation is similar to a combination of the unpacking and transfer operations, except that packing and unpacking is unnecessary, and only a single pass is made through the transfer operations before the data is written back into the framebuffer.

Fragment Operations

If texturing is enabled, a texel is generated from texture memory for each fragment and applied to the fragment. Then fog calculations are performed, if they're enabled, followed by coverage (antialiasing) calculations if antialiasing is enabled.

Next comes scissoring, followed by the alpha test (in RGBA mode only), the stencil test, the depth-buffer test, and dithering. All of these operations can be disabled. Next, if in index mode, a logical operation is applied if one has been specified. If in RGBA mode, blending is performed.

The fragment is then masked by a color mask or an index mask, depending on the mode, and drawn into the appropriate buffer. If fragments are being written into the stencil or depth buffer, masking occurs after the stencil and depth tests, and the results are drawn into the framebuffer without performing the blending, dithering, or logical operation.

Odds and Ends

Matrix operations deal with the current matrix stack, which can be the modelview, the projection, or the texture matrix stack. The commands **glMultMatrix*()**, **glLoadMatrix*()**, and **glLoadIdentity()** are applied to the top matrix on the stack, while **glTranslate*()**, **glRotate*()**, **glScale*()**, **glOrtho()**, and **glFrustum()** are used to create a matrix that's multiplied by the top matrix. When the modelview matrix is modified, its inverse is also generated for normal vector transformation.

The commands that set the current raster position are treated exactly like a vertex command up until when rasterization would occur. At this point, the value is saved and is used in the rasterization of pixel data.

The various **glClear()** commands bypass all operations except scissoring, dithering, and writemasking.

OpenGL State Variables

This appendix lists the queryable OpenGL state variables, their default values, and the commands for obtaining the values of these variables. It also describes OpenGL's error handling facility, and how to save and restore sets of state variables. The *OpenGL Reference Manual* contains detailed information on all the commands and constants discussed in this appendix. This appendix has these major sections:

- "The Query Commands"

- "Error Handling"

- "Saving and Restoring Sets of State Variables"

- "OpenGL State Variables"

The Query Commands

There are four commands for obtaining simple state variables, and one for determining whether a particular state is enabled or disabled.

---

void **glGetBooleanv**(GLenum *pname*, GLboolean **params*);
void **glGetIntegerv**(GLenum *pname*, GLint **params*);
void **glGetFloatv**(GLenum *pname*, GLfloat **params*);
void **glGetDoublev**(GLenum *pname*, GLdouble **params*);

Obtains Boolean, integer, floating-point, or double-precision state variables. The *pname* argument is a symbolic constant indicating the state variable to return, and *params* is a pointer to an array of the indicated type in which to place the returned data. The possible values for *pname* are listed in the tables in "OpenGL State Variables" on page 422. A type conversion is performed if necessary to return the desired variable as the requested data type.

GLboolean **glIsEnabled**(GLenum *cap*);

Returns GL_TRUE if the mode specified by *cap* is enabled; otherwise, returns GL_FALSE. The possible values for *cap* are listed in the tables in "OpenGL State Variables" on page 422.

Other specialized commands return specific state variables. The prototypes for these commands are listed here; to find out when you need to use these commands, use the tables in "OpenGL State Variables" on page 422. Also see the *OpenGL Reference Manual*. OpenGL's error handling facility and the **glGetError**() command are described in more detail in the next section.

void **glGetClipPlane**(GLenum *plane*, GLdouble **equation*);

GLenum **glGetError**(void);

void **glGetLight**{if}**v**(GLenum *light*, GLenum *pname*, TYPE **params*);

void **glGetMap**{ifd}**v**(GLenum *target*, GLenum *query*, TYPE **v*);

void **glGetMaterial**{if}**v**(GLenum *face*, GLenum *pname*, TYPE **params*);

void **glGetPixelMap**{f ui us}**v**(GLenum *map*, TYPE **values*);

void **glGetPolygonStipple**(GLubyte *mask*);

const GLubyte * **glGetString**(GLenum *name*);

void **glGetTexEnv**{if}**v**(GLenum *target*, GLenum *pname*,
TYPE *params*);

void **glGetTexGen**{ifd}**v**(GLenum *coord*, GLenum *pname*,
TYPE *params*);

void **glGetTexImage**(GLenum *target*, GLint *level*, GLenum *format*,
GLenum *type*, GLvoid *pixels*);

void **glGetTexLevelParameter**{if}**v**(GLenum *target*, GLint *level*,
GLenum *pname*, TYPE *params*);

void **glGetTexParameter**{if}**v**(GLenum *target*, GLenum *pname*,
TYPE *params*);

Error Handling

When OpenGL detects an error, it records a current error code. The command that caused the error is ignored, so it has no effect on OpenGL state or on the framebuffer contents. (If the error recorded was GL_OUT_OF_MEMORY, however, the results of the command are undefined.) Once recorded, the current error code isn't cleared—that is, additional errors aren't recorded—until you call the query command **glGetError**(), which returns the current error code. In distributed implementations of OpenGL, there might be multiple current error codes, each of which remains set until queried. Once you've queried all the current error codes, or if there's no error, **glGetError**() returns GL_NO_ERROR. Thus, if you obtain an error code, it's good practice to continue to call **glGetError**() until GL_NO_ERROR is returned to be sure you've discovered all the errors. Table B-1 lists the defined OpenGL error codes.

You can use the GLU routine **gluErrorString**() to obtain a descriptive string corresponding to the error code passed in. This routine is described in more detail in "Describing Errors" on page 453. Note that GLU routines often return error values if an error is detected. Also, the GLU defines the error codes GLU_INVALID_ENUM, GLU_INVALID_VALUE, and GLU_OUT_OF_MEMORY, which have the same meaning as the related OpenGL codes.

Error Code	Description
GL_INVALID_ENUM	GLenum argument out of range
GL_INVALID_VALUE	Numeric argument out of range
GL_INVALID_OPERATION	Operation illegal in current state
GL_STACK_OVERFLOW	Command would cause a stack overflow
GL_STACK_UNDERFLOW	Command would cause a stack underflow
GL_OUT_OF_MEMORY	Not enough memory left to execute command

Table B-1   OpenGL Error Codes

Saving and Restoring Sets of State Variables

You can save and restore the values of a collection of state variables on an attribute stack with the commands **glPushAttrib()** and **glPopAttrib()**. The attribute stack has a depth of at least 16, and the actual depth can be obtained using GL_MAX_ATTRIB_STACK_DEPTH with **glGetIntegerv()**. Pushing a full stack or popping an empty one generates an error.

In general, it's faster to use **glPushAttrib()** and **glPopAttrib()** than to get and restore the values yourself. Some values might be pushed and popped in the hardware, and saving and restoring them might be expensive. Also, if you're operating on a remote client, all the attribute data has to be transferred across the network connection and back as it's saved and restored. However, your OpenGL implementation keeps the attribute stack on the server, avoiding unnecessary network delays.

void **glPushAttrib**(GLbitfield *mask*);

Saves all the attributes indicated by bits in *mask* by pushing them onto the attribute stack. Table B-2 lists the possible mask bits that can be logically ORed together to save any combination of attributes. Each bit corresponds to a collection of individual state variables. For example, GL_LIGHTING_BIT refers to all the state variables related to lighting, which include the current material color, the ambient, diffuse, specular, and emitted light, a list of the lights that are enabled, and the directions of the spotlights. When **glPopAttrib()** is called, all those variables are restored. To find out exactly which attributes are saved for particular mask values, see the tables in "OpenGL State Variables."

Mask Bit	Attribute Group
GL_ACCUM_BUFFER_BIT	accum-buffer
GL_ALL_ATTRIB_BITS	--
GL_COLOR_BUFFER_BIT	color-buffer
GL_CURRENT_BIT	current
GL_DEPTH_BUFFER_BIT	depth-buffer
GL_ENABLE_BIT	enable
GL_EVAL_BIT	eval
GL_FOG_BIT	fog
GL_HINT_BIT	hint
GL_LIGHTING_BIT	lighting
GL_LINE_BIT	line
GL_LIST_BIT	list
GL_PIXEL_MODE_BIT	pixel
GL_POINT_BIT	point
GL_POLYGON_BIT	polygon
GL_POLYGON_STIPPLE_BIT	polygon-stipple

Table B-2 Attribute Groups

Mask Bit	Attribute Group
GL_SCISSOR_BIT	scissor
GL_STENCIL_BUFFER_BIT	stencil-buffer
GL_TEXTURE_BIT	texture
GL_TRANSFORM_BIT	transform
GL_VIEWPORT_BIT	viewport

Table B-2 Attribute Groups, continued

---

void **glPopAttrib**(void);

Restores the values of those state variables that were saved with the last **glPushAttrib**().

OpenGL State Variables

The following pages contain tables that list the names of queryable state variables. For each variable, the tables list a description of it, its attribute group, its initial or minimum value, and the suggested **glGet*()** command to use for obtaining it. State variables that can be obtained using **glGetBooleanv()**, **glGetIntegerv()**, **glGetFloatv()**, or **glGetDoublev()** are listed with just one of these commands—the one that's most appropriate given the type of data to be returned. These state variables can't be obtained using **glIsEnabled()**. However, state variables for which **glIsEnabled()** is listed as the query command can also be obtained using **glGetBooleanv()**, **glGetIntegerv()**, **glGetFloatv()**, and **glGetDoublev()**. State variables for which any other command is listed as the query command can be obtained only by using that command. If no attribute group is listed, the variable doesn't belong to any group. All queryable state variables except the implementation-dependent ones have initial values. If no initial value is listed, you need to consult the section where that variable is discussed (or the *OpenGL Reference Manual*) to determine its initial value.

Current Values and Associated Data

State Variable	Description	Attribute Group	Initial Value	Get Command
GL_CURRENT_COLOR	Current color	current	1, 1, 1, 1	glGetIntegerv(), glGetFloatv()
GL_CURRENT_INDEX	Current color index	current	1	glGetIntegerv(), glGetFloatv()
GL_CURRENT_TEXTURE_COORDS	Current texture coordinates	current	0, 0, 0, 1	glGetFloatv()
GL_CURRENT_NORMAL	Current normal	current	0, 0, 1	glGetFloatv()
GL_CURRENT_RASTER_POSITION	Current raster position	current	0, 0, 0, 1	glGetFloatv()
GL_CURRENT_RASTER_DISTANCE	Current raster distance	current	0	glGetFloatv()
GL_CURRENT_RASTER_COLOR	Color associated with raster position	current	1, 1, 1, 1	glGetIntegerv(), glGetFloatv()
GL_CURRENT_RASTER_INDEX	Color index associated with raster position	current	1	glGetIntegerv(), glGetFloatv()
GL_CURRENT_RASTER_TEXTURE_COORDS	Texture coordinates associated with raster position	current	0, 0, 0, 1	glGetFloatv()
GL_CURRENT_RASTER_POSITION_VALID	Raster position valid bit	current	GL_TRUE	glGetBooleanv()
GL_EDGE_FLAG	Edge flag	current	GL_TRUE	glGetBooleanv()

Table B-3   State Variables for Current Values and Associated Data

Transformation

State Variable	Description	Attribute Group	Initial Value	Get Command
GL_MODELVIEW_MATRIX	Modelview matrix stack	--	Identity	glGetFloatv()
GL_PROJECTION_MATRIX	Projection matrix stack	--	Identity	glGetFloatv()
GL_TEXTURE_MATRIX	Texture matrix stack	--	Identity	glGetFloatv()
GL_VIEWPORT	Viewport origin and extent	viewport	--	glGetIntegerv()
GL_DEPTH_RANGE	Depth range near and far	viewport	0, 1	glGetFloatv()
GL_MODELVIEW_STACK_DEPTH	Modelview matrix stack pointer	--	1	glGetIntegerv()
GL_PROJECTION_STACK_DEPTH	Projection matrix stack pointer	--	1	glGetIntegerv()
GL_TEXTURE_STACK_DEPTH	Texture matrix stack pointer	--	1	glGetIntegerv()
GL_MATRIX_MODE	Current matrix mode	transform	GL_MODELVIEW	glGetIntegerv()
GL_NORMALIZE	Current normal normalization on/off	transform/ enable	GL_FALSE	glIsEnabled()
GL_CLIP_PLANE*i*	User clipping plane coefficients	transform	0, 0, 0, 0	glGetClipPlane()
GL_CLIP_PLANE*i*	*i*th user clipping plane enabled	transform/ enable	GL_FALSE	glIsEnabled()

Table B-4   Transformation State Variables

Coloring

State Variable	Description	Attribute Group	Initial Value	Get Command
GL_FOG_COLOR	Fog color	fog	0, 0, 0, 0	glGetFloatv()
GL_FOG_INDEX	Fog index	fog	0	glGetFloatv()
GL_FOG_DENSITY	Exponential fog density	fog	1.0	glGetFloatv()
GL_FOG_START	Linear fog start	fog	0.0	glGetFloatv()
GL_FOG_END	Linear fog end	fog	1.0	glGetFloatv()
GL_FOG_MODE	Fog mode	fog	GL_EXP	glGetIntegerv()
GL_FOG	True if fog enabled	fog/enable	GL_FALSE	glIsEnabled()
GL_SHADE_MODEL	glShadeModel() setting	lighting	GL_SMOOTH	glGetIntegerv()

Table B-5   Coloring State Variables

Lighting

State Variable	Description	Attribute Group	Initial Value	Get Command
GL_LIGHTING	True if lighting is enabled	lighting /enable	GL_FALSE	glIsEnabled()
GL_COLOR_MATERIAL	True if color tracking is enabled	lighting	GL_FALSE	glIsEnabled()
GL_COLOR_MATERIAL_PARAMETER	Material properties tracking current color	lighting	GL_AMBIENT_ AND_DIFFUSE	glGetIntegerv()
GL_COLOR_MATERIAL_FACE	Face(s) affected by color tracking	lighting	GL_FRONT_ AND_BACK	glGetIntegerv()
GL_AMBIENT	Ambient material color	lighting	(0.2, 0.2, 0.2, 1.0)	glGetMaterialfv()
GL_DIFFUSE	Diffuse material color	lighting	(0.8, 0.8, 0.8, 1.0)	glGetMaterialfv()
GL_SPECULAR	Specular material color	lighting	(0.0, 0.0, 0.0, 1.0)	glGetMaterialfv()
GL_EMISSION	Emissive material color	lighting	(0.0, 0.0, 0.0, 1.0)	glGetMaterialfv()
GL_SHININESS	Specular exponent of material	lighting	0.0	glGetMaterialfv()
GL_LIGHT_MODEL_AMBIENT	Ambient scene color	lighting	(0.2, 0.2, 0.2, 1.0)	glGetFloatv()
GL_LIGHT_MODEL_LOCAL_VIEWER	Viewer is local	lighting	GL_FALSE	glGetBooleanv()
GL_LIGHT_MODEL_TWO_SIDE	Use two-sided lighting	lighting	GL_FALSE	glGetBooleanv()

Table B-6   Lighting State Variables (see also Table 6-1 and Table 6-2 for initial values)

Lighting, continued

State Variable	Description	Attribute Group	Initial Value	Get Command
GL_AMBIENT	Ambient intensity of light i	lighting	(0.0,0.0,0.0,1.0)	glGetLightfv()
GL_DIFFUSE	Diffuse intensity of light i	lighting	--	glGetLightfv()
GL_SPECULAR	Specular intensity of light i	lighting	--	glGetLightfv()
GL_POSITION	Position of light i	lighting	(0.0, 0.0, 1.0, 0.0)	glGetLightfv()
GL_CONSTANT_ATTENUATION	Constant attenuation factor	lighting	1.0	glGetLightfv()
GL_LINEAR_ATTENUATION	Linear attenuation factor	lighting	0.0	glGetLightfv()
GL_QUADRATIC_ATTENUATION	Quadratic attenuation factor	lighting	0.0	glGetLightfv()
GL_SPOT_DIRECTION	Spotlight direction of light i	lighting	(0.0, 0.0, −1.0)	glGetLightfv()
GL_SPOT_EXPONENT	Spotlight exponent of light i	lighting	0.0	glGetLightfv()
GL_SPOT_CUTOFF	Spotlight angle of light i	lighting	180.0	glGetLightfv()
GL_LIGHTi	True if light i enabled	lighting/ enable	GL_FALSE	glIsEnabled()
GL_COLOR_INDEXES	c_a, c_d, and c_s for color-index lighting	lighting/ enable	0, 1, 1	glGetFloatv()

Table B-6 Lighting State Variables, continued

Rasterization

State Variable	Description	Attribute Group	Initial Value	Get Command
GL_POINT_SIZE	Point size	point	1.0	glGetFloatv()
GL_POINT_SMOOTH	Point antialiasing on	point/enable	GL_FALSE	glIsEnabled()
GL_LINE_WIDTH	Line width	line	1.0	glGetFloatv()
GL_LINE_SMOOTH	Line antialiasing on	line/enable	GL_FALSE	glIsEnabled()
GL_LINE_STIPPLE_PATTERN	Line stipple	line	1's	glGetIntegerv()
GL_LINE_STIPPLE_REPEAT	Line stipple repeat	line	1	glGetIntegerv()
GL_LINE_STIPPLE	Line stipple enable	line/enable	GL_FALSE	glIsEnabled()
GL_CULL_FACE	Polygon culling enabled	polygon/enable	GL_FALSE	glIsEnabled()
GL_CULL_FACE_MODE	Cull front-/back-facing polygons	polygon	GL_BACK	glGetIntegerv()
GL_FRONT_FACE	Polygon front-face CW/CCW indicator	polygon	GL_CCW	glGetIntegerv()
GL_POLYGON_SMOOTH	Polygon antialiasing on	polygon/enable	GL_FALSE	glIsEnabled()
GL_POLYGON_MODE	Polygon rasterization mode (front and back)	polygon	GL_FILL	glGetIntegerv()
GL_POLYGON_STIPPLE	Polygon stipple enable	polygon/enable	GL_FALSE	glIsEnabled()
--	Polygon stipple pattern	polygon-stipple	1's	glGetPolygon-Stipple()

Table B-7 Rasterization State Variables

Texturing

State Variable	Description	Attribute Group	Initial Value	Get Command
GL_TEXTURE_x	True if x-D texturing enabled (x is 1D or 2D)	texture/ enable	GL_FALSE	glIsEnabled()
GL_TEXTURE	x-D texture image at level of detail i	--	--	glGetTexImage()
GL_TEXTURE_WIDTH	x-D texture image i's width	--	0	glGetTexLevelParameter()
GL_TEXTURE_HEIGHT	x-D texture image i's height	--	0	glGetTexLevelParameter()
GL_TEXTURE_BORDER	x-D texture image i's border width	--	0	glGetTexLevelParameter()
GL_TEXTURE_COMPONENTS	Texture image components	--	1	glGetTexLevelParameter()
GL_TEXTURE_BORDER_COLOR	Texture border color	texture	0, 0, 0, 0	glGetTexParameter()
GL_TEXTURE_MIN_FILTER	Texture minification function	texture	GL_NEAREST_ MIPMAP_ LINEAR	glGetTexParameter()
GL_TEXTURE_MAG_FILTER	Texture magnification function	texture	GL_LINEAR	glGetTexParameter()
GL_TEXTURE_WRAP_x	Texture wrap mode (x is S or T)	texture	GL_REPEAT	glGetTexParameter()
GL_TEXTURE_ENV_MODE	Texture application function	texture	GL_MODULATE	glGetTexEnviv()

Table B-8   Texturing State Variables

Texturing, continued

State Variable	Description	Attribute Group	Initial Value	Get Command
GL_TEXTURE_ENV_COLOR	Texture environment color	texture	0, 0, 0, 0	glGetTexEnvfv()
GL_TEXTURE_GEN_x	Texgen enabled (x is S, T, R, or Q)	texture/ enable	GL_FALSE	glIsEnabled()
GL_EYE_LINEAR	Texgen plane equation coefficients	texture	--	glGetTexGenfv()
GL_OBJECT_LINEAR	Texgen object linear coefficients	texture	--	glGetTexGenfv()
GL_TEXTURE_GEN_MODE	Function used for texgen	texture	GL_EYE_LINEAR	glGetTexGeniv()

Table B-8   Texturing State Variables, continued

Pixel Operations

State Variable	Description	Attribute Group	Initial Value	Get Command
GL_SCISSOR_TEST	Scissoring enabled	scissor/enable	GL_FALSE	glIsEnabled()
GL_SCISSOR_BOX	Scissor box	scissor	--	glGetIntegerv()
GL_STENCIL_TEST	Stenciling enabled	stencil-buffer/ enable	GL_FALSE	glIsEnabled()
GL_STENCIL_FUNC	Stencil function	stencil-buffer	GL_ALWAYS	glGetIntegerv()
GL_STENCIL_VALUE_MASK	Stencil mask	stencil-buffer	1's	glGetIntegerv()
GL_STENCIL_REF	Stencil reference value	stencil-buffer	0	glGetIntegerv()
GL_STENCIL_FAIL	Stencil fail action	stencil-buffer	GL_KEEP	glGetIntegerv()
GL_STENCIL_PASS_DEPTH_FAIL	Stencil depth buffer fail action	stencil-buffer	GL_KEEP	glGetIntegerv()
GL_STENCIL_PASS_DEPTH_PASS	Stencil depth buffer pass action	stencil-buffer	GL_KEEP	glGetIntegerv()
GL_ALPHA_TEST	Alpha test enabled	color-buffer/ enable	GL_FALSE	glIsEnabled()
GL_ALPHA_TEST_FUNC	Alpha test function	color-buffer	GL_ALWAYS	glGetIntegerv()
GL_ALPHA_TEST_REF	Alpha test reference value	color-buffer	0	glGetIntegerv()
GL_DEPTH_TEST	Depth buffer enabled	depth-buffer/ enable	GL_FALSE	glIsEnabled()

Table B-9 Pixel Operations

Pixel Operations, continued

State Variable	Description	Attribute Group	Initial Value	Get Command
GL_DEPTH_FUNC	Depth buffer test function	depth-buffer	GL_LESS	glGetIntegerv()
GL_BLEND	Blending enabled	color-buffer/enable	GL_FALSE	glIsEnabled()
GL_BLEND_SRC	Blending source function	color-buffer	GL_ONE	glGetIntegerv()
GL_BLEND_DST	Blending destination function	color-buffer	GL_ZERO	glGetIntegerv()
GL_LOGIC_OP	Logical operation enabled	color-buffer/enable	GL_FALSE	glIsEnabled()
GL_LOGIC_OP_MODE	Logical operation function	color-buffer	GL_COPY	glGetIntegerv()
GL_DITHER	Dithering enabled	color-buffer/enable	GL_TRUE	glIsEnabled()

Table B-9   Pixel Operations, continued

Framebuffer Control

State Variable	Description	Attribute Group	Initial Value	Get Command
GL_DRAW_BUFFER	Buffers selected for drawing	color-buffer	--	glGetIntegerv()
GL_INDEX_WRITEMASK	Color-index writemask	color-buffer	1's	glGetIntegerv()
GL_COLOR_WRITEMASK	Color write enables; R, G, B, or A	color-buffer	GL_TRUE	glGetBooleanv()
GL_DEPTH_WRITEMASK	Depth buffer enabled for writing	depth-buffer	GL_TRUE	glGetBooleanv()
GL_STENCIL_WRITEMASK	Stencil-buffer writemask	stencil-buffer	1's	glGetIntegerv()
GL_COLOR_CLEAR_VALUE	Color-buffer clear value (RGBA mode)	color-buffer	0, 0, 0, 0	glGetFloatv()
GL_INDEX_CLEAR_VALUE	Color-buffer clear value (color-index mode)	color-buffer	0	glGetFloatv()
GL_DEPTH_CLEAR_VALUE	Depth-buffer clear value	depth-buffer	1	glGetIntegerv()
GL_STENCIL_CLEAR_VALUE	Stencil-buffer clear value	stencil-buffer	0	glGetIntegerv()
GL_ACCUM_CLEAR_VALUE	Accumulation-buffer clear value	accum-buffer	0	glGetFloatv()

Table B-10 Framebuffer Control State Variables

Pixels

State Variable	Description	Attribute Group	Initial Value	Get Command
GL_UNPACK_SWAP_BYTES	Value of GL_UNPACK_SWAP_BYTES	--	GL_FALSE	glGetBooleanv()
GL_UNPACK_LSB_FIRST	Value of GL_UNPACK_LSB_FIRST	--	GL_FALSE	glGetBooleanv()
GL_UNPACK_ROW_LENGTH	Value of GL_UNPACK_ROW_LENGTH	--	0	glGetIntegerv()
GL_UNPACK_SKIP_ROWS	Value of GL_UNPACK_SKIP_ROWS	--	0	glGetIntegerv()
GL_UNPACK_SKIP_PIXELS	Value of GL_UNPACK_SKIP_PIXELS	--	0	glGetIntegerv()
GL_UNPACK_ALIGNMENT	Value of GL_UNPACK_ALIGNMENT	--	4	glGetIntegerv()
GL_PACK_SWAP_BYTES	Value of GL_PACK_SWAP_BYTES	--	GL_FALSE	glGetBooleanv()
GL_PACK_LSB_FIRST	Value of GL_PACK_LSB_FIRST	--	GL_FALSE	glGetBooleanv()
GL_PACK_ROW_LENGTH	Value of GL_PACK_ROW_LENGTH	--	0	glGetIntegerv()
GL_PACK_SKIP_ROWS	Value of GL_PACK_SKIP_ROWS	--	0	glGetIntegerv()
GL_PACK_SKIP_PIXELS	Value of GL_PACK_SKIP_PIXELS	--	0	glGetIntegerv()
GL_PACK_ALIGNMENT	Value of GL_PACK_ALIGNMENT	--	4	glGetIntegerv()
GL_MAP_COLOR	True if colors are mapped	pixel	GL_FALSE	glGetBooleanv()
GL_MAP_STENCIL	True if stencil values are mapped	pixel	GL_FALSE	glGetBooleanv()

Table B-11 Pixel State Variables

Pixels, continued

State Variable	Description	Attribute Group	Initial Value	Get Command
GL_INDEX_SHIFT	Value of GL_INDEX_SHIFT	pixel	0	glGetIntegerv()
GL_INDEX_OFFSET	Value of GL_INDEX_OFFSET	pixel	0	glGetIntegerv()
GL_x_SCALE	Value of GL_x_SCALE; x is GL_RED, GL_GREEN, GL_BLUE, GL_ALPHA, or GL_DEPTH	pixel	1	glGetFloatv()
GL_x_BIAS	Value of GL_x_BIAS; x is one of GL_RED, GL_GREEN, GL_BLUE, GL_ALPHA, or GL_DEPTH	pixel	0	glGetFloatv()
GL_ZOOM_X	x zoom factor	pixel	1.0	glGetFloatv()
GL_ZOOM_Y	y zoom factor	pixel	1.0	glGetFloatv()
GL_x	glPixelMap() translation tables; x is a map name from Table 8-5	pixel	0's	glGetPixelMap()
GL_x_SIZE	Size of table x	pixel	1	glGetIntegerv()
GL_READ_BUFFER	Read source buffer	pixel	--	glGetIntegerv()

Table B-11 Pixel State Variables, continued

Evaluators

State Variable	Description	Attribute Group	Initial Value	Get Command
GL_ORDER	1D map order	--	1	glGetMapiv()
GL_ORDER	2D map orders	--	1, 1	glGetMapiv()
GL_COEFF	1D control points	--	--	glGetMapfv()
GL_COEFF	2D control points	--	--	glGetMapfv()
GL_DOMAIN	1D domain endpoints	--	--	glGetMapfv()
GL_DOMAIN	2D domain endpoints	--	--	glGetMapfv()
GL_MAP1_x	1D map enables: x is map type	eval/enable	GL_FALSE	glIsEnabled()
GL_MAP2_x	2D map enables: x is map type	eval/enable	GL_FALSE	glIsEnabled()
GL_MAP1_GRID_DOMAIN	1D grid endpoints	eval	0, 1	glGetFloatv()
GL_MAP2_GRID_DOMAIN	2D grid endpoints	eval	0, 1; 0, 1	glGetFloatv()
GL_MAP1_GRID_SEGMENTS	1D grid divisions	eval	1	glGetFloatv()
GL_MAP2_GRID_SEGMENTS	2D grid divisions	eval	1,1	glGetFloatv()
GL_AUTO_NORMAL	True if automatic normal generation enabled	eval	GL_FALSE	glIsEnabled()

Table B-12 Evaluator State Variables

Hints

State Variable	Description	Attribute Group	Initial Value	Get Command
GL_PERSPECTIVE_CORRECTION_HINT	Perspective correction hint	hint	GL_DONT_CARE	glGetIntegerv()
GL_POINT_SMOOTH_HINT	Point smooth hint	hint	GL_DONT_CARE	glGetIntegerv()
GL_LINE_SMOOTH_HINT	Line smooth hint	hint	GL_DONT_CARE	glGetIntegerv()
GL_POLYGON_SMOOTH_HINT	Polygon smooth hint	hint	GL_DONT_CARE	glGetIntegerv()
GL_FOG_HINT	Fog hint	hint	GL_DONT_CARE	glGetIntegerv()

Table B-13 Hint State Variables

Implementation-Dependent Values

State Variable	Description	Attribute Group	Minimum Value	Get Command
GL_MAX_LIGHTS	Maximum number of lights	--	8	glGetIntegerv()
GL_MAX_CLIP_PLANES	Maximum number of user clipping planes	--	6	glGetIntegerv()
GL_MAX_MODELVIEW_STACK_DEPTH	Maximum modelview-matrix stack depth	--	32	glGetIntegerv()
GL_MAX_PROJECTION_STACK_DEPTH	Maximum projection-matrix stack depth	--	2	glGetIntegerv()
GL_MAX_TEXTURE_STACK_DEPTH	Maximum depth of texture matrix stack	--	2	glGetIntegerv()
GL_SUBPIXEL_BITS	Number of bits of subpixel precision in x and y	--	4	glGetIntegerv()
GL_MAX_TEXTURE_SIZE	Maximum height or width of a texture image (w/o borders)	--	64	glGetIntegerv()
GL_MAX_PIXEL_MAP_TABLE	Maximum size of a glPixelMap() translation table	--	32	glGetIntegerv()
GL_MAX_NAME_STACK_DEPTH	Maximum selection-name stack depth	--	64	glGetIntegerv()
GL_MAX_LIST_NESTING	Maximum display-list call nesting	--	64	glGetIntegerv()

Table B-14 Implementation-Dependent State Variables

Implementation-Dependent Values, continued

State Variable	Description	Attribute Group	Initial Value	Get Command
GL_MAX_EVAL_ORDER	Maximum evaluator polynomial order	--	8	glGetIntegerv()
GL_MAX_VIEWPORT_DIMS	Maximum viewport dimensions	--	--	glGetIntegerv()
GL_MAX_ATTRIB_STACK_DEPTH	Maximum depth of the attribute stack	--	16	glGetIntegerv()
GL_AUX_BUFFERS	Number of auxiliary buffers	--	0	glGetBooleanv()
GL_RGBA_MODE	True if color buffers store RGBA	--	--	glGetBooleanv()
GL_INDEX_MODE	True if color buffers store indices	--	--	glGetBooleanv()
GL_DOUBLEBUFFER	True if front & back buffers exist	--	--	glGetBooleanv()
GL_STEREO	True if left & right buffers exist	--	--	glGetFloatv()
GL_POINT_SIZE_RANGE	Range (low to high) of antialiased point sizes	--	1, 1	glGetFloatv()
GL_POINT_SIZE_GRANULARITY	Antialiased point-size granularity	--	--	glGetFloatv()
GL_LINE_WIDTH_RANGE	Range (low to high) of antialiased line widths	--	1, 1	glGetFloatv()
GL_LINE_WIDTH_GRANULARITY	Antialiased line-width granularity	--	--	glGetFloatv()

Table B-14 Implementation-Dependent State Variables, continued

Implementation-Dependent Pixel Depths

State Variable	Description	Attribute Group	Initial Value	Get Command
GL_RED_BITS	Number of bits per red component in color buffers	--	--	glGetIntegerv()
GL_GREEN_BITS	Number of bits per green component in color buffers	--	--	glGetIntegerv()
GL_BLUE_BITS	Number of bits per blue component in color buffers	--	--	glGetIntegerv()
GL_ALPHA_BITS	Number of bits per alpha component in color buffers	--	--	glGetIntegerv()
GL_INDEX_BITS	Number of bits per index in color buffers	--	--	glGetIntegerv()
GL_DEPTH_BITS	Number of depth-buffer bitplanes	--	--	glGetIntegerv()
GL_STENCIL_BITS	Number of stencil bitplanes	--	--	glGetIntegerv()
GL_ACCUM_RED_BITS	Number of bits per red component in the accumulation buffer	--	--	glGetIntegerv()
GL_ACCUM_GREEN_BITS	Number of bits per green component in the accumulation buffer	--	--	glGetIntegerv()
GL_ACCUM_BLUE_BITS	Number of bits per blue component in the accumulation buffer	--	--	glGetIntegerv()
GL_ACCUM_ALPHA_BITS	Number of bits per alpha component in the accumulation buffer	--	--	glGetIntegerv()

Table B-15 Implementation-Dependent Pixel-Depth State Variables

Miscellaneous

State Variable	Description	Attribute Group	Initial Value	Get Command
GL_LIST_BASE	Setting of glListBase()	list	0	glGetIntegerv()
GL_LIST_INDEX	Number of display list under construction; 0 if none	--	0	glGetIntegerv()
GL_LIST_MODE	Mode of display list under construction; undefined if none	--	0	glGetIntegerv()
GL_ATTRIB_STACK_DEPTH	Attribute stack pointer	--	0	glGetIntegerv()
GL_NAME_STACK_DEPTH	Name stack depth	--	0	glGetIntegerv()
GL_RENDER_MODE	glRenderMode() setting	--	GL_RENDER	glGetIntegerv()
--	Current error code(s)	--	0	glGetError()

Table B-16 Miscellaneous State Variables

The OpenGL Utility Library

OpenGL provides a powerful but small set of drawing operations, and all higher-level drawing must be done in terms of these. To help simplify some of your programming tasks, the OpenGL Utility Library (GLU) includes several routines that encapsulate OpenGL commands. Many of these routines are described in earlier chapters as their topics arise; these routines are briefly listed here for completeness. GLU routines that aren't discussed earlier are described in more depth here. Nevertheless, you might want to consult the *OpenGL Reference Manual* for more detailed descriptions of all these routines. This appendix groups the GLU routines functionally as follows:

- **"Manipulating Images for Use in Texturing"**
- **"Transforming Coordinates"**
- **"Polygon Tessellation"**
- **"Rendering Spheres, Cylinders, and Disks"**
- **"NURBS Curves and Surfaces"**
- **"Describing Errors"**

Manipulating Images for Use in Texturing

As you set up texture mapping in your application, you'll probably want to take advantage of mipmapping, which requires a series of reduced images (or texture maps). To support mipmapping, the GLU includes a general routine that scales images (**gluScaleImage**()) and routines that generate a complete set of mipmaps given an original image in one or two dimensions (**gluBuild1DMipmaps**() and **gluBuild2DMipmaps**()). These routines are all discussed in some detail in Chapter 9, so here only their prototypes are listed:

GLint **gluScaleImage**(GLenum *format*, GLint *widthin*, GLint *heightin*,
GLenum *typein*, const void **datain*,
GLint *widthout*, GLint *heightout*,
GLenum *typeout*, void **dataout*);

GLint **gluBuild1DMipmaps**(GLenum *target*, GLint *components*,
GLint *width*, GLenum *format*, GLenum *type*,
void **data*);

GLint **gluBuild2DMipmaps**(GLenum *target*, GLint *components*,
GLint *width*, GLint *height*, GLenum *format*,
GLenum *type*, void **data*);

Transforming Coordinates

The GLU includes routines that create matrices for standard perspective and orthographic viewing (**gluPerspective**() and **gluOrtho2D**()). In addition, a viewing routine allows you to place your eye at any point in space and look at any other point (**gluLookAt**()). These routines are discussed in Chapter 3. In addition, the GLU includes a routine to help you create a picking matrix (**gluPickMatrix**()); this routine is discussed in Chapter 12. For your convenience, the prototypes for these four routines are listed here.

void **gluPerspective**(GLdouble *fovy*, GLdouble *aspect*, GLdouble *zNear*,
GLdouble *zFar*);

void **gluOrtho2D**(GLdouble *left*, GLdouble *right*, GLdouble *bottom*,
GLdouble *top*);

void **gluLookAt**(GLdouble *eyex*, GLdouble *eyey*, GLdouble *eyez*,
GLdouble *centerx*, GLdouble *centery*,
GLdouble *centerz*, GLdouble *upx*, GLdouble *upy*,
GLdouble *upz*);

void **gluPickMatrix**(GLdouble *x*, GLdouble *y*, GLdouble *width*,
GLdouble *height*, GLint *viewport*[4]);

In addition, GLU provides two routines that convert between object coordinates and screen coordinates, **gluProject()** and **gluUnProject()**.

GLint **gluProject**(GLdouble *objx*, GLdouble *objy*, GLdouble *objz*,
const GLdouble *modelMatrix*[16],
const GLdouble *projMatrix*[16],
const GLint *viewport*[4], GLdouble **winx*,
GLdouble **winy*, GLdouble **winz*);

Transforms the specified object coordinates *objx*, *objy*, and *objz* into window coordinates using *modelMatrix*, *projMatrix*, and *viewport*. The result is stored in *winx*, *winy*, and *winz*. A return value of GL_TRUE indicates success, and GL_FALSE indicates failure.

GLint **gluUnProject**(GLdouble *winx*, GLdouble *winy*, GLdouble *winz*,
const GLdouble *modelMatrix*[16],
const GLdouble *projMatrix*[16],
const GLint *viewport*[4], GLdouble **objx*,
GLdouble **objy*, GLdouble **objz*);

Transforms the specified window coordinates *winx*, *winy*, and *winz* into object coordinates using *modelMatrix*, *projMatrix*, and *viewport*. The result is stored in *objx*, *objy*, and *objz*. A return value of GL_TRUE indicates success, and GL_FALSE indicates failure.

Polygon Tessellation

As discussed in "Describing Points, Lines, and Polygons" on page 28, OpenGL can directly display only simple convex polygons. A polygon is simple if the edges intersect only at vertices, there are no duplicate vertices, and exactly two edges meet at any vertex. If your application requires the display of simple nonconvex polygons or of simple polygons containing holes, those polygons must first be subdivided into convex polygons before they can be displayed. Such subdivision is called *tessellation*. GLU provides a collection of routines that perform tessellation. Note that the GLU tessellation routines can't handle nonsimple polygons; there's no standard OpenGL method to handle such polygons.

Since tessellation is often required and can be rather tricky, this section describes the GLU tessellation routines in detail. These routines take as input arbitrary simple polygons that might include holes, and they return some combination of triangles, triangle meshes, and triangle fans. You can insist on only triangles if you don't want to have to deal with meshes or fans. If you care about performance, however, you should probably take advantage of any available mesh or fan information.

The Callback Mechanism

To tessellate a polygon using the GLU, first you need to create a tessellation object, and then provide a series of callback routines to be called at appropriate times during the tessellation. After you specify the callbacks, you describe the polygon and any holes using GLU routines, which are similar to the OpenGL polygon routines. When the polygon description is complete, the tessellation facility invokes your callback routines as necessary.

The callback routines typically save the data for the triangles, triangle meshes, and triangle fans in user-defined data structures, or in OpenGL display lists (see Chapter 4). To render the polygons, other code traverses the data structures or calls the display lists. Although the callback routines could call OpenGL commands to display them directly, this is usually not done, as tessellation can be computationally expensive. It's a good idea to save the data if there is any chance that you want to display it again. The GLU tessellation routines are guaranteed never to return any new vertices, so interpolation of vertices, texture coordinates, or colors is never required.

The Tessellation Object

As a complex polygon is being described and tessellated, it has associated data, such as the vertices, edges, and callback functions. All this data is tied to a single tessellation object. To do tessellation, your program first has to create a tessellation object using the routine **gluNewTess()**.

GLUtriangulatorObj* **gluNewTess**(void);

Creates a new tessellation object and returns a pointer to it. A null pointer is returned if the creation fails.

If you no longer need a tessellation object, you can delete it and free all associated memory with **gluDeleteTess()**.

void **gluDeleteTess**(GLUtriangulatorObj *tessobj);

Deletes the specified tessellation object, *tessobj*, and frees all associated memory.

A single tessellation object can be reused for all your tessellations. This object is required only because library routines might need to do their own tessellations, and they should be able to do so without interfering with any tessellation that your program is doing. It might also be useful to have multiple tessellation objects if you want to use different sets of callbacks for different tessellations. A typical program, however, allocates a single tessellation object and uses it for all its tessellations. There's no real need to free it because it uses a small amount of memory. On the other hand, if you're writing a library routine that uses the GLU tessellation, you'll want to be careful to free any tessellation objects you create.

Specifying Callbacks

You can specify up to five callback functions for a tessellation. Any functions that are omitted are simply not called during the tessellation, and any information they might have returned to your program is lost. All are specified by the single routine **gluTessCallback()**.

void **gluTessCallback**(GLUtriangulatorObj *tessobj*, GLenum *type*, void (*fn*)());

Associates the callback function *fn* with the tessellation object *tessobj*. The type of the callback is determined by the parameter *type*, which can be GLU_BEGIN, GLU_EDGE_FLAG, GLU_VERTEX, GLU_END, or GLU_ERROR. The five possible callback functions have the following prototypes:

GLU_BEGIN	void **begin**(GLenum *type*);
GLU_EDGE_FLAG	void **edgeFlag**(GLboolean *flag*);
GLU_VERTEX	void **vertex**(void *data*);
GLU_END	void **end**(void);
GLU_ERROR	void **error**(GLenum *errno*);

To change a callback routine, simply call **gluTessCallback()** with the new routine. To eliminate a callback routine without replacing it with a new one, pass **gluTessCallback()** a null pointer for the appropriate function.

As tessellation proceeds, these routines are called in a manner similar to the way you would use the OpenGL commands **glBegin()**, **glEdgeFlag*()**, **glVertex*()**, and **glEnd()**. (See "Marking Polygon Boundary Edges" on page 51 for more information about **glEdgeFlag*()**.) The error callback is invoked during the tessellation only if something goes wrong.

The GLU_BEGIN callback is invoked with one of three possible parameters: GL_TRIANGLE_FAN, GL_TRIANGLE_STRIP, or GL_TRIANGLES. After this routine is called, and before the callback associated with GLU_END is called, some combination of the GLU_EDGE_FLAG and GLU_VERTEX callbacks is invoked. The associated vertices and edge flags are interpreted exactly as they are in OpenGL between **glBegin**(GL_TRIANGLE_FAN), **glBegin**(GL_TRIANGLE_STRIP), or **glBegin**(GL_TRIANGLES) and the matching **glEnd()**. Since edge flags make no sense in a triangle fan or triangle strip, if there is a callback associated with GLU_EDGE_FLAG, the GLU_BEGIN callback is called only with GL_TRIANGLES. The GLU_EDGE_FLAG callback works exactly analogously to the OpenGL **glEdgeFlag*()** call.

The error callback is passed a GLU error number. A character string describing the error can be obtained using the routine **gluErrorString()**. See "Describing Errors" on page 453 for more information about this routine.

Describing the Polygon to Be Tessellated

The polygon to be tessellated, possibly containing holes, is specified using the following four routines: **gluBeginPolygon()**, **gluTessVertex()**, **gluNextContour()**, and **gluEndPolygon()**. For polygons without holes, the specification is exactly as in OpenGL: start with **gluBeginPolygon()**, call **gluTessVertex()** for each vertex in the boundary, and end the polygon with a call to **gluEndPolygon()**. If a polygon consists of multiple contours, including holes and holes within holes, the contours are specified one after the other, each preceded by **gluNextContour()**. When **gluEndPolygon()** is called, it signals the end of the final contour and starts the tessellation. You can omit the call to **gluNextContour()** before the first contour. The detailed descriptions of these functions follow.

---

void **gluBeginPolygon**(GLUtriangulatorObj *tessobj*);

Begins the specification of a polygon to be tessellated and associates a tessellation object, *tessobj*, with it. The callback functions to be used are those that were bound to the tessellation object using the routine **gluTessCallback()**.

---

void **gluTessVertex**(GLUtriangulatorObj *tessobj*,
           GLdouble *v*[3], void *data*);

Specifies a vertex in the polygon to be tessellated. Call this routine for each vertex in the polygon to be tessellated. *tessobj* is the tessellation object to use, *v* contains the three-dimensional vertex coordinates, and *data* is an arbitrary pointer that's sent to the callback associated with GLU_VERTEX. Typically, it contains vertex data, texture coordinates, color information, or whatever else the application may find useful.

void **gluNextContour**(GLUtriangulatorObj *tessobj*, GLenum *type*);

Marks the beginning of the next contour when multiple contours make up the boundary of the polygon to be tessellated. *type* can be GLU_EXTERIOR, GLU_INTERIOR, GLU_CCW, GLU_CW, or GLU_UNKNOWN. These serve only as hints to the tessellation. If you get them right, the tessellation might go faster. If you get them wrong, they're ignored, and the tesselation still works. For a polygon with holes, one contour is the exterior contour and the others interior. **gluNextContour**() can be called immediately after **gluBeginPolygon**(), but if it isn't, the first contour is assumed to be of type GLU_EXTERIOR. GLU_CW and GLU_CCW indicate clockwise- and counterclockwise-oriented polygons. Choosing which are clockwise and which are counterclockwise is arbitrary in three dimensions, but in any plane, there are two different orientations, and the GLU_CW and GLU_CCW types should be used consistently. Use GLU_UNKNOWN if you don't have a clue.

void **gluEndPolygon**(GLUtriangulatorObj *tessobj*);

Indicates the end of the polygon specification and that the tessellation can begin using the tessellation object *tessobj*.

Rendering Spheres, Cylinders, and Disks

The GLU includes a set of routines to draw various simple surfaces (spheres, cylinders, disks, and parts of disks) in a variety of styles and orientations. These routines are described in detail in the *OpenGL Reference Manual*; their use is discussed briefly in the following paragraphs, and their prototypes are also listed.

To create a quadric object, use **gluNewQuadric**(). (To destroy this object when you're finished with it, use **gluDeleteQuadric**().) Then specify the desired rendering style, as follows, with the appropriate routine (unless you're satisfied with the default values):

- Whether surface normals should be generated, and if so, whether there should be one normal per vertex or one normal per face: **gluQuadricNormals()**

- Whether texture coodinates should be generated: **gluQuadricTexture()**

- Which side of the quadric should be considered the outside and which the inside: **gluQuadricOrientation()**

- Whether the quadric should be drawn as a set of polygons, lines, or points: **gluQuadricDrawStyle()**

After you've specified the rendering style, simply invoke the rendering routine for the desired type of quadric object: **gluSphere()**, **gluCylinder()**, **gluDisk()**, or **gluPartialDisk()**. If an error occurs during rendering, the error-handling routine you've specified with **gluQuadricCallBack()** is invoked.

It's better to use the *Radius, height,* and similar arguments to scale the quadrics rather than the **glScale*()** command, so that unit-length normals that are generated don't have to be renormalized. Set the *loops* and *stacks* arguments to values other than 1 to force lighting calculations at a finer granularity, especially if the material specularity is high.

The prototypes are listed in three categories.

Manage quadric objects:

```
GLUquadricObj* gluNewQuadric (void);
void gluDeleteQuadric (GLUquadricObj *state);
void gluQuadricCallback (GLUquadricObj *qobj, GLenum which,
                void (*fn)());
```

Control the rendering:

```
void gluQuadricNormals (GLUquadricObj *quadObject,
                GLenum normals);
void gluQuadricTexture (GLUquadricObj *quadObject,
                GLboolean textureCoords);
void gluQuadricOrientation (GLUquadricObj *quadObject,
                GLenum orientation);
void gluQuadricDrawStyle (GLUquadricObj *quadObject,
                GLenum drawStyle);
```

Specify a quadric primitive:

> void **gluCylinder** (GLUquadricObj *qobj*, GLdouble *baseRadius*,
> > GLdouble *topRadius*, GLdouble *height*, GLint *slices*,
> > GLint *stacks*);
>
> void **gluDisk** (GLUquadricObj *qobj*, GLdouble *innerRadius*,
> > GLdouble *outerRadius*, GLint *slices*, GLint *loops*);
>
> void **gluPartialDisk** (GLUquadricObj *qobj*, GLdouble *innerRadius*,
> > GLdouble *outerRadius*, GLint *slices*, GLint *loops*,
> > GLdouble *startAngle*, GLdouble *sweepAngle*);
>
> void **gluSphere** (GLUquadricObj *qobj*, GLdouble *radius*, GLint *slices*,
> > GLint *stacks*);

NURBS Curves and Surfaces

NURBS routines provide general and powerful descriptions of curves and surfaces in two and three dimensions. They're used to represent geometry in many computer-aided mechanical design systems. The GLU NURBS routines can render such curves and surfaces in a variety of styles, and they can automatically handle adaptive subdivision that tessellates the domain into smaller triangles in regions of high curvature and near silhouette edges. All the GLU NURBS routines are described in Chapter 9; their prototypes are listed here.

Manage a NURBS object:

> GLUnurbsObj* **gluNewNurbsRenderer** (void);
> void **gluDeleteNurbsRenderer** (GLUnurbsObj *nobj*);
> void **gluNurbsCallback** (GLUnurbsObj *nobj*, GLenum *which*,
> > void (*fn*)());

Create a NURBS curve:

> void **gluBeginCurve** (GLUnurbsObj *nobj*);
> void **gluEndCurve** (GLUnurbsObj *nobj*);
> void **gluNurbsCurve** (GLUnurbsObj *nobj*, GLint *nknots*, GLfloat *knot*,
> > GLint *stride*, GLfloat *ctlarray*,
> > GLint *order*, GLenum *type*);

Create a NURBS surface:

> void **gluBeginSurface** (GLUnurbsObj *nobj*);
> void **gluEndSurface** (GLUnurbsObj *nobj*);

void **gluNurbsSurface** (GLUnurbsObj *nobj*, GLint *uknot_count*,
GLfloat *uknot*, GLint *vknot_count*, GLfloat *vknot*,
GLint *u_stride*, GLint *v_stride*, GLfloat *ctlarray*,
GLint *uorder*, GLint *vorder*, GLenum *type*);

Define a trimming region:

void **gluBeginTrim** (GLUnurbsObj *nobj*);
void **gluEndTrim** (GLUnurbsObj *nobj*);
void **gluPwlCurve** (GLUnurbsObj *nobj*, GLint *count*, GLfloat *array*,
GLint *stride*, GLenum *type*);

Control NURBS rendering:

void **gluLoadSamplingMatrices** (GLUnurbsObj *nobj*,
const GLfloat *modelMatrix*[16],
const GLfloat *projMatrix*[16],
const GLint *viewport*[4]);
void **gluNurbsProperty** (GLUnurbsObj *nobj*, GLenum *property*,
GLfloat *value*);
void **gluGetNurbsProperty** (GLUnurbsObj *nobj*, GLenum *property*,
GLfloat *value*);

Describing Errors

The GLU provides a routine for obtaining a descriptive string for an error code. For information about OpenGL's error handling facility, see "Error Handling" on page 419.

---

const GLubyte* **gluErrorString**(GLenum *errorCode*);

Returns a pointer to a descriptive string that corresponds to the OpenGL, GLU, or GLX error number passed in *errorCode*. The defined error codes are described in the *OpenGL Reference Manual* along with the command or routine that can generate them.

The OpenGL Extension to the X Window System

This appendix briefly discusses the routines defined as part of the OpenGL Extension to the X Window System (GLX). These routines are discussed in more detail in the *OpenGL Reference Manual*. You need to have some knowledge of X to fully understand the following and to use GLX successfully. This appendix has the following major sections:

- "Initialization"
- "Controlling Rendering"
- "GLX Prototypes"

In the X Window System, OpenGL rendering is made available as an extension to X in the formal X sense: Connection and authentication are accomplished with the normal X mechanisms. As with other X extensions, there is a defined network protocol for OpenGL's rendering commands encapsulated within the X byte stream. Since performance is critical in three-dimensional rendering, the OpenGL extension to X allows OpenGL to bypass the X server's involvement in data encoding, copying, and interpretation and instead render directly to the graphics pipeline.

Initialization

Use **glXQueryExtension()** and **glXQueryVersion()** to determine whether the GLX extension is defined for an X server, and if so, which version is present. The **glXChooseVisual()** routine returns a pointer to an XVisualInfo structure describing the visual that best meets the client's specified attributes. You can query a visual about its support of a particular OpenGL attribute with **glXGetConfig()**.

Controlling Rendering

Several GLX routines are provided for creating and managing an OpenGL rendering context. You can use such a context to render off-screen if you want. Routines are also provided for such tasks as synchronizing execution between the X and OpenGL streams, swapping front and back buffers, and using an X font.

Managing an OpenGL Rendering Context

An OpenGL rendering context is created with **glXCreateContext()**. One of the arguments to this routine allows you to request a direct rendering context that bypasses the X server as described previously. (Note that to do direct rendering, the X server connection must be local, and the OpenGL implementation needs to support direct rendering.) You can determine whether a GLX context is direct with **glXIsDirect()**.

To make a rendering context current, use **glXMakeCurrent()**; **glXGetCurrentContext()** returns the current context. You can also obtain the current drawable with **glXGetCurrentDrawable()**. Remember that only one context can be current for any thread at any one time. If you have multiple contexts, you can copy selected groups of OpenGL state variables from one context to another with **glXCopyContext()**. When you're finished with a particular context, destroy it with **glXDestroyContext()**.

Off-Screen Rendering

To render off-screen, first create an X Pixmap and then pass this as an argument to **glXCreateGLXPixmap()**. Once rendering is completed, you can destroy the association between the X and GLX Pixmaps with **glXDestroyGLXPixmap()**. (Off-screen rendering isn't guaranteed to be supported for direct renderers.)

Synchronizing Execution

To prevent X requests from executing until any outstanding OpenGL rendering is completed, call **glXWaitGL()**. Then, any previously issued OpenGL commands are guaranteed to be executed before any X rendering calls made after **glXWaitGL()**. Although the same result can be achieved with **glFinish()**, **glXWaitGL()** doesn't require a round trip to the server and thus is more efficient in cases where the client and server are on separate machines.

To prevent an OpenGL command sequence from executing until any outstanding X requests are completed, use **glXWaitX()**. This routine guarantees that previously issued X rendering calls are executed before any OpenGL calls made after **glXWaitX()**.

Swapping Buffers

For drawables that are double-buffered, the front and back buffers can be exchanged by calling **glXSwapBuffers()**. An implicit **glFlush()** is done as part of this routine.

Using an X Font

A shortcut for using X fonts in OpenGL is provided with the command **glXUseXFont()**.

GLX Prototypes

Initialization

Determine whether the GLX extension is defined on the X server:

Bool **glXQueryExtension** (Display *dpy*, int *errorBase*, int *eventBase*);
Bool **glXQueryVersion** (Display *dpy*, int *major*, int *minor*);

Obtain the desired visual:

XVisualInfo* **glXChooseVisual** (Display *dpy*, int *screen*, int *attribList*);
int **glXGetConfig** (Display *dpy*, XVisualInfo *vis*, int *attrib*, int *value*);

Controlling Rendering

Manage or query an OpenGL rendering context:

GLXContext **glXCreateContext** (Display *dpy*, XVisualInfo *vis*,
                GLXContext *shareList*, Bool *direct*);
void **glXDestroyContext** (Display *dpy*, GLXContext *ctx*);
void **glXCopyContext** (Display *dpy*, GLXContext *src*,
                GLXContext *dst*, GLuint *mask*);
Bool **glXIsDirect** (Display *dpy*, GLXContext *ctx*);
Bool **glXMakeCurrent** (Display *dpy*, GLXDrawable *draw*,
                GLXContext *ctx*);
GLXContext **glXGetCurrentContext** (void);
GLXDrawable **glXGetCurrentDrawable** (void);

Perform off-screen rendering:

GLXPixmap **glXCreateGLXPixmap** (Display *dpy*, XVisualInfo *vis*,
                Pixmap *pixmap*);
void **glXDestroyGLXPixmap** (Display *dpy*, GLXPixmap *pix*);

Synchronize execution:

void **glXWaitGL** (void);
void **glXWaitX** (void);

Exchange front and back buffers:

void **glXSwapBuffers** (Display *dpy*, Window *window*);

Use an X font:

> void **glXUseXFont** (Font *font*, int *first*, int *count*, int *listBase*);

The OpenGL Programming Guide
Auxiliary Library

This appendix describes the auxiliary library that was written using OpenGL for this guide. It has the following major sections:

- "Initializing and Exiting a Window"

- "Handling Window and Input Events"

- "Loading the Color Map"

- "Initializing and Drawing Three-Dimensional Objects"

- "Managing a Background Process"

- "Running the Program"

See "How to Obtain the Sample Code" on page vii for information about how to obtain the source code for the auxiliary library.

With the auxiliary library, your application structures its event handling to use callback functions. (This method is similar to using the Xt Toolkit, also known as the X Intrinsics, with a widget set.) For example, first you open a window and register callback routines for specific events. Then you create a main loop without an exit. In that loop, if an event occurs, its registered callback functions are executed. Upon completion of the callback functions, flow of control is returned to the main loop.

Initializing and Exiting a Window

Before you can open a window, you must specify its characteristics: Should it be single-buffered or double-buffered? Should it store colors as RGBA values or as color indices? Where should it appear on your display? To specify the answers to these questions, call **auxInitDisplayMode()** and **auxInitPosition()** before you call **auxInitWindow()** to open the window.

---

void **auxInitWindow**(GLbyte *titleString*);

Opens a window with the characteristics specified by **auxInitDisplayMode()** and **auxInitPosition()**. The string *titleString* appears in the title bar, if your window system does that sort of thing. The Escape key is bound to an exiting function that kills the window, exits the program, and generally cleans up. Also, the default color for the background is set to black for an RGBA window and to color index 0 for a color-index window.

---

void **auxInitDisplayMode**(GLbitfield *mask*);

Tells **auxInitWindow()** whether to create an RGBA or color-index window, or a single- or double-buffered window. You can also specify that the window have an associated depth, stencil, and/or accumulation buffer. The *mask* argument is a bitwise ORed combination of AUX_RGBA or AUX_INDEX, AUX_SINGLE or AUX_DOUBLE, and any of the buffer-enabling flags: AUX_DEPTH, AUX_STENCIL, or AUX_ACCUM. For example, for a double-buffered, RGBA-mode window with a depth and stencil buffer, use AUX_DOUBLE | AUX_RGBA | AUX_DEPTH | AUX_STENCIL. The default value is AUX_INDEX | AUX_SINGLE, or a color-index, single-buffered window.

void **auxInitPosition**(GLint *x*, GLint *y*, GLsizei *width*, GLsizei *height*);

Tells **auxInitWindow**() where to position a window on the screen. The arguments (*x*, *y*) indicate the location of the lower left corner of the window, and *width* and *height* indicate the window's size (in pixels). The default values are (0, 0) for (*x*, *y*) and (100, 100) for *(width, height)*.

Handling Window and Input Events

After the window is created, but before you enter the main loop, you should register callback functions using the following three routines.

void **auxReshapeFunc**(void (**function*)(GLsizei, GLsizei));

Specifies the function that's called whenever the window is resized, moved, or exposed. The argument *function* is a pointer to a function that expects two arguments, the new width and height of the window. Typically, *function* calls **glViewport**(), so that the display is clipped to the new size, and it redefines the projection matrix so that the aspect ratio of the projected image matches the viewport, avoiding aspect ratio distortion. If you don't call **auxReshapeFunc**(), a default reshape function is called, which assumes a two-dimensional orthographic projection. With this auxiliary library, the window is automatically redrawn after every reshaping event.

void **auxKeyFunc**(GLint *key*, void (**function*)(void));

Specifies the function, *function*, that's called when the keyboard key indicated by *key* is pressed. Use one of the defined auxiliary library constants for *key*: AUX_A through AUX_Z, AUX_a through AUX_z, AUX_0 through AUX_9, AUX_LEFT, AUX_RIGHT, AUX_UP, AUX_DOWN (the arrow keys), AUX_ESCAPE, AUX_SPACE, or AUX_RETURN. With this auxiliary library, the window is automatically redrawn after every processed key event, although in a real application, you might wait for several events to be completed before drawing.

void **auxMouseFunc**(GLint *button*, GLint *mode*,
                         void (**function*)(AUX_EVENTREC *));

Specifies the function, *function*, that's called when the mouse button indicated by *button* enters the mode defined by *mode*. The *button* argument can be AUX_LEFTBUTTON, AUX_MIDDLEBUTTON, or AUX_RIGHTBUTTON (assuming a right-handed setup). The *mode* argument indicates whether the button is clicked, AUX_MOUSEDOWN, or released, AUX_MOUSEUP. The *function* argument must take one argument, which is a pointer to a structure of type AUX_EVENTREC. The **auxMouseFunc**() routine allocates memory for the structure. For example, to determine the pointer coordinates at the time of the event, you might define *function* like this:

```
void function(AUX_EVENTREC *event)
{ GLint x, y;
    x = event->data[AUX_MOUSEX];
    y = event->data[AUX_MOUSEY];
    ...
}
```

Loading the Color Map

If you're using color-index mode, you might be surprised to discover there's no OpenGL routine to load a color into a color lookup table. This is because the process of loading a color map depends entirely on the window system. The auxiliary library provides a generalized routine to load a single color index with an RGB value, **auxSetOneColor**(). You need to implement this routine for your particular system.

void **auxSetOneColor**(GLint *index*, GLfloat *red*, GLfloat *green*,
                           GLfloat *blue*);

Loads the index in the color map, *index*, with the given *red*, *green*, and *blue* values. These values are normalized to lie in the range [0.0,1.0].

Initializing and Drawing Three-Dimensional Objects

Many sample programs in this guide use three-dimensional models to illustrate various rendering properties. The following drawing routines are included in the auxiliary library to avoid having to reproduce the code to draw these models in each program. Each three-dimensional model comes in two flavors: wireframe without surface normals, and solid with shading and surface normals. Use the solid version when you're applying lighting. The argument for these routines allows you to scale the object that's drawn.

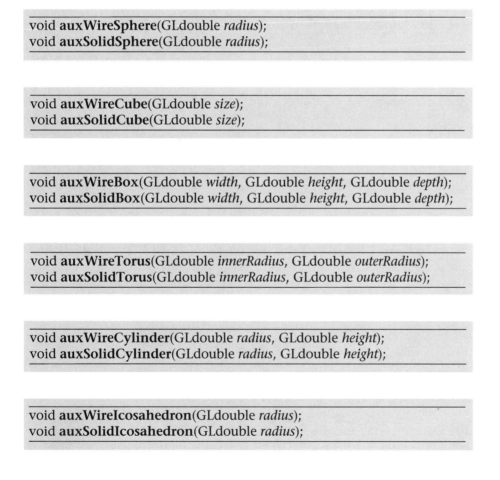

```
void auxWireSphere(GLdouble radius);
void auxSolidSphere(GLdouble radius);
```

```
void auxWireCube(GLdouble size);
void auxSolidCube(GLdouble size);
```

```
void auxWireBox(GLdouble width, GLdouble height, GLdouble depth);
void auxSolidBox(GLdouble width, GLdouble height, GLdouble depth);
```

```
void auxWireTorus(GLdouble innerRadius, GLdouble outerRadius);
void auxSolidTorus(GLdouble innerRadius, GLdouble outerRadius);
```

```
void auxWireCylinder(GLdouble radius, GLdouble height);
void auxSolidCylinder(GLdouble radius, GLdouble height);
```

```
void auxWireIcosahedron(GLdouble radius);
void auxSolidIcosahedron(GLdouble radius);
```

void **auxWireOctahedron**(GLdouble *radius*);
void **auxSolidOctahedron**(GLdouble *radius*);

void **auxWireTetrahedron**(GLdouble *radius*);
void **auxSolidTetrahedron**(GLdouble *radius*);

void **auxWireDodecahedron**(GLdouble *radius*);
void **auxSolidDodecahedron**(GLdouble *radius*);

void **auxWireCone**(GLdouble *radius*, GLdouble *height*);
void **auxSolidCone**(GLdouble *radius*, GLdouble *height*);

void **auxWireTeapot**(GLdouble *size*);
void **auxSolidTeapot**(GLdouble *size*);

Draws the specified wireframe or solid object. These routines are self-initializing; that is, the first time a rendering request is made, a display list is created for the object. Every subsequent time the routine is called, the same display list is executed. All these models are drawn centered at the origin. When drawn with unit scale factors, these models fit into a box with all coordinates from −1 to 1. Use the arguments for these routines to scale the objects.

Managing a Background Process

You can specify a function that's to be executed if no other events are pending—for example, when the event loop would otherwise be idle—with **auxIdleFunc**(). This routine takes a pointer to the function as its only argument. Pass in zero to disable the execution of the function.

void **auxIdleFunc**(void *_func_);

Specifies the function, _func_, to be executed if no other events are pending. If zero is passed in, execution of _func_ is disabled.

Running the Program

The examples in the book typically draw the scene each time the window is created, moved, or reshaped, or if some input event occurs. Use **auxMainLoop**() to specify the routine that draws the scene.

void **auxMainLoop**(void(*_displayFunc_)(void));

Specifies the function, _displayFunc_, that's called when the window needs to be updated. _displayFunc_ should redraw the objects in your scene.

Calculating Normal Vectors

This appendix describes how to calculate normal vectors for surfaces. You need to define normals to use OpenGL's lighting facility, which is described in Chapter 6. "Normal Vectors" on page 52 introduces normals and the OpenGL command for specifying them. This appendix goes through the details of calculating them. It has the following major sections:

- "Finding Normals for Analytic Surfaces"
- "Finding Normals from Polygonal Data"

Since normals are perpendicular to a surface, you can find the normal at a particular point on a surface by first finding the flat plane that just touches the surface at that point. The normal is the vector that's perpendicular to that plane. On a perfect sphere, for example, the normal at a point on the surface is in the same direction as the vector from the center of the sphere to that point. For other types of surfaces, there are other, better means for determining the normals, depending on how the surface is specified.

Recall that smooth curved surfaces are approximated by a large number of small flat polygons. If the vectors perpendicular to these polygons are used as the surface normals in such an approximation, the surface appears faceted, since the normal direction is discontinuous across the polygonal boundaries. In many cases, however, an exact mathematical description exists for the surface, and true surface normals can be calculated at every point. Using the true normals improves the rendering considerably, as shown in Figure F-1. Even if you don't have a mathematical description, you can do better than the faceted look shown in the figure. The two major sections in this appendix describe how to calculate normal vectors for these two cases:

- **"Finding Normals for Analytic Surfaces"** explains what to do when you have a mathematical description of a surface.

- **"Finding Normals from Polygonal Data"** covers the case when you have only the polygonal data to describe a surface.

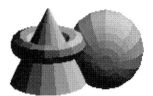 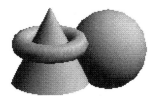

Figure F-1 Rendering with Polygonal Normals vs. True Normals

Finding Normals for Analytic Surfaces

Analytic surfaces are smooth, differentiable surfaces that are described by a mathematical equation (or set of equations). In many cases, the easiest surfaces to find normals for are analytic surfaces for which you have an explicit definition in the following form:

$$\mathbf{V}(s,t) = [\ \mathbf{X}(s,t)\ \ \mathbf{Y}(s,t)\ \ \mathbf{Z}(s,t)\ ]$$

where s and t are constrained to be in some domain, and $\mathbf{X}$, $\mathbf{Y}$, and $\mathbf{Z}$ are differentiable functions of two variables. To calculate the normal, find

$$\frac{\partial V}{\partial s} \text{ and } \frac{\partial V}{\partial t}$$

which are vectors tangent to the surface in the s and t directions. The cross product

$$\frac{\partial V}{\partial s} \times \frac{\partial V}{\partial t}$$

is perpendicular to both, and hence to the surface. The following shows how to calculate the cross product of two vectors. (Watch out for the degenerate cases where the cross product has zero length!)

$$\begin{bmatrix} v_x\ v_y\ v_z \end{bmatrix} \times \begin{bmatrix} w_x\ w_y\ w_z \end{bmatrix} = \begin{bmatrix} (v_y w_z - w_y v_z)\ \ (w_x v_z - v_x w_z)\ \ (v_x w_y - w_x v_y) \end{bmatrix}$$

You should probably normalize the resulting vector. To normalize a vector $[x\ y\ z]$, calculate its length

$$\text{Length} = \sqrt{x^2 + y^2 + z^2}$$

and divide each component of the vector by the length.

As an example of these calculations, consider the analytic surface

$$\mathbf{V}(s,t) = [\ s^2\ t^3\ 3{-}st\ ]$$

From this we have

$$\frac{\partial V}{\partial s} = \begin{bmatrix} 2s\ 0\ {-}t \end{bmatrix}, \frac{\partial V}{\partial t} = \begin{bmatrix} 0\ 3t^2\ {-}s \end{bmatrix}, \text{ and } \frac{\partial V}{\partial s} \times \frac{\partial V}{\partial t} = \begin{bmatrix} {-}3t^3\ 2s^2\ 6st^2 \end{bmatrix}$$

So, for example, when $s=1$ and $t=2$, the corresponding point on the surface is (1, 8, 1), and the vector (−24, 2, 24) is perpendicular to the surface at that point. The length of this vector is 34, so the unit normal vector is (–24/34, 2/34, 24/34) = (–0.70588, 0.058823, 0.70588).

For analytic surfaces that are described implicitly, as $F(x, y, z) = 0$, the problem is harder. In some cases, you can solve for one of the variables, say $z = G(x, y)$, and put it in the explicit form given previously:

$$\mathbf{V}(s, t) = \begin{bmatrix} s & t & \mathbf{G}(s, t) \end{bmatrix}$$

Then continue as described earlier.

If you can't get the surface equation in an explicit form, you might be able to make use of the fact that the normal vector is given by the gradient

$$\nabla F = \begin{bmatrix} \dfrac{\partial F}{\partial x} & \dfrac{\partial F}{\partial y} & \dfrac{\partial F}{\partial z} \end{bmatrix}$$

evaluated at a particular point (x, y, z). Calculating the gradient might be easy, but finding a point that lies on the surface can be difficult. As an example of an implicitly defined analytic function, consider the equation of a sphere of radius 1 centered at the origin:

$$x^2 + y^2 + z^2 - 1 = 0$$

This means that

$$\mathbf{F}(x, y, z) = x^2 + y^2 + z^2 - 1$$

which can be solved for z to yield

$$z = \pm\sqrt{1 - x^2 - y^2}$$

Thus, normals can be calculated from the explicit form

$$\mathbf{V}(s, t) = \begin{bmatrix} s & t & \sqrt{1 - s^2 - t^2} \end{bmatrix}$$

as described previously.

If you could not solve for z, you could have used the gradient

$$\nabla F = \begin{bmatrix} 2x & 2y & 2z \end{bmatrix}$$

as long as you could find a point on the surface. In this case, it's not so hard to find a point—for example, (2/3, 1/3, 2/3) lies on the surface. Using the gradient, the normal at this point is (4/3, 2/3, 4/3). The unit-length normal is (2/3, 1/3, 2/3), which is the same as the point on the surface, as expected.

Finding Normals from Polygonal Data

As mentioned previously, you often want to find normals for surfaces that are described with polygonal data such that the surfaces appear smooth rather than faceted. In most cases, the easiest way for you to do this (though it might not be the most efficient way) is to calculate the normal vectors for each of the polygonal facets and then to average the normals for neighboring facets. Use the averaged normal for the vertex that the neighboring facets have in common. Figure F-2 shows a surface and its polygonal approximation. (Of course, if the polygons represent the exact surface and aren't merely an approximation—if you're drawing a cube or a cut diamond, for example—don't do the averaging. Calculate the normal for each facet as described in the following paragraphs, and use that same normal for each vertex of the facet.)

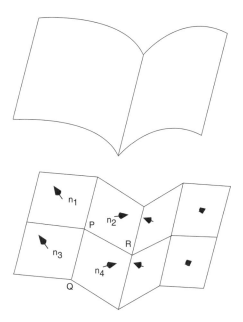

Figure F-2   Averaging Normal Vectors

To find the normal for a flat polygon, take any three vertices v_1, v_2, and v_3 of the polygon that do not lie in a straight line. The cross product

$$[v_1 - v_2] \times [v_2 - v_3]$$

is perpendicular to the polygon. (Typically, you want to normalize the resulting vector.) Then you need to average the normals for adjoining facets, to avoid giving too much weight to one of them. For instance, in the example shown in Figure F-2, if n_1, n_2, n_3, and n_4 are the normals for the four polygons meeting at point P, calculate $n_1 + n_2 + n_3 + n_4$ and then normalize it. The resulting vector can be used as the normal for point P.

Sometimes, you need to vary this method for particular situations. For instance, at the boundary of a surface (for example, point Q in Figure F-2), you might be able to choose a better normal based on your knowledge of what the surface should look like. Sometimes the best you can do is to average the polygon normals on the boundary as well. Similarly, some models have some smooth parts and some sharp corners (point R is on such an edge in Figure F-2). In this case, the normals on either side of the crease shouldn't be averaged. Instead, polygons on one side of the crease should be drawn with one normal, and polygons on the other side with another.

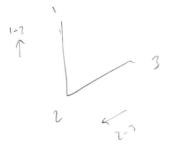

Homogeneous Coordinates and Transformation Matrices

This appendix presents a brief discussion of homogeneous coordinates. It also lists the form of the transformation matrices used for rotation, scaling, translation, perspective projection, and orthographic projection. These topics are introduced and discussed in Chapter 3. For a more detailed discussion of these subjects, see almost any book on three-dimensional computer graphics—for example, *Computer Graphics: Principles and Practice*, by Foley, Van Dam, Feiner, and Hughes (Reading, Mass.: Addison-Wesley)—or a text on projective geometry—for example, *The Real Projective Plane*, by H. S. M. Coxeter, 2nd ed. (Cambridge: Cambridge University Press, 1961). In the discussion that follows, the term *homogeneous coordinates* always means three-dimensional homogeneous coordinates, although projective geometries exist for all dimensions.

This appendix has the following major sections:

- "Homogeneous Coordinates"
- "Transformation Matrices"

Homogeneous Coordinates

OpenGL commands usually deal with two- and three-dimensional vertices, but in fact all are treated internally as three-dimensional homogeneous vertices comprising four coordinates. Every column vector $(x, y, z, w)^T$ represents a homogeneous vertex if at least one of its elements is nonzero. If the real number a is nonzero, then $(x, y, z, w)^T$ and $(ax, ay, az, aw)^T$ represent the same homogeneous vertex. (This is just like fractions: $x/y = (ax)/(ay)$.) A three-dimensional euclidean space point $(x, y, z)^T$ becomes the homogeneous vertex with coordinates $(x, y, z, 1.0)^T$, and the two-dimensional euclidean point $(x, y)^T$ becomes $(x, y, 0.0, 1.0)^T$.

As long as w is nonzero, the homogeneous vertex $(x, y, z, w)^T$ corresponds to the three-dimensional point $(x/w, y/w, z/w)^T$. If $w = 0.0$, it corresponds to no euclidean point, but rather to some idealized "point at infinity." To understand this point at infinity, consider the point $(1, 2, 0, 0)$, and note that the sequence of points $(1, 2, 0, 1)$, $(1, 2, 0, 0.01)$, and $(1, 2.0, 0.0, 0.0001)$, corresponds to the euclidean points $(1, 2)$, $(100, 200)$, and $(10000, 20000)$. This sequence represents points rapidly moving toward infinity along the line $2x = y$. Thus, you can think of $(1, 2, 0, 0)$ as the point at infinity in the direction of that line.

Note: OpenGL might not handle homogeneous clip coordinates with $w < 0$ correctly. To be sure that your code is portable to all OpenGL systems, use only nonnegative w values.

Transforming Vertices

Vertex transformations (such as rotations, translations, scaling, and shearing) and projections (such as perspective and orthographic) can all be represented by applying an appropriate 4×4 matrix to the coordinates representing the vertex. If **v** represents a homogeneous vertex, and **M** is a 4×4 transformation matrix, then **Mv** is the image of **v** under the transformation by **M**. (In computer-graphics applications, the transformations used are usually nonsingular—in other words, the matrix **M** can be inverted. This isn't required, but some problems arise with nonsingular transformations.)

After transformation, all transformed vertices are clipped so that x, y, and z are in the range $[-w, w]$ (assuming $w > 0$). Note that this range corresponds in euclidean space to $[-1.0, 1.0]$.

Transforming Normals

Normal vectors don't transform in the same way as vertices, or position vectors. Mathematically, it's better to think of normal vectors not as vectors, but as planes perpendicular to those vectors. Then, the transformation rules for normal vectors are described by the transformation rules for perpendicular planes.

A homogeneous plane is denoted by the row vector (a, b, c, d), where at least one of a, b, c, or d is nonzero. If q is a nonzero real number, then (a, b, c, d) and (qa, qb, qc, qd) represent the same plane. A point $(x, y, z, w)^T$ is on the plane (a, b, c, d) if $ax+by+cz+dw = 0$. (If $w = 1$, this is the standard description of a euclidean plane.) In order for (a, b, c, d) to represent a euclidean plane, at least one of a, b, or c must be nonzero. If they're all zero, then $(0, 0, 0, d)$ represents the "plane at infinity," which contains all the "points at infinity."

If $\mathbf{p}$ is a homogeneous plane and $\mathbf{v}$ is a homogeneous vertex, then the statement "$\mathbf{v}$ lies on plane $\mathbf{p}$" is written mathematically as $\mathbf{pv} = 0$, where $\mathbf{pv}$ is normal matrix multiplication. If $\mathbf{M}$ is a nonsingular vertex transformation (that is, a 4×4 matrix that has an inverse $\mathbf{M}^{-1}$), then $\mathbf{pv} = 0$ is equivalent to $\mathbf{pM}^{-1}\mathbf{Mv} = 0$, so $\mathbf{Mv}$ lies on the plane $\mathbf{pM}^{-1}$. Thus, $\mathbf{pM}^{-1}$ is the image of the plane under the vertex transformation $\mathbf{M}$.

If you like to think of normal vectors as vectors instead of as the planes perpendicular to them, let $\mathbf{v}$ and $\mathbf{n}$ be vectors such that $\mathbf{v}$ is perpendicular to $\mathbf{n}$. Then, $\mathbf{n}^T\mathbf{v} = 0$. Thus, for an arbitrary nonsingular transformation $\mathbf{M}$, $\mathbf{n}^T\mathbf{M}^{-1}\mathbf{Mv} = 0$, which means that $\mathbf{n}^T\mathbf{M}^{-1}$ is the transpose of the transformed normal vector. Thus, the transformed normal vector is $(\mathbf{M}^{-1})^T\mathbf{n}$. In other words, normal vectors are transformed by the inverse transpose of the transformation that transforms points. Whew!

Transformation Matrices

Although any nonsingular matrix $\mathbf{M}$ represents a valid projective transformation, a few special matrices are particularly useful. These matrices are listed in the following paragraphs.

Translation

The call **glTranslate***(x, y, z) generates **T**, where:

$$\mathbf{T} = \begin{bmatrix} 1 & 0 & 0 & x \\ 0 & 1 & 0 & y \\ 0 & 0 & 1 & z \\ 0 & 0 & 0 & 1 \end{bmatrix} \text{ and } \mathbf{T^{-1}} = \begin{bmatrix} 1 & 0 & 0 & -x \\ 0 & 1 & 0 & -y \\ 0 & 0 & 1 & -z \\ 0 & 0 & 0 & 1 \end{bmatrix}$$

Scaling

The call **glScale***(x, y, z) generates **S**, where:

$$\mathbf{S} = \begin{bmatrix} x & 0 & 0 & 0 \\ 0 & y & 0 & 0 \\ 0 & 0 & z & 0 \\ 0 & 0 & 0 & 1 \end{bmatrix} \text{ and } \mathbf{S^{-1}} = \begin{bmatrix} \frac{1}{x} & 0 & 0 & 0 \\ 0 & \frac{1}{y} & 0 & 0 \\ 0 & 0 & \frac{1}{z} & 0 \\ 0 & 0 & 0 & 1 \end{bmatrix}$$

Notice that **S**$^{-1}$ is defined only if x, y, and z are all nonzero.

Rotation

The call **glRotate***(a, x, y, z) generates **R** as follows.

Let $\mathbf{v} = (x, y, z)^{\mathrm{T}}$, and $\mathbf{u} = \mathbf{v}/\|\mathbf{v}\| = (x', y', z')$.

Also let

$$\mathbf{S} = \begin{bmatrix} 0 & -z' & y' \\ z' & 0 & -x' \\ -y' & x' & 0 \end{bmatrix} \text{ and } \mathbf{M} = \mathbf{uu}^{\mathrm{T}} + (\cos a)\,(\mathbf{I} - \mathbf{u}\,\mathbf{u}^{\mathrm{T}}) + (\sin a)\,\mathbf{S}$$

Then

$$R = \begin{bmatrix} m & m & m & 0 \\ m & m & m & 0 \\ m & m & m & 0 \\ 0 & 0 & 0 & 1 \end{bmatrix}$$ where m represents elements from M, which is a 3×3 matrix.

The R matrix is always defined. If $x=y=z=0$, then R is the identity matrix. You can obtain the inverse of R, R^{-1}, by substituting $-a$ for a, or by transposition.

The **glRotate*()** command generates a matrix for rotation about an arbitrary axis. Often, you're rotating about one of the coordinate axes; the corresponding matrices are as follows.

glRotate*(a, 1, 0, 0): $\begin{bmatrix} 1 & 0 & 0 & 0 \\ 0 & \cos a & -\sin a & 0 \\ 0 & \sin a & \cos a & 0 \\ 0 & 0 & 0 & 1 \end{bmatrix}$

glRotate*(a, 0, 1, 0): $\begin{bmatrix} \cos a & 0 & \sin a & 0 \\ 0 & 1 & 0 & 0 \\ -\sin a & 0 & \cos a & 0 \\ 0 & 0 & 0 & 1 \end{bmatrix}$

glRotate*(a, 0, 0, 1): $\begin{bmatrix} \cos a & -\sin a & 0 & 0 \\ \sin a & \cos a & 0 & 0 \\ 0 & 0 & 1 & 0 \\ 0 & 0 & 0 & 1 \end{bmatrix}$

As before, the inverses are obtained by transposition.

Perspective Projection

The call **glFrustum**(l, r, b, t, n, f) generates **R**, where:

$$\mathbf{R} = \begin{bmatrix} \dfrac{2n}{r-l} & 0 & \dfrac{r+l}{r-l} & 0 \\[2mm] 0 & \dfrac{2n}{t-b} & \dfrac{t+b}{t-b} & 0 \\[2mm] 0 & 0 & \dfrac{-(f+n)}{f-n} & \dfrac{-2fn}{f-n} \\[2mm] 0 & 0 & -1 & 0 \end{bmatrix} \text{ and } \mathbf{R^{-1}} = \begin{bmatrix} \dfrac{r-l}{2n} & 0 & 0 & \dfrac{r+l}{2n} \\[2mm] 0 & \dfrac{t-b}{2n} & 0 & \dfrac{t+b}{2n} \\[2mm] 0 & 0 & 0 & -1 \\[2mm] 0 & 0 & \dfrac{-(f-n)}{2fn} & \dfrac{f+n}{2fn} \end{bmatrix}$$

R is defined as long as $l \neq r$, $t \neq b$, and $n \neq f$.

Orthographic Projection

The call **glOrtho***(l, r, b, t, u, f) generates **R**, where:

$$\mathbf{R} = \begin{bmatrix} \dfrac{2}{r-l} & 0 & 0 & -\dfrac{r+l}{r-l} \\[2mm] 0 & \dfrac{2}{t-b} & 0 & -\dfrac{t+b}{t-b} \\[2mm] 0 & 0 & \dfrac{-2}{f-n} & -\dfrac{f+n}{f-n} \\[2mm] 0 & 0 & 0 & 1 \end{bmatrix} \text{ and } \mathbf{R^{-1}} = \begin{bmatrix} \dfrac{r-l}{2} & 0 & 0 & \dfrac{r+l}{2} \\[2mm] 0 & \dfrac{t-b}{2} & 0 & \dfrac{t+b}{2} \\[2mm] 0 & 0 & \dfrac{f-n}{-2} & \dfrac{n+f}{2} \\[2mm] 0 & 0 & 0 & 1 \end{bmatrix}$$

R is defined as long as $l \neq r$, $t \neq b$, and $n \neq f$.

Programming Tips

This appendix lists some tips and guidelines that you might find useful. Keep in mind that these tips are based on the intentions of the designers of the OpenGL, not on any experience with actual applications and implementations! This appendix has the following major sections:

- **"OpenGL Correctness Tips"**
- **"OpenGL Performance Tips"**
- **"GLX Tips"**

OpenGL Correctness Tips

- Do not count on the error behavior of an OpenGL implementation—it might change in a future release of OpenGL. For example, OpenGL 1.0 ignores matrix operations invoked between **glBegin()** and **glEnd()** commands, but OpenGL 1.1 might not. Put another way, OpenGL error semantics may change between upward-compatible revisions.

- Use the projection matrix to collapse all geometry to a single plane. If the modelview matrix is used, OpenGL features that operate in eye coordinates (such as lighting and application-defined clipping planes) might fail.

- Do not make extensive changes to a single matrix. For example, do not animate a rotation by continually calling **glRotate()** with an incremental angle. Rather, use **glLoadIdentity()** to initialize the given matrix for each frame, then call **glRotate()** with the desired complete angle for that frame.

- Count on multiple passes through a rendering database to generate the same pixel fragments only if this behavior is guaranteed by the invariance rules established for a compliant OpenGL implementation. (See Appendix I for details on the invariance rules.) Otherwise, a different set of fragments might be generated.

- Do not expect errors to be reported while a display list is being defined. The commands within a display list generate errors only when the list is executed.

- Place the near frustum plane as far from the viewpoint as possible to optimize the operation of the depth buffer.

- Call **glFlush()** to force all previous OpenGL commands to be executed. Do not count on **glGet*()** or **glIs*()** to flush the rendering stream. Query commands flush as much of the stream as is required to return valid data but don't guarantee to complete all pending rendering commands.

- Turn dithering off when rendering predithered images (for example, when **glCopyPixels()** is called).

- Make use of the full range of the accumulation buffer. For example, if accumulating four images, scale each by one-quarter as it's accumulated.

- If exact two-dimensional rasterization is desired, you must carefully specify both the orthographic projection and the vertices of primitives that are to be rasterized. The orthographic projection should be specified with integer coordinates, as shown in the following example:

```
gluOrtho2D(0, width, 0, height);
```

where *width* and *height* are the dimensions of the viewport. Given this projection matrix, polygon vertices and pixel image positions should be placed at integer coordinates to rasterize predictably. For example, **glRecti**(0, 0, 1, 1) reliably fills the lower left pixel of the viewport, and **glRasterPos2i**(0, 0) reliably positions an unzoomed image at the lower left of the viewport. Point vertices, line vertices, and bitmap positions should be placed at half-integer locations, however. For example, a line drawn from $(x_1, 0.5)$ to $(x_2, 0.5)$ will be reliably rendered along the bottom row of pixels int the viewport, and a point drawn at (0.5, 0.5) will reliably fill the same pixel as **glRecti**(0, 0, 1, 1).

An optimum compromise that allows all primitives to be specified at integer positions, while still ensuring predictable rasterization, is to translate x and y by 0.375, as shown in the following code fragment. Such a translation keeps polygon and pixel image edges safely away from the centers of pixels, while moving line vertices close enough to the pixel centers.

```
glViewport(0, 0, width, height);
glMatrixMode(GL_PROJECTION);
glLoadIdentity();
gluOrtho2D(0, width, 0, height);
glMatrixMode(GL_MODELVIEW);
glLoadIdentity();
glTranslatef(0.375, 0.375, 0.0);
/* render all primitives at integer positions */
```

- Avoid using negative w vertex coordinates and negative q texture coordinates. OpenGL might not clip such coordinates correctly and might make interpolation errors when shading primitives defined by such coordinates.

OpenGL Performance Tips

- Use **glColorMaterial()** when only a single material property is being varied rapidly (at each vertex, for example). Use **glMaterial()** for infrequent changes, or when more than a single material property is being varied rapidly.

- Use **glLoadIdentity()** to initialize a matrix, rather than loading your own copy of the identity matrix.

- Use specific matrix calls such as **glRotate*()**, **glTranslate*()**, and **glScale*()**, rather than composing your own rotation, translation, and scale matrices and calling **glMultMatrix()**.

- Use **glPushAttrib()** and **glPopAttrib()** to save and restore state values. Use query functions only when your application requires the state values for its own computations.

- Use display lists to encapsulate potentially expensive state changes. For example, place all the **glTexImage*()** calls required to completely specify a texture, and perhaps the associated **glTexParameter*()**, **glPixelStore*()**, and **glPixelTransfer*()** calls as well, into a single display list. Call this display list to select the texture.

- Use display lists to encapsulate the rendering calls of rigid objects that will be drawn repeatedly.

- Use evaluators even for simple surface tessellations to minimize network bandwidth in client-server environments.

- Provide unit-length normals if it's possible to do so, and avoid the overhead of GL_NORMALIZE. Avoid using **glScale*()** when doing lighting because it almost always requies that GL_NORMALIZE be enabled.

- Set **glShadeModel()** to GL_FLAT if smooth shading isn't required.

- Use a single **glClear()** call per frame if possible. Do not use **glClear()** to clear small subregions of the buffers; use it only for complete or near-complete clears.

- Use a single call to **glBegin**(GL_TRIANGLES) to draw multiple independent triangles, rather than calling **glBegin**(GL_TRIANGLES) multiple times, or calling **glBegin**(GL_POLYGON). Even if only a single triangle is to be drawn, use GL_TRIANGLES rather than GL_POLYGON. Use a single call to **glBegin**(GL_QUADS) in the same manner, rather than calling **glBegin**(GL_POLYGON) repeatedly. Likewise, use a single call to **glBegin**(GL_LINES) to draw multiple independent line segments, rather than calling **glBegin**(GL_LINES) multiple times.

- In general, use the vector forms of commands to pass precomputed data, and use the scalar forms of commands to pass values that are computed near call time.

- Avoid making redundant mode changes, such as setting the color to the same value between each vertex of a flat-shaded polygon.

- Be sure to disable expensive rasterization and per-fragment operations when drawing or copying images. OpenGL will apply textures to pixel images if asked to!

GLX Tips

- Use **glXWaitGL()** rather than **glFinish()** to force X rendering commands to follow GL rendering commands.

- Likewise, use **glXWaitX()** rather than **glXSync()** to force GL rendering commands to follow X rendering commands.

- Be careful when using **glXChooseVisual()** because boolean selections are matched exactly. Since some implementations won't export visuals with all combinations of boolean capabilities, you should call **glXChooseVisual()** several times with different boolean values before you give up. For example, if no single-buffered visual with the required characteristics is available, check for a double-buffered visual with the same capabilities. It might be available, and it's easy to use.

OpenGL Invariance

OpenGL is not a pixel-exact specification. It therefore doesn't guarantee an exact match between images produced by different OpenGL implementations. However, OpenGL does specify exact matches, in some cases, for images produced by the same implementation. This appendix describes the invariance rules that define these cases.

The obvious and most fundamental case is repeatability. A conforming OpenGL implementation generates the same results each time a specific sequence of commands is issued from the same initial conditions. Although such repeatability is useful for testing and verification, it's often not useful to application programmers, because it's difficult to arrange for equivalent initial conditions. For example, rendering a scene twice, the second time after swapping the front and back buffers, doesn't meet this requirement. So repeatability can't be used to guarantee a stable, double-buffered image.

A simple and useful algorithm that counts on invariant execution is erasing a line by redrawing it in the background color. This algorithm works only if rasterizing the line results in the same fragment x,y pairs being generated in both the foreground and background color cases. OpenGL requires that the coordinates of the fragments generated by rasterization be invariant with respect to framebuffer contents, which color buffers are enabled for drawing, the values of matrices other than those on the top of the matrix stacks, the scissor parameters, all writemasks, all clear values, the current color, index, normal, texture coordinates, and edge-flag values, the current raster color, raster index, and raster texture coordinates, and the material properties. It is further required that exactly the same fragments be generated, including the fragment color values, when framebuffer contents, color buffer enables, matrices other than those on the top of the matrix stacks, the scissor parameters, writemasks, or clear values differ.

OpenGL further suggests, but doesn't require, that fragment generation be invariant with respect to the matrix mode, the depths of the matrix stacks, the alpha test parameters (other than alpha test enable), the stencil parameters (other than stencil enable), the depth test parameters (other than depth test enable), the blending parameters (other than enable), the logical operation (but not logical operation enable), and the pixel-storage and pixel-transfer parameters. Because invariance with respect to several enables isn't recommended, you should use other parameters to disable functions when invariant rendering is required. For example, to render invariantly with blending enabled and disabled, set the blending parameters to GL_ONE and GL_ZERO to disable blending, rather than calling glDisable(GL_BLEND). Alpha testing, stencil testing, depth testing, and the logical operation can all be disabled in this manner.

Finally, OpenGL requires that per-fragment arithmetic, such as blending and the depth test, be invariant to all OpenGL state except the state that directly defines it. For example, the only OpenGL parameters that affect how the arithmetic of blending is performed are the source and destination blend parameters and the blend enable parameter. Blending is invariant to all other state changes. This invariance holds for the scissor test, the alpha test, the stencil test, the depth test, blending, dithering, logical operations, and buffer writemasking.

As a result of all these invariance requirements, OpenGL can guarantee that images rendered into different color buffers, either simultaneously or separately using the same command sequence, are pixel identical. This holds for all the color buffers in the framebuffer, or all the color buffers in an off-screen buffer, but it isn't guaranteed between the framebuffer and off-screen buffers.

Glossary

aliasing

A rendering technique that assigns to pixels the color of the primitive being rendered, regardless of whether that primitive covers all of the pixel's area or only a portion of the pixel's area. This results in jagged edges, or *jaggies*.

alpha

A fourth color component. The alpha component is never displayed directly. It's typically used to control color blending. By convention, OpenGL alpha corresponds to the notion of opacity rather than transparency, meaning that an alpha value of 1.0 implies complete opacity, and an alpha value of 0.0 complete transparency.

animation

Generating repeated renderings of a scene, with smoothly changing viewpoint and/or object positions, quickly enough that the illusion of motion is achieved. OpenGL animation almost always is done using double-buffering.

antialiasing

A rendering technique that assigns pixel colors based on the fraction of the pixel's area that's covered by the primitive being rendered. Antialiased rendering reduces or eliminates the jaggies that result from aliased rendering.

application-specific clipping

Clipping of primitives against planes in eye coordinates; the planes are specified by the application using **glClipPlane()**.

back face

See *face*.

bit

Binary digit. A state variable having only two possible values: 0 or 1. Binary numbers are constructions of one or more bits.

bitmap

A rectangular array of bits. Also, the primitive rendered by the **glBitmap()** command, which uses its *bitmap* parameter as a mask.

bitplane

A rectangular array of bits mapped one-to-one with pixels. The framebuffer is a stack of bitplanes.

blending

Reduction of two color components to one component, usually as a linear interpolation between the two components.

buffer

A group of bitplanes that store a single component (such as depth or green) or a single index (such as the color index or the stencil index). Sometimes the red, green, blue, and alpha buffers together are referred to as the color buffer, rather than the color buffers.

C

God's programming language.

client

The computer from which OpenGL commands are issued. The computer that issues OpenGL commands can be connected via a network to a different computer that executes the commands, or commands can be issued and executed on the same computer. See also *server*.

client memory

The main memory (where program variables are stored) of the client computer.

clip coordinates

The coordinate system that follows transformation by the projection matrix and that precedes perspective division. View-volume clipping is done in clip coordinates, but application-specific clipping is not.

clipping

Elimination of the portion of a geometric primitive that's outside the half-space defined by a clipping plane. Points are simply rejected if outside. The portion of a line or of a polygon that's outside the half-space is eliminated, and additional vertices are generated as necessary to complete the primitive within the clipping half-space. Geometric primitives and the current raster position (when specified) are always clipped against the six half-spaces defined by the left, right, bottom, top, near, and far planes of the view volume. Applications can specify optional application-specific clipping planes to be applied in eye coordinates.

color index

A single value that represents a color by name, rather than by value. OpenGL color indices are treated as continuous values (for example, floating-point numbers) while operations such as interpolation and dithering are performed on them. Color indices stored in the framebuffer are always integer values, however. Floating-point indices are converted to integers by rounding to the nearest integer value.

color-index mode

An OpenGL context is in color index mode if its color buffers store color indices, rather than red, green, blue, and alpha color components.

color map

A table of index-to-RGB mappings that's accessed by the display hardware. Each color index is read from the color buffer, converted to an RGB triple by lookup in the color map, and sent to the monitor.

component

A single, continuous (for example, floating-point) value that represents an intensity or quantity. Usually, a component value of zero represents the minimum value or intensity, and a component value of one represents the maximum value or intensity, though other normalizations are sometimes used. Because component values are interpreted in a normalized range, they are specified independent of actual resolution. For example, the RGB triple (1, 1, 1) is white, regardless of whether the color buffers store 4, 8, or 12 bits each.

Out-of-range components are typically clamped to the normalized range, not truncated or otherwise interpreted. For example, the RGB triple (1.4, 1.5, 0.9) is clamped to (1.0, 1.0, 0.9) before it's used to update the color buffer. Red, green, blue, alpha, and depth are always treated as components, never as indices.

concave

Nonconvex.

context

A complete set of OpenGL state variables. Note that framebuffer contents are not part of OpenGL state, but that the configuration of the framebuffer is.

convex

A polygon is convex if no straight line in the plane of the polygon intersects the polygon more than twice.

convex hull

The smallest convex region enclosing a specified group of points. In two dimensions, the convex hull is found conceptually by stretching a rubber band around the points so that all of the points lie within the band.

coordinate system

In n-dimensional space, a set of n linearly independent vectors anchored to a point (called the origin). A group of coordinates specifies a point in space (or a vector from the origin) by indicating how far to travel along each vector to reach the point (or tip of the vector).

culling

The process of eliminating a front face or back face of a polygon so that it isn't drawn.

current matrix

A matrix that transforms coordinates in one coordinate system to coordinates of another system. There are three current matrices in OpenGL: the modelview matrix transforms object coordinates (coordinates specified by the programmer) to eye coordinates; the perspective matrix transforms eye coordinates to clip coordinates; the texture matrix transforms specified or generated texture coordinates as described by the matrix. Each current matrix is the top element on a stack of matrices. Each of the three stacks can be manipulated with OpenGL matrix-manipulation commands.

current raster position

A window coordinate position that specifies the placement of an image primitive when it's rasterized. The current raster position, and other current raster parameters, are updated when **glRasterPos()** is called.

depth

Generally refers to the *z* window coordinate.

depth-cuing

A rendering technique that assigns color based on distance from the viewpoint.

display list

A named list of OpenGL commands. Display lists are always stored on the server, so display lists can be used to reduce network traffic in client-server environments. The contents of a display list may be preprocessed, and might therefore execute more efficiently than the same set of OpenGL commands executed in immediate mode. Such preprocessing is especially important for computing intensive commands such as **glTexImage()**.

dithering

A technique for increasing the perceived range of colors in an image at the cost of spatial resolution. Adjacent pixels are assigned differing color values; when viewed from a distance, these colors seem to blend into a single intermediate color. The technique is similar to the halftoning used in black-and-white publications to achieve shades of gray.

double-buffering

OpenGL contexts with both front and back color buffers are double-buffered. Smooth animation is accomplished by rendering into only the back buffer (which isn't displayed), then causing the front and back buffers to be swapped. See **auxSwapBuffers()** in Appendix E.

element

A single component or index.

evaluation

The OpenGL process of generating object-coordinate vertices and parameters from previously specified Bézier equations.

execute

An OpenGL command is executed when it's called in immediate mode or when the display list that it's a part of is called.

eye coordinates

The coordinate system that follows transformation by the modelview matrix and that precedes transformation by the projection matrix. Lighting and application-specific clipping are done in eye coordinates.

face

One side of a polygon. Each polygon has two faces: a front face and a back face. Only one face or the other is ever visible in the window. Whether the back or front face is visible is effectively determined after the polygon is projected onto the window. After this projection, if the polygon's edges are directed clockwise, one of the faces is visible; if directed counterclockwise, the other face is visible. Whether clockwise corresponds to front or back (and counterclockwise corresponds to back or front) is determined by the OpenGL programmer.

flat shading

Refers to coloring a primitive with a single, constant color across its extent, rather than smoothly interpolating colors across the primitive. See *Gouraud shading*.

fog

A rendering technique that can be used to simulate atmospheric effects such as haze, fog, and smog by fading object colors to a background color based on distance from the viewer. Fog also aids in the perception of distance from the viewer, giving a *depth cue*.

font

A group of graphical character representations usually used to display strings of text. The characters may be roman letters, mathematical symbols, Asian ideograms, Egyptian hieroglyphs, and so on.

fragment

Fragments are generated by the rasterization of primitives. Each fragment corresponds to a single pixel and includes color, depth, and sometimes texture-coordinate values.

framebuffer

All the buffers of a given window or context. Sometimes includes all the pixel memory of the graphics hardware accelerator.

front face

See *face*.

frustum

The view volume warped by perspective division.

gamma correction

A function applied to colors stored in the framebuffer to correct for the nonlinear response of the eye (and sometimes of the monitor) to linear changes in color-intensity values.

geometric model

The object-coordinate vertices and parameters that describe an object. Note that OpenGL doesn't define a syntax for geometric models, but rather a syntax and semantics for the rendering of geometric models.

geometric object

Geometric model.

geometric primitive

A point, a line, or a polygon.

Gouraud shading

Smooth interpolation of colors across a polygon or line segment. Colors are assigned at vertices and linearly interpolated across the primitive to produce a relatively smooth variation in color. Also called *smooth shading*.

group

Each pixel of an image in client memory is represented by a group of one, two, three, or four elements. Thus, in the context of a client memory image, a group and a pixel are the same thing.

half-space

A plane divides space into two half-spaces.

homogeneous coordinates

A set of $n+1$ coordinates used to represent points in n-dimensional projective space. Points in projective space can be thought of as points in euclidean space together with some points at infinity. The coordinates are homogeneous because a scaling of each of the coordinates by the same nonzero constant doesn't alter the point to which the coordinates refer. Homogeneous coordinates are useful in the calculations of projective geometry, and thus in computer graphics, where scenes must be projected onto a window.

image

A rectangular array of pixels, either in client memory or in the framebuffer.

image primitive

A bitmap or an image.

immediate mode

Execution of OpenGL commands when they're called, rather than from a display list. No immediate-mode bit exists; the *mode* in immediate mode refers to usage of OpenGL, rather than to a specific bit of OpenGL state.

index

A single value that's interpreted as an absolute value, rather than as a normalized value in a specified range (as is a component). Color indices are the names of colors, which are dereferenced by the display hardware using the color map. Indices are typically masked, rather than clamped, when out of range. For example, the index 0xf7 is masked to 0x7 when written to a 4-bit buffer (color or stencil). Color indices and stencil indices are always treated as indices, never as components.

indices

Preferred plural of index. (The choice between the plural forms indices or indexes—as well as matrices or matrixes and vertices or vertexes—has engendered much debate between the authors and principal reviewers of this guide. The authors' compromise solution is to use the -ices form but to state clearly for the record that the use of indice [*sic*], matrice [*sic*], and vertice [*sic*] for the singular forms is an abomination.)

IRIS GL

Silicon Graphics' proprietary graphics library, developed from 1982 through 1992. OpenGL was designed with IRIS GL as a starting point.

jaggies

Artifacts of aliased rendering. The edges of primitives that are rendered with aliasing are jagged rather than smooth. A near-horizontal aliased line, for example, is rendered as a set of horizontal lines on adjacent pixel rows, rather than as a smooth, continuous line.

lighting

The process of computing the color of a vertex based on current lights, material properties, and lighting-model modes.

line

A straight region of finite width between two vertices. (Unlike mathematical lines, OpenGL lines have finite width and length.) Each segment of a strip of lines is itself a line.

luminance

The perceived brightness of a surface. Often refers to a weighted average of red, green, and blue color values that gives the perceived brightness of the combination.

matrices

Preferred plural of matrix. (See *indices*.)

matrix

A two-dimensional array of values. OpenGL matrices are all 4×4, though when they are stored in client memory they're treated as 1×16 single-dimension arrays.

modelview matrix

The 4×4 matrix that transforms points, lines, polygons, and raster positions from object coordinates to eye coordinates.

monitor

The device that displays the image in the framebuffer.

motion blurring

A technique that simulates what you get on a piece of film when you take a picture of a moving object, or when you move the camera when you take a picture of a stationary object. In animations without motion blur, moving objects can appear jerky.

network

A connection between two or more computers that allows each to transfer data to and from the others.

nonconvex

A polygon is nonconvex if there exists a line in the plane of the polygon that intersects the polygon more than twice.

normal

A three-component plane equation that defines the angular orientation, but not position, of a plane or surface.

normalize

Divide each of the components of a normal by the square root of the sum of their squares. Then, if the normal is thought of as a vector from the origin to the point (nx', ny', nz'), this vector has unit length.

$$factor = \sqrt{nx^2 + ny^2 + nz^2}$$

$nx' = nx / factor$

$ny' = ny / factor$

$nz' = nz / factor$

normal vector

Same as *normal*.

NURBS

Non-Uniform Rational B-Spline. A common way to specify parametric curves and surfaces. See GLU NURBS routines in Appendix C.

object

An object-coordinate model that's rendered as a collection of primitives.

object coordinates

Coordinate system prior to any OpenGL transformation.

orthographic

Nonperspective projection, as in some engineering drawings, with no foreshortening.

parameter

A value passed as an argument to an OpenGL command. Sometimes one of the values passes by reference to an OpenGL command.

perspective division

The division of x, y, and z by w, carried out in clip coordinates.

pixel

Picture element. The bits at location (x, y) of all the bitplanes in the framebuffer constitute the single pixel (x, y). In an image in client memory, a pixel is one group of elements. In OpenGL window coordinates, each pixel corresponds to a 1.0×1.0 screen area. The coordinates of the lower left corner of the pixel named x,y are (x, y), and of the upper right corner are $(x+1, y+1)$.

point

An exact location in space, which is rendered as a finite-diameter dot.

polygon

A near-planar surface bounded by edges specified by vertices. Each triangle of a triangle mesh is a polygon, as is each quadrilateral of a quadrilateral mesh. The rectangle specified by **glRect*()** is also a polygon.

primitive

A point, a line, a polygon, a bitmap, or an image. (Note: Not just a point, a line, or a polygon!)

projection matrix

The 4×4 matrix that transforms points, lines, polygons, and raster positions from eye coordinates to clip coordinates.

quadrilateral

A polygon with four edges.

rasterize

Convert a projected point, line, or polygon, or the pixels of a bitmap or image, to fragments, each corresponding to a pixel in the framebuffer. Note that all primitives are rasterized, not just points, lines, and polygons.

rectangle

A quadrilateral whose alternate edges are parallel to each other in object coordinates. Polygons specified with **glRect*()** are always rectangles; other quadrilaterals might be rectangles.

rendering

Conversion of primitives specified in object coordinates to an image in the framebuffer. Rendering is the primary operation of OpenGL—it's what OpenGL does.

RGBA

Red, Green, Blue, Alpha.

RGBA mode

An OpenGL context is in RGBA mode if its color buffers store red, green, blue, and alpha color components, rather than color indices.

server

The computer on which OpenGL commands are executed. This might differ from the computer from which commands are issued. See *client*.

shading

The process of interpolating color within the interior of a polygon, or between the vertices of a line, during rasterization.

single-buffering

OpenGL contexts that don't have back color buffers are single-buffered. You can use these contexts for animation, but take care to avoid visually disturbing flashes when rendering.

singular matrix

A matrix that has no inverse. Geometrically, such a matrix represents a transformation that collapses points along at least one line to a single point.

stipple

A one- or two-dimensional binary pattern that defeats the generation of fragments where its value is zero. Line stipples are one-dimensional and are applied relative to the start of a line. Polygon stipples are two-dimensional and are applied with a fixed orientation to the window.

tessellation

Reduction of a portion of an analytic surface to a mesh of polygons, or of a portion of an analytic curve to a sequence of lines.

texel

A texture element. A texel is obtained from texture memory and represents the color of the texture to be applied to a corresponding fragment.

texture

A one- or two-dimensional image that's used to modify the color of fragments produced by rasterization.

texture mapping

The process of applying an image (the texture) to a primitive. Texture mapping is often used to add realism to a scene. As an example, you could apply a picture of a building facade to a polygon representing a wall.

texture matrix

The 4×4 matrix that transforms texture coordinates from the coordinates that they're specified in to the coordinates that are used for interpolation and texture lookup.

transformation

A warping of space. In OpenGL, transformations are limited to projective transformations that include anything that can be represented by a 4×4 matrix. Such transformations include rotations, translations, (nonuniform) scalings along the coordinate axes, perspective transformations, and combinations of these.

triangle

A polygon with three edges. Triangles are always convex.

vertex

A point in three-dimensional space.

vertices

Preferred plural of vertex. See *indices*.

viewpoint

The origin of either the eye- or the clip-coordinate system, depending on context. (For example, when discussing lighting, the viewpoint is the origin of the eye-coordinate system. When discussing projection, the viewpoint is the origin of the clip-coordinate system.) With a typical projection matrix, the eye-coordinate and clip-coordinate origins are at the same location.

view volume

The volume in clip coordinates whose coordinates satisfy the three conditions

$-w \leq x \leq w$

$-w \leq y \leq w$

$-w \leq z \leq w$

Geometric primitives that extend outside this volume are clipped.

window

A subregion of the framebuffer, usually rectangular, whose pixels all have the same buffer configuration. An OpenGL context renders to a single window at a time.

window-aligned

When referring to line segments or polygon edges, implies that these are parallel to the window boundaries. (In OpenGL, the window is rectangular, with horizontal and vertical edges). When referring to a polygon pattern, implies that the pattern is fixed relative to the window origin.

window coordinates

The coordinate system of a window. It's important to distinguish between the names of pixels, which are discrete, and the window-coordinate system, which is continuous. For example, the pixel at the lower left corner of a window is pixel (0, 0); the window coordinates of the center of this pixel are (0.5, 0.5, z). Note that window coordinates include a depth, or z, component, and that this component is continuous as well.

wireframe

A representation of an object that contains line segments only. Typically, the line segments indicate polygon edges.

X Window System

A window system used by many of the machines on which OpenGL is implemented. GLX is the name of the OpenGL extension to the X Window System (see Appendix D).

Index

Page numbers for command summaries are in bold; page numbers for code examples are in italics.

object, 68
window, 69
correcting for perspective, 208
correctness of an OpenGL implementation, 482
coverage, 207
cross product, 88, 471
culling back-facing polygons, 47
curved surfaces, 54
curves, 32, 452
curves, *see* evaluators or NURBS

D

data types, in OpenGL, 8
decals, 302, 397
depth buffer, 27, 293, 295
    clearing, 23, 28
    for drawing static background, 404
    masking, 298
    optimizing performance of, 482
    using for decals, 397
    using for Dirichlet domains, 406
    using for three-dimensional blending, 204
    using to create a common background, 299
depth coordinate, 98
depth test, 307
depth values, using for picking, 371
depth-of-field effect, 319, *320*
diffuse light, 160, 167
diffuse material color, 179
Dirichlet domains, 405
display lists, 21, 117, *119*
    deleting, 131
    executing, 127
    executing multiple, 132, *133*
    hierarchical, 129, *130*
    nesting, 129
    no error reporting while being defined, 482
    obtaining indices for, 131
    optimizing performance with, 484
    performance with, 121, 137
    state changes and, *128*
    using for changing mode settings, 137, *138*

using for fonts, 231
using for matrix operations, 122
using for stippling, 137
using to create a font, 133
using with lighting, 165
what can be stored in, 127
distorted images, 390
dithering, 146, 309, 482
dof.c, *320*
double-buffering, 15
double.c, *17*
drawf.c, *228*
drawing
    an icosahedron, 56
    clearing the window before, 21
    curves, 452
    forcing completion of, 25
    points, 34
    polygons, 34, 45
    preparing for, 21
    rectangles, 32
    spheres, cylinders, and disks, 450
drawing pixel data, *see* pixel data

E

edges of a polygon, 51, *52*
emission, 180, 182
enabling blending, 198
enabling lighting, 179
endianness, 245
environment mapping, 287
error codes, 420
error handling, 419, 453
error round-off, 84
evaluators, 325, 328
    one-dimensional, 328
    two-dimensional, 334, *336*
    using for textures, 340
    using to tessellate, 484
eye coordinates, 68, 107